YOUNG AND INNOCENT?

The Cinema in Britain, 1896–1930

This book brings together the study of silent cinema and the study of British cinema, both of which have seen some of the most exciting developments in Film Studies in recent years. The result is a comprehensive survey of one of the most important periods of film history. Most of the acknowledged experts on this period are represented, joined by several new voices. Together they chart the development of cinema in Britain from its beginnings in the 1890s to the conversion to sound in the late 1920s. From these accounts the youthful British cinema emerges as far from innocent. On the contrary, it was a fascinatingly complex field of cultural and industrial practices.

Andrew Higson is Professor of Film Studies at the University of East Anglia and Director of the British Cinema History Research Project.

Exeter Studies in Film History
General Editors: Richard Maltby and Duncan Petrie

Exeter Studies in Film History is devoted to publishing the best new scholarship on the cultural, technical and aesthetic history of cinema. The aims of the series are to reconsider established orthodoxies and to revise our understanding of cinema's past by shedding light on neglected areas in film history.

Published by University of Exeter Press in association with the Bill Douglas Centre for the History of Cinema and Popular Culture, the series includes monographs and essay collections, translations of major works written in other languages, and reprinted editions of important texts in cinema history. The series editors are Richard Maltby, Associate Professor of Screen Studies, Flinders University, Australia, and Duncan Petrie, Director of the Bill Douglas Centre for the History of Cinema and Popular Culture, University of Exeter.

Parallel Tracks: The Railroad and Silent Cinema
Lynne Kirby (1997)

The World According to Hollywood, 1918–1939
Ruth Vasey (1997)

'Film Europe' and 'Film America': Cinema, Commerce and Cultural Exchange 1920–1939
edited by Andrew Higson and Richard Maltby (1999)

A Paul Rotha Reader
edited by Duncan Petrie and Robert Kruger (1999)

A Chorus of Raspberries: British Film Comedy 1929–1939
David Sutton (2000)

The Great Art of Light and Shadow: Archaeology of the Cinema
Laurent Mannoni, translated by Richard Crangle (2000)

Popular Filmgoing in 1930s Britain: A Choice of Pleasures
John Sedgwick (2000)

Alternative Empires: European Modernist Cinemas and Cultures of Imperialism
Martin Stollery (2000)

Hollywood, Westerns and the 1930s: The Lost Trail
Peter Stanfield (2001)

University of Exeter Press also publishes the celebrated five-volume series looking at the early years of English cinema, *The Beginnings of the Cinema in England*, by John Barnes.

YOUNG AND INNOCENT?

The Cinema in Britain
1896–1930

edited by
Andrew Higson

UNIVERSITY
of
EXETER
PRESS

First published in 2002 by
University of Exeter Press
Reed Hall, Streatham Drive
Exeter, Devon EX4 4QR
UK
www.ex.ac.uk/uep/

© 2002 University of Exeter Press

British Library Cataloguing in Publication Data
A catalogue record for this book is available from the British Library

Paperback ISBN 0 85989 717 6
Hardback ISBN 0 85989 659 5

Typeset in 11/13pt Adobe Caslon by
Kestrel Data, Exeter, Devon

Printed in Great Britain by
Short Run Press Ltd, Exeter, Devon

Contents

List of Illustrations   viii
Picture Credits   x
Acknowledgements   xi

Introduction
Andrew Higson   1

Section A—Putting the Pioneers in Context: Films and Filmmakers before the First World War

1. 'But the Khaki-Covered Camera is the *Latest* Thing': The Boer War
   Cinema and Visual Culture in Britain
   Simon Popple   13

2. James Williamson's Rescue Narratives
   Frank Gray   28

3. Cecil Hepworth, *Alice in Wonderland* and the Development
   of the Narrative Film
   Andrew Higson   42

4. Putting the World before You: The Charles Urban Story
   Luke McKernan   65

5. 'It would be a Mistake to Strive for Subtlety of Effect': *Richard III*
   and Populist, Pantomime Shakespeare in the 1910s
   Jon Burrows   78

Section B—Going to the Cinema: Audiences, Exhibition and Reception from the 1890s to the 1910s

6. 'Indecent Incentives to Vice': Regulating Films and Audience Behaviour from the 1890s to the 1910s
   Lise Shapiro Sanders   97

7. 'Nothing More than a "Craze" ': Cinema Building in Britain from 1909 to 1914
   Nicholas Hiley   111

8. Letters to America: A Case Study in the Exhibition and Reception of American Films in Britain, 1914–1918
   Michael Hammond   128

Section C—A Full Supporting Programme: Serials, Cinemagazines, Interest Films, Travelogues and Travel Films, and Film Music in the 1910s and 1920s

9. British Series and Serials in the Silent Era
   Alex Marlow-Mann   147

10. The Spice of the Perfect Programme: The Weekly Magazine Film during the Silent Period
    Jenny Hammerton   162

11. Shakespeare's Country: The National Poet, English Identity and British Silent Cinema
    Roberta E. Pearson   176

12. Representing 'African Life': From Ethnographic Exhibitions to *Nionga* and *Stampede*
    Emma Sandon   191

13. Distant Trumpets: The Score to *The Flag Lieutenant* and Music of the British Silent Cinema
    Neil Brand   208

Section D—The Feature Film at Home and Abroad: Mainstream Cinema from the End of the First World War to the Coming of Sound

14. Writing Screen Plays: Stannard and Hitchcock
    Charles Barr   227

15. H.G. Wells and British Silent Cinema: The War of the Worlds
    Sylvia Hardy   242

16. War-Torn Dionysus: The Silent Passion of Ivor Novello
    Michael Williams   256

17. Tackling the Big Boy of Empire: British Film in Australia,
    1918–1931
    Mike Walsh   271

Section E—Taking the Cinema Seriously: The Emergence of an Intellectual Film Culture in the 1920s

18. The Film Society and the Creation of an Alternative Film
    Culture in Britain in the 1920s
    Jamie Sexton   291

19. Towards a Critical Practice: Ivor Montagu and British Film
    Culture in the 1920s
    Gerry Turvey   306

20. Writing the Cinema into Daily Life: Iris Barry and the
    Emergence of British Film Criticism in the 1920s
    Haidee Wasson   321

Section F—Bibliographical and Archival Resources

21. A Guide to Bibliographical and Archival Sources on British
    Cinema before the First World War
    Stephen Bottomore   341

22. A Guide to Bibliographical and Archival Sources on British
    Cinema from the First World War to the Coming of Sound
    Jon Burrows   356

23. Bibliography: British Cinema before 1930
    compiled by Andrew Higson, Michael Williams and Jo-Anne Blanco 371

Notes on Contributors   405
Index   411

Illustrations

Plates

1. 1901 advertisement listing Mitchell and Kenyon's 'Boer War Films'
    (from *The Showman*, 6 September 1901).
    Source: personal collection of Simon Popple   18

2. Frame still from *Fire!* (Williamson, 1901).
    Source/copyright: BFI Collections and South-East Film and
    Video Archive   35

3, 5, 7.   Reproductions of Sir John Tenniel's illustrations
    for *Alice's Adventures in Wonderland*.   49, 50, 52

4, 6.   Frame stills from *Alice in Wonderland* (Hepworth, 1903).
    Source: BFI Collections; copyright: The Hepworth Estate   49, 51

8–11.   Frame stills from *Richard III* (London Cinematograph
    Company, 1910–11).
    Source: BFI Collections   87, 89

12. Frame still from *Kiss in the Tunnel* (Riley and Bamforth, 1899).
    Source: BFI Stills, Posters and Designs   103

13. Postcard, *c.*1914 (postmark on back): 'Do Take Me to See the
    Pictures Again'.
    Source/copyright: The Bill Douglas Centre for History of Cinema
    and Popular Culture   105

14. Advertisement for Cinematograph Supplies, 1911
    Source: *The Modern Bioscope Operator* (London: Ganes Ltd, 1911)   117

15. Southampton Picture Palace, 1912.
    Source/copyright: Southampton Archive Services   133

16. Poster for *Lieut. Rose R.N. and the Boxers* (Stowe, 1911).
    Source: BFI Stills, Posters and Designs   150

17. Frame still from *Ultus and the Grey Lady* (Pearson, 1916), featuring
    Aurele Sydney as Ultus
    Source: BFI Stills, Posters and Designs   157

18. 'Hair Fashions', from *Eve's Film Review* (Pathé, 1921)—the
    direct look at the camera.
    Source/copyright: British Pathe plc   171

19. Advertisement for *Nionga* (Stoll, 1925).
    Source: *Kinematograph Weekly*, 21 May 1925   195

20–21. Frame stills from *Nionga* (Stoll, 1925).
    Source: BFI Collections; copyright: Stoll Moss Theatres Ltd   196, 197

22. Frame still from *Stampede* (Court Treatt, 1929).
    Source: BFI Collections   199

23. Front cover of music score for *The Flag Lieutenant* (Elvey, 1926).
    Source: personal collection of Neil Brand   209

24. 'Musical Suggestions for *Stage Struck*'.
    Source: *Paramount Services*, 14 August 1926   212

25–26. Pages from the music score for *The Flag Lieutenant*
    (Elvey, 1926).
    Source: personal collection of Neil Brand   220, 221

27. The title pages from Eliot Stannard, 'Writing Screen Plays,'
    Lesson Six in the series *Cinema—in Ten Complete Lessons*
    (London: Standard Art Book Company, 1920).   229

28. Production still from *Bluebottles* (Montagu/Wells, 1928),
    featuring Elsa Lanchester.
    Source/copyright: The Estate of Frank Wells   250

29. Production still from *The Rat* (Cutts, 1925), featuring
    Ivor Novello as The Rat.
    Source: BFI Stills, Posters and Designs   257

30. Cartoon by Bernard Partridge: 'Hold That, John!'
    Source: *Punch*, 23 March 1927; copyright: The Punch
    Cartoon Library and Archive   281

31. Frame still from *C.O.D.—A Mellow Drama* (Dickinson *et al.*, 1929).
    Source: BFI Collections   299

32. Production still from *Bluebottles* (Montagu/Wells, 1928).
    Source/copyright: The Estate of Frank Wells   309

33. The painting 'Praxitella' (1920–21) by Wyndham Lewis.
    Source: Leeds Museums and Galleries (City Art Gallery);
    copyright: The Trustees of the Estate of Percy Wyndham Lewis   328

Unless otherwise indicated, we have been unable to trace copyright holders.

Figures

1. The pattern of construction of purpose-built cinemas, 1907–1918   119

2. The growth of film exhibition in Britain, 1908–1916   121

3. Average percentage dividend paid by cinema companies,
   1909–1918   124

Tables

1. London venues used regularly for film exhibition in January 1908   113

2. The transformation of film exhibition in Britain, 1910–1913   120

3. Cinema exhibition companies registered and liquidated, 1908–1914   123

Picture credits

We are grateful to the following for supplying illustrative material: Simon Popple (1), British Film Institute and South East Film and Video Archive (2), British Film Institute (front cover, 4, 6, 8–12, 16, 17, 19–22, 27, 29, 31), the Bill Douglas Centre for the History of Cinema and Popular Culture (13), Nicholas Hiley (14, 24), Southampton Archive Services (15), British Pathe plc (18), Neil Brand (23, 25, 26), Sylvia Hardy and Martin Wells (28, 32), the Punch Cartoon Library and Archive (30), Museum of Modern Art, New York (33).

We are grateful to the following for granting permission to reproduce images: British Film Institute and South East Film and Video Archive (2), British Film Institute and The Hepworth Estate (front cover, 4, 6), the Bill Douglas Centre for the History of Cinema and Popular Culture (13), Southampton Archive Services (15), British Pathe plc (18), British Film Institute and Stoll Moss Theatres Ltd (20, 21), the Estate of Frank Wells (28, 32), Leeds Museums and Galleries—City Art Gallery (33), the Punch Cartoon Library and Archive (30).

The editor and publishers have made every effort to trace original copyright holders in order to obtain their permission. We would like to take this opportunity of making acknowledgement to any copyright holder that we may have failed to contact.

Acknowledgements

This book has its origins in a conference on British cinema held at the University of East Anglia in July 1998, *Cinema, Identity, History*. About half of the chapters were first presented as papers at the conference and I would like to thank all those involved with the organization of the conference, especially Jayne Morgan. The rest of the chapters were commissioned especially for the book. My gratitude goes to all the contributors for their admirable scholarship and dedication and for responding gracefully to an often enthusiastic editor. Some of them deserve further thanks for persevering with me when the going was slow; others deserve thanks for responding to very late commissions after one or two of the original contributors had to pull out. Jon Burrows in particular has taken on responsibilities beyond those one would expect of a contributor; his support has been vital. The bibliographical section has benefited considerably from input from many people besides the listed authors and compilers, including Stephen Bottomore, Jon Burrows, Christine Gledhill, Mike Hammond, Nicholas Hiley, Luke McKernan, Jamie Sexton and Gerry Turvey; my thanks go to all of them, but especially to Michael Williams and Jo Blanco, who made sure the listings were as comprehensive as they are. Thanks too to Luci Cummings for secretarial support.

I am grateful to Richard Maltby and Duncan Petrie, the series editors, for their faith in this project and to Simon Baker and all at the University of Exeter Press for seeing the book through from start to finish. The index was compiled by Miranda Bayer, who has done a thoroughly professional job.

The Film Studies sector at the University of East Anglia (UEA) has been the ideal base from which to edit this book, given its long-term commitment to the study of both silent cinema and British cinema. My colleagues as usual have been extremely supportive and encouraging, not least in ensuring the strength and vitality of our research culture. I should also thank several cohorts of students who have helped me discover the intricacies of British cinema in the silent period, especially those members of my MA seminar on the topic. That several of them have stayed on to undertake doctoral work in this area has been especially encouraging. That nearly half of the contributions to the book are from scholars who have either taught or studied at UEA speaks volumes. Further stimulus has been provided by the participants at and organizers of the annual Silent British Cinema Weekend at Nottingham Broadway (and previously Phoenix Arts, Leicester). UEA's School of English and American Studies provided funding for the conference where some of the papers originated. Parts of my own contributions to the book were completed during a sabbatical granted by the University and partly paid for by an Arts and Humanities Research Board Research Leave Award.

Finally, Val, Billie and Luisa have continued to provide all the support and love I could possibly want. Thank you!

Introduction

Andrew Higson

The study of the pre-history of cinema, the early years of film, the transition to a classical narrative cinema and the period up to the conversion to sound in the late 1920s, has in the last couple of decades yielded some of the most important and exciting research and writing in film studies and cultural history. The study of British cinema history has taken off in this same period, but it is only in the last few years that a significant number of historians have focused on the British silent period. There has of course long been an interest in the silent period, as demonstrated by Rachael Low's Herculean enterprise, *The History of the British Film*, begun in the 1940s, the publication in the 1950s of memoirs by some of the key figures from the silent period, and, more recently, John Barnes's trailblazing efforts to chart the early period.[1] Of course, too, at either end of the silent period there are well-known films and filmmakers who are cited in most film histories, the so-called pioneers from the turn of the century (Cecil Hepworth, James Williamson and R.W. Paul, for instance), and the silent films of Alfred Hitchcock in the late 1920s.

Young and Innocent was the title of one of the string of extremely influential and successful British sound films Hitchcock made in the 1930s. To invoke that title here, followed by a question mark, is in part to suggest that it is high time our understanding of British cinema history looked beyond the Hitchcock legacy. The emergence of an intellectual film culture in Britain in the late 1920s consolidated a particular way of looking at cinema internationally that valorized the likes of Hitchcock but left little room for the appreciation of the routine, and of so much of the popular or the middlebrow British cinema. If we are to make sense of the way in which cinema developed in Britain in its first three decades, then we need to see beyond Hitchcock and the value judgements of the intellectual film culture of the inter-war years. This is not to ignore either Hitchcock or intellectual film culture—indeed, there are chapters taking a fresh look at both later in this book. But it is to make a plea for a more rounded understanding of the experience of watching films and the institution of cinema in Britain in the silent period.

'Young and Innocent?' The phrase, with that question mark again, also works in another way as a metaphor for British silent cinema, questioning the assumption that that cinema was youthful and immature. In one sense it was, but in the problematically teleological sense that cinema can only be understood retrospectively in relation to what it would become. To adopt such a perspective is often to overlook what cinema was at the time—what its constituent parts were, how they operated together, but also how they related to other contemporary cultural practices, other media, entertainment and leisure activities of the period. The first film shows were inserted into well-established cultural frameworks, as one of the acts on a music hall bill, for instance, or as one of the attractions at a fairground. It makes much more sense to see these film shows in their own terms, as attractions in their own right, than as primitive, embryonic forms of the twenty-first-century Hollywood blockbuster. In any case, cinema has always been much more than moving pictures, much more than just films, and an adequate historiography needs to take that fact into account. It needs to look at the films, yes, but it also needs to look at the conditions that enabled filmmakers to adopt a particular film form, subject matter and concerns. It needs to look at the ways in which those films were made available to their audiences, the circumstances in which they were exhibited, and the ways in which audiences, critics, reformers and the trade made sense of them. It also needs to acknowledge that it was not only British-made films that were shown in Britain, and that film culture was organized around the full range of films available.

Again, it is important to recognize that Low's work had already forged just such an all-embracing view of cinema and film history. In the last few years, however, there has been much more sense of a community of scholars and archivists working together to move beyond the most familiar landmarks, the best-known inventors and *auteurs*, and the often negative assumptions about silent British cinema that have for so long been taken for granted. That sense of a relatively coherent project has been vitalized by a series of events that have brought together academics, archivists, collectors and historians. It is widely recognized that the FIAF conference at Brighton in 1978 and more recently the annual Pordenone Festival of Silent Cinema in Italy have had an important effect on the study of silent cinema internationally. In the same way, *Cinema, Identity, History: An International Conference on British Cinema*, held at the University of East Anglia in 1998, and the *British Silent Cinema Weekend*, held annually since 1998, first in Leicester and subsequently at the Broadway Media Centre in Nottingham, have provided catalysts to those working specifically on British cinema.

In the last few years, several publications have emerged that foreground such work, but they have tended either to deal with much more than just British cinema, or they have focused on particular companies, genres or themes.[2] This book is, then, the first all-embracing survey of British cinema in the silent period to take on board the new research on British cinema and silent film history. It has its beginnings in the *Cinema, Identity, History* conference, in that thirteen of the chapters were first presented as papers at the conference. Another nine chapters were specially commissioned for this collection. The book thus brings together both established writers and those who are carrying out significant research but who are relatively new to publishing. While most of the contributors are academics, several are archivists, curators or freelance historians, who are able to bring different sorts of expertise and understanding to their writing. Together, they provide a wide-ranging survey of the development of cinema and film culture in Britain in the silent period, but also of the state of current research and scholarship on these topics. The rationale for the book has been to proceed by way of exemplary case study rather than to attempt to offer a comprehensive history. The case study approach has been adopted partly to play to the strengths of the contributors and to avoid generalization, and partly because most scholars of the period would agree that the time is not yet right to attempt to write a comprehensive history, despite the wealth of work that has already been carried out. In any case, no book of this length can possibly hope to be exhaustive.

In this context, one of the most crucial parts of the book is the section on bibliographical and archival sources. If a comprehensive history of British cinema in the silent period is to be written, then those undertaking the research must have the best possible access to resources. To this end, the book includes an ambitious and expansive bibliography, covering both material published in Britain at the time and more recent publications; catalogues, source books and websites as well as critical surveys and case studies; and autobiographies and interviews as well as thoroughly researched histories, on local, regional, national and international developments. There are also two essays offering guides to researching British cinema, one, by Stephen Bottomore, on the period up to 1914, the other, by Jon Burrows, on the period from the beginning of the First World War to the conversion to sound in the late 1920s. Both writers guide their readers through the most important historical writing on their respective periods and draw attention to a huge wealth of material available to researchers at archives, libraries and elsewhere. This includes trade publications and fan magazines, collected papers and other special collections, and a whole range of contemporary reports and treatises.

The other sections of this book are organized in part chronologically and in part thematically. Thus the first section deals with the pioneer period up to the beginning of the First World War. Some of the chapters in this section look at key filmmakers such as James Williamson, Cecil Hepworth and Charles Urban, and the contributions they made to the emergence of the narrative film on the one hand and the non-fiction film, and especially the scientific film, on the other (see the chapters by Frank Gray, Andrew Higson and Luke McKernan respectively). Simon Popple's chapter looks at the use of moving pictures to document and comment upon the Boer War, while Jon Burrows considers the penchant for adaptations of Shakespeare and the discourses and practices of acting they drew upon in the late 1900s and early 1910s. Each of the chapters in this section focuses on the processes of innovation and enterprise, whether they are to be found in the development of film form or in the finessing of business practices. Equally, though, it is clear that in each case the films in question are heavily dependent on pre-existing cultural and/or economic activities. Thus Popple demonstrates the extent to which producers of moving pictures concerned with the Boer War drew on representational traditions established by the printed image, the photograph and theatrical, music hall and fairground performance. Gray shows the extent to which Williamson's films from the early 1900s work with a well-established rescue narrative formula. Higson shows how Hepworth was able to create one of the longest fiction films of the early period by adapting a much-reproduced Victorian classic, *Alice's Adventures in Wonderland*. Burrows looks at F.R. Benson's film version of his own stage production of *Richard III* and the modes of performance adopted by the cast in the context of contemporary debates about the ideal acting style for films. McKernan tells a slightly different story, presenting Urban as a dynamic entrepreneur who was able to combine a good business sense with an interest in science and education to forge a distinctive career in the film industry of the period.

Looking towards the end of the silent period, at the other end of the book is a section that focuses on the post-war feature film. Again, some of the chapters are organized around key figures of the period, including writers H.G. Wells and Eliot Stannard, the director Alfred Hitchcock, and the leading British male star of the 1920s, Ivor Novello. Charles Barr looks at the innovative work of Stannard, a screenwriter with strong views on the filmmaking process, who collaborated with some of the leading directors of the period, including Hitchcock. Sylvia Hardy's chosen writer is the novelist H.G. Wells, who also had strong views on how films should work, and several of whose stories were adapted for the screen, including *Kipps* (Harold Shaw, 1921) and *The Passionate Friends* (Maurice Elvey, 1922). Looking at such productions allows Hardy to consider the relationship between literature and film and the process of adaptation. In Michael Williams's contribution, the focus of attention has shifted from behind the camera to in front of it, and the cultural significance of Novello's charismatic and luminous star image. Williams argues that Novello's appeal owed much to his associations with the horrors of the First World War (he had composed the great war-time hit 'Keep the Home Fires Burning') and that his film roles play out a morbid fascination with both horror and beauty. From a rather different perspective, Mike Walsh explores the role that British feature films played in the Australian market in the post-war period. In so doing, he reminds us that British films were not made simply for the domestic market, that the export market was more than the USA, and that Hollywood's struggle for supremacy over British cinema was fought in part on Australian territory.

With the first section of the book taking us up to the First World War and this latter section picking up the story in the post-war period, there is clearly a chronology at work, with the history of the silent period in Britain divided into periods. Such attempts at periodisation are always problematic. In this case, the war in fact functions less as a moment of radical change in the film industry than as a convenient point at which to begin and end a set of discussions. In fact, film historians now conventionally distinguish four periods between the mid-1890s and the early 1930s.[3] First, there is the early period, the period of the cinema of attractions, which is generally considered to last from the mid-1890s to the mid-1900s. Next comes a transitional period, between the mid-1900s and the mid-1910s, as the story film begins to take prominence and the features of the classical narrative film emerge and become established. The classical period proper is usually seen as beginning in the mid-1910s—only to enter a further transitional period in the late 1920s and early 1930s, as the process of converting to sound takes place.

There are two problems with this conventional periodisation of the silent period. First, it is premised on developments in the USA more than anywhere else, and secondly it leaves little room for all the other types of film that continue to circulate around the mainstream narrative feature film well into the 1920s and beyond. It is certainly difficult to identify a classical British cinema emerging in the mid-1910s. While some British filmmakers might have been moving in the same direction as their American counterparts, others, such as Cecil Hepworth, were deliberately trying to do something different, to make what they saw as distinctively British films and thereby to create a national cinema. After all, what is sometimes loosely referred to as classical cinema is much better identified as classical *Hollywood* cinema. To some extent, because American cinema was by the late 1910s the strongest cinema in the world, its standards were applied internationally. But this was only intermittently the case with British production in the 1910s. Indeed, perhaps because the industry was less well organized, there was much less standardization in British films of the period—or, to put it another way, there were several competing standards. While commentators both at the time and subsequently have criticized British filmmakers for lagging behind American developments in the post-First World War period, it is important to recognize that American standards were not the only ones being applied. One of the functions of this book is then to consider British cinema in its own terms, rather than simply in relation to developments elsewhere. That some sections of the book use the First World War as a cut-off point is not intended to indicate that a marked historical break takes place in British cinema at this moment: it is simply a pragmatic means of organizing material.

This brings us to the second problem with the arguments about periodization, and the place of the classical Hollywood model in those arguments. It is not simply that mainstream feature filmmaking in Britain in the 1910s was more heterogeneous, and so less standardized than in the USA. It is also the case that there were in both countries many other filmic models in circulation, since the long narrative film was by no means the only film on the bill.

Sandwiched between the sections of this book on pre-war film-making and the post-war feature film, therefore, is a section looking at other aspects of the 'full supporting programme' that would have been a feature of most film shows of the 1910s and 1920s. Alex Marlow-Mann charts the surprisingly large number of British-made serials and other series films that were so popular with filmgoers in this period, investigating their characteristic modes of narration, the genres they typically fell into, and the ways in which they were distributed, promoted and exhibited. Jenny Hammerton looks at another key feature of the film programme, the weekly cinemagazine, which virtually all cinemas in Britain showed during the silent period. Hammerton describes the ways in which these short non-narrative films were organized and exhibited. She also argues that, like so many other items on the full supporting programme, the cinemagazine reworked aspects of the cinema of attractions, generally associated with the early period. Roberta Pearson examines a range of short travelogues, newsreels and interest films—and the occasional feature film—all of which have something to say about Shakespeare and Stratford-upon-Avon. Her interest is in the way they presented Shakespeare to their audiences and what this says about ideas of English national identity. Emma Sandon also looks at travel films, but of a very different sort. The objects of her study are two ethnographic films of the 1920s, *Nionga* (1925) and *Stampede* (1929), both set and shot in Africa. Where Pearson relates her chosen films to contemporary travel writing and Shakespeare biography and criticism, Sandon shows how her two films draw on the traditions of live ethnographic displays and exhibitions and early actuality films, photographs and lantern slides from the turn of the century. Another key feature of the filmgoing experience in the 1910s and 1920s was the live music played between and during films, and Neil Brand's chapter in this section looks at the sorts of music and other sound effects that were used to accompany film screenings in Britain in this period. In particular, he focuses on the recently rediscovered score for *The Flag Lieutenant*, a big hit at the British box-office in 1926–7. It is the presence of serials, cinemagazines, travelogues, live music and the like on the film programme well into the so-called classical period that complicates the idea that film history charts a simple linear movement towards narrative integration;

on the contrary, historical development is always both uneven and complex.

Another section of the book concentrates on the point of exhibition as much as—and sometimes much more than—the films being shown. Several questions are addressed here. What sorts of audiences did film shows attract? What do we know of their tastes and preferences? How did the trade attempt to cater for specific audiences, but also how did they, and the various social reformers of the period, attempt to regulate the behaviour of those audiences? And what sorts of spaces were provided within which film shows might take place? Nicholas Hiley's chapter is about the exhibition space itself, and more specifically about how a boom in roller-skating paved the way for a concerted bout of cinema building between 1909 and 1914. Lise Shapiro Sanders, on the other hand, is more concerned with the behaviour of audiences within such spaces, and the ways in which their behaviour was regulated. In particular, she is interested in the presence of women in the audiences for film shows, and the moral concerns their presence triggered. Michael Hammond uses an archive of correspondence between an American distributor and British exhibitors to build up a picture of the distribution, exhibition and reception of American films in Britain in the mid-1910s, at the moment when Hollywood product began to dominate British screens.

The last remaining section of the book deals with another aspect of film reception, namely the emergence of an intellectual film culture in Britain in the 1920s. It was in this period that, in a concerted way, film began to be taken seriously as an art form. A key development here, as Jamie Sexton shows, was the formation of the Film Society in London in 1925, the first of its kind in Britain, and dedicated to showing a range of world cinema and documenting key developments in film practice. Another key development was the publication of film reviews in 'serious' publications, including the British-based film journal *Close Up*, the upmarket weekly magazine the *Spectator*, the daily news-paper the *Daily Mail* and the Sunday newspaper the *Observer*. Haidee Wasson's chapter looks at Iris Barry's writing for the *Spectator* and the *Daily Mail*, while Gerry Turvey considers Ivor Montagu's writing for the *Observer*. Both Barry and Montagu were key figures within the intellectual film culture of the period and both were involved in the Film Society. Montagu was also active in the post-production end of the film business and as a reformer, and he and his business partner Adrian Brunel made a series of short independent films, which Sexton looks at in his chapter.

The various contributors to this book adopt a range of historiographical methods. Several deal with the development of film form, charting the ways in which both fiction and non-fiction films changed between the late 1890s and the late 1920s. Across the book as a whole, but also within particular chapters, however, films are always situated historically, in relation to developments in the cinema business both nationally and internationally, in relation to other cultural practices such as literature, live performance and the visual media, and in relation to audiences, exhibition and reception. The same is true of the various individuals foregrounded in the book. Whether they are filmmakers, businessmen or cultural commentators, their contributions to the development of cinema or film culture are treated not as the actions of free agents apparently in command of their destiny, but as historically determined, caught up in the web of interconnected activities that we call history.

It is this attention to historical context, and the copious use of primary archival sources, that all the book's contributors share. The function of the historian is not simply to accumulate material, however, but to interpret it, to marshal it into an argument, to tell a particular story—albeit one that intersects with other stories. The combined effect of the stories that the various contributors tell here is to advance our understanding of how cinema developed in Britain as a complex business and cultural practice, from the first public film shows of 1896 to the conversion to sound in the late 1920s. But there are many other stories still to be told, and different ways of telling old stories. It is hoped that the section on bibliographical and archival sources will enable others to tell some of those stories.

Notes

My thanks to Justine Ashby for commenting on an earlier draft of the Introduction.

1. Rachael Low and Roger Manvell, *The History of the British Film, 1896–1906* (London: Allen and Unwin, 1948); Low, *The History of the British Film, 1906–1914* (London: Allen and Unwin, 1949), *1914–1918* (London: Allen and Unwin, 1950), *1918–1929* (London: Allen and Unwin/BFI, 1971; all volumes reissued by London: Routledge, 1997). Cecil Hepworth, *Came the Dawn: Memories of a Film Pioneer* (London: Phoenix House, 1951); George Pearson, *Flashback: The Autobiography of a British Film-maker* (London: George Allen and Unwin, 1957). John

Barnes, *The Beginnings of the Cinema in England*, 5 volumes, covering 1894–1900 (Exeter: University of Exeter Press, 1996–8; first published 1977–97).

2. See e.g. John Fullerton, ed., *Celebrating 1895: Proceedings of the International Conference on Film Before 1920* (Sydney: John Libbey, 1998); Richard Brown and Barry Anthony, *A Victorian Film Enterprise: The History of the British Mutoscope and Biograph Company* (Trowbridge: Flicks Books, 1999); Alan Burton and Laraine Porter, eds, *Pimple, Pranks and Pratfalls: British Film Comedy Before 1930* (Trowbridge: Flicks Books, 2000); Linda Fitzsimmons and Sarah Street, eds, *Moving Performance: British Stage and Screen, 1890s–1920s* (Trowbridge: Flicks Books, 2000); Alan Burton and Laraine Porter, eds, *The Showman, the Spectacle and the Two-Minute Silence: Performing British Cinema Before 1930* (Trowbridge: Flicks Books, 2001); Simon Popple and Vanessa Toulmin, eds, *Visual Delights: Essays on the Popular and Projected Image in the 19th Century* (Trowbridge: Flicks Books, 2001).

3. See e.g. David Bordwell, Janet Staiger and Kristin Thompson, *The Classical Hollywood Cinema, 1917–1960* (London: Routledge and Kegan Paul, 1985).

SECTION A

Putting the Pioneers in Context
Films and Filmmakers before
the First World War

1

'But the Khaki-Covered Camera is the *Latest* Thing'
The Boer War Cinema and Visual Culture in Britain

Simon Popple

This essay is concerned with refocusing attention on the varying types of cinema produced during the Boer War period. Previous work has provided insights into the scale and nature of the many films produced during the Boer War period, and the personalities involved in their production.[1] I want to extend this work by positioning films portraying this conflict within the broader context of British visual culture at the time. I want to demonstrate the extent to which cinema, as the *latest* form of visual culture, draws on the representational traditions established by the printed image, the photograph, and theatrical, music hall and fairground performance.

The 'Latest Thing'

Photographic and cinematic images were at the heart of this representational nexus, providing a new technological iconography of the war, a new form of evidence considered far more legitimate than that of the war correspondent or the special artist. The war itself straddled the end of the old and the beginning of the new century, and marked the end of a tradition dominated by the manual transcription of information and impressions. New media based predominantly on the technologies of the camera and the telegraph altered not only the speed with which the war could be covered but also the nature of its representation.

The public's appetite for these new forms of imagery and their display at traditional sites such as the music hall or the fairground is hard to quantify, particularly when one attempts to read it within the context of a popular imperial war. The demand for visual representations of the war were doubtless magnified by the distance at which the war was fought and the guerrilla nature of its prosecution. This demand was highlighted in an article in the *Windsor Magazine* in 1900:

> It is just possible that the indifference of British painters to battle-scenes and military subjects generally will disappear in consequence of the importunate public demand that now manifests itself on all sides for pictures dealing with the war in South Africa . . . [T]he universal desire, amounting to a positive craving, for pictorial commentaries on the doings of our Army in South Africa points to the existence of a genuine instinct, not wholly brutal, which our painters would do well to satisfy. A nation of shopkeepers, no doubt we are; but the man in the street who perhaps serves behind a counter, none the less knows and feels with pride that he belongs to a conquering race.[2]

There is also evidence that indicates the rejection of such nineteenth-century traditions by the classes whose visual stimuli were more likely to be the magazine or newspaper. In the preface to *The Anglo Boer War 1899–1900* the editor makes it clear that one can no longer rely on 'manufactured' illustrations, a clear nod towards the photograph and the cinematograph:

> The 'Faked' war picture is a production of the times, and gives no true conception of what it is supposed to represent. Imagination is brought into play in many of these, but though well and ingeniously drawn, they are not truthful.[3]

The sensitivity with which the new media were regarded was picked up by those who leapt to the defence of the noble art of the war correspondent and special artist. W.B. Wollen, in a letter to the editor of the *Friend*, concluded that, 'the Kodak cannot compete for one single moment with the individual who is using the pencil'.[4] This contrasts strongly with the caption to a striking image of the Biograph camera posed next to a 4.7 inch gun in *The Black and White Budget*: 'Two fearful weapons on the battlefield.'[5]

The obvious advantage enjoyed by the technologically reproduced image was one of scientific objectivity, or so one might suppose. The notion of truth or more bluntly realism is something which overlays our readings of these cultural forms. The extent to which audiences differentiated between the real and the imagined, the actual and the artificial is one of the most difficult questions to answer. By examining the nature and reception of a range of material I hope to be able to suggest that these oppositions are in fact not fixed, and that a complex and often knowing series of negotiations took place between the audience and the visual spectacle, particularly film. What is certain is that spectatorship was not a passive, naive process, but one of complex, knowing complicity.

Black and White: Texts and Contexts

Film historians have often made clear distinctions between the actuality film and the fake or staged patriotic display. While there are clear and obvious differences this process of demarcation has precluded readings of how they were consumed at the time. It has also hidden their related themes and preoccupations and obscured their relationship with other cultural forms such as journalism and literary fiction. Their 'new' technological status has also hidden the traditions of narrative and performance that so obviously inform them. The production and subject matter of actuality or topical films has received a great deal of attention from film historians.[6] My concern here will be to situate these topicals in relation to wider developments in popular entertainment. The other category, the fake or patriotic display, has largely been analysed in the context of propaganda, and is presented as distinctly different and contained. I want to test the boundaries of these distinctions and integrate both categories within a largely theatrical or performance-based milieu.

The magazine *Photogram* published a revealing song in 1900, 'The Khaki-Covered Camera', which considers the centrality of both photographic and cinematographic imagery in representing events in South Africa.

PHOTOMERRIMENT: And Songs of The Camera
By Ward Muir
No. 2. THE KHAKI-COVERED CAMERA.

We've songs about Pretoria (which rhymes with Queen Victoria):
We've patriotic photo-frames and soap and statuettes;
For war we are all gluttons, e'en to wearing portrait buttons,
And decking out with tri-colors our harmless household pets;
But the Khaki-covered camera is the *latest* thing,
To use the Emerald language, 'it's the natest thing!'
Your Kodak's in disgrace
If not in a Khaki case,
For it's positively quite the up-to-datest thing!

The Special Correspondent need never be despondent
If a Khaki-Covered camera forms a portion of his kit,
For the mere fact that it's there will save him from the snare
Of over-gory writing in the wish to make a 'hit.'
Yes, the Khaki-covered camera is the latest thing:
For saving printers' ink it is the greatest thing;
Each exposure states a fact,
Plain, unvarnished, and compact;
As historian it's quite the up-to-datest thing!

But every blessed journal—monthly, weekly, or diurnal—
Is filled with 'our exclusive snap-shots of the Transvaal War';
And it all is very clever, for 'our artist' often never
Heard a louder cannon's thunder than Fleet Street's traffic roar!
But he's got a Khaki camera—it's the latest thing;
For absolute straightforwardness the straightest thing.
You can make a 'Scene at Paard-
eburg' in your back yard
If you understand this truly up-to-datest thing.

Then the dizzling Kinetograph and its brave undaunted staff
Who've rented a secluded park not far from gay Paree;
Their methods, though dramatic, are a little bit erratic,
For they can't resist the joy of making British soldiers flee!
Their Khaki-covered camera is the latest thing,
As a fabrication-mill it is the greatest thing;
Two hundred lies a minute!
Why, Kruger isn't in it
With this quite unanswerable film-beats-platest thing![7]

The song, although a humorous skit, draws attention to the role
of mechanical means of reproduction in representing the war. It
highlights not only their realistic character, but also their propensity
towards artifice and deception, demonstrating an implicit recognition

of the unreal and the fake. It also highlights the myriad forms of visual display the average citizen was exposed to, from advertising to the decorated domestic pet.

Pears, Ogden's Gold Flake and most explicitly Monkey Brand Soap made heavy use of war subjects and military personalities to advertise their products and promote their patriotic credentials. Popular magazines were awash with war-orientated imagery, much of it meant for public display. Campaign maps, colour lithographs, special supplements, serialized commentaries, instructions on the construction of Mafeking and Ladysmith hats and war games were frequent additions to the usual fare of this burgeoning sector, as well as novelty articles touching on some of the more bizarre displays of patriotic fervour. One, 'The War in Toyland',[8] outlined the extent and desirability of patriotic toys for children, with an inflatable pig's bladder bearing the face of Kruger and a doll that demonstrated bayonet drill. Another, 'Strange Things Seen in Shop Windows', praised patriotic window displays, including one which exhibited scale models of shells used by forces in South Africa, and another acting as a gallery for pictures and cartoons culled from the popular press.[9]

These conspicuously patriotic displays and their associated narratives were mirrored in popular entertainment forms. The cinema acted as an interface between these media and absorbed existing narrative concerns and traditions of performance to achieve its status as the key mediator of the war at home. A central narrative concerned the nature and conduct of the Boers, and their behaviour on the field of battle was obsessively contrasted with that of the British Tommy.

Racial stereotyping was endemic and themes such as hygiene played throughout the war. The advertising campaigns constructed by the soap manufacturers were augmented by pictorial representations of the dirty Boer. A series of comic sketches drawn by Captain Clive Dixon of the 16th Lancers and published in 1901 contains typical references.[10] One image, with the caption, 'Between the hours of 7 and 8 am the Boer Prisoners are expected to perform their ablutions', depicts a group of bewildered Boer prisoners examining a bar of soap bearing a notice which reads, 'This is Soap'. Another shows a group of British troops bathing in a river under shellfire; the caption reads, 'The sight of our men washing so infuriated the Boers that they immediately opened fire'.

The other central narrative of the Boer War concerned the abuse of the conventions of civilized warfare. Atrocity stories, perhaps more familiar to us from the First World War, received constant attention.

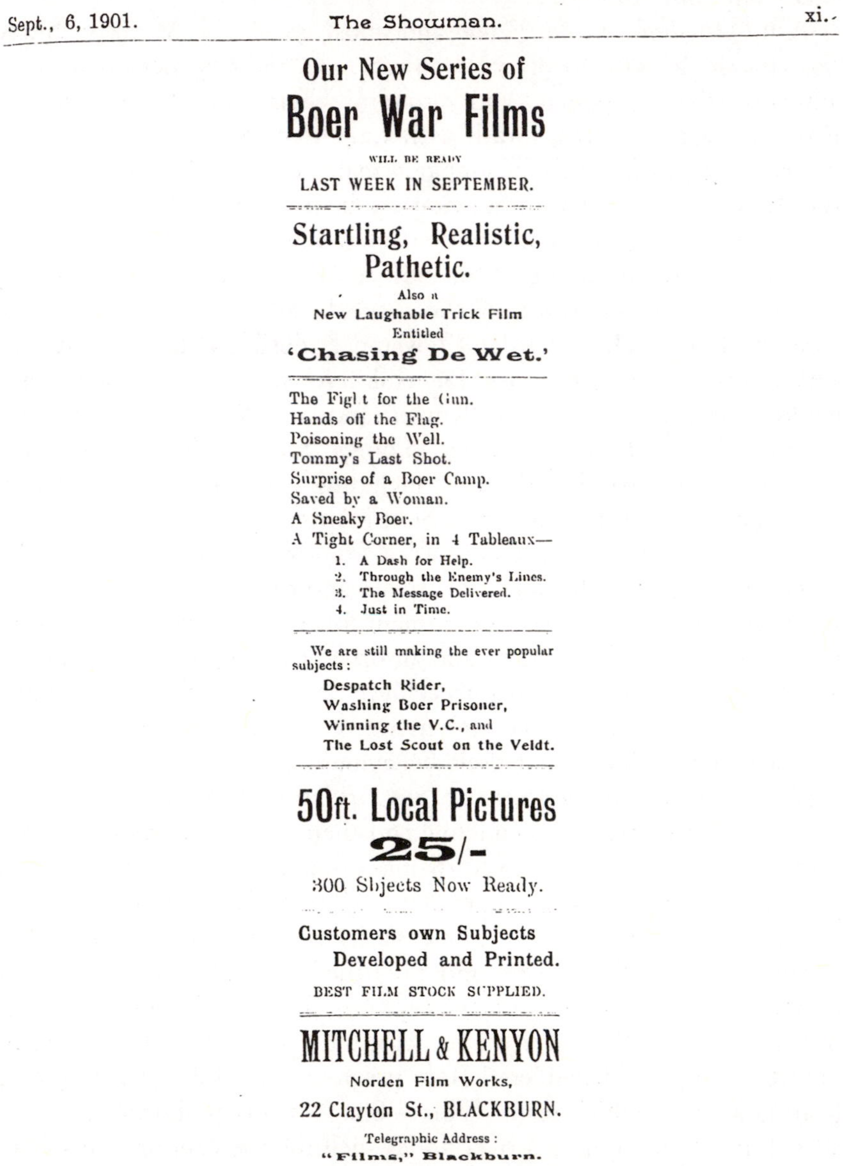

Sept., 6, 1901. The Showman. xi.

Our New Series of

Boer War Films

WILL BE READY

LAST WEEK IN SEPTEMBER.

Startling, Realistic, Pathetic.

Also a

New Laughable Trick Film

Entitled

'Chasing De Wet.'

The Fight for the Gun.
Hands off the Flag.
Poisoning the Well.
Tommy's Last Shot.
Surprise of a Boer Camp.
Saved by a Woman.
A Sneaky Boer.
A Tight Corner, in 4 Tableaux—

1. A Dash for Help.
2. Through the Enemy's Lines.
3. The Message Delivered.
4. Just in Time.

We are still making the ever popular subjects:

Despatch Rider,
Washing Boer Prisoner,
Winning the V.C., and
The Lost Scout on the Veldt.

50ft. Local Pictures

25/-

300 Sbjects Now Ready.

Customers own Subjects
Developed and Printed.

BEST FILM STOCK SUPPLIED.

MITCHELL & KENYON

Norden Film Works,

22 Clayton St., BLACKBURN.

Telegraphic Address:

"Films," Blackburn.

Plate 1. 1901 advertisement listing Mitchell and Kenyon's 'Boer War Films' (from *The Showman*, 6 September 1901)

Reports of well poisoning, the use of poisoned bullets, shelling Red Cross ambulances and the terrible treatment of British troops were commonplace.[11] But what upset the military civilian population more than anthing else was the abuse of the white flag. Reports of 'White Flag' incidents, where British troops were fired upon by surrendering Boers, reached a crescendo in the early months of 1900. The myriad press reports were soon augmented by literary and visual representations highlighting the British sense of fair play and the Boer disregard for international law, let alone good manners.[12] The narrative was even evoked in a children's serial run in *Chatterbox* during the summer of 1902. *Lost Sir Brian*, told in twenty-nine thrilling instalments, is the story of an orphaned member of the British aristocracy, brought up by Zulus and Boer farmers, who discovers his true identity during the Boer War and has to choose sides. The story, which covers activities during the campaign, features not one but two incidents in which the Boers abuse the white flag.[13] Reference is also made to such abuses in a music hall song entitled 'Tommy's Flag' by W.M. Elkington.[14]

These popular concerns were also taken up in films of the period. A series of staged patriotic films produced by the Mitchell and Kenyon Company in Blackburn between 1900 and 1902 illustrate this process (see Plate 1).[15] These films, dealing with events in South Africa, presented short tableaux replaying familiar narratives in an overtly theatrical manner and were made for display in staged, theatrical contexts. Whilst the advertising puff described them as depicting 'heroism, bravery and pluck set forth with perfect realism',[16] their reception by audiences is difficult to confirm. Their subjects were familiar: *Poisoning the Well* (1901), *White Flag Treachery* (1900), *Shelling the Red Cross* (1900), *A Sneaky Boer* (1900) and *Washing Boer Prisoners* (*Washing A Boer Prisoner in Camp*) (1900). Such titles are drawn from the list of atrocity stories illustrated above and display a strong journalistic sensibility.

Audiences were well aware of the presence of faked films, and that certain filmmakers and exhibitors did indeed attempt to deceive, as this reply to a letter to the *Optical Magic Lantern Journal* indicates:

> Sham War Cinematograph Films.—A correspondent asks us how he is to know real from sham war films, seeing that several subjects are made up at home from life models? The subject lends itself so well to life model work that one has to a great extent to rely on common sense: for instance in one film we have heard

about, there is a hand-to-hand encounter between Boers and British, all realistic in its way, but the effect is somewhat spoilt by reason of the fringe of an audience appearing in the picture occasionally. Thus, when one sees gentlemen with tall hats, accompanied by ladies, apparently looking on, common sense would at once pronounce the film of the sham order. The same may be said of films showing soldiers lying and firing from behind 'earthworks,' composed of nicely arranged straw.[17]

The Mitchell and Kenyon films draw on the standard Boer narratives, in which the patriotic behaviour of the Tommy is contrasted with the devious and unchivalrous conduct of the Boer. *Shelling the Red Cross* depicts wounded being carried into a tent, with female nurses in attendance. A smoking bomb is thrown into the tent, removed and thrown away. The subsequent explosion wounds the occupants of the tent further, and they are brought out, along with an injured nurse. The film ends with a shell-shocked orderly giving water to the wounded. *Hands off the Flag* similarly demonstrates the lack of civilized values as an outpost, occupied by nurses, is attacked. The Union Jack is torn down and defiled, the nurses, tied to the flagpole, are about to face summary execution by firing squad. The tableau ends with the return of the British troops and the salvation of the nurses and the flag.

The films are unrealistic and mimic narrative and compositional conventions evident in a broad range of representational contexts. They also employ two basic trick devices. The action in some of the films is exaggerated by scratches applied to the negative,[18] while in *Chasing De Wet* (1901) stop-start substitution is employed to make De Wet appear and disappear at will. Staged elements are even more evident in two other well-known patriotic films of the period, Warwick Trading Company's *The Set-to Between John Bull and Paul Kruger* (1900), and R.W. Paul's *Kruger's Dream Of Empire* (1900). Both use humour and sophisticated technical devices to develop an imperial polemic. The Warwick film is a staged boxing match between John Bull and Paul Kruger, in which Kruger deploys various dirty tricks, but Bull is finally triumphant. Paul's trick film is far more complex and indicative of the combination of pure entertainment and polemic evident in other contexts, especially the music hall and fairground.

> Trick Films Tableau:—Those who have had much experience in connection with taking pictures on cinematographic films, know that it is by no means a difficult task to produce the most absurd, yet realistic looking effects by means of judicious stops, rejoining

and other devices. One of the latest 'fakes' has been produced by Mr R.W. Paul, entitled 'Kruger's Dream of Empire.' When the scene opens the stage is occupied by a bust of Oom Paul and a large frame on which is boldly written 'On Majuba Day England was defeated.' Oom Paul enters and observes this with evident delight. He sits down in an arm-chair and dozes. The legend in the frame changes to a striking cartoon entitled 'Kruger the Conqueror,' in which Kruger himself is seen with one foot on a recumbent figure of Lord Roberts, and a rifle in one hand and a Bible in the other. To the real Kruger in his chair enters Mr Joseph Chamberlain with the British Crown on a silken cushion. He kneels and presents this to Kruger, but, as Kruger stretches forth his hands to grasp it, it vanishes in a puff of smoke. Kruger is rudely awakened from his illusion, and while he gazes on the cartoon suddenly changes to the words 'On Majuba Day Cronje surrendered.'

In his rage he rushes to seize Chamberlain, but the latter suddenly disappears, and at the same time the bust of Kruger changes to a bust of Queen Victoria, which Kruger endeavours to overthrow. While doing so four men in Khaki enter and seize him, placing him on a pedestal. They drape him with the Union Jack. Two of the men step forward and fire on Kruger. As the shot is fired Kruger vanishes and his place is taken by a stately figure of Britannia.[19]

These domestically staged films, along with their American counter-parts,[20] seemingly existed in opposition to the topical material produced by various companies during the campaign. Topicals acted in some respects as a living newspaper and an extension of received journalistic practice. This was certainly one of the key strategies employed in selling these films to the public and in attempting to retain an audience under difficult circumstances. The vicissitudes of operating in the field are well chronicled in W.K.L. Dickson's *The Biograph in Battle*,[21] and once the rigours of the veldt and the censor were overcome the resulting product had to be transported half-way around the globe and marketed. Initial responses to these films were enthusiastic, even though there was a delay of several months between the outbreak of the campaign and the receipt of the first images from the front. Yet somehow topicals ultimately failed to supply the vicarious displays of patriotism provided by more theatrical entertainments.

Apart from the touring Biograph Company presentations, which consisted of an extended cinematic programme, the other 'realistic' films were increasingly integrated into the broad context of theatrical performances and patriotic entertainment. I would argue that topicals provided a framework for understanding staged films and performances. They worked both as a theatrical backdrop and a limited evidential form, lending legitimacy to other cultural forms. These forms predated not only the arrival of the topicals and the staged patriotic films, but the medium of film itself. The contexts into which films entered provided a sophisticated and demanding set of audiences, used to spectacle and hyperbole.

Before the arrival of films dealing with the campaign, audiences had been presented with screenings of stock footage, lantern slides and dramatic representations of the conflict. The Belle Vue Zoological gardens in Manchester, for instance, provided a series of spectacular entertainments representing and recreating events from South Africa. These open air performances, staged on an artificial island in the middle of the boating lake and at other venues on the massive site, combined music, fireworks displays, light shows, tableaux vivants and a mock battle often involving more than a hundred participants. Events included 'The Siege of Ladysmith', in summer 1900 and, in 1902, 'The Battle of Paardeberg'. The following handbill advertising 'The Siege of Ladysmith' provides a flavour of the spectacle:

> In the evening, at dusk, are reproduced the stirring incidents in the
> SIEGE OF LADYSMITH
> with the final and successful struggle that drove the Boers northward.
>
> The flickering camp fires show the Burghers dotted in the picturesque positions among the rocks cooking their evening meal. A Kaffir runner trying to steal through their lines is captured, stripped and flogged. The Boers next cut the telegraph, and blow up the railway bridge in a most realistic manner. Then lie in wait for the armoured train. This, seen in the distance, rushes on until a displaced rail overthrows a truck under the enemy's fire. After a desperate but useless struggle, many of the English are taken prisoners.
> The beleaguered garrison revenge themselves by smashing a Long Tom, and clearing their way back at bayonet's point. President Kruger then arrives, exhorting his Burghers to drive back the Khaki multitudes advancing under Buller. They fight desperately until the British, throwing Pontoons across the river, turn their flank with men and guns.

They then fall back along the line, our mounted infantry hurrying the retreat. The town guns then boom the glad tidings of the relief, and a tableau represents

THE ENTRY OF LORD DUNDONALD INTO LADYSMITH

amid the joyful acclamations of the besieged. Next are seen illuminated portraits, framed in Shamrock, Rose, and Thistle, of our victorious commander-in-chief

LORD ROBERTS and the HEROES OF LADYSMITH and MAFEKING

supported by representative figures of our home and colonial forces, and surmounted by the motto, in dazzling points of variegated fire,

FOR QUEEN AND COUNTRY.

Then the final glory of soaring rockets and bursting shells, a myriad electric lights flash forth the honoured title: DEFENDERS OF THE EMPIRE.[22]

Such spectacular entertainment was not unusual. Indeed the Warwick Trading Company produced a film of the Savage South Africa Troop at Earls Court in 1899.[23] The troop, which re-enacted events from the Zulu Wars, and the film, subsequently toured several venues during the war.

'Fresh from the Front'

One of the venues visited by the Savage South Africa Troop was the city of Leeds.[24] A brief look at the variety of war-related entertainments on offer in the city in this period will provide a good sense of the context in which Boer War films were produced and consumed. Leeds had a thriving theatrical scene around the turn of the century, with a range of theatres and music halls including the Tivoli Theatre of Varieties, the Leeds Coliseum, the Empire Palace and the Leeds City Varieties, catering for a broad, but increasingly integrated audience.[25] During the first year of the war, between October 1899 and October 1900, film played an increasingly central role as part of popular stage entertainments, but was rarely presented as a single or indeed primary attraction. Films were integrated into general variety bills, as was the norm in such venues, but they increasingly entered the context of the 'patriotic' display, or became the focus of or patriotic interlude within a programme following the outbreak of hostilities. If one begins to analyse specific programmes and existing reviews there is a discernible move away from the general variety bill within music halls and theatres to fully integrated patriotic performances.

The initial status of topical and staged films, in the early months of 1900, was as a distinct, individual entertainment. Advertising played up the unique, immediate nature of the images as 'Fresh from the Front', or 'From the seat of battle'.[26] One of the earliest reviewed film shows at the Empire in January 1900 provides an insight into the mood of the audience and the initial impact of these films:

> There is a tremendously popular feature in this week's Empire programme in the form of a bio-tableaux, representing 'Living Pictures' from the seat of war. Last night's audience cheered wildly when the presentment of Lord Roberts was shown on the screen, and everyone must have felt that in the spontaneous outburst of enthusiasm there was considerable significance. . . . One and all of these patriotic pictures stirred deeply the emotions of the crowded audience.[27]

The arrival of the Biograph Company's show in Leeds in March 1900[28] created great interest and attracted glowing reviews, but importantly marked the brief highpoint achieved by film as the single focus of such entertainments. The scale and reach of the advertising, which included mention of the quality and size of the images, would prove an impossible act to follow,[29] a fact well evidenced in contemporary reviews:

> The biograph is now a recognized institution in both peace and war, and of all the varying types of machine which are now ministering to the martial spirit of the public, that showing at the Leeds Coliseum is perhaps the most perfect. Great enterprise has been shown in obtaining photographic films depicting exciting scenes at the scene of hostilities, and quite a unique picture is that giving a panoramic of the North camp and Chievenley. One sees how the 4.7 guns were worked by 'the jollies, Her Majesty's Jollies,' how the Red Cross men did their work at the Tugels, where shot and shell rained death on the troops: how bridges were

re-constructed, and how Tommy looks on the field of battle; everything is clear and free from blur, and the biograph is indeed a new chronicle and brief abstract of these moving times. A special patriotic programme has been arranged for Wednesday night, when the Black Dyke Band will be in attendance.[30]

The 'special patriotic programme' increasingly became the standard context for the exhibition of films, which were often used to illustrate and complement other visual representations of the war. In the same month as the Biograph visit, Mr Luscombe Searle was delivering his 'Celebrated "chat" (humorous and instructive) illustrated with songs, the latest cinematograph and limelight views from the seat of the war'.[31] There were also presentations by Eugene Sandow, and Harry. H. Hamilton's *Deeds that Won the Empire*, both of which integrated war films into the body of the programmes.[32] These patriotic entertainments were mirrored by purely theatrical reviews of events in South Africa, such as *The Tommy Atkins Review, Our Navy* and *Our War with the Transvaal*, which combined tableaux vivants, songs, short dramatic recreations and demonstrations of drill and uniforms.

Audience reception of these entertainments is notoriously difficult to assess. Brief press notices do little to illuminate the nature and atmosphere inside the halls and theatres. Some reported accounts point to the overtly theatrical attempts to affect audiences and create patriotic feeling. The display outside the venue, redolent of fairground barkers and paraders, was a common ploy. The use of uniformed actors and veterans added to the excitement of the event.[33] One report of a performance in Manchester detailed the use not only of uniformed actors, but also of live cartridges during the screening of films; another noted the interaction of stooges in the audience.[34] The ambience of the performance naturally conditioned the reception of the war films and unquestioningly positioned them at the heart of an ideologically informed hyper-narrative.

There is more work to be done on the composition of these narratives and their relationship with Boer war films.[35] But what is evident from this tentative appraisal is the symbiotic relationship between the various representational forms of the period. As entertainment, and as a news medium, the war films, in their broadest sense, both mirror and mediate cultural and political concerns within the emergent mass visual culture of the early twentieth century. They operate as visual stimuli, as original texts, and as sites of confirmation and comparison. The crucial mediating role they assume in relation to other popular entertainment forms and cultural practices, and their complex relationship with audiences, demands further investigation. If we are to understand the true nature of these relationships, film historians must increasingly consider interpretative models that focus on the intersection of different media, cultural forms and narratives.

Notes

1. See, for example, John Barnes, *The Beginnings of the Cinema in England: Volume Four, 1899* (Exeter: University of Exeter Press, 1996; first published 1992, as *Filming the Boer War*), Stephen Bottomore, 'Frederic Villiers, War Correspondent,' *Sight and Sound*, vol. 49, no. 4, Autumn 1980, pp. 250–5, and Bottomore, 'The Most Glorious Profession,' *Sight and Sound*, vol. 52, no. 4, Autumn 1983, pp. 260–5.
2. Robert Machray, 'A Group of Battle Painters and War Artists,' *Windsor Magazine*, vol. 12, June–November 1900, pp. 261–2.
3. Preface, *The Anglo Boer War 1899–1900* (Capetown: Denis Edwards & Co., 1900).
4. W.B. Woollen, Letter to the Editor, *Friend* (Bloemfontein), 13 April 1900, p. 379.
5. *The Black and White Budget*, vol. 2, no. 19, 17 February 1900, p. 22.
6. See, for example, Richard Brown and Barry Anthony, *A Victorian Film Enterprise: The History of the British Mutoscope and Biograph Company, 1897–1915* (Trowbridge: Flicks Books, 1999).
7. *Photogram*, July 1900, p. 300.
8. Arthur C. Banfield, 'The War in Toyland,' *Royal Magazine*, vol. 4, May–October 1900, pp. 396–9.
9. Robert Machray, 'Strange Things Seen in Shop Windows,' *Royal Magazine*, vol. 3, November 1899–April 1900, pp. 515–21.
10. Captain Clive Dixon, *The Leaguer of Ladysmith* (London: Eyre and Spottiswood, 1901).
11. See, for example, 'Firing on the Ambulance,' Supplement to the *Illustrated London News*, vol. 115, 9 December 1899, p. 3; and 'Notes o' War,' *The Black and White Budget*, vol. 1, no. 9, 9 December 1899, p. 6.
12. See for example, 'Abuse of the White Flag,' *Illustrated London News*, vol. 115, 9 December 1899, p. 827.
13. *Chatterbox*, 1902, pp. 162, 170, 182, 186, 194, 202, 214, 218, 230, 238, 242, 250, 258, 270, 278, 286, 294, 302, 307, 318, 326, 334, 338, 350, 358, 366, 370, 382, 386.
14. *The Black and White Budget*, vol. 3, no. 29, 28 April 1900, p. 128.
15. Robin Whalley and Peter Worden, 'Forgotten Firm: A Short Chronological Account of Mitchell and Kenyon, Cinematographers,' *Film History*, vol. 10, 1998, pp. 35–51.

16. *Showman*, 6 September 1901, p. xi.
17. *Optical Magic Lantern Journal*, March 1900, p. 3.
18. This device was employed in many of the films, most notably in *Tommy's Last Shot*.
19. *Optical Magic Lantern Journal*, June 1900, p. 70.
20. A series of staged Boer War films were produced for the Edison Company by James White. For full details and to download these films visit the Library of Congress website. http://memory.loc.gov/.
21. W.K.L. Dixon, *The Biograph in Battle* (Trowbridge: Flicks Books, 1997; first published 1901).
22. This handbill is kindly reproduced from the Jennison Collection, Cheethams Library, Manchester.
23. *Savage South Africa—Attack and Repulse*, Warwick Trading Company (1899).
24. The troop performed in Leeds for three weeks, commencing 8 October 1900.
25. For a discussion of the music hall audience, see Dagmar Hoher, 'The Composition of Music Hall Audiences 1850–1900,' in Peter Bailey, ed., *The Business of Pleasure* (Milton Keynes: Open University Press, 1986), pp. 72–92.
26. Such descriptions were common throughout this period.
27. *Yorkshire Post*, 9 January 1900, frontis.
28. The Biograph run commenced on 19 March 1900. It was advertised for two weeks, but actually ran until 7 April.
29. A subsequent engagement commenced on 7 January 1901, for three weeks. It was advertised on Christmas Eve 1900, especial mention being made of the size of the images, 25 feet by 22 feet. *Yorkshire Post*, 24 December 1900, frontis.
30. *Yorkshire Post*, 3 April 1900, p. 8.
31. Ibid., 20 March 1900, p. 9.
32. Eugene Sandow review: *Yorkshire Post*, 16 March 1900, p. 10. Harry Hamilton review: *Yorkshire Post*, 6 October 1900, frontis.
33. 'William Clarke,' *Showman*, 1 February 1901, p. 73. I am indebted to the National Fairground Archive for supplying this reference.
34. 'A Cinematographic Incident,' *British Journal of Photography* (Supplement) 1 November 1901, p. 83. I am indebted to Richard Brown for this reference.
35. I am currently pursuing this research for a forthcoming book.

2

James Williamson's Rescue Narratives

Frank Gray

James Williamson, the Hove chemist, magic lanternist, photographer and X-Ray photographer, began to make animated photographs in 1897. The first productions by this leading British film pioneer were single-shot, one-minute actualities. In 1900, he began to make his first multi-shot fiction films. In this chapter, I want to examine three important works made by Williamson between 1900 and 1905 in order to reveal how they conform broadly to the general characteristics of what I call the rescue narrative. They are: *Attack on a China Mission—Bluejackets to the Rescue* (1900), *Two Little Waifs* (1905) and the film I shall deal with in most detail, *Fire!* (1901). While each film sets up a threat, a victim and a rescuer in its own way, they all draw on well-established cultural conventions.

Rescue narratives, typically, are stories in which familiar representatives of the dominant culture—a woman, a child or a family—are thrown into a crisis precipitated by the arrival of a disruptive force. This causal agent takes on many guises. It can be natural forces (fire, the sea) but usually takes bodily form through a manifestation of an 'other', such as other races or ethnicities, the psychotic, the criminal or the supernatural. This other, indeed this 'evil', places the 'good' in a position of danger. The restoration of normality can only be achieved through the intervention of a rescuer. The rescuer, as that force for good which can and will restore order, is traditionally played a man. Such saviours, in modern texts, are embodied usually by fathers, the military, the police or the fire service. Rescue narratives generally function to provide emotive depictions of survival, security, comfort and hope for a 'real' world that suffers from terror, tragedy and death. It can be argued that the rescue narrative's relationship with the dialectics of life and death, good and evil, provides it with its cultural purpose and significance.

In nineteenth-century Britain, rescue narratives could be found in popular melodrama, magic lantern lectures, news stories, short stories and novels—and even through live spectacles created for circus tents and Buffalo Bill's Wild West show. In the twentieth century, rescue narratives have become an essential part of popular cinema. They have been employed as a narrative framework across many film genres, including horror, science fiction, holocaust films, crime and the western. From the actions of the Ku Klux Klan in Griffith's *Birth of a Nation* (1915) to the Cavalry doing its duty in *Stagecoach* (1939), from Moses leading the Israelites across the Red Sea in *The Ten Commandments* (1956) to the military saving the planet in *Independence Day* (1996), in all such films powerful and successful solutions are brought to bear and the 'good' are saved. The rescue narrative has also found its place within television. Typical examples from British television in the 1990s include the drama series *London's Burning* and the documentary series, *Rescue 999*. By returning to Williamson's films from the early 1900s, we can look at the way in which the rescue format provided an important structuring device for early narrative films.

Attack on a China Mission—Bluejackets to the Rescue

Attack on a China Mission—Bluejackets to the Rescue (abbreviated to *Attack* for the remainder of this chapter) was made in the autumn of 1900 and was Williamson's first edited multi-shot narrative film. This four-shot work of 230 feet came after a summer of inspired filmmaking by George Albert Smith, his Hove friend and counterpart. Smith's films of 1900—*As Seen Through the Telescope* (three shots), *Grandma's Reading Glass* (eleven shots), *The House That Jack Built* (two shots) and *Let Me Dream Again* (two shots)—were innovative in their creation of subjective and objective point-of-view shots and dream-time, and their use of reversing and interpolative close-ups. It is in the context of this development of English film form that Williamson conceived and executed *Attack*. Its appearance marks his move from the production of non-continuous to continuous narratives.[1]

The production and reception of *Attack*, Williamson's first rescue narrative, was informed by events in China in 1900. Williamson created the film at the end of a year in which the Boxer Rebellion had overshadowed the ongoing Boer War and become the most important international incident of the year. In its review of 1900, *The Times* devoted much attention to the 'China Crisis'. It articulated the conflict between the Boxers and the 'Powers' (Britain, Germany, Austria, America, France, Italy, Japan and Russia) as a symbolic and dramatic struggle between the West and the East, in which the victory of the Powers over the Boxers marked the return to order and the 'triumph' of the West.[2]

Williamson's film was one of a small film genre of 'faked incidents' representing the 'China Crisis' of 1900. They were all informed by the Western interpretation of the Boxer Rebellion and were all imagined, dramatized scenes of the conflict. The English film company of Mitchell and Kenyon, based in Blackburn, produced four Boxer films in July 1900, including *Attack on a Mission Station*. This single-shot, 86-foot film provided Williamson with a simple prototype. It depicts a missionary and his family, the subsequent attack by the Boxers and the rescue of the family by the British Army.

The making of Williamson's more sophisticated film was undertaken after the release of this film. It is a chronological arrangement of four shots with an adequately defined sense of simultaneity and consecutive action, in which the individual shots have been unified into a plausible whole. We can read the four shots as an edited sequence without ellipsis. It has a very straightforward structure:

> Shot 1: Chinese Boxers break into the grounds of the Mission Station.
> Shot 2: The Missionary and his household, surprised by the Boxer attack, begin to take defensive action. The Missionary is killed instantly.
> Shot 3: Almost simultaneously, the British Bluejackets arrive at the Station to rescue the family and fire volleys of shots at the Boxers.
> Shot 4: The Boxers are overwhelmed and taken prisoner, and the Station is saved.

The events of the Boxer Rebellion provided Williamson with a 'closed' text which functioned to present a state of crisis and siege—the attack on the mission and the killing of the missionary—and the subsequent relief provided by the arrival of the Bluejackets and their rescue of the missionary's family and household. The film, like Mitchell and Kenyon's, was an abstraction of the actual attacks on the Christian communities by the Boxers throughout 1899 and 1900 and the siege and liberation of the legations in Peking from June to August 1900. It was thus an imagined view in which world affairs could be addressed from the official British perspective. It became, therefore, a mythic and moral distillation of the imperial narrative.

For the location, Williamson had 'rented a derelict house with a large garden, called Ivy Lodge'.[3] This Victorian villa in Hove, set within a walled garden, was very suitable for his Boxer drama, as contemporary reports had described the British Legation in Peking as 'a garden of some ten acres, partly occupied by buildings, and surrounded with a high wall of sun-dried clay'.[4] The dense foliage around Ivy Lodge enabled Williamson to keep the everyday life of Hove out of his shots thereby creating a rough illusion of a Chinese scene. Williamson's daughter, Florence, was cast as the 'young girl'. The 'Missionary' was performed by Ernest Lepard, Manager of the Brighton Alhambra Opera House and Music Hall. It is likely that the Bluejackets were members of the Hove Coast Guard and the Royal Naval Volunteer Reserve.

When exhibited in Brighton and elsewhere, Williamson's film was placed in a commercial context devoted to pleasure and national celebration. It was probably irrelevant to the late Victorian audience that Williamson's film was staged in Hove, England, and displayed the Boxers in absurd ceremonial dress. We can imagine the audience's applause for the victory of Empire, Christendom and the West. Against the spectre of the 'yellow peril' and an international war founded on racial, cultural and religious differences, victory had been secured.

Fire!

Williamson's next major film, *Fire!*, depicts a household being rescued from the threat of a fire. As such, it needs to be related to the wider cultural history of the fire service, fire rescue narratives and the late Victorian bourgeois world. As Victorian urban society grew exponentially throughout the second half of the century, the fireman, the fire service and the fire rescue became important symbols of this modern environment. The heroic fireman, as cast in an epic manner by John Millais in his painting *The Rescue* of 1855, epitomized a new sense of civic duty and honour. Rarely was the fireman named. This new hero was altruistic and devoted to the defence of lives and property. Fire rescue dramas were represented through song, performed on stage, adapted into sets of magic lantern slides with accompanying readings, recorded on film from 1894 and even, by 1904, performed 'live' out-of-doors at Coney Island. International fire congresses, in London in 1893 and Paris in 1900, mounted competitions between brigades from different countries. One of the events in London began with firemen in bed, followed by the sounding of the alarm, their descent down a flight of stairs, the harnessing of the horses and the departure from the engine house. Such narratives and performances would be informed by the experience of 'actual' fire stories and their written and visual documentation in newspapers and periodicals.

The first issue in 1891 of the *Strand* magazine, an illustrated English monthly periodical, contained an article devoted to the contemporary fascination with 'fire culture'. It is a fine example because of its evocation of the successful rescue:

> Suddenly arises a yell—a wild unearthly cry, which almost makes one's blood run cold in that atmosphere. A tremor seizes us as a female form appears at an upper window, framed in flame, curtained with smoke and noxious fumes.
>
> 'Save her! Save her!'
>
> The crowd sways and surges; women scream; strong men clench their hands and swear—Heaven only knows why. But before the police have headed back the people the escape is on the spot, two men are on it, one outstrips his mate, and darting up the ladder, leaps into the open window.
>
> He is swallowed up in a moment—lost to our sight. Will he ever return out of that fiery furnace? Yes, here he is, bearing a senseless female form, which he passes out to his mate, who is calmly watching his progress, though the ladder is in imminent danger. Quick! The flames approach!
>
> The man on the ladder does not wait as his mate again disappears and emerges with a child about fourteen. Carrying this burden easily, he descends the ladder. The first man is already flying down the escape, head-first, holding the woman's dress round her feet. The others, rescuer and rescued, follow. The ladder is withdrawn, burning. A mighty cheer arises 'mid the smoke. Two lives saved! The fire is being mastered. More engines gallop up. 'The Captain' is on the spot, too. The Brigade is victorious.
>
> In the early morning hour, as I strolled home deep in thought, I determined to see these men who nightly risk their lives and stalwart limbs for the benefit and preservation of helpless fire-scorched people. Who are these men who go literally through

fire and water to assist and save their fellow creatures, strangers to them—unknown, save in that they require help and succour?[5]

The magic lantern industry in Britain in the late 1880s and early 1890s produced several sets of lantern slides with readings on the theme of both fire and sea rescues. Williamson would have known of such material as he was a practising lanternist during this period and sold lanterns and lantern supplies from his chemist's shop in Hove. The lantern series of c.1890, *Bob the Fireman, or, Life in the Red Brigade*, was particularly popular. It consisted of twelve slides with a reading of approximately 1,600 words and very closely followed the structure of the *Strand* article:

> Firemen are brave as I said before, sir, but it seemed utter folly and madness to attempt what most of us felt was an impossible task. Just then Bob's voice rang out, 'Run the escape up again, boys, I'll chance it.' We knew if anyone could do it, Bob would; but there was not one of us but what expected he would lose his life. The escape must be burnt through if it remained leaning against that wall of living fire three minutes . . . Up he sprang like a cat; there was not an instant to lose. The flames leaped round him. Once he paused and threw back his head and we thought all was over. The flames were singeing his hair and blackening his face. Then he went up again and at last reached the window, but to our astonishment we saw him, instead of seizing the child and coming down, enter the room . . . And he appeared with not the girl only, but a boy also, clasped in his arms. But would he ever get down alive? The escape was on fire now . . . Suddenly a voice cries, 'Jump, Bob, quick.' He is within six feet of the ground, the escape snaps, but with a bound at just the very critical moment, he springs off and alights on the ground shaken but safe. His hands and feet are terribly scorched, and for nearly three weeks he was under the doctor's hands, but he didn't seem to care. The precious lives saved seemed sufficient recompense to him for what he had gone through.[6]

A news story from 1891, from a Brighton newspaper, provides a succinct 'real life' complement to these two depictions of a fire rescue:

> A fire, which had it not been for the prompt measures of one or two members of the Brighton Police Fire Brigade, would certainly have resulted in the death of a woman who was in bed, occurred

on Saturday night at 3, Brunswick Row. The fire was discovered by some persons living in the same row, when flames were seen issuing from an upper bedroom of the cottage. News of the fire soon reached the Level Police Station and a posse of firemen and constables were not long in arriving at the scene with a hose reel. While water was being applied to the flames the door of the cottage was forced open. Chief-engineer Holloway rushed upstairs and groping about amid the smoke discovered the wife of the occupier, Mr. Clark, lying on a bed in an insensible condition and partly suffocated, with the assistance of Auxiliary-engineer Parker he managed to convey her downstairs. She was taken to some neighbours and after a few minutes was restored to consciousness.[7]

These three examples of fire dramas, despite their differences in context and prose styles, share much in terms of narrative development and suggest a composite dramatic framework that might be broken down into the following stages:

1. detection/raising the alarm
2. preparation/departure
3. journey: the race to the blaze
4. fighting the flames
5. the successful rescue.

All of the early fire rescue films made in Europe and America relate to this pattern. The clear emphasis on chronological order and linear causality was maintained and, indeed, provided a rationale for the arrangement of shots. The history of this subject in film begins with single-shot, non-fiction 'views' of fire services in action. The earliest of these was the Edison Company's one-shot *Fire Rescue Scene* (1894), followed in 1897 by Edison's series of four single-shot films: *A Morning Alarm, Starting for the Fire, Going to the Fire* and *Fighting the Fire*. As the titles indicate, these films began to express the various narrative elements of the fire rescue structure, each part roughly identifying with one of the stages. They were sold as separate films but could be exhibited together as a sequence. In Europe contributions to the fire genre were made by many film companies in the late 1890s. In 1897 the Lumière Company released a four-part work with a similar structure: *Firemen—Getting Ready, Firemen—Departure of Fire Engine, Firemen—Playing at the Fire* and *Firemen— Life Saving*. In 1899 in Britain, the Warwick Trading Company, Robert Paul and Charles

Plate 2. Frame still from *Fire!* (Williamson, 1901)

Goodwin Norton all made single-shot films that shared some aspect of the fire rescue.

From their catalogue descriptions, the two films produced in the summer of 1900 by Eberhard Schneider for the Edison Company appear conceptually to be the most ambitious fire films made to date. *Fire Drills at Breslau, Germany* and *Breslau Fire Department in Action* were each 200 feet in length and consisted of a sequence of exterior shots depicting various different stages of the fire rescue. They may have provided Williamson with a significant template because the Schneider films were both presented as single films possessing all of the actions associated with a fire rescue.[8]

Williamson's fire rescue film of 1901 appears to be very conscious of this history in the way in which it follows the established narrative model. In this five-shot film, a policeman discovers a house in flames, he informs the fire brigade, fire escapes and fire engine are prepared and depart, a fireman rescues a 'helpless' man from his burning bedroom and, in the concluding shot, all of the members of the household are saved. Williamson was evidently very proud of this film, describing it in his 1902 catalogue as 'undoubtedly the most sensational fire scene which has yet been kinematographed, ... [which] never fails to arouse the utmost enthusiasm. To enhance the effect, portions of the film are stained red.'[9]

The transitions from shot to shot, the sense of temporal economy and the effective staging reflect Williamson's interest in creating an intense drama. The policeman makes his discovery and therefore initiates the rescue narrative. He runs out of shot, to the right, only to immediately run into the next shot from the left in order to arouse the sleeping fire station. The firemen quickly prepare and race out of frame on their horse-drawn carriages, exiting left. This movement binds these first two shots together, the ellipsis in time and space being comprehensible and contributing to a sense of urgency. The next shot maintains this pulse. From a low angle, a horse-drawn fire escape moves from the background to the foreground, followed by a fire engine. Through careful planning and by working with his local fire brigade, Williamson created a shot of unique graphic power. As the last carriage races past the camera and out of frame, a jump cut takes the viewer into the next shot, which is tinted red and located within the heart of the fire. A man is trapped in his burning bedroom, unable to escape. A fireman breaks in through the window, places the man on his shoulder, and steps out of the window. A crude continuity edit, probably the first of its kind, links this shot to the final 'scene'—a long shot, also tinted red, of the exterior of the house. It begins with the fireman climbing out of the window, onto the ladder and descending the escape. From a studio set to a location—the edit bridges the two and attempts to bind them into a seamless whole.

Fire! reflects Williamson's understanding of the rescue narrative and his ambition to find the means to develop, on film, a more complex and arresting interpretation of the fire rescue drama. By designing a work of fiction which employed the apparatus and staff of a real fire brigade, used locations and a set, and possessed careful shot construction and a clear editing strategy, Williamson created a film with a passionate, dramatic energy. This quality was missing from the non-fiction fire rescues on film but had always been part of the rescue dramas found in print, on stage and on the screen at the lantern lecture. Williamson demonstrates in *Fire!*, as he had done in his China film of the previous year, his interest in visualizing a drama so that the viewer became intrigued by the unfolding of the narrative. This is best expressed in the film by the scene in the bedroom of the burning house. Previous fire films had all focused on the exterior events whereas Williamson brought an innovation to the fire rescue narrative by employing both exterior and interior spaces. It is this expansion of

'hero' finds the Gypsy's home and, across two shots, effectively liberates the girl from it. The use of a left- and right-hand mask on the interior shot of the stairwell, which he descends as he cradles the rescued girl amidst the smoke from the fire, creates a concentrated and intense expression of this moment. He then emerges, in the following shot, from the burning building to daylight. His achievement is timed perfectly because the very next shot depicts the Gypsy's quarters being destroyed by flames. Williamson's use of cross-cutting in this sequence, from the exterior of the house to the interior, upstairs room of the Gypsy and his wife, creates a sense of urgency and, as a result of the father's action, relief. In this fundamentalist drama, good has been victorious. The perpetrator of the crime of child abduction has died. In the final shot, the rescued girl and her new family express love and security, suggesting that the trauma has passed.

Rescued by Rover, by Cecil Hepworth, was also produced in 1905 and is similar to *Two Little Waifs* since it too is a rescue narrative based on child abduction.[15] The kidnapper is described in the Hepworth catalogue as both 'a wicked-looking beggar woman' and 'the gipsy woman'. The baby is rescued through the combined efforts of the family's 'faithful Collie dog' and the Father: '. . . he rushes home again, and places the baby in its mother's arms, while the dog, almost dancing for joy, impartially licks the faces of master, mistress and little playmate.' Unlike the villains of Williamson's film, the 'drunken old woman' does not die in her 'filthy attic' as a result of her crime. But like Williamson, Hepworth makes an important distinction between two very different worlds. They are defined, in class terms, by the comfortable, 'luxurious' environment of the family and the gypsy woman's 'slum'.[16]

We can interpret Williamson's *Attack, Fire!* and *Two Little Waifs* as depictions of attacks on middle-class spaces and their occupants. The responsible agents of civil society—the military, the fire service, fathers—come to the rescue and save those in peril. In some respects, these altruistic heroes become the defenders of a public culture in an era that was beginning to recognize the value of public services. We can position these films as advertisements for a modern, civilized nation that can appear to protect itself, and therefore its subjects, from any threat.

They also contributed to the foundation of the dominant narrative paradigm in the American and European film industries. As Bordwell has written:

the classical film respects the canonic pattern of establishing an initial state of affairs which gets violated and which must then be set right. Indeed, Hollywood screenplay-writing manuals have long insisted on a formula that has been revived in recent structural analysis: the plot consists of an undisturbed stage, the disturbance, the struggle, and the elimination of the disturbance.[17]

The late Victorian and early Edwardian rescue narrative could not allude either to modern rescue missions which resulted in failure—as encapsulated by the memory of General Gordon—or to news stories of everyday tragedy. It worked to provide comfort and confidence in a world of uncertainty and change. The rescue narrative's popularity throughout Victorian culture led easily to its early and successful entry into 'animated photography' and the subsequent commercial benefits derived from its exploitation.

Notes

1. A longer analysis of this film and its context can be found in my paper, 'James Williamson's "Composed Picture": *Attack on a China Mission— Bluejackets to the Rescue* (1900),' in John Fullerton, ed., *Celebrating 1895: The Centenary of Cinema* (Sydney: John Libbey, 1998), pp. 203–11.
2. *The Times*, 31 December 1900, p. 11.
3. Extract from Florence Williamson's hand-written notes on the production of the film (held in the South East Film and Video Archive [SEFVA] Collection). Ivy Lodge also served as the location of the burning house in Williamson's *Fire!*.
4. *The Times* 31 December 1900, p. 12.
5. 'The Metropolitan Fire Brigade. Its Home and its Work,' *Strand*, vol. 1, January 1891, pp. 22–3.
6. 'Bob the Fireman: Or Life in the Red Brigade,' *Descriptive Lectures For the Complete Series of Lithographic Lantern Slides* (London: A.W. Gamage, *c*.1890), pp. 126–9 (SEFVA Collection).
7. 'Fire,' *Brighton Guardian*, 1 April 1891, p. 8.
8. Charles Musser, *Edison Motion Pictures, 1890–1900, An Annotated Filmography* (Washington: Smithsonian Institute Press, 1997), p. 617.
9. *Williamson's Kinematograph Films*, September 1902, pp. 27–8 (SEFVA Collection).
10. Martin Sopocy examines the relationship between these two films in *James Williamson, Studies and Documents of a Pioneer of the Film Narrative* (London: Associated University Presses, 1998), pp. 46–60. Musser explores the cultural origins of Porter's film and positions it, as we can do with *Fire!*, as a key work within the early evolution of the 'story film'.

Charles Musser, *Before the Nickeklodeon, Edwin S. Porter and the Edison Manufacturing Company* (Berkeley: University of California Press, 1991), pp. 212–34.

11. Gaston Bachelard, *The Poetics of Space* (Boston: Beacon Press, 1969), p. 17.

12. F.M.L. Thompson, *The Rise of Respectable Society, A Social History of Victorian Britain 1830–1900* (London: Fontana, 1988), p. 175.

13. Hove Museum possesses a Williamson family photograph album. It covers the years *c.*1890–1910.

14. The title of the film is borrowed from Mrs Molesworth's children's novel of 1883. This story is about two young children and their stay in Paris during the mysterious absence of their father. It has very little connection with the film's narrative. Mrs Molesworth, *Two Little Waifs* (London: Macmillan, 1883).

15. The Edison Company also made a child abduction film in 1905, *Stolen by Gypsies*.

16. From the film's catalogue description as found in Rachael Low and Roger Manvell, *The History of the British Film 1896–1906* (London: George Allen & Unwin, 1948), pp. 109–10.

17. David Bordwell, *Narration in the Fiction Film* (London: Methuen, 1985), p. 157.

3

Cecil Hepworth, *Alice in Wonderland* and the Development of the Narrative Film

Andrew Higson

Hepworth's *Alice* and Early English Cinema

Cinema, in England as elsewhere, was not in the first instance primarily a narrative medium.[1] It was only over time that filmmakers developed strategies for producing extended story films and rendering them intelligible to contemporary audiences. They had to find ways of transforming the contingency of the turn-of-the-century film programme—a string of short attractions, many of them non-fiction, related if at all only thematically—into the consequentiality of narrative. They had to discover how to create a coherent, comprehensible experience out of a series of images, a visual variety show. Several strategies emerged. Some were internal to the film text, notably the use of the chase as a means of linking similar actions in disparate spaces; others were external to the text, notably the reliance on an audience's prior knowledge of a story to fill in the gaps between the narrative fragments presented on screen.[2]

Alice in Wonderland, an adaptation of Lewis Carroll's 'nonsense' children's story, made by Cecil Hepworth and Percy Stow for the Hepworth Manufacturing Company in 1903, provides an admirable case study of how such strategies were developed.[3] By the standards of the time, this comic drama was both a longer and a more complex narrative film than the average. I will argue that one of the main reasons why such an ambitious piece of filmic story-telling might succeed with contemporary audiences was that the story it was trying to tell was already so well known. Indeed, the adaptation of literary source-texts was one of the most important strategies by which English cinema in the 1900s and 1910s negotiated the development of more elaborate and extensive narrative films and attempted to attract a more upmarket, respectable audience and reputation.[4] But if *Alice* could be appreciated by some as an extended narrative, audiences could also appreciate it as a series of relatively discrete attractions. This was partly because of the quality of the production and partly because of the way in which it was promoted to showmen, both as a single complete film and as a series of short scenes that could be purchased separately.

Cecil Hepworth was already one of England's leading filmmakers, and would remain so until the early 1920s. The qualities of *Alice* are typical of both his (and his company's) work and his contributions to the history of English cinema. If the film is ambitious, it is also quaint. If it is well made, there is at the same time nothing too challenging about it. If it has a surreal or absurdist edge, it is also shot through with middlebrow, Home Counties respectability. The fact that it is a literary adaptation, and, more specifically, a reworking of a favourite, culturally mainstream, Victorian text, also establishes it as typical of the Hepworth company's subsequent output, which included several Dickens adaptations in the early 1910s, and several other feature-length adaptations, such as the two versions of Helen Mathers's *Comin' Thro' The Rye* in 1916 and 1923.[5]

The idea of taking on as rich, complex and word-driven a text as *Alice* was enterprising to say the least in a period when single-scene films and films made up of just a handful of shots were still very common. In the pages that follow, I want to explore the ways in which the literary source-text was reworked in pictorial terms, partly by focusing on what was already pictorial in the source-text. I also want to explore the ways in which the simple single-shot attraction of so many early films was absorbed into and re-presented in this multi-shot narrative. It is certainly one of the most remarkable achievements of *Alice* that it mixed the residue of the single-shot film into a more complex and extended narrative form. There is nothing particularly unique in the way Hepworth achieved this complexity. In that sense, the film is typical of the more ambitious films of the period, typical of the ways in which some filmmakers were embracing and developing more elaborate stories—very often by relying on audience familiarity with the source-text, or with a range of intertexts. As Charles Musser has written of an American film of 1903, Edwin S. Porter's *Uncle Tom's Cabin*, 'the narrative was not presented as if the audience was seeing it for the first time, but existed in reference to a story assumed to be already present in the audience's mind'.[6]

Although *Alice* was made in 1903, it was still being heavily promoted in the Hepwix catalogue of 1906, suggesting that it was a success with showmen and audiences.[7] Hepworth himself was clearly proud of the film, recalling it in his autobiography as 'a more ambitious effort' by comparison with 'the usual little comedies' and the topicals and actualities of the period.[8] At 800 feet, it was indeed a long film for the period, 'the longest ever at that time', according to Hepworth. 'We had by now definitely broken away from the fifty-foot tradition and our films took whatever length, in reason, that the subject demanded [although] the great majority of them varied from 100 to 200 feet at that time.'[9] Indeed the average length of British-made fiction films in 1903 was 167 feet, and by 1905 still only 251 feet. *Alice* was thus considerably longer than the norm, and by some way the longest fiction film made in Britain to date.[10] The sixteen scenes and eleven different sets or locations that comprised the film when it was released are testament to its narrative complexity. The film is thus an important prelude to the even more impressive narrational accomplishments of Hepworth's *Rescued by Rover* (which incidentally was only a little over half the length of *Alice*, at 425 feet) and *Falsely Accused*, both made in 1905.

The film was also impressive for its technical achievements: the quality of its camerawork, the use of dissolves, the colouring of the film ('toned and stained in various beautiful colours'[11]), the mix of exterior location shots and sets, the quality of the costumes, the undemonstrative naturalism of the acting and the use of intertitles.[12] Inevitably for a film of this period, *Alice* is composed mainly in long shot, with the majority of the scenes consisting of a single shot, although cut-ins are inserted in two scenes to film details on a larger scale. While the staging is often quite frontal, at least two of the scenes are staged at an angle to the camera, thus creating a greater sense of depth and dynamic movement within the frame. The film also avoids an overly theatrical mode of presentation, with promotional material in the 1906 company catalogue proclaiming that 'no pantomime or stage effect is introduced in this film; the whole of the various scenes having been produced in pretty natural surroundings'.[13]

Carroll's *Alice* and the Middle-class Victorian Worldview

It is unlikely that such a long and complex film could have been successful at the time without the wide familiarity of the source-text from which it was adapted (and indeed of the various other adaptations and re-workings of that source-text). The intertextual knowledge of contemporary audiences, and especially their foreknowledge of Carroll's illustrated novella, in effect served as one of the main vehicles for carrying the multiple episodes and images that made up the narrative. It is also surely significant that even if the word, and the play on words, is vital in the print versions of *Alice*, they too relied heavily for their reputation on both Carroll's visual imagery and Sir John Tenniel's drawings: this was already in part a pictorial text.

Alice's Adventures in Wonderland was first published in 1865, for the Christmas children's market. Initial reviews of the book were mixed and the success of the book was gradual.[14] By the time of Carroll's death in 1898, however, its success was beyond doubt, 160,000 copies having been sold to date, across several editions and numerous reprints.[15] This was a huge number at the time for a children's book, and it had become a firm favourite 'in the Victorian nursery'.[16] As well known as Carroll's story were the illustrations by Tenniel, who was already well established as an illustrator and cartoonist when Carroll asked him to work on *Alice*; indeed, on its publication in 1865, it was Tenniel's drawings that made the book noteworthy, not the nonsense text by an unknown writer. According to one of the very few scholarly studies of Tenniel, he was 'one of the most popular artists in England', not least for his regular contributions to *Punch*, in which capacity he became the country's 'quasi-official political cartoonist'.[17] Carroll's story and Tenniel's images had also been widely reproduced in magic lantern presentations, as children's lectures at the Regent Street Poly-technic, as songs, as a musical play or operetta, as a charade and as a legitimate stage play.[18] The film version was thus following in an already long and well-established tradition of adaptation and inter-textual activity.

As Jackie Wullschläger suggests, these various intertexts need to be seen in the context of the Victorian cult of the child and childhood. The close-knit and caring nuclear family and the adoration of the child were increasingly pervasive features of late Victorian culture and society, and a mass production industry developed to cater for this culture, manufacturing toys, clothes and books.[19] The *Alice* phenomenon was a key part of this industry. By the time of the film version in 1903, it did not therefore seem unreasonable for Hepworth to claim in his promotional material that Carroll's story was 'familiar to most people'.[20] Yet was the fascination with and commodification of *Alice* not primarily a middle-class phenomenon? As Wullschläger points out

> children's books, one of the most profitable parts of the Victorian publishing industry . . . were imbedded in middle-class culture. Lewis Carroll, hoping for a wide middle-class readership for *Alice*, advised his publishers that 'below that I don't think it would be appreciated'.[21]

A bourgeois sensibility certainly pervades Carroll's story, in terms of language, iconography, manners and milieu, but also in terms of specific references to class and social status.

Did Hepworth also have a middle-class target audience in mind? The very idea of making an ambitious film version of a middle-class nursery favourite suggests that he may well have sought to address a relatively upmarket audience with this film. The bourgeois sensibility of the novella is perhaps less blatant in the film version, yet there is still a recognizably middle-class iconography, carried in *Alice*'s dress and demeanour, her ease at the tea-party and the general sense of suburban homeliness, the absurdities of the text notwithstanding. The film is also certainly a much more gentle and refined production than the vast numbers of films from the period that indulged in slapstick, violence and frenetic chases.

In fact the class composition of both the reading public and audiences for films in this early period is more complex than might be evident at first glance. Thus the publishing history of *Alice's Adventures in Wonderland* reveals that among the several editions of the book published in the forty years after the first edition there were at least two low-cost versions addressed to a wider readership: a People's Edition, published by Macmillan in 1887 and reprinted in 1893, and an even cheaper edition in Macmillan's Sixpenny Series of 1898, reissued the next year.[22] In the same way, films were enjoyed in turn-of-the-century England by both working-class and middle-class audiences, who were to some extent catered for in different venues and entertainment spaces. Thus the itinerant showmen catered primarily for working-class audiences at fairs and the like, while the more respectable music halls could attract more middle-class audiences.

Equally, some filmmakers such as William Haggar, Frank Mottershaw and Alf Collins made films primarily for working-class audiences, while many of the films produced by what Noël Burch calls the gentlemen filmmakers like Hepworth seem more suitable for respectable middle-class audiences.[23]

But even if *Alice*'s bourgeois sensibility is indicative of Hepworth's own class identity, it seems unlikely that circulation of the film would have been restricted to middle-class venues. This well-made fantasy film would surely have appealed to a variety of audiences in a variety of settings. It would also be wrong to conceptualize the target audience solely in class terms, since the one clear indication Hepworth gives of audience appeal is the suggestion in the catalogue that the film is 'especially suitable for children's entertainments'.[24] Even here, though, there is a class veneer: the more reputable venues in which films were shown may well have jumped at the chance to put on some children's fare since a family audience would have enhanced their bid for respectability still further.

In the 1910s and early 1920s, Hepworth was both outspoken and widely celebrated as a maker of specifically *English* films, films that articulated a nostalgic, pre-modern, semi-ruralist sensibility.[25] This sensibility—associated above all with the respectable middle classes —can be seen at work in his earlier films too. His comedies were gentle, his dramas expressed a middle-class suburban angst, his protagonists, while often exuberant, were generally respectable, his topicals and interest films were patriotic, his panoramic films, scenics, travelogues and actualities often delighted in displaying the soft, cultivated, pastoral landscapes of Home Counties England. *Alice* fits into this worldview in various ways. Its exteriors, the carefully chosen 'pretty natural surroundings', for instance, are very much part of this English pastoral, with their leafy gardens and well-tended parkland with cows grazing in the background.[26]

In the case of *Alice*, this sensibility is in part inherited from the source-text, and from Victorian and Edwardian children's literature more generally. Wullschläger sees the work of Carroll, Edward Lear, J.M. Barrie, Kenneth Grahame and others as suggestive of 'a golden age, of a secure, prosperous, optimistic country', but notes that such authors

> also celebrate escape, the flight into an unknown dream world. They point to one of the strongest influences on the Victorian and Edwardian cult of childhood and on children's books: the

regressive desire for a pre-industrial rural world and the identification of the child with purity, a pre-sexual life, moral simplicity.[27]

Such a sentimental worldview would have held great appeal for Hepworth and for a respectable, middle-class suburban audience. As Wullschläger points out, *Alice* combines 'the idea of an escapist Paradise, with its resonance of lost innocence and unattainability', with another cultural tradition, 'the comic, anarchic spirit of nonsense, with its roots in English nursery rhymes'.[28] The same cultural tendencies come together not simply in Hepworth's *Alice* but in his filmmaking career more generally. The comic, anarchic trajectory can be traced from his early trick films such as *How It Feels to be Run Over* and *The Exploding Motor Car* (both 1900) to the series of *Tilly* comedies made in the early 1910s, while the longing for the paradisical innocence of childhood reaches its height in the post-war version of *Comin' Thro' The Rye* (1923).

Tenniel's *Alice* and Pictorial Authenticity

This sense of drawing on well-established traditions was vital to the reception of the film version of *Alice*. The production and promotion of the film clearly played on the assumed audience foreknowledge of the story and the images. The Hepworth catalogue, for instance, stated not simply that the story was 'familiar to most people', but that 'in producing a film of this well-known tale, the lines of the book have been strictly adhered to, and in nearly every instance Sir John Tenniel's famous illustrations have been reproduced in animated form with remarkable fidelity'.[29] Hepworth later recalled the film in very similar terms: 'Every situation was dealt with with all the accuracy at our command and with reverent fidelity, so far as we could manage it, to Tenniel's famous drawings.'[30] What is interesting about these statements is not simply that a 'famous' source-text was acknowledged, but that the cited authority was less Carroll than Tenniel. The claim rings true, since the film is more faithful to the visual detail of Tenniel (and Carroll's descriptions) than to the verbal detail which is half the fun of the story in book form.

This pictorial authenticity can be seen in the way the film's *mise-en-scène* picks up on Tenniel's drawings of Alice, the White Rabbit, the Mad Hatter, the Duchess, the Queen of Hearts and the pack of cards (compare Plates 3 and 4). The angle of vision, the framing

Plate 3. Tenniel's drawing of the pack of cards from
Alice's Adventures in Wonderland

Plate 4. The pack of cards from the film version of *Alice in Wonderland*
(Hepworth, 1903)

and the spatial relationships of the scenes inside and outside the Rabbit's house, showing a giant Alice cramped in the Rabbit's house with her arm poking out of the window, are also almost exactly as in Tenniel (compare Plates 5 and 6). The scene when she meets the Duchess and the cook in the kitchen is again graphically very similar, as is the *mise-en-scène* and angle of vision at the Mad Tea-party (compare plate 7 and the front cover). This sort of pictorial authenticity, or art-historical realism, subsequently became a familiar feature of later English heritage films and quality costume dramas.

Integrating Attractions into a Narrative Framework

If the film cannibalizes the *Alice* cultural industry, it also reworks and absorbs several aspects of earlier filmmaking. Filmic material familiar from the previous seven or eight years is here integrated into a longer and more complex narrative framework. Thus various special effects are taken over from early trick films and comic gag films, demonstrating the extent to which filmmakers—and Hepworth in particular—were by 1903 able and willing to incorporate into a longer and more respectable

Plate 5. Tenniel's drawing of Alice in the White Rabbit's house

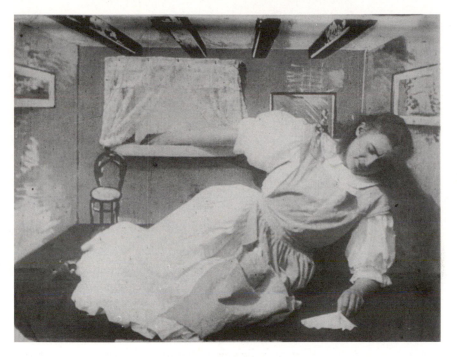

Plate 6.   Alice in the White Rabbit's house in the film version
(Hepworth, 1903)

dramatic framework familiar photographic devices that had once been
the *raison d'être* of the short film. Indeed, Rachael Low and Roger
Manvell, in their standard work on the first decade of British cinema,
classify *Alice* as a trick film, although its narrative is far more elaborate
than most films so categorized.[31] It was in part by narrativizing trick
effects that a relatively sophisticated and extensive narrative could be
achieved. The same process can be seen at work in slightly earlier
English dramatic narrative films or films adapted from well-known
literary sources. G.A. Smith, for instance, made a series of short films
that were based on well-known titles but that were promoted equally
as trick films, including *The Corsican Brothers, Cinderella and the Fairy
Godmother, Faust and Mephistopheles* (all 1898), *Dick Whittington*
and *Aladdin and the Wonderful Lamp* (both 1899). R.W. Paul's early
Dickens film *Scrooge, or Marley's Ghost* (1901) was more like *Alice*,
in that it was considerably longer than the Smith films but still
incorporated trick effects.

Various examples of this process can be cited from *Alice*. At the start
of the film, Alice follows the Rabbit down its hole and underground,

Plate 7.   Tenniel's drawing of the Mad Tea-party
(the same scene from the film is illustrated on the front cover)

an effect that is achieved via a dissolving fade that brings together
location and set, absorbing the magic of editing into a narrative
framework. In the Hall of Many Doors, Alice shrinks as she drinks
from the bottle marked 'Drink Me', then grows as she eats from the
box marked 'Eat Me'. The effect is achieved via a combination of jump
cuts, stop frame animation, staging and framing. Later Alice fans
herself with the fan the Rabbit has dropped, gradually disappearing
courtesy of a superimposed fade, a device later used to transform the
Duchess's baby into a very lively pig, and to allow the Cheshire Cat to
disappear and reappear in a bush. In earlier films, the illusion of
cinema, the magical effect of the superimposition or the dissolve,
might have been a sufficient attraction in itself. Now it has been
harnessed to narrative purpose—yet the trick effect in itself still has
some appeal, judging by the number of times the Hepworth catalogue
entry refers to 'the weird and beautiful dissolving effects [which] have a
very fine and startling effect'.[32]
　The Royal Procession at the end of the film allows Hepworth to
rework another aspect of early films, the fascination with pageantry and

procession that is such a feature of topicals, actualities and interest films of the period. Indeed, in the film version of *Alice*, the procession is a much bigger event than in the book, is built up as much more of a visual attraction and is virtually the climax of the film (a function which it patently does not have in the book). The scene is followed by Alice's confrontation with the Queen of Hearts, who orders the executioner to cut off Alice's head. When Alice retaliates, the pack of cards that made up the Procession turns on Alice and chases her off-screen. This is in effect a reworking of the violent and comic crowd chase scenes that featured in so many comic and dramatic chase films in the first two decades of cinema history, from *The Miller and the Sweep* (G.A. Smith, 1897) to *A Daring Daylight Burglary* (Frank Mottershaw/Sheffield Photo Company, 1903), *Our New Errand Boy* (James Williamson, 1905) and *Tilly's Party* (Lewin Fitzhamon/ Hepworth Manufacturing Co., 1911).

The typical film programme of 1903 might still have included a trick film, a comic gag film, a topical or interest film and a chase film. One of the attractions of *Alice* was that it incorporated all of these genres into a single extended drama. And it was the familiarity of the *Alice* story as much as anything else that was used to bind these disparate elements together, to integrate what in other circumstances would have been separate films, separate attractions, into a single, coherent and relatively cohesive whole. By working with a familiar story, and knowing that exhibitors would use various means of introducing additional information prior to and during screenings, filmmakers were able to assume a fair degree of extra-diegetic narrative comprehension on the part of audiences. It was therefore possible to present relatively discontinuous narrative fragments without jeopardizing the audience's ability to understand the narrative development. Indeed, we can put it more strongly than that: the story makes little sense *without* some foreknowledge. Narrative meaning and sense is to some degree imparted to individual scenes by the audience's intertextual understanding, by their recollection of the place of the scenes within the overall scheme of *Alice's Adventures in Wonderland*.

Thus the Royal Procession at the end of the film is introduced with a title card that states simply 'The Royal Procession' (before going on to explain events that take place later in the scene). There is no explanation of why there should be a Royal Procession, just as the previous scene gives us no indication that such might be the next logical step in the narrative. In other words, there is no apparent narrative motivation for the scene to take place, no causal relationship evident from the film itself between this scene and the previous one. The assumption is that we should know why there should be a Royal Procession: it is what happens in the book. The function of the intertitle, then, is to prime the viewer, to help recall the larger narrative from which this scene is but a fragment.[33] The same is true of the insertion of the Mad Tea-party in the film: there is no necessary reason for it to take place; it is deemed sufficient motivation that the plot of the film in this instance follows the plot of the novella.

Carroll's *Alice's Adventures in Wonderland* is of course an extremely episodic and digressive text whose twists and turns owe more to the illogic of dreams than the causal logic of classical narratives. This illogic, this non-sense, was apparently part of the creative process, Carroll later writing: 'I distinctly remember . . . how, in a desperate attempt to strike out some new line of fairy-lore, I had sent my heroine straight down a rabbit-hole . . . without the least idea what was to happen afterwards.'[34] One scholarly commentary on *Alice*, writing about the various filmic adaptations of Carroll's source-text, suggests that 'the structure of *Alice* is so episodic that it does not translate [easily] into the narrative demands of the 90 minute motion picture'.[35] Those demands did not of course apply in 1903; indeed, it may have been that it was precisely that episodic quality that allowed the film to be adapted as early as 1903, for there was little obligation on the filmmaker to provide the sort of internal narrative motivation that might have been expected for a plot with a tighter cause-effect line of development.

Low and Manvell describe the film as 'an exceptionally interesting series of scenes'.[36] The phrase captures perfectly the lack of continuity from one scene to the next, for there is indeed a strong sense of discrete attractions, fragments or scenes from a longer and familiar story. The film is thus in effect a series of tableaux. Even so, narrative movement is not solely dependent on extra-diegetic or intertextual knowledge and there are some internal indicators of motivation and explanation. Individual shots and scenes are not always entirely discrete but do in various ways on occasion establish causal connections with the shot or scene that follows. On at least two occasions the action moves around a window or a doorway from interior to exterior, or vice versa. To the modern eye, the transition can seem clumsy or primitive, since the degree of matching is much less than we would expect from a film of today, while dissolves or fades are sometimes used where we would now expect a cut. Thus the transition from the interior of the Rabbit's house, with a giant Alice squeezed into the room, to the exterior showing her arm poking out of the window, seems fine on paper. On screen, however, Alice actually disappears (as she waves the fan) before the cut to the exterior shot, when her arm is miraculously still visible. Even so, the narrative continuity across the two shots is perfectly legible, as is the 'primitive' matching on movement in various other shot transitions, or the cutting in to closer shots in the Hall of Many Doors scene.

Such shot transitions and scene constructions were already familiar from earlier English films, if not yet by any means standardized. Matching on movement was thus vital to the legibility of the chase film, the cut in to closer shots had appeared in films like *As Seen Through the Telescope* or *Grandma's Reading Glass* (both G.A. Smith, 1900), and films like the two versions of *Kiss in the Tunnel* (G.A. Smith, and Riley and Bamforth, both 1899) and *Fire!* (James Williamson, 1901) had demonstrated the possibilities of cutting between an interior and an exterior. It is possible too that Hepworth saw the dissolve, his favoured mode of shot transition, as a means of ensuring continuity between and across scenes, which are described in the company catalogue as 'dissolving very beautifully from one to another'.[37] The dissolve did not yet have a standard meaning; it would seem that for Hepworth at this time, it was both aesthetically pleasing and a continuity device. According to Barry Salt, the use of the dissolve as a continuity device, quite rare in films of this period, though of course typical of scene transitions in magic lantern displays, was probably influenced by the work of Georges Méliès. As Salt notes, Hepworth even uses dissolves when moving to a closer shot within the same scene, and when Alice walks out of one shot into the next ('despite the fact that the position matching from one shot to the next . . . would have been considered quite satisfactory a few years later').[38]

Producing a Comprehensible Narrative

As others have noted, 1903 was an important year for the development of the multi-shot chase film, both in England, with *A Daring Daylight Burglary* and *A Desperate Poaching Affray* (William Haggar), and in the USA, with *The Great Train Robbery* (Edwin S. Porter).[39] Films such as these used the chase across different spaces as a means of binding shots together, the dynamic continuity of the movement across those

spaces creating both energy and cohesion. It was this same sense of
continuous movement across multiple spaces that was to be used to
such dramatic effect in that later Hepworth film, *Rescued by Rover*.[40]
This sense of dynamic, continuous movement is much weaker in
Alice, yet as we have seen there is still a reasonably strong sense of
narrative integration and development. While that integration is partly
dependent on intertextual, extra-diegetic knowledge, the differences
between source-text and film version suggest that some effort was
made to strengthen the sense of narrative continuity and causality in
the plotting of the film.

The broad parameters of Carroll's story and many though by no
means all of the details have been preserved in the adaptation. Thus, as
in the novella, the film begins with Alice falling asleep and dreaming
and ends with her waking, although she has no accompanying sister in
the film version. Some of the business of shrinking and growing is
retained as she tries to follow the Rabbit underground, but the whole
of chapter III, with its sea of tears and its menagerie of animals and
tales within tales has been lost. While the scene in the Rabbit's house
follows the actions and events of Carroll's story fairly closely, minus the
attempts to evict Alice, her encounter with the caterpillar and his nonsense rhymes is entirely missing (the hookah was perhaps thought too
risky . . .). The kitchen scene ('Pig and Pepper') and the Mad
Tea-party are again close to Tenniel and Carroll, though more to the
former than the latter since both the illustrations and the film offer
only fragments from each scene. I noted earlier that the procession of
the pack of cards takes on a greater significance in the film than in the
novella. By making this scene into the film's visually compelling climax
most of the final four chapters of the novella have been ousted from
the plot, so that we see and hear nothing of the croquet game
with flamingos for mallets, Alice's talk with the Duchess, the Mock
Turtle's story and the lobster quadrille, and the ensuing trial of the
Knave of Hearts. All that remains of these chapters is the final attack
by the deck of cards, which eventually wakes Alice up from her
dreaming.

What is the effect of this pruning? Arguably, the sections of
Carroll's story that have been omitted from the film are the most
glaring digressions in what is admittedly always a digressive picaresque
narrative. Gone are most of the secondary tales within the main tale of
Alice's journey through Wonderland, gone are those sections which
depend most on word-play. As a result, there is a stronger sense of
continuous action across the different segments of the film—or at

least, there is to those members of the audience who are familiar with the broad parameters of the plot, since without such knowledge, as already noted, it is still very difficult to construct the logic of Alice's journey.

There are two further ways in which such knowledge was made available to audiences. First, there are the intertitles. Secondly, there would have been various on-site exhibition aids, notably the live accompaniment of a lecturer or narrator, as well as promotional material such as printed programmes or 'the fairground barker's spiel, which *primed* the audience by explaining in advance the images it would see inside the tent'.[41] The function of intertitles is indicated quite clearly in the Hepworth catalogue: 'The film is composed of sixteen scenes, dissolving very beautifully from one to another, but preceded, where necessary for the elucidation of the story, by short descriptive titles.'[42] The implication would seem to be that, if the dissolve and the internal logic of the shots are insufficient as means of ensuring informed narrative progression, then the device of the intertitle has been brought into play. This was a device that Méliès had already demonstrated to good effect in multiple shot films even before 1900, notably in *L'Affaire Dreyfus* (1899). As Salt points out, in this period, in 'films adapted from stage or literary works, or even actual events, . . . a more complex narrative was handled within several minutes running time by using narrative or descriptive titles before all (or most of) the scenes.'[43]

Even so, according to Martin Sopocy, until 1904 intertitling was an *atypical* trade practice. Films like *Alice* were thus 'exceptions to the general practice of the time'.[44] The five intertitles in *Alice* are entirely expositional, preceding the scenes in which the described action takes place, functioning in some way as chapter headings, and thereby imparting narrative meaning and significance to the action. Thus the final three shots of the film (which are linked by dissolves) are preceded by the following title: 'The Royal Procession.—The Queen invites Alice to join—Alice unintentionally offends the Queen who calls the executioner to behead her. But Alice, growing bolder, boxes his ears and in the confusion which results she awakes.' Very little of this narrative could be discerned by an audience from the images alone, especially the second of the three images, which in extreme long shot depicts details of Alice's confrontation with the Queen and her entourage. Familiarity with the source-text might explain why Alice is witnessing a Royal Procession, but it cannot provide all the details necessary for a smooth narrative reading of the three shots in question. Legibility and meaning would probably have been further enhanced at contemporary screenings by the live narrator or lecturer who accompanied so many film events in the period, explaining details not self-evident from the image, literally reading the image, rendering it intelligible.

Between the Cinema of Attractions and the Cinema of Narrative Integration

What should be clear from the preceding discussion is the sense of a relatively strong tension between narrative continuity on the one hand, and discrete scenes on the other, each an attraction in its own right. This tension between narrative and attractionist aesthetics, typical of so many films from this period, is underlined by three facts in particular. First, the incorporation of a range of comic attractions, visual gags and absurd images to some extent sets the appeal of the image at odds with the forward drive of the narrative. Secondly, the emphasis on pictorialist authenticity, on the faithful reproduction of Tenniel's drawings, resulted in a film in which visual spectacle, the pictorial, is as important as story or narrative flow. Thirdly, the tension between narrative and attractionist aesthetics is underlined by the fact that some of the sixteen 'scenes' of the film could be bought separately by showmen, as discrete films or attractions in their own right.

The 1906 Hepwix Catalogue notes that 'in response to repeated requests, we have decided to print some of the more popular portions of the film . . . separately . . . [They] will be found especially suitable for children's entertainments.'[45] Four such scenes are listed as being available individually: *Alice's Adventures in the Beautiful Garden* (75 feet); *The Duchess and the Pig-Baby* (200 feet); *The Mad Tea Party* (50 feet); and the *Procession of the Pack of Cards* (150 feet), 'the beautiful dream scene from *Alice in Wonderland*.'[46]

The fact that showmen could buy just one scene from the whole film makes it very clear that the longer and more complex narrative was by no means the only filmic standard at the time. Indeed, the film was produced in a culture that could enjoy the re-enactment or the pictorialization of just a single scene or a handful of scenes from a well-known and ambitious dramatic text. Short scenes from popular or prestigious plays occasionally appeared as sketches in music-hall programmes, condensed versions of Shakespeare were not unusual and, right from the earliest years of cinema, films depicting scenes from celebrated plays and novels were being produced. Most such films were initially very short, although four film versions of the *Passion Play* made in 1897 and 1898 in Paris, Bohemia and New York were remarkably long for the period.[47] In England, early and very short 'extracts' from plays were often based on current stage productions, such as the Mutoscope and Biograph Company films *Fencing Contest from 'The Three Musketeers'* (1898), based on a contemporary production of the Dumas novel, *King John* (1899), which reworked scenes from Beerbohm Tree's Shakespeare production at Her Majesty's Theatre, and *English Nell* (1900), which presented a scene from the second act of a Prince of Wales Theatre production of a play by Anthony Hope and Edward Rose. Films such as these, presenting short fragments from stage productions, might be presented almost as news items (topicals, in the language of the period) or even as advertisements for the productions.[48]

Presentations of scenes from novels were also common, such as several 'adaptations' by R.W. Paul of material from Dickens. *Mr Bumble the Beadle* was a period scene from *Oliver Twist*, made in 1898; *Mr Pickwick's Christmas at Wardle's* and *Scrooge, or Marley's Ghost*—originally 620 feet long—were both made in 1901, probably for the Christmas market. Another relatively elaborate film for the period was a 500-foot version of the ever popular *East Lynne* (Dicky Winslow, 1902) in five scenes. In the same year as *Alice*, there were versions of *Rip Van Winkle* and *Dotheboys Hall, or Nicholas Nickleby* (both Alf Collins/Gaumont) and an 800-foot, 20-scene version of Longfellow's poem *Hiawatha* (Joe Rosenthal/Urban).[49] Filmmakers also reworked the practice of presenting fairy tales and other traditional children's stories as lantern shows for children in the late nineteenth century. The fairy tale film subsequently became a popular genre around the turn of the century, with both Georges Méliès and G.A. Smith producing several such films.[50]

Two tendencies can be discerned here. First, there is the practice of adaptation, although in this early period adaptation often meant extreme condensation, in which context the meaning of fragments from longer source-narratives was heavily dependent on intertextual knowledge. Second, there is the move towards longer, multi-scene films based on already well-known narratives. Thus the longest British-made fiction film produced in 1896 or 1897 was *The Death of Nelson* (Philip Wolff), based on the popular song of the same name; *Scrooge, or Marley's Ghost* was the longest British-made fiction film until *Alice*; and all four of the fiction films of 600 feet or more made in

Britain in 1903 were based on pre-existing narratives (*Dorothy's Dream* [G.A. Smith], *The Adventurous Voyage of 'The Arctic'* [R.W. Paul], *Hiawatha* and *Alice in Wonderland*).[51]

The separation of single scenes from the 'full' film version of *Alice* suggests that the presentation of fragments from longer narratives could still command a following, and that the aesthetics and expectations of narrative integration had by no means displaced the aesthetics of attractionism. Filmmakers in the early period often shot short interest films, topicals and actualities in series that could be combined by exhibitors into a longer experience. At one level, this is how *Alice* too operates. But it also works in the opposite direction, as a long film, carefully conceived as such, which could yet be broken down into shorter entertainments, 'to make them saleable to a few of our more prudent customers'.[52]

Some Conclusions

Alice in Wonderland is a good indication of the trend towards the production of fiction films, where the first few years of filmmaking had been dominated by non-fiction films. It may have been fairly unique as a long and carefully designed English costume drama, but the means by which it sustained interest over its 800 feet were typical of developments in narrative filmmaking in this early period. It is this innovative typicality which enables the film to work so effectively as a case study in early film history, demonstrating how the adaptation of a familiar pre-cinematic text and worldview, and the absorption of the pleasures and principles of early single-shot films, enabled filmmakers to achieve an unprecedented filmic complexity.

At the same time, it would be wrong to imply that 1903 was a key moment from which there could be no turning back. History is never that neat. The filmmakers had latched onto several means of enabling audiences to enjoy *Alice* as a coherent, continuous, integrated narrative. That the film could also be enjoyed as a series of discrete attractions, or even the single attraction of a scene separated from the rest of the film, is indicative of the degree of flux and the lack of standardization in the cinema of the period. The sense of uneven development is underlined still further if we recall that the 1906 Hepwix catalogue was still offering individual scenes as short films in their own right, in effect encouraging showmen to dismantle the longer filmic narrative.

As numerous film historians have pointed out, early films were often marked by the externality of their narration, since they were reliant on the intertextual or extra-diegetic knowledge of their audiences, the live presentation of narrative information by a narrator or lecturer, or other on-site exhibition aids.[53] The subsequent development of an integrated narrative cinema and self-sufficient film shows in dedicated exhibition spaces in part involved internalizing as much narrational information as possible. *Alice* goes some way towards internalizing the process of narration in its incorporation of intertitles; at the same time, it still falls some way short of providing the degree of internally legible causal connections between story elements, or the clear motivation for plot developments that we expect of classical narratives. That the film would seem to have been successful suggests that audiences at that time did not necessarily expect such attributes in the fiction films they watched.

Notes

1. A version of this chapter was presented at the Second British Silent Cinema Weekend, Broadway, Nottingham, in 1999. My thanks to Peter Krämer for comments on an earlier draft.
2. See Tom Gunning, 'Non-Continuity, Continuity, Discontinuity: A Theory of Genres in Early Films', and Charles Musser, 'The Nickelodeon Era Begins: Establishing the Framework for Hollywood's Mode of Representation,' both in Thomas Elsaesser with Adam Barker, eds, *Early Cinema: Space, Frame, Narrative* (London: BFI, 1990), pp. 86–94 and 256–73; Musser, *Before the Nickelodeon: Edwin S. Porter and the Edison Manufacturing Company* (Berkeley: University of California Press, 1991); Musser, *The Emergence of Cinema: The American Screen to 1907* (New York: Scribner's, 1990).
3. Denis Gifford, *The British Film Catalogue, 1895–1985: A Reference Guide* (Newton Abbot: David & Charles, 1986), entry 651.
4. See my 'Heritage Discourses and British Cinema before 1920,' in John Fullerton, ed., *Celebrating 1895: The Centenary of Cinema* (Sydney: John Libbey and Co., 1998), especially pp. 186–8.
5. See my *Waving The Flag: Constructing a National Cinema in Britain* (Oxford: Clarendon Press, 1995), pp. 26–97.
6. Musser, *Before the Nickelodeon*, p. 243.
7. *A Selected Catalogue of the Best and Most Interesting 'Hepwix' Films* (London: Hepworth Manufacturing Company, 1906), entry no. 430, pp. 55–8.

8. Cecil Hepworth, *Came The Dawn: Memories of a Film Pioneer* (London: Phoenix House Ltd, 1951), p. 63.
9. Ibid.
10. According to film lengths given in Gifford, *The British Film Catalogue*. The next longest film, *Scrooge, or Marley's Ghost*, was only 620 feet. Thanks to Ann-Marie Cook for calculating the averages.
11. *A Selected Catalogue*, p. 56.
12. Unfortunately the viewing copy at the National Film and Television Archive of the British Film Institute is from a poor nitrate original, now badly decomposed, missing some 300 feet of the original 800 feet, without the original colour toning and staining and with some of the shots in the wrong order.
13. *A Selected Catalogue*, p. 56.
14. Jackie Wullschläger, *Inventing Wonderland: the Lives and Fantasies of Lewis Carroll, Edward Lear, J.M. Barrie, Kenneth Grahame and A.A. Milne* (London: Methuen, 1995), p. 54.
15. Ibid., p. 54; see also the British Library catalogue of holdings.
16. Ibid., p. 55.
17. Michael Hancher, *The Tenniel Illustrations to the 'Alice' Books* (Columbus: Ohio State University Press, 1985), pp. xv, 26.
18. See Morton N. Cohen and Anita Gandolfo, eds, *Lewis Carroll and the House of Macmillan* (Cambridge: Cambridge University Press, 1987), passim. A two-act operetta prepared by Henry Savile Clark was first performed on 23 December 1886, at the Prince of Wales Theatre, and revived in December 1888 at the Globe Theatre. See Anne Clark, *Lewis Carroll—A Biography* (London: Dent, 1979), pp. 235–40. See also Lewis Carroll/C.L. Dodgson, 'Alice on the Stage,' *Theatre*, April 1887, available on-line at http://www.bibliomania.com/Fiction/Caroll/CompleteWorks/p3-wm.html#Ch5. A *Charade* based on the novella was published in 1898 (London: Samuel French).
19. Wullschläger, *Inventing Wonderland*, pp. 11ff., especially pp. 15–16.
20. *A Selected Catalogue*, 55.
21. Wullschläger, *Inventing Wonderland*, p. 16, quoting Lewis Carroll, letter to Macmillan, 15 December 1869, in Cohen and Gandolfo, eds, *Lewis Carroll*, p. 77.
22. See Hancher, *The Tenniel Illustrations to the 'Alice' Books*, pp. 121–2; see also the British Library catalogue of holdings.
23. Burch, *Life to Those Shadows* (London: BFI, 1990), pp. 80–108.
24. *A Selected Catalogue*, p. 56; Macmillan also brought out children's editions of the book, including *The Nursery 'Alice'* (1890) and a 1903 'Little Folks' edition.
25. See my *Waving The Flag*, pp. 26ff.
26. *A Selected Catalogue*, p. 56.

27. Wullschläger, *Inventing Wonderland*, p. 17.
28. Ibid., p. 43.
29. *A Selected Catalogue*, p. 55.
30. Hepworth, *Came The Dawn*, p. 63.
31. Low and Manvell, *The History of the British Film, 1896–1906* (London: Allen and Unwin, 1948; reprinted London: Routledge, 1997), pp. 83–5.
32. *A Selected Catalogue* p. 57.
33. Musser, *Before the Nickelodeon*, pp. 243–4.
34. Carroll/Dodgson, 'Alice on the Stage'.
35. Jones and Gladstone, *The Alice Companion*, p. 90.
36. Low and Manvell, *The History of the British Film*, p. 83.
37. *A Selected Catalogue*, p. 55.
38. Salt, *Film Style and Technology: History and Analysis* (London: Starwood, 1983), p. 53.
39. See for example Martin Sopocy, 'The Role of the Intertitle in Film Exhibition, 1910–1914,' in Christopher Williams, ed., *Cinema: The Beginnings and the Future* (London: University of Westminster Press, 1996), p. 121 and note 5, p. 131; and Musser, *Before the Nickelodeon* and *The Emergence of Cinema*.
40. See Charles Barr, 'Before *Blackmail*: British Silent Cinema,' in Robert Murphy, ed., *The British Cinema Book* (London: BFI, 1997), pp. 7–10.
41. Sopocy, 'The Role of the Intertitle in Film Exhibition,' p. 123.
42. *A Selected Catalogue*, p. 55.
43. Salt, *Film Style and Technology, p. 56.*
44. Sopocy, 'The Role of the Intertitle in Film Exhibition,' p. 124.
45. *A Selected Catalogue*, p. 56.
46. Ibid., p. 58.
47. See Burch, *Life to Those Shadows*, pp. 144–7; Musser, *The Emergence of Cinema*, pp. 208–21.
48. See Gifford, *The British Film Catalogue*; Low and Manvell, *The History of the British Film*; Luke McKernan, 'Beerbohm Tree's *King John* Re-discovered: the First Shakespeare Film, September 1899,' *Shakespeare Bulletin*, Winter 1993, pp. 35–6; McKernan, 'Further Notes on Beerbohm Tree's *King John*,' *Shakespeare Bulletin*, Spring 1993, pp. 49–50; and Geoff Brown, ' "Sister of the Stage": British Films and British Theatre,' in Charles Barr, ed., *All Our Yesterdays: 90 Years of British Cinema*, esp. p. 146.
49. See Gifford, *The British Film Catalogue*; Low and Manvell, *The History of the British Film*; and Rachael Low, *A History of the British Film, 1906–14* (London: Allen and Unwin, 1949; reprinted London: Routledge, 1997), p. 185.
50. Musser, *Before the Nickelodeon*, p. 200.

51. See Gifford, *The British Film Catalogue*.
52. Hepworth, *Came the Dawn*, p. 63.
53. See Burch, *Life to Those Shadows*, pp. 186 ff; also Sopocy, 'The Role of the Intertitle in Film Exhibition'.

4

Putting the World Before You
The Charles Urban Story

Luke McKernan

We put the world before you. That was the proud boast of Charles Urban when he put on his 'Urbanora' shows of scientific, nature and travel films at the height of his career in the late 1900s. It is a phrase that neatly encapsulates his ambition for what cinema was or should be, and put Urban himself as master of that world. Urban was the dominant figure in the British film industry before 1914, pre-eminent in the fields of documentary and educational film, a master entrepreneur of colour film, and the image of the world is one that is particularly pertinent when considering his story. There was the world he offered on the screen, the world in its every height and depth and breadth as illustrated in the catalogues of his film companies, there was the film world that he came to dominate for a while, in Britain at least, and the larger world-wide film industry in which he ultimately became lost. And there was Urban himself, an internationalist figure in a nationalist industry, and of himself very much a man of the world.

American Beginnings

He was born in Cincinnati in 1867, one of ten children of recent immigrants from the Austro-Hungarian empire. Brought up among the German-speaking community of Ohio, Urban left school at 15, working in a variety of jobs and first making his mark as a travelling book agent, specializing in fine art productions.[1] In 1889 he moved to Detroit, where he set up a stationery and office supplies business with one John T. Doan. It was through this business that Urban came into contact with Robert L. Thomae of the North American Phonograph Company, and so found himself on the first step towards the career that was to find him fame and fortune in a business that did not at that time even exist, namely motion pictures.

Thomas Edison's Phonograph, as well as playing commercial sound recordings, was also used as a kind of proto-Dictaphone for office work, which is what interested Urban, and in 1893 he became agent for the Phonograph for the Michigan area. His connections with Edison then grew with the appearance of the Kinetoscope, the peepshow device that showed a miniature image from a loop of film and which first introduced motion pictures to the American public in 1894. Early in 1895 the Kinetoscope made its first appearance in Michigan, at a music publisher's showrooms on Woodward Avenue, the centre of town. The Kinetoscopes were initially demonstrated by Edison agents Raff and Gammon, before the Michigan agency was sold to the Michigan Electric Company. Urban was naturally excited by the potential of motion pictures, approached the Michigan Electric Company, and merged his Phonograph business with their Kineto-scopes, becoming manager of a combined Phonograph and Kinetoscope at 101 Woodward Avenue on the ground floor of the Michigan Electric Company's building, early in 1895.[2]

Urban was keen to pursue each advance in motion pictures, and journeyed up to New York to witness the introduction of projected film with the Edison Vitascope, followed shortly afterwards by the Lumière Cinématographe. This was clearly the future, and Urban wanted no more of the restrictions of peepshows and coin-operated machines. However, the Vitascope and the Cinématographe could only be leased, not purchased. At some time in 1896 he acquired a Vitascope agency for the Michigan area, while also developing his own projector that would free him from the strictures of leasing, as well as improving on some of the technical deficiencies of the Vitascope. This was the genesis of the famous Bioscope projector, an invention that would make his name. Urban asked an associate from his Phonograph days, Walter Isaacs, to design a projector which was not tied to an electricity supply, which fact was limiting the exploitation of the Vitascope in Michigan as still too few towns in the area had any electrical facilities. It had to be hand operated, to use an ordinary source of light such as limelight, and needed to be able to handle several films threaded together rather than be tied to changing the film each time a 50-foot spool came to an end. Isaacs set about its construction to Urban's instructions, but by the time the first Bioscopes were ready in February 1897 Urban was engaged on the next stage in his career.[3]

On a business trip to New York late in 1896 he met Robert Thomae once again, now manager of the New York offices of Maguire and Baucus, who as the Continental Commerce Company were one of the three major licensees of Edison films and film projectors. Thomae told Urban that the company was looking for a new manager for its London office. Maguire and Baucus were very interested in Urban, the resourceful and ambitious young salesman, though they were undoubtedly also very interested in his Bioscope projector, which could free them from too great a tie to Edison and its product.

A Yank in Britain

After a period working in the New York office, Urban and his wife sailed from New York to Liverpool in August 1897. He was taking a considerable risk, as what he was being offered as salary was considerably less than he was earning from his Bioscope business, but the opportunities offered by the managership, as well as the chance to go to Europe, were too great, and he always had the good sense to move on to a new position of promise when one presented itself.

The London office of Maguire and Baucus was based at Dashwood House, Broad Street, near Liverpool Street railway station. The company had been established in Britain since 1894, when it introduced the Kinetoscope, but it now acted as a general film agency, as well as conducting such ancillary business as supplying weighing machines to railway stations. The business was run by Joseph Baucus, an American lawyer, and the largely absent American-Irishman Franck Maguire whose business it was to seek out new machines for the company to exploit. Urban found a business heavily in debt to the New York parent company and the victim of high interest loans taken out on a fatal business policy of short termism. Although the company's film business was full of potential, since it held the rights to exploit both Edison film and four-perforation gauge Lumière film, it was not profitable.[4]

Urban changed all this with a dynamism that shook all those around him severely. His first action was to relocate the company. He saw that the burgeoning film industry was not centred around Liverpool Street but around the High Holborn and Gray's Inn Road area: among the leading film concerns at this period, Robert Paul was in Hatton Garden, John Wrench and Son were in Gray's Inn Road, and Urban found premises at Warwick Court, close by Chancery Lane, moving the firm there by September 1897, within a month of his arrival. He next changed the name of the company. Noting a certain anti-Americanism in the film business, he opted for the solidly British and reliable-sounding name Warwick Trading Company, after their new location.

The effect of Urban's management of the company can be seen quite simply by the huge rise in sales figures: sales were £10,500 in 1897, but had risen to £45,000 by 1901.[5] Urban soon had the company making films, and determined that it should be dedicated to a particular kind of film, namely news or actuality material. Urban acquired the distribution rights to the work of a number of prominent fiction film makers, including James Williamson and G.A. Smith of Brighton and Georges Méliès of Paris. Such acquisitions were necessary if the premier film company in Britain was to offer exhibitors a complete service, but the Warwick Trading Company itself was to specialize in films of reality, which became the company's trademark—and Urban's throughout his film career.

The reputation of the company was primarily based on the dependability of the Bioscope projector. Urban instigated another trend which was to feature throughout his career, that of depending on the mechanical abilities of a succession of technicians whose skills he encouraged and financed, sharing in the reflected glory. First of these was Cecil Hepworth, who constructed an automatic developer and printer in the short time he was with Urban. There then followed Alfred Darling, a Brighton engineer, who undertook the construction of the various pieces of equipment marketed under the Warwick name, including the various modifications to the Bioscope projector. Others technicians and scientists Urban employed and supported and through whose efforts he satisfied some need to be seen as a master of technology included G.A. Smith, F. Martin Duncan, Theodore Brown, Percy Smith and Henry Joy.

A commitment to the actuality film, and especially in the early years, to the travel film, meant a team of travelling cameramen. Among these were the mountaineering specialist Frank Ormiston-Smith, Jack Avery (Urban's brother-in-law), and most famously Joseph Rosenthal, who became especially noted for his filming of the Anglo-Boer War, exploits given due prominence in the regular film catalogues that Urban issued, with increasingly lavish descriptions, illustrations and advertising.

Urban had clearly been the making of the Warwick Trading

Company, yet he was still the employee of Maguire and Baucus and was naturally eager to assert his independence. Maguire and Baucus tried to hold on to Urban first by offering a high salary, then generous share terms, and then unsuccessfully through the courts trying to prove he had no right to operate as an individual. The legal proceedings reveal much of the arrogant, confident, uncontrollably impulsive and often naive personality that exasperated the steadier and much less brilliant Maguire and Baucus. Inevitably, Urban broke away in 1903 to form his own Charles Urban Trading Company.[6]

Independence and Education

As an independent businessman, Urban continued to flourish, and especially to market his own name and that of his products as hallmarks of quality. The bedrock of his product continued to be the travel and topical film, with Joe Rosenthal and George Rogers reporting the Russo-Japanese War of 1904–5 from the Japanese and Russian sides respectively. But he now began to take an increased interest in promoting scientific film, starting his campaign for the cinema to be recognized as an educative force. Urban's understanding of what education might mean does not bear much analysis, but it was undoubtedly sincere, and even courageous, though at a time when the film industry was frowned upon for its lowly status and largely confined to an impoverished working-class audience, anything that stressed the higher values of the medium was probably good business. Other filmmakers tried to attract a moneyed middle-class audience by providing film versions of the classics; Urban gave them the world through a microscope.

Urban progressively diversified his film business interests. He created the Kineto Company to produce his scientific and travel films, formed the Eclipse company in France, and once he had the colour film system Kinemacolor he created the Natural Color Kinematograph Company to exploit it. Urban cameramen continued to tour the globe and to put the truth behind that slogan, 'We Put the World Before You', which Urban used to advertise his 'Urbanora' programmes of popular education subjects. Urban was an internationalist, and although he became deeply fond of his adopted country, and a naturalized British subject in 1907,[7] he retained the global outlook and lack of nationalist partiality which was beginning to hamper some of his rivals in the British film industry, as they felt the threat of American competition and responded with chauvinism. Urban's

American nationality had been a mixed blessing—he carried with him the glamour of the United States, but he also had to deal repeatedly with anti-American sentiments and being treated as an outsider. His change of nationality was as much a sound commercial move as an expression of undying loyalty to his new homeland.

Urban produced few fiction films throughout his career, and those he did produce were stilted, gauche and poorly made even by the low standards of much British film production of the time. Most of what he offered as Urban fiction films were in any case productions of his French company Eclipse. Urban loved reality, loved packaging it and making it palatable to a general public that on the back of the Education Act was newly literate, absorbed popular magazines, and was keen to see the world if not to learn as such. Motion pictures, when first invented, were not immediately viewed as a long-lasting entertainment medium. Film was seen as a means to record reality or history, or as a tool of scientific study, and a number of scientists in the 1890s experimented with film as a means to record surgical operations, or to show the growth of plants, the nature of human ailments, or life under the microscope. Urban sought out such men and commercialized them. It is easy to forget the vision it took to think that a general audience might be transported by scenes of scientific study. At a time when the cinema was increasingly moving down the road towards fiction film entertainments for a mass cinema audience, Urban's belief in a higher purpose for the medium was acclaimed in the press and recognized as being what cinema should be if it was to have any value at all.[8] He gave particular expression to this belief in a 1907 booklet, *The Cinematograph in Science, Education, and Matters of State*. This text in praise of the 'accurate and truthful eye of the camera' puts forward many of what would become the classic arguments in favour of the moving image as a medium of instruction, while also containing probably the first use in English of the word 'documentary' in a cinematic sense.[9]

Urban's first scientific associate was F. Martin Duncan, a zoologist with a history of experimentation in moving-image technology and a special interest in microphotography. Martin Duncan's work came to the attention of Urban, who naturally responded to the promise of science as entertainment. Martin Duncan's films were marketed by Urban as 'The Unseen World', as filmed by the Urban-Duncan Micro-Bioscope, a perfect example of how Urban absorbed and shared in the brilliance of others.

Best known among Urban's talented protégés was Percy Smith, a shy and retiring functionary at the Board of Education, who had a passion for animal life and photography. Urban got to know of his work (reputedly after seeing a Smith photograph of a bluebottle's tongue) in 1908 and persuaded him to make films along similar lines for Urban to exploit commercially. Smith was a painstaking and dedicated scientist who pioneered many of the techniques of nature cinematography, particularly in his use of stop motion photography, and saw in Urban someone with enthusiasm but also the necessary patience to let him work under the best conditions. He joined Urban full-time in 1910, and made his famous *The Birth of a Flower*, which Urban released in Kinemacolor.

Kinemacolor

It was to be another Smith who would prove to be Urban's closest and most important associate. G.A. Smith was a commercial film processor and producer based in Brighton who did much business with the Warwick Trading Company and subsequently with the Charles Urban Trading Company, building up a good business and personal relationship with Urban. In 1901 Urban was approached by an inventor named Edward R. Turner, who had patented a complicated and fundamentally impractical three-colour film projection system and who had financial backing from speculator F. Marshall Lee. Lee withdrew that backing in 1901 and Turner approached Urban, who took to the prospect of natural colour pictures with all of his expected enthusiasm. A projector was constructed by Alfred Darling, but the three separate colour pictures would never stay in register; shortly afterwards Turner died. Undaunted, Urban purchased the patent rights from his widow and invited G.A. Smith to work on the problem of how to achieve natural colours on the screen.

Smith abandoned the impractical three-colour system, and made the happy discovery that a quite satisfactory colour record could be achieved by using only two colour filters, red and green. The results did not display the full colour range, but were pleasing and effective, and crucially reproduced flesh tones very well. This was Kinemacolor. Urban, who worked closely with Smith on the project, later wrote of the moment when they both realized what they had achieved:

> One Sunday we were ready for the first real two-colour test. It was
> a beautiful sunshiny day. Smith dressed his little boy and girl in a
> variety of colours, the girl was in white with a pink sash, the boy

in sailor blue waving a Union Jack. We had the green grass and the red brick house for a setting. This was July 1906. It took about thirty seconds to make the exposure on a specially prepared negative after which we went into Smith's small darkroom to develop the results in absolute darkness. Within two hours we had dried the negative, made a positive print of the 50 feet length, developed and dried it—and then for the grand test. Even today —after seventeen years, I can feel the thrill of that moment, when I saw the result of the two-colour process—I yelled like a drunken cowboy—'We've got it—We've got it'.[10]

There is always a certain amount of unreliable romanticism about Urban's various written records of his achievements, but this was clearly how he wanted to remember it, and it was with that sense of excitement that he produced and marketed his Kinemacolor films. He wanted to make the public as excited as he was about colour films, and his campaign was conducted in real style.

Kinemacolor was patented in November 1906, and first exhibited on 1 May 1908 at the inauguration of Urban's new premises at Urbanora House in Wardour Street. (Urban was the first person in the film business to move to the street that was to become the heart of the British film industry.) The audience was mainly newspapermen, while a second show in July was presented to the Lord Mayor of London and other civic dignitaries. Urban always knew how to do things in style, building up anticipation and gaining approval from on high, though part of the reason why they did not go public straight away was simply that they had not made sufficient Kinemacolor films at this time. A very important screening for both Smith and Urban took place at the Royal Society of Arts in December 1908, after which Smith was awarded the Society's Silver Medal.

In 1909 the Natural Color Kinematograph Company was formed, and Urban started producing Kinemacolor films commercially. Kinemacolor became so important to Urban that it dominated his life to the exclusion of almost anything else. He resigned as manager of the Charles Urban Trading Company in 1910 and opened new premises at 80–82 Wardour Street, which he named Kinemacolor House. He looked for a venue that could be solely devoted to showing Kinemacolor, and took a two-year lease out on the Scala, a small theatre just off Tottenham Court Road.

At the Scala all the new Kinemacolor productions were premiered, including the fiction films made at Hove and in Nice, and here it was that Urban demonstrated his greatest triumph, the film record of the Delhi Durbar, the elaborate ceremony held in India to welcome King George V as the Emperor of India. The Durbar took place in December and the film, a phenomenal two and a half hours long, was shown at the Scala in February 1912. Urban, as ever, put on a superb show, with a stage setting based on the Taj Mahal, specially composed music with a forty-eight piece orchestra and a chorus of twenty-four, bagpipes and electrical effects. Urban made £150,000 from the film.[11]

Two events, both in December 1913, brought Urban tumbling down from his pedestal. First was the building of a special theatre for Kinemacolor films in Paris, the Théâtre Edouard VII. A wildly over-ambitious project, the theatre was too small, over-priced and inaccessible, and lost him thousands. More damaging still was the challenge to the monopolistic Urban-Smith Kinemacolor patent launched in the same month by the inventor William Friese-Greene, anxious to promote his own Biocolour system. Friese-Greene claimed the Kinemacolor patent was insufficiently detailed, but the petition was dismissed, only to be reversed on appeal, a decision upheld in the House of Lords. Kinemacolor claimed to show natural colours, but the appeal judge pointed out that with only red and green filters this could not be true. The patent was invalid.[12]

Return to America

The effective end of Kinemacolor as a commercial force coincided with the outbreak of the First World War. Rather surprisingly, in view of his German antecedents, Urban was not impeded in any way in his attempts to interest British propaganda outfits in using film. Urban's route was to approach the covert propaganda outfit based at Wellington House under Charles Masterman, employing his always admirable persuasive powers to produce a documentary feature entitled *Britain Prepared* (1915). With some Kinemacolor sequences, and filmed by four cameramen including Urban himself, the film showed impressive scenes of Britain's military preparedness. As an American with an assumed understanding of that country's people, Urban was sent to the USA with the film to try to get British propaganda films on to American screens.

In the wider world of the American film industry, Urban began for the first time to look out of his depth. American exhibitors showed little interest in the British war films, and a company formed by British sympathizers to distribute the films, the Patriotic Film Corporation, eventually collapsed. Urban also made an exceedingly unwise approach to the Hearst organization to distribute the films, when William Randolph Hearst was widely seen as a German sympathizer. The action irritated Urban's British superiors at Wellington House, even if the misplaced initiative came to nothing. His salvation came with America's entry into the war, which ended resistance to the British propaganda that Americans had so resented previously. British footage was added to American Signal Corps film in a propaganda news-reel, *Official War Review*, which Urban edited and printed for the Committee on Public Information.[13]

When the war ended, Urban decided to maintain operations in the United States. His business interests were many, but mostly speculative, certainly not at the stage where they could yield much revenue, and in any case the situation in the world film industry had changed considerably since the pre-war era in which Urban had flourished. Furthermore, he was in America, not Britain, and like a subject previously viewed through F. Martin Duncan's microscope, where once he had seemed a colossus, now he was revealed to be microscopic indeed, a small man in a cinema industry growing larger and richer every day on the proceeds of the fiction film. For Urban still placed his faith in the film that was good for you, the educational film, but it seemed fewer people wanted to learn than wanted to see entertaining stories.

In 1919 he co-founded a small, independent newsreel called *Kinograms*. Although it bore the distinctive K title of several of Urban's creations, he seems to have had little to do with its subsequent operations.[14] Together with engineer Henry Joy (a loyal associate from his pre-war days) he was developing a colour film system that would improve on Kinemacolor and enable him to make further commercial use of his huge Kinemacolor library. The system was to be called Kinekrom, but it never really got beyond the trial stage. Also with Joy he was hoping to market a projector called the Spirograph, originally invented in 1907 by Theodore Brown, another of the inventors who benefited from Urban's kindly purse over a number of years. This showed films on a celluloid disc, and again would be a way of re-marketing the Urban library. This was a common theme, because Urban had also founded a new film company, the Kineto Company of America, whose chief product was a series of shorts called *Movie Chats*, showing mostly travel and industrial films of light interest, many of which were simply Urban productions from the pre-war period.

In 1922 Urban moved all of his business interests to a huge building at Irvington-on-Hudson, New York. This he named the Urban Institute, home of his new parent company Urban Motion Picture Industries Inc. His increasingly visionary ideas were unfocused but impressively ambitious. He wrote of creating 'The Living Book of Knowledge' (a title with interesting echoes of the kind of works Urban had peddled many years before as a book salesman), offering his library, either on film or on Spirograph disks, to schools and other educational bodies. Many Irvington investors were attracted, unwisely, by Urban's idealism and the impressive Urban Institute building. For the inevitable occurred, and the Irvington-on-Hudson business in its grand building with all of its grand notions of supplying a motion picture encyclopaedia, collapsed into a prolonged and awkward bankruptcy in 1924–5. Former investors tried for a while to continue the business as the Urban-Kineto Corporation, but the effort was short-lived. It was the end of the name Urban as an active concern in the world of film.[15]

Of Urban himself, his feelings on the matter and his activities in America over the next five years, we know virtually nothing. He was not in penury, because his second wife Ada (they married in 1910), who had wisely kept much of her personal resources separate from his, remained comparatively wealthy. Tragically, the two million feet of film, much of it Kinemacolor, that he reportedly had at Irvington disappeared, probably destroyed or melted down for its silver content, its only true worth as a tangible asset to the industry, when Urban had had such high hopes of its enduring, educational worth. The Urbans had moved back to London by 1930. In 1937 his wife Ada died. That same year Urban donated all of his papers to the Science Museum, where they remain to this day, continuing to be a considerable boon to researchers, if daunting in the sheer scale of the collection. Urban himself died in Brighton, aged 75, in 1942.

Conclusion

Charles Urban was a typical example of the rider on the wheel. For a while the wheel lifted him up and it appeared that he was on top of the world, a man of substance, 'The King's Kinemacolorist' as one cartoon of him had it. Then he discovered that the wheel was turning, that he was subject to forces over which he had no control, and down he went again. The upturn was the economic expansion and confidence of the 1890s that was a breeding ground for enterprising, ambitious salesmen such as Urban; the peak of that turn was the nebulous nature of the early film industry, when all was unsettled and no one truly knew what the medium was for or for long it would last. In that climate, a confident man could thrive. In the emerging British film industry in particular, Urban stood out as an internationalist, unencumbered by parochialism, his outlook reflected in the cosmopolitan nature of his film catalogues. He stood out equally as both a hard-headed business-man (to the extent of trying to create a monopoly in colour film itself) and an idealist, espousing the educational film beyond the point where commercial sense might have led him.

Then the film market hardened and simplified—no longer could anyone think big and think documentary at the same time. And Urban made one too many wild gambles. His downturn was swift, and he found that there was little place for someone whose expertise lay in producing and promoting the pre-war film of actuality in the expanding post-war American market, where 'interest' films occupied a shrinking corner of the cinema programme. His legacy, however, is that he, more than anyone, established, encouraged and financed a native aptitude for films of fact which has ever since been a hallmark of British filmmaking. When he first encountered Edison's films in 1895 they were peepshow gimmicks, showing dancers and strongmen; Charles Urban simply showed that the cinema could embrace the world.

Notes

1. Much of the information on Urban's early years comes from his recently discovered unfinished memoirs, now published as Luke McKernan, ed., *A Yank in Britain: The Lost Memoirs of Charles Urban, Film Pioneer* (Hastings: The Projection Box, 1999).
2. Gordon Hendricks, *The Kinetoscope: America's First Commercially Successful Motion Picture Exhibitor* (New York, 1966), pp. 58–60.
3. A useful distillation from legal sources of Urban's Vitascope and proto-Bioscope period can be found in Richard Brown, ' "England is Not Big Enough . . .": American Rivalry in the Early English Film Business: The Case of Warwick v Urban,' *Film History*, vol. 10, 1998, pp. 21–34.
4. McKernan, *A Yank in Britain*, pp. 42–3.
5. Receipt of sales for the Warwick Trading Company, April 1897 to December 1901, Charles Urban papers, Science Museum, URB 3/2, p. 66 verso.
6. Brown, 'England is Not Big Enough . . .'
7. Public Record Office, HO/334/44.
8. See for example Urban's film catalogues, copies of which are held by the

Science Museum Library (which holds Urban's personal collection of papers) and by the National Film and Television Archive, and which are filled with often lavish press notices in praise of his various film programmes.

9. Charles Urban, *The Cinematograph in Science, Education, and Matters of State* (London: Charles Urban Trading Company, 1907), p. 33. The word 'documentary' comes in a translation of part of a lecture given in 1903 by Dr Eugène-Louis Doyen, a pioneer of the surgical film, who was associated with Urban: 'The Cinematograph will also allow of the preservation in documentary form of the operations of the older surgeons . . . The documents that we shall have henceforth will, thanks to the Cinematograph, allow the surgeon of the future to judge better of the progress achieved.'

10. Charles Urban, 'Terse History of Colour Kinematography' (1921), unpublished document, Charles Urban papers, Science Museum, URB 9/1-1.

11. Urban, 'Terse History,' also quoted in D.B. Thomas, *The First Colour Motion Pictures* (London: HMSO, 1969), pp. 26–7.

12. Thomas, *The First Colour Motion Pictures*, pp. 33–4. The full court proceedings can be found in the Charles Urban papers, Science Museum, URB 7/2-6.

13. Kevin Brownlow, *The War, The West and The Wilderness* (London: Secker and Warburg, 1979), pp. 51–4.

14. Raymond Fielding, *The American Newsreel 1911–1967* (Norman: University of Oklahoma Press, 1972), p. 83.

15. McKernan, *A Yank in Britain*, pp. 82–3 (afterword).

5

'It would be a Mistake to Strive for Subtlety of Effect'
Richard III and Populist, Pantomime Shakespeare in the 1910s

Jon Burrows

In 1911 the Co-operative Film Company released a 1,385-foot version of a production of *Richard III* that had been filmed at the Shakespeare Memorial Theatre in Stratford-upon-Avon. The play was originally staged and performed by the distinguished company of Frank Benson for the annual Shakespearean Festival held there. Benson was one of the most prolific and well-known actor-managers of the era, and he had been in charge of organizing this prestigious event since 1885.

In the mid to late 1900s, fiction films classed in the category of drama had become the dominant product of the film industry internationally. Before the widespread advent of multi-reel productions, or 'feature' films, around 1912–13, the period between 1908 and 1911 witnessed a small but prominent degree of experimentation in the filming of theatrical successes featuring established actors from the legitimate stage. The Co-operative's *Richard III* was neither the first nor the most celebrated British example of such an adaptation. It was not even the only celluloid recording of a Frank Benson Shakespearean performance, since its producers also filmed five more plays from his Stratford repertoire. It is, however, the only one to have survived in a viewable condition. This historical 'accident' has frequently placed it at the centre of debates about the merits of early British cinema in this transitional period.

In the only detailed general historical account of post-1900 silent British filmmaking, Rachael Low categorically denounces the film as a 'mistake'. She claims that its unashamedly theatrical methodology led the producers to ignore the obvious narrative resources implicit in cinematic technology, resulting in a film that compensates for its visual poverty and incomprehensibility only with an abundance of 'wild gestures'.[1] Robert Hamilton Ball has amplified these criticisms. He similarly attributes what he perceives to be the failings of the performances to the extreme long shot scale. As a result of this distant camera placement, and a concomitantly crowded, confusing stage picture, the players apparently resort to an 'exaggeration of gesture' and 'overregistration of emotions [which] with no suitable aesthetic distance becomes ridiculous'.[2]

More recently, there have been some welcome revisionist attempts to understand the film within its original historical context. John Collick argues that the very extravagance of gesture in the film represents a pronounced foregrounding of its theatrical origins, and is part of an attempt to create, by association with the stage, 'a unique and distinctive national film idiom. Shakespeare, or more specifically, Victorian Shakespeare production, was an ideal expression of a uniquely English, high-class culture . . . In this context *King Richard III* isn't a primitive film at all.'[3] Andrew Higson has similarly categorized the film as an early example of a subsequently ubiquitous tradition of British 'heritage' cinema. It thus belongs to a conscious effort 'to define a distinctive national cinema by engaging with . . . indigenous cultural traditions', which saw its 'target audience' as the 'respectable middle-class public, more used to visiting the theatre than the cinema'.[4]

The main problem with this latter approach is that it simply compensates for the film's abject status within conventional teleological accounts of the historical evolution of film form by creating an alternative narrative: a fully formed 'national tradition', within which *Richard III* becomes an originary pioneering model. Neither one of these critical constructions of the film seems to me to be sensitive enough to the often contingent and contradictory dynamic forces which shaped the production and consumption of British cinema in the early 1910s. It is also problematic to talk unreflexively about 'the theatre' at this time as if it constituted a singular, self-evident object. Within the Edwardian theatre there was no single set of theatrical conventions, no single theatrical style. Instead, the stage of 1911, in all its multifarious manifestations, housed an incredible diversity of performance practices that appealed to different and sometimes mutually exclusive audience constituencies, both in terms of class and regional specificity. So when British films drew upon some of these practices they were making an intervention into a complex network of divergent critical canons and audience affiliations which often resulted in historically provisional and nonsynchronous conceptions of the kind of imaginary ideal spectator that they aimed to attract and to please.

This chapter is an attempt to remedy these oversights. I will situate the film in relation to a series of international developments in the cinematic employment of theatrical stars between 1908 and 1911. I will also compare it with other similarly ambitious products of the British industry, like the famous lost film of Sir Herbert Beerbohm Tree's production of Shakespeare's *Henry VIII* (1911). I will argue that *Richard III* should partly be seen as the product of a general discourse about the art of moving picture acting that influenced the industries of several film-producing nations for a time. These all looked towards the very specific theatrical tradition of Continental pantomime as a suitable artistic model that the cinema could aspire to in order both to exploit its signifying peculiarities to the full and enhance its cultural kudos. I will attempt to demonstrate the degree to which the performance style showcased in *Richard III* fulfilled the prescriptions for an appropriately cinematic form of acting which were tentatively enunciated within this pantomimic discourse. A better understanding of this acting style will help us to see how character movement is actually very carefully choreographed within the film as an aid to spectatorial clarity and comprehensibility, rather than just a badly digested hangover from another medium. More contentiously, perhaps, I will also argue that *Richard III*'s cast, subject matter and style of presentation contained sufficient appeal and intelligibility for a much broader class stratum of spectators than the middle-class theatre-going public.

French Lessons

The Co-operative Shakespeare films belong to a relatively self-contained period of experimentation with certain theatrical modes of performance in British cinema between 1908 and 1911. This is not to say that there are no continuities with developments extending beyond these dates, but they have certainly been exaggerated in previous surveys. George Perry, for example, sees the release of W.G. Barker's aforementioned adaptation of Tree's famous presentation of *Henry VIII* at His Majesty's Theatre in 1911 as a great turning point in British film history: 'there was a rush of stage performers after Tree had paved the way, and many other West End actors turned to films.'[5] In fact, apart from H.B. Irving a month later, and for the same company, not a single British 'footlights favourite' followed Tree's example until a full two years later—an immense gap for such a rapidly evolving and expanding industry.

I would argue that Tree's much-fêted decision to appear before the cameras at this time was more a consummation of a pre-existent trend than a trailblazing blueprint that the rest of his profession straight-forwardly copied. Low and Ball have both assumed that the release of the Benson films in the immediate aftermath of the heavily publicized *Henry VIII* illustrates the influence of Tree's legacy,[6] but there is compelling evidence to suggest that the Co-operative Cinemato-graph Company had actually made their Stratford films nearly twelve months earlier. The delay in Benson's appearance on the nation's moving picture screens would seem to have been caused by the financial dissolution of the London Cinematograph Company, which had originally made the films, in the middle of 1910. The company had already by this time posted numerous advertisements announcing their release, and Benson himself had given a speech in the spring of 1910 at the Shakespearean Festival in which he talks of having just 'represented Shakespeare without words for the benefit of a cinematograph'.[7]

Back in 1910, the obvious inspiration for Benson's producers' decision to hire a theatrical luminary of his calibre would have been provided less by their British peers than by the efforts of the French Film d'Art company, along with its numerous imitators and plagiarists. Following the public premiere of a package of films, including *La Mort du Duc de Guise*, in Paris and London during November 1908, the world's motion picture exhibitors could now offer their patrons privileged access to the work of various elite Parisian theatres' most distinguished performers, including Albert Lambert, Le Bargy and Cecile Sorel.

French theatre—or at least a stereotyped perception of what French theatre stood for—also played an important role internationally in debates about the new art of cinema acting. The discourse which promulgated such ideas actually predated the *films d'art*. One of the earliest references to the subject of screen acting that I have found comes from the American trade periodical *Moving Picture World* in 1907:

The actor who is too reposeful on the stage, and expresses his
meaning and feeling merely by the tones of his voice or in subtle
movements, is utterly worthless for the moving picture.
Sometimes the actor who has risen no higher than to scrub parts
or the chorus can be made good use of for the moving picture
because of his great proneness to gesture and motion.[8]

Actorly performance is conceived of here in exactly the same terms as
one of the main attractions of cinema back in the 1890s: what is
admired is simply pure kineticism. The emphasis on movement to the
proscribed detriment of depth or subtlety may seem like a mechanistic
denial of art, but very similar ideas were reformulated a year later in the
British trade paper the *Bioscope*. This time the perfect screen actors
were defined not as rough and ready supernumeraries but as Continental European performers who had either been trained in, or were
temperamentally inclined towards, a school of pronounced gestural
expression. Such performers could provide the requisite frantic physical
motion (and had the added advantage of carrying with them the
attached weight of a culturally prestigious performance tradition with
deep historical roots):

> Strange as it may seem, the best moving picture actors or actresses
> are not found in the ranks of American and English professionals.
> The best material is found in the Latin races. The French and
> Italian people are notably successful. The explanation of this is
> that the Anglo-Saxon is more phlegmatic. By reason of his natural
> suppression of powers of expression he fails to attain the same
> ends that the others mentioned do. There is a lack of required
> action.[9]

The same sentiments were expressed in the *Kinematograph and Lantern
Weekly*:

> English actors are, both by temperament and education, unable to
> equal the Continental performer in the graphic gestures which in
> films must take the place of dialogue. The typical English style of
> acting is quiet and restrained, and if an artiste is unable to forget
> the traditions of his profession and throw himself into a piece
> with the abandon of a French or Italian actor, the manufacturer is
> hardly to be blamed.[10]

I could quote literally dozens of similar pronouncements made in this particular period. Some commentators did not simply enunciate the differences in national gestural tendencies but advocated a specific mode of Southern European theatrical performance, artistic panto-mime, as the model to which the cinema should aspire. It is important to understand precisely what is meant by this term. It does not refer to the familiar kind of English seasonal pantomimes that have survived intact from the Victorian era to the present day. These retained the title of 'pantomimes' by virtue of their emphasis on some form of fairytale narrative presented through spectacular staging techniques, but in practice their generic format incorporated spoken word elements drawn from a mixture of influences such as variety theatre and musical comedy.

As the word's etymology suggests, true pantomime is a form of wordless drama in which emotions and ideas are expressed purely through gesture and movement. In itself this definition is still inadequate, since all silent film acting is in one sense necessarily pantomimic. Furthermore, a comparison of the illustrations in the specialized acting manuals which professed to teach the techniques of pantomime with those of more generalized acting guides published in the eighteenth and nineteenth centuries shows that exactly the same kinds of conventionalized poses are recommended in both sources. However, Ben Brewster and Lea Jacobs have recently distinguished what they define as a *pictorial* style of acting, which can be seen to persist in European cinema to at least 1918, from pantomime *per se*.[11] Whilst pantomime may share a similar gestural repertoire, it is more intensely stylized than the broader tradition of pictorial acting and foregrounds constant performative movement within more stereo-typically ritualized dramatic situations. Unlike the pictorial style, which used pronounced gestures to emphasize and illustrate key emotional points of dialogue, pantomime abhorred even the imitation of speak-ing and listening and placed the focus of attention entirely upon summary gestures. These gestures distilled narrative content into a quick succession of instantly readable semaphoric messages. As a result, pantomimic gestures articulated significantly more compressed meanings and followed each other with greater rapidity and much less intermediate gradation.

My source for much of this information is Charles Aubert's *L'Art Mimique*, an acting manual dedicated to teaching the art of panto-mime, published in France in 1901. Some of Aubert's more programmatic statements are surprisingly similar to the language used to describe cinema at the end of the 1900s, and often anticipate the style of acting presented in *Richard III*:

> Pantomimes are theatrical performances played in the language of action . . . Its rapid and noiseless action causes a very different emotion than the drama does . . . Pantomime speaks only of the visible . . . Expressions which require too many explanatory gestures must be rejected or modified because they cause length. Also expressions whose meaning is equivocal, or which could signify several things, must be rejected or modified because they cause confusion. Length and confusion are two dangers to be shunned. A pantomimic movement should be executed with great precision . . . Let the spectacle of a pantomime be a series of moving pictures which each gesture changes every moment.[12]

One regularly finds forthright calls in the British trade press for producers to emulate and adapt the stylistic principles of Continental pantomimes. In 1911, for instance, Laurence Trevelyan called for 'The Revival of Pantomime' within the cinema, since 'in the picture play—which depends upon pantomime for its presentation—the producer has to consider an entirely different set of conditions from those which obtain on the legitimate stage'.[13] Even as late as 1913, a contributor to the *Kinematograph Weekly* could define 'The Artistic Possibilities of the Kinema' in exactly the same terms:

> The problem of the kinema drama resolves itself into the problem of artistic pantomime. Pantomime throws aside all the conventional restrictions of motion as set by every-day life and finds its peculiar means of expression in the language of movements . . . The only artistic possibilities for the kinema lie in the direction of pantomime in all its various forms.[14]

This belief was put into practice in all the major film-producing nations around this time by the filming of specialist pantomime performers and even complete productions. The mime artist Séverin appeared in one of the very first *films d'art* in 1908, *La Main Rouge*, and over the next few years was the star of several Pathé films featuring the archetypal pantomime character of the minstrel Pierrot. One of the most celebrated modern wordless pantomimes of the late nineteenth century was Michel Carré's *L'Enfant Prodigue*, which Gaumont filmed in 1907 and again in 1911. Carré's pantomime expertise induced Pathé to recruit him as a scenarist and director on a number of films made between 1909 and 1911. Carré was also later hired by the German Menschen company to help supervise the filming of Max Reinhardt's mimed production of *The Miracle* in 1912. The Italian Celio Company were still adapting stage pantomimes like Bessier's *Histoire d'un Pierrot* during 1913. In the United States, the lead actress in one successful stage revival of *L'Enfant Prodigue*, Mlle Pilar Morin, was given a contract by the Edison company, and for a short time in 1909–10 she was its most heavily promoted picture personality. Not only did she feature in a series of prestige productions that received unusually hyperbolic praise from trade reviewers, she also authored articles on the art of pantomime and its suitability for cinematic presentation in the trade press. Morin even orchestrated a special revival of *L'Enfant Prodigue* at the Liberty Theatre in New York, which curious and momentarily receptive industry representatives attended in large numbers.[15]

Robust Shakespeare

The trend caught on in Britain as well. Native theatrical actors with a greater penchant for demonstrative and ostentatious attitudinizing than many of their more fashionably reserved countrymen were for a time assiduously courted by film producers. When playing in *Henry VIII* on the stage Beerbohm Tree was reported to have demonstrated an 'art [that] largely consists in the invention and elaboration of gesture and "business" of which he is a consummate master . . . [He] must always be doing something, must always be on the move.'[16] This is probably in part what made him so attractive as a new recruit to the ranks of cinematograph actors. The gestural largesse seems to have been played up even further in the film version, one reviewer noting that several of the performers 'appeared to have purposely emphasized and exaggerated their gestures for the occasion'.[17]

Perhaps the best source of information about the kind of acting that was featured in the (missing) film version of the play can be found in an article on screen acting contributed to a popular *Handbook of Kinematography* in 1911. The author is Henry Morrell, a member of Tree's company, and one of the featured players in *Henry VIII*. His comments chime very neatly with the discourse on moving picture acting that I have delineated:

> The kinematograph actor will need . . . to be above all things an accomplished pantomimist . . . For this reason it would be a

mistake to strive for subtlety of effect . . . It is therefore necessary
to adopt a style which shall be impressionistic rather than otherwise; a style wherein effects are obtained by methods at once
broad, deliberate and incisive . . . [T]he kinematograph actor must
be a master pantomimist, and the writer of kinematograph plays
must write for pantomime.[18]

It is plausible to speculate, then, that *Henry VIII* most likely had a
marked formal kinship with the kinds of films that can be seen as
products of this pantomimic discourse. I would certainly argue that
this is demonstrably the case for Co-operative's earlier *Richard III*.
The surviving evidence about Benson's performance practices on the
stage indicates that, like Tree, he preferred the vigorously gesticulatory
grammar of the 'old school' to the 'reserved force' which was often
characterized as the genetic calling of the English actor on the West End
stage. Benson never got any kind of foothold as a manager in the West
End. Many of his productions there were perceived as failures and his
reputation was largely forged in the provinces. Given the repetition
of particular complaints by dismissive metropolitan critics, Benson's
biographer surmises that he was prone to 'gestures, too many and far too
fidgety', and that throughout his career 'he could not escape from
a carpet-beating fling of the right arm'.[19] If we bear in mind the emphasis
of the pantomimic discourse on constant motion and uninhibited
articulacy in the representation of emotional poses, there is an obvious
logic behind his selection as a cinema actor, especially since he was a
performer who could, as one of his more sympathetic reviewers wrote
in 1907, make his 'movements tell more than his words'.[20]

I would argue that the much-criticized and fairly extreme long shot
framing adhered to in the film version of *Richard III* is actually
deliberately employed to maximize this kind of pantomimic style and
its plastic effects. The exorbitant use of pronounced gestures in the film
is thus not simply the sloppily unintended by-product of the camera
placement as Low and Ball have suggested. The scale of each shot
provides extra width to the image, which is used to create a space for
constant, vigorous performative movement. It is, for example, patently
exploited in the various fight scenes that are presented in the film,
which even Low describes as 'cover[ing] the stage like a ballet'. In a
similar way, in the ostensibly more sedate scene where Richard woos
Lady Anne, the width of the playing area is actually used as a concrete
physical summation and correlative for the latter's alternating hostility
and submission: she moves from the left of the screen to the right, and

Plates 8 and 9. Frame stills from *Richard III*
(London Cinematograph Company, 1910–11)

then back to the left again on five separate occasions as she wavers in
her resolutions.

Through these kinds of effects, speech is translated into a different
realm of broadly symbolic *action*. Perhaps an even better example of the
condensation of Richard's lengthy rhetoric into pure physical motion is
the way this scene represents the influence of his charm over Anne as a
form of hypnotism. Richard holds his hand above hers and—without
physical contact—guides it upwards like a snake charmer, so that he

87

can place a ring upon it as she stands in a passive trance (see Plates 8 and 9).

Such purely pictorial touches are consolidated by the fact that there is very little attempt by the characters to simulate speech in a scene originally dedicated to verbal dissembling. Although there are occasional lapses from an authentically pantomimic refusal of lip movement, compared with the majority of films made afterwards—and even a great many made concurrently—the rarity of simulated conversational moments is quite striking.

An embargo on mimed speech was, of course, one of the prescriptive rules of pantomimic acting laid down by Charles Aubert. Another of his more emphatic injunctions was a warning against letting two actors make different gestures simultaneously, unless they were physically interacting in close proximity. This rule responded to the fact that in wordless drama the spectator had to be able to read any isolated gesture in its entirety without distraction, since there was no speech and few other signifying devices to corroborate interpretation. This injunction is again fairly scrupulously observed in *Richard III*: we frequently see Richard 'freeze' and hold poses whilst another actor performs the next significant gesture.

Aubert also suggests that, in the interests of further clarity, if a group of actors representing a gathered throng have to perform significant actions in unison, they should all reproduce the same gesture. This contravenes the advice of many orthodox theatrical acting manuals, since, as one early-nineteenth-century book of technical instruction put it, 'nothing is more ugly, than for two Actors to stand alike, because contrasts must hold in the whole of the tableau'.[21] Aubert's pantomime technique is regularly used in *Richard III*, however, as a means of directing attention within a crowded stage picture. In the scene where Buckingham and the Lord Mayor and various assembled clergy and dignitaries try to persuade Richard to accept the crown, we see them all perform exactly the same gestures in unison. To begin with, they all kneel and, in exact synchronization, extend their open right palms to him in supplication (see Plate 10). When Richard finally accedes to their entreaty all of the men raise their right arms in the air to celebrate, and are, once again, scrupulous in their symmetry and unity of gesticulation (see Plate 11).

These are definitely not the kinds of random and confused sets of groupings which Low and Ball have stigmatically assigned to *Richard III*. One might in fact characterize these groupings as a relatively sophisticated form of narration, controlled purely by the carefully

Plates 10 and 11.   Frame stills from *Richard III*
(London Cinematograph Company, 1910–11)

orchestrated movements of the actors. They effectively give us editing
within the shots as a workable alternative to editing *between* them.

Popular Shakespeare?

The logic behind this kind of pantomime choreography would, of
course, lose much of its justification if the source material was itself
deemed to be an inappropriate or even incomprehensible attraction for

cinema patrons at the time. This is the final question that I would like to pose here: at whom was this Shakespearean adaptation really aimed, and what kind of audiences would have appreciated the kind of pantomimic display it foregrounds? The heritage discourse that Higson has invoked to classify the film is undoubtedly relevant in some respects. It seems particularly appropriate to consider the decision to film Benson and his company on the actual stage of the Shakespeare Memorial Theatre in this light. Such a location represents a curious choice because it does necessitate the sacrifice of any significant depth in the image. Large theatrical spaces, unlike a two-dimensional projected cinema image, had to maintain a relatively shallow *mise-en-scène* to ensure the consistent visibility of the action from every seat in the auditorium. One explanation for the producers' willingness to accommodate this formal limitation may lie with the fact that in the summer of 1910 a lavish ceremony took place in which the Corporation of Stratford-upon-Avon conferred the Freedom of the Borough upon Benson in recognition of his services in having organized the Shakespeare Festivals there for the past twenty-five years. He thus became only the second Freeman of Stratford after David Garrick in 1769, and the legal document was laid alongside Garrick's in a casket of sixteenth-century oak fashioned from the old woodwork of Stratford Church.[22] This symbolic assertion of a great and glorious yet simultaneously elite and exclusive tradition of English acting stretching back through the centuries created enormous publicity, which the Benson films may well have intended to capitalize upon. Benson's newsworthy connection with the theatre would seem to provide a justifiable pretext to film him in his most rarefied natural environment.

But just how elite was the appeal of this tradition of great Shakespearean actors? Recent work by Roberta Pearson and William Uricchio on the American cinema of the same period—specifically on a series of potted Shakespeare films that the Vitagraph company made between 1908 and 1910—suggests that heavily butchered fifteen to twenty minute versions of Shakespearean plays actually predated the cinema. They were often staged for the benefit of lower-class and immigrant audiences, as part of a popular culture in which Shakespeare played a surprisingly pervasive part. As one sign of their adaptation to different constituencies, the plays were regularly presented in formats that highlighted their most spectacular and violent elements and recoded the characters as stock generic types resembling the inhabitants of 'the rankest cheap melodrama'.[23]

There is no comparable work that I am aware of that has explored the place of Shakespeare within British popular culture, or his centrality to working-class educational provision and self-improvement courses. There are some pertinent features of the Stratford Shakespeare Festivals in 1910, though, that bear thinking about in this context. For the first time, the plays that Benson performed were carefully selected to correspond with those taught on the national schools syllabus, and large parties of schoolchildren flocked to Stratford for this reason.[24] At the very least, this indicates the existence of a democratizing educational impulse behind the festival, rather than a strictly elite appeal. Also in 1910, the festival underwent the final process of its commercial transformation into a major cultural industry. A second summer festival was set up to capitalize upon the hordes of American tourists who seasonally gravitated towards Stratford. This hint that the event was increasingly directed towards creating a greater mass appeal is strengthened by the fact that cheaper rail fares were offered to people who could only afford the gallery and pit seats.[25] In other words, the festival was constructing itself as subsidized public culture, and not as an emblem of hierarchical distinction. As such, it is a significant intertext for our understanding of the adapted films.

One might want to bear in mind the fact that this version of *Richard III* crams no fewer than five fights and slayings into its short running length. Three of these are only mentioned and not directly represented in Shakespeare's original play, and even Benson's stage presentation at the Stratford Festival showed less bloodthirstiness than the film by having all incidents relating to the murder of the princes 'wrought off'.[26] Habitual consumers of blood-and-thunder melodrama might feasibly have appropriated Benson's film version of *Richard III* as a text in the same vein, offering comparable pleasures. There is certainly little cultural snobbery or special treatment evident in the way that some of the Benson films were programmed in cinemas. *Macbeth*, for example, was shown on its first West End run at the Theatre de Luxe on the Strand alongside two westerns, *The Indian and the Maid* and *Only a Sister*, and a comedy, *Wiffle's Best Friend*.[27] The same film shared the bill at the Falmouth Polytechnic Picture Hall with a live act featuring 'little Miss Dot Moss, the Toy Comedienne, and the World's Smallest Banjo Soloist and Dancer'.[28]

This is not to deny the vicarious prestige that was being forged here by association with an established theatrical star, a work of great cultural capital, and emphasis upon a style of pantomimic acting with a distinguished artistic lineage. But this is very much a text that different groups of viewers could activate in different ways. It followed what were defined at the time as legitimate cinematic imperatives, rather than a simplistic urge to replicate refined theatrical pleasures. Furthermore, no single privileged social formation necessarily monopolized the ability to understand the source narrative inter-textually. The Co-operative Cinematograph Company's *Richard III* may ultimately belong to a long-term historical effort to upgrade the cinema's cultural status, but at this stage some care was taken not to leave the medium's existing loyal viewers behind in the process.

Notes

1. Rachael Low, *The History of the British Film 1906–1914* (London: George Allen and Unwin, 1949), p. 225.
2. Robert Hamilton Ball, *Shakespeare on Silent Film: A Strange Eventful History* (London: George Allen and Unwin, 1968), p. 87.
3. John Collick, *Shakespeare, Cinema and Society* (Manchester: Manchester University Press, 1989), pp. 45–6.
4. Andrew Higson, 'Heritage Discourses and British Cinema before 1920,' in John Fullerton, ed., *Celebrating 1895: The Centenary of Cinema* (London: John Libbey, 1998), pp. 183, 187.
5. George Perry, *The Great British Picture Show: From the Nineties to the Seventies* (London: Paladin, 1975), p. 36.
6. See Low, *The History of the British Film*, p. 187; Ball, *Shakespeare on Silent Film*, p. 82.
7. As reported in the *Stratford-upon-Avon Herald and South Warwickshire Advertiser*, 22 April 1910, p. 8.
8. *Moving Picture World*, 13 July 1907, p. 298.
9. 'Film-Picture Actors,' *Bioscope*, 2 October 1908, p. 18.
10. *Kinematograph and Lantern Weekly*, 1 July 1909, p. 349.
11. Ben Brewster and Lea Jacobs, *Theatre to Cinema: Stage Pictorialism and the Early Feature Film* (Oxford: Oxford University Press, 1997), p. 82.
12. Charles Aubert, *The Art of Pantomime*, trans. Edith Sears (London: George Allen and Unwin, 1927; first published in French in 1901), pp. 3, 152, 156, 198, 201.
13. 'The Revival of Pantomime,' *Bioscope*, 21 December 1911, p. 815.
14. Alexander Bakshy, 'The Artistic Possibilities of the Kinema,' *Kinematograph and Lantern Weekly*, 21 August 1913, p. 1781.
15. See *Moving Picture World*, 23 September 1910, p. 687, and *Kinematograph and Lantern Weekly*, 22 September 1910, p. 1315 for further details.
16. *Evening News*, 2 September 1910; clipping held in the University of Bristol's Herbert Beerbohm Tree Collection.
17. ' "Henry VIII" on the Bioscope,' *Morning Post*, 21 February 1911;

clipping held in the University of Bristol's Herbert Beerbohm Tree Collection.

18. Henry Morrell, 'On Acting Before the Kinematograph,' in Colin N. Bennett, ed., *The Handbook of Kinematography: The History, Theory and Practice of Motion Photography and Projection* (London: The Kinematograph Weekly, 1911), pp. 218–19. For analysis of the exhibition and reception of *Henry VIII*, and for more details about the production of the Benson Shakespeare films, see Jonathan Burrows, '*The Whole English Stage to be Seen for Sixpence!': Theatrical Actors and Acting Styles in British Cinema, 1908–1918*, unpublished PhD thesis, University of East Anglia, 2000.

19. J.C. Trewin, *Benson and the Bensonians* (London: Barrie and Rockcliff, 1960), p. 91.

20. Allan Monkhouse, *Manchester Guardian*, quoted in Trewin, *Benson and the Bensonians*, p. 162.

21. Johannes Jelgerhuis, *Theoretische Lessen over de Gesticulatie en Mimiek* (Amsterdam: P.M. Warnars, 1827), quoted in Brewster and Jacobs, *Theatre to Cinema*, p. 92.

22. Sir Frank Benson, *My Memoirs* (London: Ernest Benn, 1930), p. 321.

23. William Uricchio and Roberta Pearson, *Reforming Culture: The Case of the Vitagraph Quality Films* (New Jersey: Princeton University Press, 1993), p. 69.

24. T.C. Kemp and J.C. Trewin, *The Stratford Festival: A History of the Shakespeare Memorial Theatre* (Birmingham: Cornish Brothers, 1953), p. 90.

25. *Stratford-upon-Avon Herald*, 22 July 1910, p. 8.

26. *Era*, 29 April 1911, p. 12.

27. *Picture Theatre News*, 19 April 1911, p. 6.

28. *Cornish Echo*, 12 May 1911, p. 5.

SECTION B

Going to the Cinema
Audiences, Exhibition and Reception from the 1890s to the 1910s

6

'Indecent Incentives to Vice'[1]
Regulating Films and Audience Behaviour from the 1890s to the 1910s

Lise Shapiro Sanders

While we know an increasing amount about the British films of the silent period and the artisanal or industrial contexts in which they were produced, we know much less about the audiences that watched those films and how they watched them. Yet audiences and audience behaviour were vital subjects of debate in the first decades of cinema, especially among middle-class social reformers and moral commentators. My chapter will focus on some of these debates, drawing on recent research on early film audiences in an effort to illuminate contemporary concerns about women's moral and social practice. My principal argument will be that the presence of women in the audience resulted in a heightened focus on the cinema as a vehicle for subversive sexual practices taking place both on and off the screen.

The constitution and behaviour of film audiences altered dramatically between the 1890s and the 1910s; in particular, audiences became less participatory and more subject to social control and regulation. This shift in audience behaviour was due to several influences. The first was the wide-scale effort to 'improve' the moral status of working-class entertainments by encouraging women and children to join the audience, thereby differentiating new forms of leisure like the cinema from older ones like the pub. The second was the impact of various reform movements, such as the purity campaigns of the 1880s and 1890s, and other expressions of middle-class anxiety about popular

leisure activities, which resulted amongst other things in the formaliza-
tion of film censorship in the 1910s. The third was the transition from
the music hall and variety form of performance to the extended realist
dramas that began to dominate film programmes in the mid-1910s.
Classical narrative form thus began to exert an influence on audience
behaviour: audiences were increasingly encouraged to watch the longer
feature films in relative silence and with less interaction between
members of the audience in the darkened viewing space of the cinema
theatre. These influences on audience behaviour were, in fact, causally
related: contemporary sources reveal a subtle but crucial exchange
between the behaviour of the audience and the films viewed. Accounts
describing either audience behaviour or the moral status of the film
image invariably lapse from one subject to the other and back again,
seemingly unable to separate the two. This slippage occurs, I contend,
because of the widely held belief that the subjects represented on
screen might somehow affect the behaviour of audience members, and
that audience *mis*behaviour might negatively influence not only the
viewing experience but also the morals of other audience members.
Consequently, middle-class social reformers, among them representatives of the clergy, purity and vigilance campaigners, and
temperance groups, sought to improve the morals of both the audience
and the subjects presented on the screen.

One of the first and most important exhibition contexts for films
was in the many music halls already catering to mass audiences. It is
not surprising, then, that the concern about and regulation of music
hall audiences in the latter part of the Victorian period affected
attitudes towards film audiences in the Edwardian period and beyond.
In this sense, the struggle to create 'rational recreations' or morally and
socially acceptable forms of leisure described by Peter Bailey as a
mid-Victorian phenomenon continued well into the twentieth century,
subjecting new technologies of leisure like the cinema to censorship
and ideological control in an endeavour to distribute middle-class
codes of social practice to the 'lower' classes.[2]

Of course, not all audiences were the same. Music halls and cinemas
targeted specific social groups and were in turn shaped by the
audiences who patronized them. Contemporary accounts readily
demonstrate the variety of actual audiences, from the elite crowds who
patronized London's West End music halls and theatres to the middle-
and working-class populations attending local entertainments in the
provinces, the suburbs and the East End.[3] My concern in this chapter
will be primarily with lower middle-class and working-class audiences,

and especially the newest segment of the consuming public, young single women from these social groups. Women became an increasingly significant part of the cinema-going audience—according to some estimates, by 1916 they made up over 50 per cent of the total audience—and were gradually incorporated into the ideology of respectability that was becoming increasingly dominant within the industry.[4]

Initially, however, the presence of young women at exhibitions of moving images was a subject of concern, because of both what they might see and how they might behave. Young single working women often spent their leisure time in each others' company, or alternatively went to the music hall, the variety theatre or the cinema with a male suitor. Popular leisure practices and courtship rituals thus became intertwined as working women, unable to afford the luxurious experience of an evening on the town on their own, accepted the offers of men in order to provide themselves with stimulation and diversion. In such music hall environments as the Empire or the Alhambra, where the nightly promenades served as a meeting place for prostitutes and their clients, single women were apt to be mistaken for prostitutes; of course, by accepting a man's invitation for an evening's entertainment, they risked placing themselves in a similar, if less explicitly articulated, situation. As first-hand accounts of the courtship experience for working- and lower-middle-class couples are scarce, we may never know the extent of actual commercial exchange present in such relationships. However, we can presume that the contemporary perception—that the music hall provided couples with the licence to pursue their romantic and sexual desires—was based to some extent on the actual practices of the men and women who attended the performance together; they may well have used the interactive environment of the halls as a cover for intimate activities pursued of necessity in public. The potential confusion over the identity and behaviour of women in the music hall audience signalled sexual and social risk to those middle-class critics concerned to raise the tone of music halls and variety theatres from their 'degraded' position.

The situation in cinemas was somewhat different; as the working and lower middle classes became subject to industry efforts to broaden social patterns of attendance, there was an increasing emphasis on cinema's role as educator and enforcer of moral codes for public conduct. The significant aspect of this attention to morality and social practice is the focus on the exhibition space as a site of conflict in sexual terms: the darkened theatre provided a space where prostitutes might locate prospective clients, and where couples might find the solitude they desired within the crowd. In an attempt to regulate the behaviour of patrons in the cinema auditorium, reformers and censors turned a critical gaze on the subjects presented on screen, assuming a direct relationship between the practices of the viewer and the films viewed. Increasingly, the films themselves were subject to scrutiny and eventually censorship, a transformation that entailed the gradual assimilation of popular cinema into a more standardized mode of presentation and leisure practice.[5] In this context, women moved to the centre of the struggle for ideological and legislative control at the same time that their presence as participants in the mass audience came to signify a new arena of conflict in the history of leisure at the turn of the century.

'Lewd Pictures'[6]: The Development of Film Audiences

In the closing decades of the nineteenth century, reformers increasingly sought to establish legal and social control over the practice of vice and corruption in London's streets and social institutions. Since the early 1880s, the missionary efforts of reformers had contributed to an atmosphere of militant agitation in an attempt to suppress drunkenness, obscenity and sexual vice. Temperance, purity and vigilance campaigners perceived the late-Victorian music hall as a culture of sexual and social risk, a perception that extended to early film shows and their patrons. This was no coincidence, given that films were shown so widely in music halls and variety theatres during the first decades of cinema. As the new technology of the cinema developed from a novelty item to a legitimate form of popular leisure, films began to be included as one of the music hall 'turns', usually occupying a twenty- to thirty-minute period toward the end of the evening's programme. Like performers, operators might give more than one turn per night, maximizing their exposure and profits from a number of different halls. Although early film exhibition in London began in West End halls like the Empire and the Alhambra, it was not limited to those locations: as public exhibitions became more frequent in city centres and suburban areas, the film experience became available to working- and lower-middle-class viewers through the cheaper halls and in the 'penny gaff' or shop-show, the peepshow street cinematograph, and the travelling or fairground exhibition.[7] By the end of the first decade of film exhibition, purpose-built cinemas began to take the place of these transitional exhibition contexts, and by 1916 the public displayed their commitment to this form of entertainment by spending more on it than on all other public forms of leisure combined.[8] With the increasing attention paid to cinema as a leisure entertainment came a concern over the behaviour of the audience, particularly its female members, and discussion over how that behaviour might be affected by the cinematic image. The transformation of the audience into a controllable entity paralleled efforts by the industry and reformers to improve the moral condition of the narratives taking place on as well as off the screen.

The concern over 'immoral' films and their alleged impact on audience behaviour can be seen in complaints to the press and to local administrative bodies throughout this period. In 1899, for instance, Samuel Smith, MP, wrote a letter to *The Times* about what he saw as a dangerous new technology for representing sexual vice and indecency, and its likely effect on viewers:

> Will you allow me to call the attention of the public, through your columns, to a new source of evil which has recently sprung up at our popular watering places? I refer to vicious, demoralising pictures shown in penny-in-the-slot machines . . . It is hardly possible to exaggerate the corruption of the young that comes from exhibiting, under a strong light, nude female figures represented as living and moving, going in and out of baths, sitting as artists' models &c. ... If nothing is done to stop this, we shall see a rapid decay of English morals to the level of Paris, with the same deadly results on the life of the nation.[9]

A similar view was expressed in the *Daily Chronicle* by a correspondent who made a 'personal investigation' of such exhibitions:

> I frankly admit that some of the pictures were refined and beautiful, but these were interspersed with others of a lewd nature. Those which were not flagrantly obscene were suggestive of evil and calculated to engender foul imaginations and impure thoughts. Around one of the most impure of these exhibits I watched a group of girls, ranging in age from ten to fifteen years. An outer circle was formed by youths and men [who], with leering eyes and base language, supplemented any vicious suggestions these pictures had already made.[10]

The kinetoscopes, mutoscopes and other machines designed for individual viewing had, of course, always been associated with the peepshow, and were morally and legally suspect for this reason. In the public exhibition context of the cinema auditorium, however, similarly immoral activities were thought to be encouraged by both the darkened theatre and the on-screen images.

Kissing in the Cinema: Courtship Films

An example of the slippage between on-screen images and the (mis)behaviour of the audience can be found in the genre of courtship or 'kissing' films, seemingly a popular subject in early cinema, if we may judge from extant prints and catalogue descriptions. Numerous short films showed one or more scenes in which a man steals a kiss from his female acquaintance, or gradually woos her, proposes, and is rewarded with an embrace. The 1896 Edison film of a kiss between stage actors, *The May Irwin–John C. Rice Kiss*, is a now famous example of this genre; others include those catalogued in the National Film and Television Archive under assumed titles such as *The Kissing Couple*, showing 'a close shot of an amorous couple engaging in a series of prolonged kisses'.[11] These films took what was seen by many as a private activity to be shared between two lovers and offered it as one of the 'attractions' to be consumed by the early film audience.[12] Some of the films in this genre showed a kiss repeated several times, layering successive versions of this formerly private activity as a public spectacle. In so doing, these films suggested the presence of private sexual acts taking place alongside the exhibition of the image in the public environment of the early cinema auditorium.

Two films produced around 1899 represent scenes of kissing couples in such a way that they underscore the parallel between the events happening on screen and the possible activities occurring within the cinema auditorium. These films, both entitled *The Kiss in the Tunnel*, are significant to the history of early cinema in that each was designed as a scene that might be inserted into another film or between two other films depicting a train going into and emerging from a tunnel. In the first film, by G.A. Smith, the opening and closing shots are part of a continuous 'phantom ride' shot which places the viewer in the position of the train itself, entering the tunnel and then emerging into daylight on the other side.[13] Inserted in the middle of this phantom ride is a staged scene that shows the interior of a railway car, with windows darkened to achieve the effect of the tunnel interior; a well-dressed man and woman (played by Smith and his wife), surrounded by luggage, interrupt their reading for an affectionate

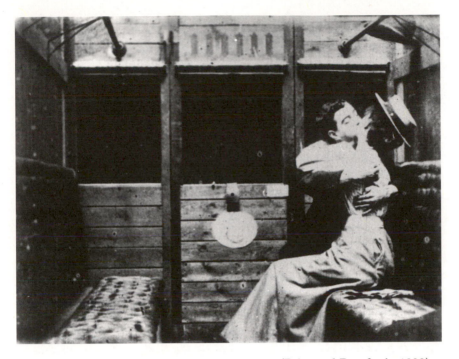

Plate 12.   Frame still from *Kiss in the Tunnel* (Riley and Bamforth, 1899)

embrace. The man stands, kisses the woman, sits briefly, and then stands again to kiss her several more times. At the close of the scene the couple resume their previous positions seated across from one another and go back to their reading. The Warwick Trading Company's 1899 catalogue describes a very similar (possibly the same) film: 'as the train enters the tunnel this couple is supposed to take advantage of the surrounding darkness by giving vent to their pent-up feelings, and indulging in a loving kiss or two.'[14] This description of a couple using a darkened space for the expression of their 'pent-up' desire reveals the perceived dangers of representing such activity to a mixed audience: in the eyes of reformers anxious about the behaviour of men and women in the cinema auditorium, the parallel between two darkened spaces used for 'illicit' activity could hardly be more evident.

The second film, co-produced by Riley Brothers and James Bamforth, depicts a similar kissing scene intercut between two scenes of an actual train entering and then leaving the tunnel.[15] This short piece extends the tunnel kiss concept by providing a complete three-shot sequence. The interior scene shows a man stubbing out a lit cigarette and moving to sit next to his female companion, who throws aside her magazine to embrace him (see Plate 12). This scene places the couple in a more intimate physical relation, allowing for an extended embrace which continues to the end of the shot. The seated placement of the couple mimics that of a couple seated beside one another in an auditorium, furthering the parallel between the on-screen events and the intimate behaviour of cinema patrons within the darkened theatre.

This display of private intimacy in a public context can be found in other films of the early period. While the kissing sequences described above occur in a private (because solitary) compartment, many early films showed such acts taking place in public, to both humorous and (in the eyes of reformers and proto-censors) titillating ends. For example, a short film entitled *An Interrupted Courtship* (Warwick Trading Company, 1899) depicts a young lady awaiting her companion in a hotel lobby; when he arrives, the couple 'indulge[s] in most friendly demonstrations', 'hugs and osculation, and so forth', despite repeated intrusions by hotel guests and employees. The catalogue for this film described it as 'full of human interest'.[16] For some members of the clergy and others seeking to abolish the 'indecent' activity taking place within the auditorium, this element of 'interest' suggested the perception of barely restrained sexual activity in the audience and furthered the sense of moral self-endangerment on the part of early film viewers. A Newcastle court case revealed in detail the controversy over the alleged indecency of kissing and courtship films: a local vicar had interfered with the cinema programme exhibited in a parish hall because of a picture called *Courtship*, in which a gentleman came up behind a lady seated on a garden bench and kissed her. The vicar was being sued by the exhibitor to recover the profits from the show had it been completed. The vicar had objected to the film as 'unfit to be shown to an audience', consisting as it did of 'a most violent windmill performance [by the couple], with their arms in a most elaborate and grotesque style, and . . . utterly low'. The judge found in favour of the vicar, arguing that the defendant was within his rights in stopping such an 'entirely vulgar' entertainment, and lamenting the fact that there was as yet no formalized structure of film censorship that would control the subjects presented and thereby regulate the morality of the audience.[17]

Plate 13.   Postcard, *c.*1914 (postmark on back): 'Do take me to see the pictures again'

Regulating Audiences, Censoring Films

Nicholas Hiley has argued that the transition from the participatory experience of the music hall to the silent spectatorship of the classical cinema was an effect of managerial and government efforts to maximise profits and standardize the early film industry.[18] It is certainly true that the cinema constituted a vast new market to be exploited by filmmakers and distributors, theatre owners and management alike; but this argument, grounded in economic analysis, does not account for the cultural concern over the presence of sexuality in the audience as well as on the cinema screen. The records of rulings and decisions made by the London County Council and the British Board of Film Censors (established in 1913) suggest that the industry concern for profits was intimately linked to a national effort to improve the moral and social environment of the cinema through the simultaneous control of the acts taking place on and off the screen.

For the first decade of cinema in Britain there were few direct legislative controls by local or national government which addressed the cinema's effects on public morals and social relations. This is not to say that contemporary critics did not express their anxiety over the cinema's influence on mass audiences; on the contrary, as we have seen, they blamed the cinema for its escapist function and its tendency to foster juvenile delinquency and crime, and saw cinema theatres as sites which, like the music hall, licensed prostitution and facilitated the spread of contagious diseases.[19] The only way to control this potentially dangerous new medium, many believed, was to institute a formal structure for film censorship and disciplinary measures for controlling the unruly or transgressive behaviour of audience members. Hence the formation of the British Board of Film Censors in 1913, a regulatory board proposed by representatives from the film industry and headed by G.A. Redford, formerly a stage censor on the Lord Chamberlain's staff. This was thus not an official body but something run by the trade for the trade, to avoid the peculiarities of local censorship. Films were judged as to whether or not they included 'anything repulsive and objectionable to the good taste and better feelings of English audiences', a principle which embodied the ideology of 'rational' and 'healthy' amusement for the masses.[20] The board's 1914 report specified twenty-two grounds on which films were either cut or banned, including vulgar or immoral behaviour, excessive violence, and the disparagement of public figures or sacred subjects.[21]

By 1917, when the National Council of Public Morals undertook an

investigation of the cinema,[22] social reformers were arguing simultaneously for increased supervision of the audience and a greater reliance on
educational subjects rather than romances or adventure films. Nonetheless, the focus remained on the effects of inappropriate film
narratives on audience behaviour. A social worker in the East End
described the darkness of the theatre as a central point of contention,
for 'if you have a young lady it is very convenient to go there', and
described her visit to the Old King's Hall in Commercial Road, where
she saw one 'very objectionable' romance film:

> The hall was well ventilated and the audience composed mostly of
> adults or boys and girls over sixteen. The behaviour was on the
> whole more seemly. There were, of course, the usual couples
> absorbed in one another. The film shown was one in which a
> woman causes a man such temptation as to make him lose control
> of himself—shows him carrying her off—and was so very
> suggestive that the man next to me groaned repeatedly and could
> not keep still in his seat—he left after the climax. I am certain that
> the film could not do otherwise than have a very dangerous effect
> on any one at all given to sensuous thoughts, and could not fail to
> cause impure thoughts to any of the couples watching it.[23]

It is worth noting that this statement of anxiety about the supposed
effects of films on audiences collapses the 'climax' of the film with
sexual stimulation in the male viewer. Even the design of cinema
auditoria was suspect, since they were often built with a promenade
potentially 'allowing for the standing together promiscuously of people
at the back of the hall'.[24] This further contributed to the middle-class
perception that cinema attendance as a leisure practice endangered the
moral and physical well-being of the mass audience.

Following their investigation, the National Council of Public Morals
published a report recommending the establishment of suitable conditions for viewing and expressing support for state- rather than
industry-controlled censorship. Their findings contributed to a standardization of the cinematic experience through control of lighting,
projection standards and increased audience supervision by patrolling
attendants, as well as by influencing the types of films available to the
audience. The Council's recommendations thus played their part in
the ongoing effort to discipline public leisure experiences.[25]

Conclusion

This chapter has traced a transformation in audience behaviour during the early years of cinema, articulating efforts by middle-class social reformers and industry representatives to regulate the sexual and social practices of film's first patrons. This transformation was intimately connected to anxieties about the presence of women in the cinema audience, which were in turn founded on perceptions of women's endangered moral status and increased sexual vulnerability in public. These perceptions resulted from an assumed causal connection between films and their audiences, revealing a concern over cinema's effects on viewers that formed the basis of censorship efforts and culminated in attempts to standardize popular viewing practices. These attempts were never wholly successful; indeed, audience members continued to resist assimilation into this new model for spectatorship throughout the early period.[26] Nevertheless, a focus on the rhetoric of reform and regulation of cinema in its first decades illustrates the significance of contemporary debates over films and their effects on audiences and underscores their relevance to cultural histories of popular leisure at the turn of the twentieth century.

Notes

My thanks go to Nicholas Hiley for research suggestions, and to Lauren Berlant, Tom Gunning, Elaine Hadley, Elizabeth Helsinger, Andrew Higson and Eric Sanders for comments on earlier versions of this essay.

1. Robert P.C. Corfe, complaining about the images shown in mutoscopes and kalloscopes lining the piers and esplanades in seaside towns, 'Incentives to Vice,' *The Times*, 1 June 1901, p. 5.
2. Peter Bailey, *Leisure and Class in Victorian England: Rational Recreation and the Contest for Control, 1830–1885* (London: Routledge & Kegan Paul, 1978).
3. See Dagmar Kift, *The Victorian Music Hall: Culture, Class and Conflict* (Cambridge: Cambridge University Press, 1996), and Benny Green, ed., *The Last Empires: A Music Hall Companion* (London: Pavilion, 1986), pp. 60–1.
4. See Nicholas Hiley, 'The British Cinema Auditorium,' in Karel Dibbets and Bert Hogenkamp, eds, *Film and the First World War* (Amsterdam: Amsterdam University Press, 1994), p. 162, and 'Fifteen Questions about the Early Film Audience,' in Daan Hertogs and Nico de Klerk, eds,

Uncharted Territory: Essays on Early Non-Fiction Film (Amsterdam: Stichting Nederlands Filmmuseum, 1997), p. 112. For similar developments in the American film industry, see Miriam Hansen, *Babel and Babylon: Spectatorship in American Silent Film* (Cambridge: Harvard UP, 1991).

5. For a valuable critical study of censorship and cinema in England in this period, see Annette Kuhn, *Cinema, Censorship, and Sexuality, 1909–1925* (London: Routledge, 1988).

6. Corfe, 'Incentives to Vice,' p. 5.

7. On the general exhibition context of cinema in Britain up to the 1910s, see Rachael Low and Roger Manvell, *The History of the British Film, 1896–1906*, and Low, *The History of the British Film, 1906–1914* (London: George Allen & Unwin Ltd, 1948, 1949); John Barnes, *The Beginnings of the Cinema in England 1894–1901*, 5 vols (Exeter: University of Exeter Press, 1996–8; first published 1977–97); Michael Chanan, *The Dream that Kicks: The Prehistory and Early Years of Cinema in Britain* (London: Routledge, 1980); Ian Christie, *The Last Machine: Early Cinema and the Birth of the Modern World* (London: BFI, 1994); Hiley, 'The British Cinema Auditorium,' and 'Fifteen Questions about the Early Film Audience'.

8. Hiley, 'The British Cinema Auditorium,' p. 162.

9. Samuel Smith, MP, 'Demoralizing Moving Pictures,' *The Times*, 3 August 1899, p. 12.

10. Cited in John Barnes, *The Beginnings of the Cinema in England: Volume Four, 1899* (Exeter: University of Exeter Press, 1996; first published 1992, as *Filming The Boer War*), p. 157.

11. *National Film Archive Catalogue, Part 3: Silent Fiction Films, 1895–1930* (London: BFI, 1966), p. 71.

12. See Tom Gunning, 'The Cinema of Attractions: Early Film, Its Spectator and the Avant-Garde,' in Thomas Elsaesser with Adam Barker, ed., *Early Cinema: Space, Frame, Narrative* (London: BFI, 1990), pp. 56–62.

13. John Barnes notes that the footage of the 'phantom ride' in the NFTVA print is taken from Hepworth's *View from an Engine Front, Shilla Mill Tunnel*. See Barnes, *The Beginnings of the Cinema in England 1894–1901, Volume Five, 1900* (Exeter: University of Exeter Press, 1997), p. 265. 'Phantom rides' were another of the major genres of early film; see Gunning, 'The Cinema of Attractions,' and 'An Aesthetic of Astonishment: Early Film and the (In)Credulous Spectator,' *Art & Text*, no. 34, Spring 1989; and Lynne Kirby, *Parallel Tracks: The Railroad and Silent Cinema* (Exeter: University of Exeter Press and Durham: Duke University Press, 1997).

14. Cited in Barnes, *The Beginnings of the Cinema in England: Volume Four*, p. 45.

15. The dating and attribution of this film has proved difficult. Denis Gifford lists the film as a co-production between Riley Brothers of Bradford and James Bamforth of Holmfirth, and catalogues it under 1899. John Barnes initially concurred with this dating and attribution but later noted that this film, along with three others listed in a Hepworth catalogue of 1903, may have been among the films produced by Riley Brothers and Bamforth in 1898. See Gifford, *The British Film Catalogue 1895–1970* (Newton Abbot: David & Charles, 1973); Barnes, *The Beginnings of the Cinema in England: Volume Four*, pp. 64, 67; and *Volume Five*, pp. 271–2.

16. Catalogue description cited in Barnes, *The Beginnings of the Cinema in England: Volume Four*, p. 249.

17. 'Kissing by Cinematograph: An Amusing Case,' *British Journal of Photography*, vol. 46, no. 2030, 31 March 1899, pp. 204–5.

18. Hiley, 'The British Cinema Auditorium,' pp. 165–8.

19. For an anthology of primary sources, see Colin Harding and Simon Popple, *In the Kingdom of Shadows: A Companion to Early Cinema* (London: Cygnus Arts, 1996).

20. From the board's first annual report, published in 1914; quoted in James C. Robertson, *The British Board of Film Censors: Film Censorship in Britain, 1896–1950* (London: Croom Helm, 1985), p. 7.

21. Robertson, *The British Board of Film Censors*, pp. 7–8.

22. The investigation was undertaken by a special commission appointed to inquire into 'the physical, social, educational, and moral influences of the cinema, with special reference to young people,' with a focus on the 'nature and extent' of complaints lodged against film exhibitions, and to report on cinema's present and future. See National Council of Public Morals (NCPM), *The Cinema: Its Present Position and Future Possibilities* (London: Williams and Norgate, 1917), p. ix.

23. NCPM, *The Cinema*, p. 240.

24. Ibid., p. 151.

25. For further discussion of the NCPM and its effects on cinema in the 1910s and 1920s, see Kuhn, *Cinema, Censorship, and Sexuality*.

26. This resistance was often quite literal: patrons might slash seatbacks with pocket knives, disrupt the show by shouting at the screen, or kick the seats of those with noise complaints. See Hiley, 'The British Cinema Auditorium,' p. 163; NCPM, *Cinema*, p. 210; and *Kinematograph Weekly*, 14 March 1918, p. 87.

7

'Nothing More than a "Craze"'
Cinema Building in Britain from 1909 to 1914

Nicholas Hiley

Moving pictures are generally understood as a means of communicating images and ideas, yet even before 1914 the British film industry was far too complex for there to be any direct relationship between filmmakers and audiences. Producers sold their films to renters, who hired them to exhibitors, who in turn showed them to patrons who paid to enter their cinemas. As each group added its own interpretation so the meaning of the films changed, whether that interpretation came as bold advertising, atmospheric music, or ironic catcalls. In the same way the expression of demand changed as it passed from the audience back to the producer, until in some instances the voice of the patron was barely audible to filmmakers. As I have argued elsewhere, it thus seems possible that the growth of the 'feature film' before 1914 reflected the demands of the larger cinema owners, who wished to put their smaller rivals out of business, as much as it did the changing tastes of audiences.[1]

In this puzzling set of relationships one thing seems certain—that the appearance of the first purpose-built cinemas in Britain in 1907 and 1908, and the burst of cinema construction that followed from 1909 to 1914, must indicate a growing demand for motion pictures and represent the consolidation of the British film audience. Yet even with this 'cinema boom' historians must be cautious, for cinemas are not sold to audiences but to company promoters and speculative investors, and the pattern of construction of the first purpose-built venues may well have owed as much to the ambitions of those eager to invest in the film industry as to the growing popularity of moving pictures. This is certainly what contemporaries believed, and, as we shall see, they had the 'rinking boom' of 1909 and 1910 to support their case.

The First Permanent Shows

There had been hopes of creating an habitual audience for moving pictures as early as 1907, but the prospect still seemed remote, despite the appearance of Britain's first permanent venues for the regular projection of films. One pioneer of this new form of exhibition was the lantern showman Joshua Duckworth, but even he proceeded with considerable anxiety and later confessed to having 'many misgivings as to whether an entertainment consisting chiefly of animated pictures would continue to attract the public'. Duckworth finally decided to invest £2,000 in opening the Central Hall at Colne in Lancashire in 1907, but he still faced problems in finding a viable format for the moving pictures he intended to show. The local audience had little enthusiasm for his original mixture of films and variety acts, and Duckworth confessed that several months as a cinema exhibitor had left him with considerable problems 'in satisfying an audience to which you are playing week after week'.[2]

The truth was that in 1907 few people regarded the permanent, purpose-built show as a viable form of moving picture exhibition. Successful 'town hall lecturers' regarded Duckworth's Central Hall with undisguised amazement, continuing to believe that the only guaranteed way of making money was to keep moving, and that no town with fewer than 50,000 inhabitants could ever support a regular display of films. An experienced exhibitor like Waller Jeffs refused to stay for more than two weeks in a town of twice that size, and even in London the resistance to permanent shows remained considerable. In March 1907 the British Cinema Company was created with the intention of operating permanent film shows in the capital, and in July 1907 it began running a two-hour programme twice nightly at the Balham Empire, but this much-publicized venture proved only the continuing weakness of the permanent show. Despite its patriotic name, more than half the capital of the British Cinema Company was provided by foreign investors, and, despite the considerable novelty of its all-film shows, it failed to find an audience and was soon wound up.[3]

In 1908 it was in fact virtually impossible to establish a permanent film show in central London for the simple reason that big investors continued to treat the cinema as 'a thing liable to run out in two years', whilst the owners of freehold property objected to its being adapted for such ephemeral use, and their leaseholders demanded a sizeable increase in rent to offset the supposed risk of fire. The result, as Table 1 demonstrates, was that London film exhibition could still be characterized by the irregular performances of travelling lecturers in church halls and charitable institutions, rather than by any form of regular and permanent exhibition.[4]

Table 1: London venues used regularly for film exhibition in January 1908[5]

Music halls	58
Churches, chapels and mission halls	58
Salvation Army hostels, workhouses, etc.	53
Public halls	24
Schools	19
Shops	12
Canvas tent	1
TOTAL	225

1908 saw the start of a process that would eventually transform this situation, however, as company promoters managed to divert part of an extraordinary rush of speculative investment in rubber and oil into a whole range of new corporate ventures 'formed to provide public amusements'. The initial focus of these operations was not film exhibition but the public craze for roller-skating, whose intensity attracted numerous speculators such as Chester Crawford, who had arrived from the United States the previous year with the backing of a prominent roller-skate manufacturer and a scheme for constructing a whole chain of skating rinks across Britain. Crawford joined forces with a British theatrical contractor, Fred Wilkins, to form the American Roller Rink Company, and together they set about raising enough local capital to build a skating rink at the Tournament Hall in Liverpool. When this proved successful they opened another venue in Newcastle, and then moved south to establish a giant skating rink at London's Olympia. The Olympia rink proved so popular that within months of its opening in December 1908 they were taking £2,400 a week, and its success allowed the partners to raise sufficient capital to launch similar ventures in other parts of the country.[6]

The 'rinking boom' was now underway, and the rush of investment became so great that by March 1909 'rinking companies' were being registered at the rate of almost one a day. By the end of 1909 there were more than three hundred such ventures with a nominal capital of 'considerably over £2,000,000', whilst London possessed more than twenty functioning rinks, with a combined capital estimated at £320,000. There were said to be 'few parts of London that cannot boast a local rink', and yet the demand for roller-skating was so considerable that the major venues could still attract up to 3,000 patrons a day on weekdays, and 5,000 on Saturdays. The supporters of the new craze argued that 'not to "rink" is to be out of it altogether', and their fanaticism was such that the rinking industry was even able to support its own trade journals, entitled *Rinking and Rinks* and the *Rinking World*. By the start of 1910 the demand for skating equipment was so great that the Birmingham manufacturers were having to produce 15,000 pairs of roller-skates every week, and the rinks them- selves were employing almost 10,000 skating instructors, 'not to mention the attendants, doorkeepers, check and money takers, and musicians'.[7]

By 1909 excited investors were also being persuaded to pour their money into film exhibition, and here, as in rinking, it was said that unscrupulous promoters had gathered millions of pounds 'from igno- rant speculators . . . fascinated by the business of pleasure'. Everything capable of conversion to a cinema was bought for exploitation, includ- ing old drill halls, chapels, public houses and assembly rooms. 'Shops in the busiest thoroughfares have been converted into film shows', declared one London journalist in November 1909, whilst in the suburbs

> nearly every small hall which was formerly carrying on a precarious existence with dancing classes, lectures and meetings, has been seized upon by the enterprising living-picture syndicates, repainted, relit and newly furnished, to blossom out as cinemas, picture palaces, picturedromes, and 'electric palaces'.

The foundation of the British cinema industry was laid by men like Sam Harris, a London estate agent who specialized in finding properties suitable for cinema conversion, and Montague Pyke, a former commercial traveller and undischarged bankrupt who saw a chance of making some easy money. In October 1908 Pyke had established a company called Recreations Limited, whose nominal capital was £10,000 but whose assets, as he later admitted, were simply 'a very nice name plate on the door, and some office furniture on the hire purchase'. Pyke approached Harris for help in finding suitable premises for film shows, and Harris recalled that despite Pyke's lack of funds 'I found him two draper's shops in Edgware Road and he immediately ordered carpets, curtains, seating, everything of the best'.[8]

The key throughout was confidence, and by keeping prospective investors away from his dingy office Pyke managed to raise enough money to begin constructing his cinema, after which the building site served as his headquarters. 'I succeeded in getting every penny of the capital subscribed', he later recalled, despite the fact that most of his wealthy investors remained sceptical, 'and maintained that it would be just a phase, and the novelty would be over in a few months.' Pyke's Recreations Theatre finally opened in March 1909, and proved so popular that he had no difficulty in floating a second cinema company upon its success, nor in continuing that process until fourteen separate ventures were underway, each owning and running its own venue. Pyke always kept his current investors happy, yet his personal income rose from £1,300 to £10,000 a year and he later admitted that 'from each company . . . I received a very nice salary as managing director, not to mention bonuses and the returns on my very large holdings of shares'. Pyke was soon well known for rolling up to trade events in a big car, 'with diamonds sparkling, a special cigar, and, when weather warranted, a fur-lined overcoat', but despite this opulence the scale of investment in film exhibition was still much less than in roller-skating. The seventy-eight cinema companies registered in 1909 thus had a nominal capital of £708,000, but this was still only a third of that claimed by the three hundred rinking ventures which opened that year.[9]

The Collapse of Rinking

At the end of 1909 business indeed looked bright for the rinking industry, and yet by the start of the following year it had begun to collapse as dramatically as it had been created. Investors lost confidence in roller-skating almost overnight and suddenly, as one insider recalled, firms like Crawford and Wilkins' American Roller Rink Company found themselves badly over-extended:

Crawford had found it so easy to turn over his acquisitions to companies, that he and Wilkins had made themselves responsible for land and building contracts all over the place. When the distrust of skating-rink enterprises set in, they found it difficult to raise the money for building purposes, and became involved in a financial mess.

Showmen like Edward Bostock, who had opened a rink in Glasgow in May 1909 and had even demolished the old Hippodrome music hall in order to enlarge it, were forced to accept that rinking 'was but a passing phase', and began to close down their entire operations. Within a matter of weeks thousands of small investors had lost their savings, and yet the decline of roller-skating did not mark the end of speculative investment in mass entertainment. On the contrary, as one contemporary observed, the sudden bankruptcy of hundreds of rinking companies 'left numerous sites and building shells free' and cinema speculators rushed to colonize the wreckage of their rival industry. In July 1910 the publishers of the *Rinking World* prudently launched a new magazine, entitled the *Picture Theatre News*.[10]

The collapse of rinking not only left a ready-made audience for moving pictures, but also opened up the industry to a second rank of petty speculators, such as the theatrical manager J. Bannister Howard. By the end of 1909 even small cinemas were generating profits of £100 a week, and Howard decided to cash in on the boom by purchasing the Arcade Skating Rink in Aberdeen for £1,000 and reopening it in 1910 as the New Electric Theatre. Howard confessed to being 'sure the new craze for moving pictures would not last very long', but he was nevertheless determined to make some easy money from it. In 1911 he successfully floated the New Electric Theatre Company, in order to sell his shares in the venture for £2,000 and move on to Dundee, where the whole process could begin again. In Dundee he constructed a second Electric Theatre, but then sold up and moved to Bath, where he built two further cinemas and again floated them as a company before moving on when he 'heard the news that new cinemas were to be erected'. In a host of similar schemes across the country, company promoters and speculators fed the wreckage of the rinking industry back into commercial entertainment, using it to enlarge the flimsy bubble of credit that now supported film exhibition.[11]

The British cinema industry was indeed built upon very shaky foundations. The earliest purpose-built venues had been constructed by small showmen with their own money, but by 1909 this source of

Plate 14. Advertisement for Cinematograph Supplies, 1911, from
The Modern Bioscope Operator
(London: Ganes Ltd, 1911)

capital was exhausted and the general pattern of investment in film exhibition was by private limited company. The vast majority of capital was raised locally for the running of a single cinema, and the provincial middle classes proved themselves eager to invest in this new form of entertainment: 'in Manchester £20,000 of local money has been subscribed to open fifteen or twenty theatres; in Glasgow £10,000 for six or eight.' This rapid influx of outside investment brought a subtle change to the film industry, for whilst the earliest exhibitors had been in close touch with their audiences, and willing to stake their livelihood on the success of the purpose-built cinema, the new breed of disinterested investors and professional managers was hoping to make a quick profit from moving pictures without any commitment to their future development. The new mood of cynicism was so widespread that in August 1909 the *Bioscope* openly attacked those businessmen 'closely identified with the inner workings of the film world', who refused to conceal their belief 'that the public appreciation of the picture theatre is nothing more than a "craze" '.[12]

These cynical attitudes persisted, and when Pyke planned a new cinema on Oxford Street in 1909 the owner of the freehold was prepared to lease him the ground only on condition that his structure was 'built in such a way that, if it was not a success, it could easily be reconstructed suitable to let [*sic*] as business premises'. The collapse of rinking in 1910 did nothing to dispel the general belief that permanent cinemas were a passing fancy, and although by the end of 1911 some 575 cinema companies had been floated on a nominal capital of £4.3 million, it still appeared to many in the industry that there was 'something uncanny about it; it was almost too good to be true'. The massive injection of outside capital had transformed the musty penny gaff into the modern cinema palace, 'with its blaze of light and super-abundance of gorgeous plush and gilt edging'. Once beyond the brilliant arc-lights, however, it was not difficult to see that these buildings were still no more than large oblong halls, constructed cheaply out of concrete slabs, poorly lit, badly ventilated, and impressive only in 'the monstrous effect of their plainness'. The whole pattern of cinema exhibition, from its uniformed barkers to its garish posters, was indeed so reminiscent of the fairground bioscope that it could only serve to emphasize the air of impermanence that still hung about the industry.[13]

Yet picture palaces and electric theatres continued to open at a phenomenal rate, and by the end of 1909 the country was already said to contain 'something between six hundred and a thousand of them'.

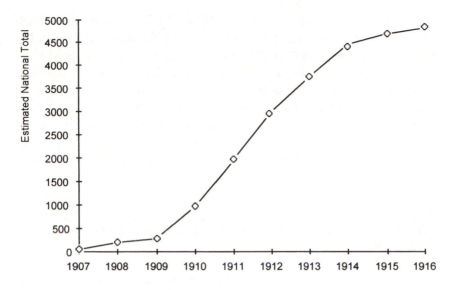

Figure 1: The pattern of construction of purpose-built cinemas, 1907–1918[14]

Contemporaries were unable to keep track of the rapid growth of these purpose-built venues, but we can nevertheless estimate the magnitude of this first rush of construction using a sample survey of representative towns. Figure 1 was compiled by taking the known dates of opening of all the purpose-built cinemas in Birmingham, Leeds, Bristol, Bradford, Hull, Newcastle and Oxford, and afterwards enlarging this limited sample to national scale. By 1911 these seven towns contained some 2.5 million inhabitants, and the resulting graph suggests that they were indeed representative of the country as a whole, for it is an almost perfect curve of adoption, demonstrating how in just eight years an entirely new form of film exhibition spread rapidly throughout Britain.[15]

Having generated these figures for the growth of purpose-built cinemas, we can combine them with the yearly figures for all venues published in the *Bioscope Annual* to reveal the sudden transformation of British film exhibition. As Table 2 demonstrates, between 1910 and 1912 the dramatic increase in purpose-built cinemas was accompanied by a sharp decline in existing venues. The rush of speculative investment in purpose-built cinemas was no doubt partly responsible for this rapid collapse of exhibition in theatres, halls and clubs, but from 1910 onwards it was accelerated by the rigorous safety inspections and yearly licensing introduced under the new Cinematograph Act. The conditions imposed on cinema exhibitors by local authorities were acknowledged as working 'to the advantage of the wealthy company or rich private owner', and seem to have played a significant part in the transformation of exhibition. By 1912 the earlier pattern of exhibition was gone, and in London only seven church or mission halls possessed cinema licences by comparison with the fifty-eight that had previously shown films. By 1914 some 82 per cent of licences in London and 88 per cent of licences in Leeds were held by purpose-built cinemas, and the picture palace had become the permanent home of film exhibition.[16]

Table 2: The transformation of film exhibition in Britain, 1910–1913

	1910	1911	1912	1913
Purpose-built cinemas	1,000	2,000	3,000	3,800
Theatres, music-halls, town halls, etc	1,900	1,100	800	200
TOTAL	2,900	3,100	3,800	4,000

The rapid closure of established film shows served only to emphasize the impermanence of the new medium, however, and at the start of 1914 the industry was still haunted by a sense of unease. It was noted with relief that film exhibition was 'no longer a wild "get-rich-quick" scandal', but the floating of almost 1,200 new cinema companies over the previous three years had still produced a dangerous instability. The *Financial Times* surveyed the numerous cinemas which these companies had erected and observed candidly that 'in London they jostle one another and other places of amusement to such an extent that the curious may justly wonder how they can all obtain a living': 'As a matter of fact they do not—a few are making large profits, many are existing from hand to mouth, and more are starving.' On the eve of war in 1914 one British cinema in five was indeed considered to be on the verge of bankruptcy, and the *Architects' and Builders' Journal* felt it prudent to warn its readers that although they might still accept contracts from cinema speculators it would be foolish 'to put actual money into an adventure which has now become distinctly precarious by reason of quite excessive competition'.[17]

Speculation and Demand

There is indeed persuasive evidence that, throughout this early period of construction, cinema speculation ran far ahead of audience demand. In 1911 it was estimated that Britain's 2,000 purpose-built cinemas were able to sell about four million tickets each week, yet three years later, with some 5,000 purpose-built cinemas in operation, the figure had only risen to seven million tickets a week. The discrepancy between the growth of exhibition and the growth of the cinema industry is clearly visible if we compare the yearly percentage increase of purpose-built cinemas during the period of rapid growth with the yearly percentage increase of entertainment films and ticket sales during their own periods of rapid growth. As Figure 2 indicates, the peak growth of British cinema construction came in 1910, but the corresponding peak of film production did not take place until 1912, and the peak growth of weekly cinema attendance did not appear until 1915. This is the reverse of the pattern that would have appeared in an industry led by audience demand, confirming the belief of contemporaries that by 1914 the level of investment in purpose-built cinemas had far exceeded the growth of their audience.[18]

The conclusion must be that the British cinema boom of 1909 to

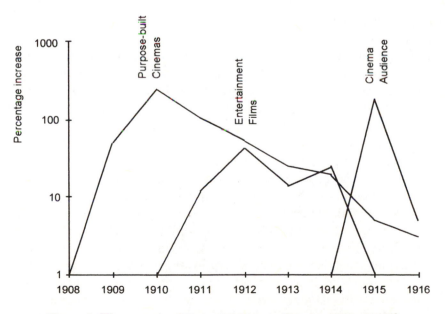

Figure 2: The growth of film exhibition in Britain, 1908–1916[19]

1914 was largely an investment boom, built upon the remarkable success of the early venues. In 1909 Biograph Theatres Limited had operated five suburban cinemas in London, and by taking 3s. 4d. per week from each seat had enjoyed weekly profits in excess of £30 per cinema. By 1910 Amalgamated Cinematograph Theatres Limited was likewise taking a massive 6s. 3d. a week from each of 2,700 seats in five London venues, producing profits of £85 a week per cinema. This level of turnover ensured a high level of interest in cinema investment, and although more than two thousand new venues were opened over the next four years, Sam Harris still had two thousand eager clients waiting for premises, and was receiving forty or fifty new enquiries each week. He launched the *Cinema News and Property Gazette* in February 1912 to cater for their needs, and by 1914, with more than four million cinema seats in operation, the rate of cinema building had exhausted the available audience. Attendance was static at about seven million visits a week; when combined with the onset of fierce price-cutting this produced a dramatic decline in profits. Biograph Theatres Limited could now raise only 1s. 5d. per seat per week, and by the time that its interest charges and managerial expenses had been taken into account this amounted to a loss of more than £1,500 a year. Associated Electric Theatres Limited was in a similar position; with three of its venues in difficulties the company lost £4,000 in just six months, and the only action it could take was to sell its unprofitable venues, cut the wages of the remaining staff and hire cheaper films.[20]

The investment boom left only a passing resemblance between the public face of cinema exhibition and its actual economic performance. At the start of 1914 the Cinematograph Exhibitors' Association accepted that an average cinema would now achieve only 1,400 attendances per week; given that an average cinema seated 850 people, and presented at least two performances every weekday plus a Saturday matinée, this represented an attendance of no more than 12.5 per cent of the potential capacity. On the eve of war most British exhibitors must have been showing to largely empty halls. A survey of Bolton, for instance, revealed that during the evening performance, when the fourteen local cinemas should have been filling to capacity, there were only 7,000 patrons for some 15,000 seats. The shareholders in cinema companies may have remained optimistic about the future of the industry, but the fierce competition for audiences had nevertheless produced a dramatic reduction in the value of their investment. As Table 3 reveals, by 1911 the capital being lost through company liquidations was equal to a fifth of the new investment; by 1914 this had risen to more than a half.[21]

Table 3: Cinema exhibition companies registered and liquidated, 1908–1914[22]

	Companies registered		Liquidated and struck off	
	No.	Capital [£]	No.	Capital [£]
1908	12	167,000	–	–
1909	78	708,000	–	–
1910	231	2,183,700	–	–
1911	254	1,214,400	36	242,800
1912	400	1,627,400	48	460,000
1913	544	2,954,700	91	686,000
1914	314	2,449,300	137	1,294,000
TOTAL	1,833	11,304,500	312	2,682,800

The investment value of the industry collapsed as the construction boom continued and by 1911 it was all too common for a shareholder to receive 'offers of shares at 80 per cent below par, when he has paid full value and waited patiently for the dividends that never came'. This unfortunate situation persisted and by 1914 there were few profits to be made from local cinema companies, despite the investment of an estimated £13.9 million of public and private capital. The truth was that the eagerness of middle-class investors to pour money into the British cinema had left it in a parlous state. As Figure 3 demonstrates, even the major public companies were paying such low dividends on their ordinary shares as to make them no longer financially attractive. Many exhibitors were only saved from ruin by the resurgence of interest in moving pictures that followed the outbreak of war in 1914, which pushed even redundant venues back into profit. By the end of 1915 the average cinema was able to attract some five times its capacity every week, equal to perhaps 4,200 attendances or 38 per cent of its potential. Such was the level of over-provision, however, that only at the start of 1917, with the average weekly audience standing at some 4,500 visits or 41 per cent of potential, did it begin to seem that the

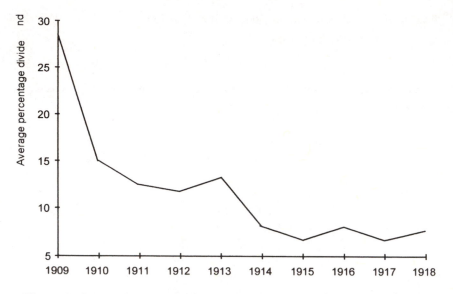

Figure 3: Average percentage dividend paid by public cinema companies, 1909–1918[23]

awful spectre of empty cinemas might finally have been banished from the industry.[24]

Conclusion

The 'cinema boom' that began in 1909 has to be approached with care by historians. There was certainly a public demand for moving pictures in Britain between 1909 and 1914, and the evidence suggests that this demand was steadily growing. It is also certain that there was public enthusiasm for the new type of purpose-built auditoria, as the first generation of exhibitors and investors could readily testify. However, the demand from audiences had first been equalled and then surpassed by the demand from speculators and investors, who saw moving pictures not as a means of communication or entertainment but as an easy way of making money. It was their eagerness for quick returns that found expression in 5,000 purpose-built cinemas, whose empty auditoria remained as testimony to this eager speculation. In 1914, with as many as 1,000 cinemas facing bankruptcy, the shadow of the 'rinking boom' still lay across the cinema industry, and there were many people who remained convinced that moving pictures were still 'nothing more than a "craze"'.

Notes

1. Nicholas Hiley, 'The British Cinema Auditorium,' in Karel Dibbets and Bert Hogenkamp, eds, *Film and the First World War* (Amsterdam: Amsterdam University Press, 1995), pp. 160–70; Hiley, 'Fifteen Questions About the Early Film Audience,' in Dan Haartogs and Nico de Klerk, eds, *Uncharted Territory: Essays on Early Nonfiction Film* (Amsterdam: Stichting Nederlands Filmmuseum, 1997), pp. 105–18. See also Hiley, ' "At the Picture Palace": The British Cinema Audience, 1895–1920,' in John Fullerton, ed., *Celebrating 1895: The Centenary of Cinema* (Sydney: John Libbey, 1998), pp. 96–103, and Hiley, ' "Let's Go to the Pictures": The British Cinema Audience in the 1920s and 1930s,' in Annette Kuhn and Sarah Street, eds, *Journal of Popular British Cinema*, issue 2, 1999, pp. 39–53.
2. 'A Lancashire Exhibitor's Success,' *Kinematograph Weekly*, 26 September 1907, p. 352; 'Mr J. Duckworth,' 2 July 1908, p. 153.
3. John H. Bird, *Cinema Parade: Fifty Years of Film Shows* (Birmingham: Cornish Bros., 1947), p. 50; 'First Kinematograph Theatre in London,' *Kinematograph Weekly*, 25 July 1907, p. 166; 'Wake Up John Bull!' 29 August 1907, p. 245; 'How Fixed Shows May be Maintained,' 30 April 1908, p. 427; 'Success in Exhibiting,' 2 July 1908, p. 173; ' "On the Road" with the Half-Reelers,' 17 June 1926, p. 56; Public Record Office, London [PRO], BT 31/11888/92496, British Cinema Company file.
4. 'A Talk with Mr C. Ivatts,' *Kinematograph Weekly*, 19 September 1907, p. 301; 'The Ground Landlord,' 3 October 1907, pp. 353–5.
5. Greater London Record Office, LCC/MIN 10,729 (f.21), minutes of LCC Theatres and Music Halls Committee, 15 January 1908. Premises licensed by the LCC were not included, but the number of music halls has been added from the *Era Annual 1908* (London: The Era, 1907), pp. 103–4, on the assumption that all were now showing films.
6. ' "Fun City" and Skating at Olympia,' *The Times*, 9 December 1908, p. 5, col. 4; 'Roller Skating,' 8 April 1909, p. 4, col. 3; PRO, BT 31/12519/99659, London Olympia Skating Rink Company file; Charles B. Cochrane, *The Secrets of a Showman* (London: William Heinemann, 1925), pp. 142–4.
7. 'Rinking Gossip,' *Era*, 17 July 1909, p. 23; 'Rinking Gossip,' 11 September 1909, p. 27; 'Rinking Gossip and Notices,' 18 December 1909, p. 27; 'Rinking Gossip,' 19 February 1910, p. 24; 'Second List of Rinking Companies,' 12 March 1910, p. 27, '£1,000,000 in Roller Skating,' *Evening News* [London], 25 November 1909, p. 3, col. 2; Philip Tovey, *Prospectuses: How To Read and Understand Them* (London: Sir Isaac Pitman & Sons, 1912), p. 94.
8. 'Miles of Films,' *Star* [London], 13 November 1909, p. 3, col. 4; William R. Titterton, *From Theatre to Music Hall* (London: Stephen Swift & Co., 1912), p. 67; Henry G. Hibbert, *Fifty Years of a Londoner's Life* (London:

Grant Richards, 1916), p. 269; E. Betts, 'When Films came to Wardour Street,' *The Times*, 20 September 1967, p. 6, cols 6–8; M.A. Pyke, 'When I Was the Cinema King,' *Picture House: The Magazine of the Cinema Theatre Association*, No. 10 (1987), p. 3; PRO, BT 31/12530/99766, Recreations Limited file.

9. 'Mr Pyke's Bankruptcy,' *The Times*, 8 September 1915, p. 3, col. 2; National Council of Public Morals (NCPM), *The Cinema: Its Present Position and Future Possibilities* (London: NCPM, 1917), p. 2; 'Two Pioneers Pass On,' *Kinematograph Weekly*, 3 October 1935, p. 5, col. 2; Pyke, 'When I Was the Cinema King,' pp. 3–4, 9.

10. Hibbert, *Fifty Years*, p. 269; Cochran, *Secrets*, p. 144; Edward H. Bostock, *Menageries, Circuses and Theatres* (London: Chapman & Hall, 1927), pp. 192–4.

11. 'London's Picture Palaces,' *Evening News* [London], 16 November 1909, p. 1, col. 4; J. Bannister Howard, *Fifty Years a Showman* (London: Hutchison & Co., 1938), pp. 152–5; Michael Thomson, *Silver Screen in the Silver City* (Aberdeen: Aberdeen University Press, 1988), pp. 49–50.

12. 'While it Lasts,' *Bioscope*, 5 August 1909, p. 3; 'London's Picture Palaces,' *Evening News* [London], 16 November 1909, p. 1, col. 4; D. Mayall, 'Leisure and the Working Class, With Special Reference to the Cinema in Birmingham, 1908–1918,' MA thesis, University of Warwick, 1977, pp. 50–1.

13. Candid Criticism,' *Bioscope*, 9 November 1911, p. 433; Colin N. Bennett, 'A Survey of the Year's Technical Progress,' *Kinematograph Year Book 1914* (London: Kinematograph Weekly Ltd, 1914), p. 22; *How to Run a Picture Theatre: A Handbook for Proprietors, Managers, and Exhibitors* (London: E.T. Heron, 1914, 2nd ed.), p. 13; R.W. Newcombe, 'Cinema Decoration,' *Building News*, 28 March 1917, p. 269; NCPM, *The Cinema*, p. 2; Leslie Wood, *The Romance of the Movies* (London: William Heinemann, 1937), p. 84; Dennis Sharp, *The Picture Palace and Other Buildings for the Movies* (London: Hugh Evelyn, 1969), p. 55; Pyke, 'When I Was the Cinema King,' p. 5.

14. This graph was first published as Figure 1 in Hiley, ' "At the Picture Palace",' p. 97.

15. 'London's Picture Palaces,' *Evening News* [London], 16 November 1909, p. 1, col. 4.

16. F.W. Ogden Smith, 'Picture Theatre Finance,' *Bioscope*, 4 June 1914, p. 1009; [London County Council (LCC)] *London Statistics, 1912–13* (London: LCC, 1913), p. 268; *London Statistics, 1913–14* (London: LCC, 1914), p. 292; *How To Run a Picture Theatre*, p. 13; Central Library, Leeds, Annual Report of Chief Constable for 1914, p. 27.

17. '1913 a Year of Progress,' *Bioscope*, 1 January 1914, p. 5; 'A Superfluity of Cinemas,' *Architects' and Builders' Journal*, 7 January 1914, p. 4; Kinematograph Competition,' *Financial Times*, 17 January 1914, p. 6, col.

3; L. Reed, '7000 Picture Houses,' *Edinburgh Evening News*, 27 June 1914, p. 7, col. 5; NCPM, *The Cinema*, p. 2.

18. ' "Palace Figures",' [London] *Evening Times*, 18 September 1911, p. 6, col. 1; 'The Cinematograph and Education,' *The Times*, 4 March 1914, p. 8, col. 5.

19. The cinema figures come from the sample survey and the film statistics from Denis Gifford, *The British Film Catalogue 1895–1985: A Reference Guide* (Newton Abbot: David & Charles, 1986). Audience figures are taken from a number of sources including Anon., 'Palace Figures (The Popularity of the Photo-Play),' *Evening Times* [London], 18 September 1911, p. 6; 'The Cinematograph and Education,' *Times*, 4 March 1914, p. 8, col. 5; 'Stroller', 'Weekly Notes,' p. 2; NCPM, *The Cinema*, p. 3.

20. 'Cinematograph Profits,' *British Journal of Photography*, 28 May 1909, p. 428; Reed, '7000 Picture Houses'; *Kineto* advertisement, *System*, June 1914, front endpapers; PRO, BT 31/19514/110118, auditors report on Amalgamated Cinematograph Theatres Limited, 14 June 1910; BT 31/18570/99828, Biograph Theatres Ltd file, 'Summary of Share Capital,' 17 February 1915; 'Summary of Share Capital,' 25 July 1917; BT 31/19440/109321, Associated Electric Theatres Ltd file, 'Summary of Share Capital,' 8 December 1914. The estimate of seating capacity in 1914 is derived from the 2,000 cinemas of stated size in the *Kinematograph Year Book 1915* (London: Kinematograph Weekly Ltd, 1915), enlarged to the estimated national total of 5,000 venues.

21. 'The Cinematograph and Education,' *The Times*, 4 March 1914, p. 8, col. 5; 'Notes from Bolton,' *Bioscope*, 15 January 1914, p. 213.

22. NCPM, *Cinema*, p. 2; 'The Kinema Death Roll,' *Financial Times*, 24 January 1918, col. 719.

23. Figures derived from the *Theatre, Music Hall and Cinema Companies' Blue Book*, June 1918 and August 1919.

24. 'Candid Criticism,' *Bioscope*, 9 November 1911, p. 433; Reed, '7000 Picture Houses'; H.B. Montgomery, 'Kinematograph Finance in 1914,' *Kinematograph Year Book 1915* (London: Kinematograph Weekly Ltd, 1915), p. 28; 'Stroller', 'Weekly notes,' *Kinematograph Weekly*, 4 November 1915, p. 2; NCPM, *Cinema*, pp. 2–3.

8

Letters to America
A Case Study in the Exhibition and Reception of American Films in Britain, 1914–1918

Michael Hammond

Between 1914 and 1918 the London Office of the American company Selig Polyscope sent the following letter to its exhibitors and renters as a matter of course following the release of selected films:

> Dear Sir,
>
> As you are just concluding running (name of film) we should much appreciate hearing from you, as to how this film went with your audiences.
> We are particularly anxious to ascertain the views of the various exhibitors with regard to this film, as it is only by doing this, that we are able to ascertain what class of film we should instruct our American house goes best over here.
> Trusting to hear that the film proved highly satisfactory.
>
> Yours very truly,
> Selig Polyscope

The Margaret Herrick Library holds British exhibitors' responses for three Selig releases: a serial, *The Adventures of Kathlyn* (USA, 1913; UK release, 1914), and two features, *The Crisis* (USA, 1916; UK release, 1917), a Civil War drama, and *The Garden of Allah* (USA, 1917; UK release, 1918), a mystical 'desert romance'.[1] The exhibitors' letters comment on their audiences' preferences and their own relationship with Selig, and in some cases offer comments and criticisms of the film themselves. As such, the letters provide valuable evidence of the nature of distribution, exhibition and reception and help to build a more complete understanding of the history of British cinema culture at the moment when Hollywood product began to dominate British screens. They indicate how exhibitors and renters conceptualized their audiences in terms of social background and 'taste preferences'. Many of the exhibitors made a direct link between taste and class, describing their audiences in terms such as 'our better class' or 'our groundlings'.[2] When referring to their own taste, they often mention the quality of the film print, or the acting or the 'artistry' involved. The letters also provide evidence of the transnational reception of American films in Britain. In various ways, then, they demonstrate how different audiences respond to specific elements in contemporary films, and offer competing interpretations not only of films but also of the function of film-going in a wide range of localities during the mid-1910s.

Underpinning these responses are the exhibitors' attempts to negotiate their need to attract paying customers with the shifting practices of production and distribution companies. Local competition was considerable at this time as the boom in fixed-site cinema construction in 1913–14 had resulted in a high ratio of seats per person in most large and medium-sized cities and towns.[3] Exhibitors were faced with further changes in the mid-1910s, including the continuing rise of the feature; the introduction of the serial; the introduction in 1916 of the Entertainments Tax; and the decline of the open market and the move to 'exclusives' and later block booking.[4] Under the open market system, films were rented from a variety of exchanges and sources; under the 'exclusives' system, films were rented as first or second run to the one exhibitor in the area solely for that run. In such an environment exhibitors vied with local competition for 'first runs' and proven successes, while production and distribution companies attempted to cater to their needs and avoid the almost 50 per cent wastage of unsold films in 1913–16.[5] Significant shifts in audience composition accompanied the demographic upheavals brought about by the war, with women dominating audiences while their men were at the front and, in cinemas near military facilities, the emergence of a new soldier audience. Many of these changes are reflected in the letters.

The letters are an example of a type of market research prevalent among American film producers at the time. Such research was taken into account in planning production strategies for film companies and remained remarkably resilient throughout the 1920s and 1930s as a means of determining audience preferences. Studios such as Selig took this type of market survey seriously in their attempt to maximize the sale of their product to renters in Britain. Renters in turn were concerned to purchase films that their exhibitors wanted. Many of them were also owners of regional chains who participated in survey exercises like Selig's in order to maintain a perspective on audience preferences in their region.

In addition to marketing surveys, Selig, like most of the major American film companies, provided exhibitors with advertising and promotional material which many of the larger cinemas took advantage of, 'showcasing' posters and advertising through newspaper stories and the circulation of handbills. Charles Burgess, the manager at the Coliseum Cinema in Leicester, wrote in response to the *Kathlyn* series:

> . . . this serial picture is the greatest attraction I have had at this hall up to now as I run all serial films here for Leicester. I have run *Lucille Love, Dolly of the Dailies* and I have *The Million Dollar Mystery* booked here too. I can safely say that *Kathlyn* is the most popular with the great audiences I get at this hall. This being the largest picture Theatre in the Midlands I get as a rule on the Saturday I am showing *Kathlyn* over 3500 on average. The seating capacity of my hall is 2000 persons. If you remember I had 1000 post cards of Kathlyn Williams and I assure you they are selling well with the film when showing. Now I have a great many photographs of the leading stars, full size, of different companies that have been sent on to me. I have these framed in gilt all round my theatre and am pleased to say they are admired by thousands of people. I shall be pleased to receive some of your leading star actors including of course Kathlyn.

The letter is an indication of the kind of marketing strategies employed at the time. The production of postcards encouraged collections and attempted to induce 'brand loyalty' for both distributors and exhibitors. Burgess's comment that he 'runs all serial films' in Leicester is probably an exaggeration as other houses ran them, but it is an indication of the exhibitor's competitiveness. The number of seats in the hall, the indication that other companies' serials were successful and the particular success of the *Kathlyn* series were inducements to Selig to maintain their relationship with Burgess. They could make more profit from the bigger halls while, for Burgess, the regularity of his clientele would have raised the profile of the cinema, perhaps enough to secure it 'first refusal' status, a valuable position in an open market system.

The high streets in Britain offered a choice of cinemas during the war. Southampton, for instance, had four cinemas either on or within easy walks of the high street and a further eight were accessible by tram car. Consequently competition for film product which worked with the audiences was considerable. In a letter reporting on the disappointing business done by *The Crisis*, the manager of Andrew's Pictures in Burnley wrote: 'Pictures of the style of *The Cobweb*, *The Girl Phillippa*, Pauline Frederick, Marge Clarke, Mary Pickford Pictures, *Freckles* are the kind the public want and if they don't find them at one place they go to another.' Films and their stars clearly played a central role in exhibitors' attempts to attract audiences.

The Adventures of Kathlyn (1914–1915)

The Adventures of Kathlyn was one of the first adventure serials to reach Britain. It featured Kathlyn Williams as Kathlyn Hare, the daughter of Colonel Hare, a collector of wild animals, who has been captured by Prince Umballah, ruler of Allaha, a small principality in East India. Kathlyn travels with her sister to Allaha and the serial depicts her adventures as she tries to rescue her father. The *Kathlyn* serial was also the first to introduce holdover action, the 'to be continued' device at the end of every episode. This device was helpful in maintaining audiences on weeknights, which were often called adventure nights. A letter from E.E. Alison of the Grove Cinema near Stockport reported that:

> *The Adventures of Kathlyn* have been a complete success from start to finish. Each part had been eagerly awaited by my audience and now there seems to be something missing every other Monday but when Miss Kathlyn Williams appears on the screen in one of Selig's pictures the appreciation is shown by the audience (as) enthusiastically as on an Adventure night.

This letter suggests that audiences were expecting particular types of films on particular nights and the fact that the exhibitor is moved to comment on the behaviour of the audience as if it was an 'adventure night' suggests that these were, when successful, boisterous affairs. It also suggests that feature films required a different kind of response, one with a more attentive 'gazing' audience.

Several letters reporting the positive reception for the *Kathlyn* series point to audience behaviour in terms of enthusiasm or applause. Charles Williams of Darlaston Cinemas in South Staffordshire wrote:

> . . . we have just shown the last instalment of this series and on Monday night at the conclusion when Kathlyn said goodbye to friends I was astounded at the applause. In fact I have never experienced anything like it. I may mention we had about 1200 folks in the hall at the time.

Another exhibitor, from the Angel Picture Theatre, Islington wrote: '. . . *Kathlyn* has been a great success. The public has asked for it and immediately the film is shown upon the screen it is greeted with a round of applause.'

The Selig letters offer a corollary to Ben Singer's suggestion that, 'Considered from the perspective of industry history, the serials can be seen as a resistance to the emergence of the feature film'.[6] For many exhibitors at this time the feature was less attractive since its length dominated the programme and reduced the opportunity of audience turnover. Exhibitors who depended largely on a regular clientele found the length of serial episodes, and their 'to be continued' format, suited their continuous programme policy. Some audiences clearly enjoyed the performative rather than merely spectatorial involvement that seems to have been part and parcel of the cinema-going experience in some houses, as the following recollection of watching serials in a working-class district in the mid-1910s suggests:

> . . . Just in front of the screen they used to have a curtain go round and an old piano there and pianist playing which kept the music for the film . . . that woman playing that piano must have had an umbrella up, because all the peels used to go there and all kiddies like, oranges and all the peel used to throw over there. How she used to play the thing I don't know. I think the lights used to go up about once every ten minutes and we'd get threatened and all thrown out if we didn't keep quiet and that was the days of old Pearl White and we used to shout out 'look who's behind you', you can imagine the kids and the uproar was terrific . . . when we got too bad the old manager used to put the lights up telling us all to keep quiet otherwise he'd throw the lot of us out. (George Cook of Southampton remembering his days as a child at the cinema.)[7]

Plate 15.   Southampton Picture Palace, 1912

Although such memories should always be treated with caution, there is no doubting that such lively audience behaviour took place, and that some audiences expected and enjoyed it. Such expectations were often referred to in local advertising and provided a means of appealing to specific audience constituencies. In February 1915, a cinema in Southampton ran *The Adventures of Kathlyn*; alongside the announcement of the first instalment, the cinema placed the following advertisement in a local paper:

> 'Oh I say, Maude, where would you like to go tonight, shall we go for a walk on the common?' 'No Charlie, it's too cold tonight, take me to the Northam Picturedrome where its warm and cosy, and we are sure to see some extra good pictures.' This conversation is frequently overheard, and judging by the continued excellent business at the above hall, it is quite evident that there is more than one who knows where the comfort is.[8]

'The common' in Southampton was the traditional place where couples could find some privacy. The advert was an invitation to couples to use the 'cosy' cinema in the same way, and emphasized the function of the cinema as a social space. Cinema exhibitors clearly addressed their patrons' expectations of pleasures at several levels, with the film itself as a part, but not all, of the overall experience. By the time *Kathlyn* was released, the building boom in picture palaces, begun in earnest in 1911, was reaching a peak and the comfort and experience of the cinema itself was a means of differentiation in a highly competitive environment.

Serials drew on forms of serial narration already familiar from newspapers and popular magazines. Even so, the introduction of *Kathlyn*'s open-ended structure seems initially to have caused some confusion. A.S. Strom of the Balsall Heath Picturedrome, Birmingham, noted that *Kathlyn* appealed

> particularly to the ladies and the disappointment of the sudden changes are audibly expressed. One patron while booking to see part three asked if that was the finish but when the worker told him there were ten more parts . . . he nearly collapsed. In the workers opinion it is good but too long.

Strom is drawing attention to the difficulties audiences had in adjusting to the serial format. The 'disappointment audibly expressed' is a disappointment that the episode has ended but also an indication of their involvement with the narrative. This was of sufficient concern to the manager of The Palace music hall in Southampton to point out in his advertising that 'Each of the *Kathlyn* episodes are complete in themselves'.[9] The male patron 'who nearly collapsed' was perhaps concerned about the repeated purchase of tickets while the cinema attendant surely felt there were too many episodes rather than each episode being too long. Is this an example of audience members adjusting to a film form based on previous experience and expectations that are primarily centred around narrative closure? Strom's linking of the serial's appeal to women with a male customer's confusion perhaps indicates that serials were more readily accepted by women. After all, popular literature addressed to women since the middle of the nineteenth century had been dominated by both sensational fiction and serial narratives.[10] It seems that from the perspective of a history of exhibition and reception serials demanded an adjustment as signifi- cant as the feature film in terms of the mode of reception and the expectations they fostered.

The Crisis

The majority of letters in the collection date from late November 1917 and concern Selig's Civil War 'superfilm' *The Crisis*. This was a prestige feature based on the 1901 best seller by American novelist Winston Churchill. The story revolves around the friendship between Judge Whipple, supporter of Abraham Lincoln, and Colonel Carvel, Southern merchant and slave owner. The judge's student Stephen Brice visits the colonel and falls in love with his daughter Virginia. They meet at a slave auction where Brice, appalled by the process of slavery, buys a 'young woman slave' in order to set her free. This gets the possible union off to a rocky start as Virginia was bidding for the woman as well. The Civil War splits apart not only the couple but also the judge and the colonel. After the war the judge and the colonel die, but not before they have made amends, while Abraham Lincoln himself brings the young couple together. The press pack sent out quoted the *Evening News* as saying:

> *The Crisis* is in many respects far greater than *The Birth of a Nation*. It is stronger in characterisation and better in story, and it has the merit of being splendidly produced and finely acted. The whole production is marked by such strong characterisations, such contrasts, such little touches revealing the souls of men, that *The Crisis* is bound to live when hundreds of other pictures have been forgotten.[11]

The press pack also included directions on how best to advertise and present the film: 'Your success is not due to the mere fact that you book films, but to the manner in which you present them to your patrons. It takes an enterprising exhibitor to make big money out of a booking.' What followed was a set of order forms for posters and music. The music had been

> Specially arranged and written by Thomas Batty who has made a thorough study of music as applied to the cinema. A number of stirring American airs have been introduced into the pot pourri. . . . See to it that you do justice to yourself and the film by ordering the accompaniment right away . . . Specially arranged music is always a good investment.

The reference to American airs indicates not only the appropriateness of the music, but also the fact that British audiences would recognize it.[12]

The film cost exhibitors a great deal in comparison to other films as some of the letters bear out. There were at least three reasons why exhibitors were prepared to take on such an expense: the reputation of the business done with *The Birth of a Nation*, the reputation of the Selig company, and the increasing fear that, like *The Birth of a Nation*, the superfilms would play only in prestige theatres and not in cinemas. For most exhibitors the gamble didn't pay off. (Among the letters from British exhibitors there are forty-four 'Testimonials' and fifty 'Adverse Criticisms', but the Testimonials are more often praise for artistry rather than reports of profitable business.) A number of exhibitors and renters even asked for their money back. One renter wrote:

> 'I wish to inform you that we have today received the copy of *The Crisis* from the Palace, Southport and with a telephone message saying it is the worst three days they have ever had since they opened, as the people simply walked out when it was put on the screen . . .

Exhibitors' explanations for their audience responses focused on the pace of the film and on the dated nature of the subject matter, the American Civil War. The manager of the Coliseum in Sheffield noted: 'It is a good picture but too quiet and not popular with audiences.' William G. Hutt of Park and Dare's Workman's Hall in Treorchy, Rhondda found that his patrons 'do not care for Civil War Films . . .'. Boyle Lawrence of Cinema House, Oxford Street, London, wrote:

> the picture as a picture is excellent but the subject is old and threadbare and English audiences are by this time tired of the American Civil War and all concerning it. It being inundated with this, no doubt, epoch making subject since cinemas have existed.

Frank Graham of Star Pictures, Sheffield found the picture: 'too long and lacking in comedy . . . The majority of the audience in a picture house are not interested in the American history of the freedom of the slaves and the war between North and South.'

The press blocks that were part of the advertising campaign for *The Birth of a Nation* had emphasized its relevance to the British public's experience of wartime. They invited audiences to 'see a nation reborn as England will be when this war is over'.[13] The relevance of American history to the British cinema audience was thus couched in terms of patriotism while the images of plantations, slaves and the use of minstrel music were easily recognizable as part of the 'exotic' iconography of Empire.

Expectations of a similar experience with *The Crisis* in many areas were dispelled by word of mouth. Selig had required exhibitors to book the film for six days and many of them subsequently commented on dwindling audiences. The Midland Amusement Company's general manager wrote: '. . . We opened all right on Monday and there was a drop all the week, which proves to me that the public will not have any more of this American Civil War Stuff.' One exhibitor remarked that his patrons stayed away because they thought it was a 'political film'. At the Alhambra in Darlington the film did well for three nights 'but we think that the name Winston Churchill, whom the majority took to be our Winston, was the draw more than the picture itself . . .'

The advertising for *The Crisis* trumpeted spectacular battle scenes, but by November 1917 the impact of such footage had become troubling. The official war film *The Battle of the Somme*, screened throughout late 1916 and 1917, as well as follow-up films such as *The Battle of the Ancre and the Advance of the Tanks*, had been successful but by early 1917 the appeal of this type of film was waning.[14] Herbert Craven of the Albion Picture Palace, Castleford, curtly observed that 'The people seem to be fed up with war stuff.' Exhibitors were proving sensitive to the fact that many of their patrons were suffering bereavement. Frank Graham of Star Pictures in Sheffield wrote:

> One must not forget that the seriousness of the affairs of to-day, and the news we are constantly reading in the press as to casualties etc., make it absolutely imperative that the entertainment at a picture house, should be of a bright and cheerful nature, so that the individual will be able to forget his worries and anxieties.
>
> The success of a Picture House depends not only upon the variety of films shown, but it is necessary that humour of a refined kind should enter into the subject of the big film, even a humorous subtitle relieves greatly a serious subject.

Other exhibitors chose to invoke a patriotic tone attaching to it the discourse of uplift associated with the advertising for 'superfilms'. The manager of the Royal Pavilion in Mossley wrote:

> When I received *The Crisis* my impression was the finest production I had seen this last ten years. The subject was

interesting the acting of the artistes brilliant. The story carried
one's mind to the present Great War and the wish that England
and the Allies will hold that faith and perseverance and will to
hold out and overcome and finally crush the central powers and
for all times end all ideas the brutal military despotism holds of
ruling the earth. Would that we had another Lincoln today so
strong, so conscientious of his right to win and with all that waive
[*sic*] of beautiful sympathy which he handed to friends and foes
alike with a great and free heart. Production of these cannot help
but win success wherever portrayed.

Many of the exhibitors' and renters' letters were anxious to differentiate their taste from that of their audience. William Thorp of
Manchester Picture House wrote: 'to me personally the production as a
production seemed good, but facts proved it anything but a money
bringer.' The letters also provide provocative anomalies, which militate
against a simplistic reading of the class prejudices informing their
perceptions of their audience. W. Harlan, manager of The Bungalow
in Portobello, Midlothian, highlighted a preference for 'modern stories'
in all of his patrons:

> . . . the story is too dry and the action too slow. Another thing
> that does not please is the period. I find that any story that calls
> for costumes of a period ante-dating the present or modern past
> never gathers the sympathetic interest of the audience unless the
> story is exceptionally strong and dramatic. *The Crisis* is not 1.2.3.
> with the 'ne'er do well' or [the] 'thy shalt not covet thy neighbour's
> wife'.

Harlan's euphemisms for class were beyond the manager of the Picture
House in Birmingham who bluntly stated: '. . . *The Crisis* was very
much appreciated by our audience here . . . particularly by the better
class.' By contrast A.W. Kenyon, manager of The New Royal Picture
Theatre in Manchester, noted:

> . . . the film went well and delighted crowded houses for three
> days . . . It was a film to give satisfaction for the exhibitor to feel
> that they have had a good show for their money. This class of
> homely film is very suitable for my class of patrons, (working class
> district).

The fact that the same film might be perceived as appealing to 'the better class' in one cinema and the working classes in another illustrates the position of the exhibitor between production and reception, and the conflict over the meaning of texts in general. For one exhibitor, the film lacks the dramatic ingredients he thinks appeal to the 'ne'er do well'; Kenyon, however, identifies other textual elements that did appeal to his working-class patrons. His reference to the film as 'homely' highlights a central theme in Civil War melodramas, and is a reading that privileges its domestic drama rather than the film's value as a historical (that is, educational) epic. Yet they each illustrate the general sense of paternalism that many of the cinema managers exhibit in their letters and indeed sought to cultivate within their respective communities.

The Garden of Allah

Several exhibitors refer to the upcoming big feature *The Garden of Allah* while lamenting the poor business of *The Crisis*. This 'Romance of the Desert' was an adaptation of the 1904 best-selling novel of the same name by Robert Hichens. The press package provided a synopsis of the story:

> At Benimora on the edge of the Sahara desert Domini Enfilden, an English girl, comes to find peace. Here she meets Boris Androvsky the stranger who flees from the sight of prayer and is afraid of women. Domini finds love for the first time with Boris and after their wedding they stay for a honeymoon in the desert to find peace together. Peace does not come to Boris however for he has a secret which is weighing on his conscience. Finally he confides to Domini that he is Father Antonio who fled worldly pleasure and found Domini. Torn between his love of her and his church through the strength of guidance by Domini he returns to the monastery.

The popularity of the novel and its undertones of sensuality provided the exhibitors with good business and with a great deal of response from their patrons. E.C. Morgan of Croydon Picture Theatre wrote:

> I am more than favourably disposed to the film because I am a great lover of Robert Hichens' work and most especially of this one. As a film I think it is splendid. IT [*sic*] is something you can handle with distinctive taste, style and showmanship and fetch the

best class audience who are the people who *think, read* and *can appreciate* unique presentations as against 'movie muck' they so often decry. Good luck to you and lets have plenty more.

This is an example of an exhibitor referencing the intertextual nature of his engagement with the film as a marker for the kind of audiences the cinema *should* have. The letter illustrates the overarching discourse of 'taste' distinctions in the production of an ideal, even utopian audience. The ideal audience in this construction coincides with the 'middle-class respectability' that was a central part of the British film industry's attempts to appeal to middle-class audiences.

For other exhibitors, however, the film's middlebrow taste references are recognized and interpreted differently. W. Earnest Maxfield, of Queens Theatre, Chatham, wrote:

> *The Garden of Allah* is in my opinion above the heads of the average picture theatre patron. By this I don't mean they cannot appreciate a first rate or even classical subject but it must be a clear and lucid story with plenty of action and characters in whom they can take a lively and sympathetic interest. Now with the two principal characters in *The Garden of Allah* I found it personally impossible to enter into their joys or sorrows. Not having read the book I had to judge Hichens' work by the film. We are introduced to a man whose actions in the early part suggest he has escaped from a lunatic asylum. Nobody would dream he is simply a monk who has come out into the world to shake a loose leg . . . though judging by his age one would have thought that he knew before joining the brotherhood 'how many beans made five' and what worldly attractions were worth. Had he only done something when he did leave 'the abode of peace' . . . [and] gone to the devil for a period and then through the love of Domini become regenerated, that would have been something but he simply bores one, the girl too. Looks as though she had a past, she certainly looks old enough to have had a lurid past but of that past, except a brief reference to her dead father and mother, [the film] tells us nothing. . . . I think [it] should have made more of the part of Boris but on different lines. When we come to the spectacular I have nothing but praise, it is beautiful but as Hamlet says 'the play's the thing' and when all is said its the play that touches the hearts of the picture patron that is the real winner. Beautiful effects by all means where necessary but first and foremost comes the story and the acting. I can imagine a story of mean streets and poverty stricken interiors or at the best only rising to the lower

middle classes the only effects from the fire or lamplight and then at the last the character transported to some glorious part of god's beautiful world to revel in sunshine and happiness. That would grip the hearts of all. I can imagine circus stories that a firm like Selig could give us and fairy stories too introducing wild beasts etc. but more *Garden of Allahs* . . . no. This of course is only my opinion.

Maxfield's letter reads like a how-to script writing manual of the period. His reference to the film being 'over the heads' of most is not a compliment to the film but an understandable lament from an exhibitor who has lost money. While both Maxfield and Morgan invoke the discourse of uplift, there are differences. Maxfield wants film product that his (British) audience understands and enjoys. He calls not for spectacle but for narrative that is inclusive rather than exclusive in its address. Morgan is content to praise the film's anticipation of an ideal 'respectable' audience.

Conclusion

The letters to the Selig company provide evidence of some of the ways in which British exhibitors and their audiences interacted in the mid-1910s. They also allow some insight into how those two groups made sense of the films they watched or handled. Audiences were, of course, crucial to the successful running of the cinema and the letters suggest how exhibitors thought of, or produced, their audiences. Throughout these accounts there exist traces of probable, or preferred, readings of films as they circulated at the time. The exhibitors give voice to available public vocabularies that speak to, and about, their audiences' preferences. Further, those readings are shaped by the climate of the business at the time, which was precarious, in spite of large national attendance figures. While the fears of total closure in the early weeks of the war proved to be unfounded, there were still many threats to the business of running a single cinema, including local competition for audiences, the changing means of obtaining films and the introduction of the Entertainments Tax.

While the letters provide an important insight into the exhibitors' response to changes in the industry they also raise questions about the reception of American cinema in Britain at a significant moment when Hollywood was consolidating its dominant position. This may be why exhibitors engaged in two activities simultaneously, both describing their audiences and explaining their patrons' taste preferences. The two were interlinked through their expression in terms of discourses of class, gender and national identity. In the case of *The Crisis* the exhibitor had a hand in redirecting the meanings to make the film more comprehensible and relevant to British audiences. This involved a transnational translation for audiences and commensurate re-translation to the Selig London office. Not surprisingly descriptions of the preferences of audiences were expressed in terms of taste and artistry and yet crucially they provide productive anomalies such as the popularity of *The Crisis* with working-class audiences in Manchester, the resistance of the patron to paying for each episode of *The Adventures of Kathlyn*, or Mr Maxfield's argument for spectacle in the service of 'story and acting' in *The Garden of Allah*. These and other examples provide evidence of the 'contested terrain' of cinema culture in Britain. Perhaps more importantly these letters give a voice, however incomplete, to the exhibitors and provide an insight into this often invisible part of cinema culture in shaping interpretations of specific films at a crucial moment in British cinema history.

Notes

1. These letters are part of the Selig Collection held at the Margaret Herrick Library, Beverly Hills, California. There are fourteen letters on *The Adventures of Kathlyn* in Folder 10, fifty letters in Folder 48, labelled *The Crisis*: Adverse Criticism,' forty-five letters in Folder 49, 'Testimonials for *The Crisis*', and eighty letters in Folder 55 concerning *The Garden of Allah*. All subsequent uncredited quotations are from this collection. I would like to thank Scott Curtis and Val Almendez at the Margaret Herrick Library for their assistance and advice during my research for this chapter.

2. It was the norm at this time for those cinemas whose seats were constructed on more than one level for the cheapest seats to be on the ground floor.

3. For example, Southampton had sixteen cinemas for a population of 119,039. The average seating capacity for these was 600, which meant that in order to operate at 50 per cent capacity almost 5,000 tickets per day needed to be sold.

4. Nicholas Hiley, 'The British Cinema Auditorium,' in Karel Dibbets and Bert Hogenkamp, eds, *Film and The First World War* (Amsterdam: Amsterdam University Press, 1995), pp. 166–7.

5. Kristin Thompson, *Exporting Entertainment: America in the World Film Market, 1903–1934* (London: BFI, 1985), p. 35.

6. Ben Singer, 'Female Power in the Serial Queen Melodrama: The Etiology of an Anomaly,' in Richard Abel, ed., *Silent Film* (London: Athlone, 1992), p. 163.

7. Quoted in Bill White, Sheila Jemima and Donald Hyslop, *Dream Palaces: Going to the Pictures in Southampton* (Southampton: Southampton City Council, 1996), p. 41. George Cook is no doubt talking of a Saturday matinée, which poses the problem always prevalent in oral histories in that, for the period of 1916, which is when *Pearl of the Army* was released, Southampton cinemas were running serials on Mondays–Wednesdays.

8. Northam Picturedome, *What's On in Southampton*, week ending 12 February 1915, no pagination.

9. 'Sunday Evening at The Palace,' *What's On in Southampton*, week ending 15 August 1914, no pagination.

10. See Kate Flint, *The Woman Reader: 1837–1914* (Oxford: Clarendon Press, 1993), especially pp. 274–93.

11. Press pack for *The Crisis*, Selig Collection, Margaret Herrick Library.

12. The technique of including well-known melodies in the score for the film had been a feature of Joseph Carl Breil's score for D.W. Griffith's *Birth of a Nation*. 'American Airs' and military marches were often a part of the programme at local public concerts.

13. Michael Hammond, ' "A Soul Stirring Appeal to Every Briton": The Reception of *Birth of a Nation* in Britain (1915–1916),' *Film History*, vol. 11, no. 3, 1999, pp. 353–70.

14. Nicholas Reeves, *Official British Film Propaganda During the First World War* (London: Croom Helm, 1986), pp. 225–6.

SECTION C

A Full Supporting Programme
Serials, Cinemagazines, Interest Films,
Travelogues and Travel Films, and Film Music
in the 1910s and 1920s

9

British Series and Serials in the Silent Era

Alex Marlow-Mann

Film serials played a key role in the British film-going experience in the silent era, but the majority of the writing on the subject concentrates on the work of Louis Feuillade or American serials. In this chapter, I will make a first step towards redressing this balance by outlining the history of the serial in Britain, considering key films in terms of narration, genre, and distribution and exhibition practices. Much of what has been written about French and American serials applies to the British situation and I will begin by briefly considering the notion of 'tie-ins' and 'cliff-hangers' and the distinction that can be made between series and serials.

The birth of the serial is generally taken to have been July 1912 with the release of *What Happened to Mary?* This was the result of an agreement between the Edison Company and a magazine, *McClure's Ladies World*, to release simultaneously a series of one-reel films and publish the same stories in literary form. The practice of 'tie-ins', as they came to be known, was commercially beneficial to both the magazine and the films and soon became standard practice in American serials. *What Happened to Mary?* had a set of characters and broad narrative logic running across the various instalments, but the individual episodes were consisted of self-contained stories. By 1913, it became evident that an audience could be better guaranteed to return by leaving the story incomplete at the end of each episode and by teasing them as to what would happen next. The concept of 'cliff-hanger' endings, in which the hero(ine) would be left in grave danger at the end of one episode only to be miraculously freed at the start of the next (often with little concern for narrative coherence or verisimilitude), was initiated with *The Adventures of Kathlyn* (Selig 1913) and was standardized by 1915.[1]

The conventional distinction between serials and series is outlined by Kalton Lahue:

> A serial contained the same leading figures in the cast, and it had a plot which inter-connected each episode, whether these divisions were complete in themselves or were cliff-hangers. A series, although it might contain the same cast, had no broad connecting plot between chapters.[2]

Raymond William Stedman argues that this is 'a misguided segregation which overlooks the fact that all chapter plays are, technically, sequential series'.[3] As will become clear from the British examples, we can in fact distinguish four main trends within the serial formula, although these are not always distinct enough to be true categories. First, there is what is often referred to as the true serial, in which key plot points remain unresolved at the end of each episode to be picked up at the start of the next (most characteristically in the form of a cliff-hanger); the true serial also shows a clear narrative progression across the individual episodes. Second, there is what I will call the semi-serial, which has an over-arching narrative premise and sense of progression and a consistent set of characters but which has clearly demarcated, self-contained chapters that contain the resolution to their own narrative goals. Third, there is the character-based series, which features recurring character(s) in a number of short films with self-contained stories but no over-arching sense of narrative progression, made by the same production company and/or director and/or screenwriter. Finally, there is the thematically based series, which utilizes different characters and self-contained narratives but maintains strong thematic links and a sense of continuity between episodes. In what follows, I will use Stedman's term sequential series to describe all forms of serial narratives, distinguishing between the individual types with the terms true serial, semi-serial, character-based series and thematically based series, according to the above descriptions.

The British film industry produced few true serials during the silent era and this is perhaps one reason why nothing has yet been written on the subject; it did however produce a number of sequential series, several of which had a significant commercial impact at the time of release. The ensuing discussion will consider the principal examples of the serial form in Britain, as understood in its widest sense. I will however exclude the various series of comic films, such as Folly Films' *Pimple* series with Fred Evans, which can be better understood in the tradition of the gag film or comedy short.[4] I will also be excluding thematically linked sequential series that lacked a consistent set of characters, such as Fred Paul's *Grand Guignol* (Screen Plays, 1921). While these films clearly share strong affinities with other forms of serial film-making, the sense of continuity between episodes is much weaker; furthermore, given the wide range of different thematically linked sequential series produced, a broadening of scope to include these films would risk either confusion or superficiality.

British Sequential Series

Although precedents to the serial form in Britain can be traced further back, the first real example of the format was *The Exploits of Three-Fingered Kate*, released between October 1909 and September 1912 and numbering seven episodes of between 600 and 1000 feet.[5] The films were produced by British and Colonial (B&C), a company which was to dominate the series film market in Britain during the 1910s. The films featured a master criminal, the eponymous Kate, and her gang who repeatedly elude the ill-fated detective Sheerluck. The series is significant not only because it marks the beginning of the formula in Britain but also because Kate anticipates the strong, dominant female protagonists that would later characterize the American serials and embody the idea of the 'New Woman' (although, as Jane Bryan has pointed out, unlike her later American counterparts, Kate is a criminal rather than a heroic crime-fighter).[6]

Three months later Clarendon released the first of its *Lieutenant Rose* films, which were to last until March 1914 with a total of sixteen episodes. Directed by Percy Stow and starring P.G. Norgate (who was replaced by P.G. Ebbutt and Harry Lorraine for some of the later episodes) the films relate the adventures of a naval officer who defends his country against spies and anarchists. In September 1911 B&C released a rival version, *Lieutenant Daring*, which was destined to be even more successful and to last until April 1914, with thirteen episodes, as well as two feature-length versions in 1924 and 1935.[7] Initially Clifford Marle starred, but the character soon became identified with the charismatic ex-circus acrobat Percy Moran, who was to appear in a number of series films including B&C's concurrent *The Adventures of Dick Turpin* (June–November 1912, four

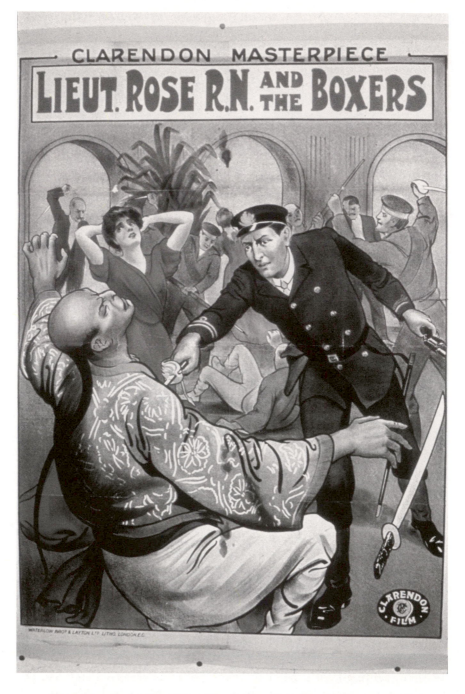

Plate 16.   Poster for *Lieut. Rose R.N. and the Boxers* (Stowe, 1911)

episodes), which related various events in the life of the famous highwayman.

In November 1912 the Franco-British Film Co. released an eight-episode series titled *Sherlock Holmes*, directed by and starring Georges Treville. This was slightly longer than the earlier series, averaging about 1,700 feet per episode. B&C's *Don Q* (December 1912), although only numbering three episodes, is notable for uniting many of the British series' main talents—it was directed by H.O. Martinek and starred Charles Raymond, Ivy Martinek and Percy Moran.

Although further episodes of the two Lieutenant series continued to be produced, no new series appeared for three years, until Ideal's six-episode *The Adventures of Deadwood Dick*, directed by and starring Fred Paul, appeared in October 1915. December 1915 saw the release of the first episode of Gaumont-Victory's *Ultus* series, directed by George Pearson and featuring Aurele Sydney as a master criminal. It was explicitly designed to replicate the success of *Fantomas* (Gaumont, 1913) in France,[8] and although numbering only four episodes (though they were of feature length, 4,000-6,000 feet), it was to be one of the most successful and popular of the British series.[9] *Boy Scouts Be Prepared* (September 1917), produced by the Transatlantic Film Co. and directed by Percy Nash, numbered eight episodes and was the first British example of a true serial. It tells of two boys who join the scouts and foil a gypsy spy supplying petrol to German U-boats. It was another two years before the release of *The Adventures of Dorcas Dene, Detective* (July 1919), directed by Frank Carlton and starring Winifred Rose. Telling of the wife of a blinded police lieutenant who becomes a detective, the series anticipated the 1920s vogue for detective series.

In August 1920 Hepworth (Imperial) released the only example of a British semi-serial, the five-episode *The Amazing Quest of Mr. Ernest Bliss*, directed by and starring Henry Edwards and based on the novel by E. Phillips Oppenheim. It tells of a rich young man who makes a bet that he can earn his own living. In each episode he unsuccessfully attempts a new profession; in so doing, however, he falls in love and wins the heart of the girl and the bet. While each episode is a self-contained story, there is an overall narrative progression and ultimate resolution in the final episode. Besides *Boy Scouts Be Prepared*, the only other British example of a true serial is *The Great London Mystery* (November 1920, twelve episodes) produced by Torquay and Paignton Photoplay Productions and directed, once again, by Charles Raymond. It stars David Devant, a popular magician of the time, and relates the story of a native priest who travels to England to recover the jewels stolen from his temple. Judging by the coverage in contemporary trade journals neither of these series was more than moderately successful.[10]

In April 1921 Stoll (who would dominate much of the later series market) released *The Adventures of Sherlock Holmes*, to be followed by *The Further Adventures of Sherlock Holmes* (April 1922) and *The Last Adventures of Sherlock Holmes* (March 1923). Numbering in total thirty-six episodes, these series were all directed by Maurice Elvey, starred Eille Norwood, and were adapted from Conan Doyle's stories. In a similar vein Stoll also released *The Mystery of Dr. Fu Manchu* (April 1923) and *The Further Adventures of Dr. Fu Manchu* (August 1924), directed by A.E. Coleby and Fred Paul respectively, starring H. Agar Lyons and adapted from the stories of Sax Rohmer.

Other companies as well as Stoll continued this cycle of detective series. Master Films released *Leaves of My Life* (April 1921, six episodes), directed by Edward R. Gordon and starring Ernest Haigh, in which a retired policeman relates various cases he solved. Stoll's *The Old Man in the Corner* (July 1924, twelve episodes), directed by Hugh Croise from the stories of Baroness Orczy and starring Rolf Leslie, copied the same idea of a retired policeman relating his past adventures. Phillips' *Pixie at the Wheel* (August 1924, three episodes), directed by Lee Morrison and starring Peggy Worth, told of an American reporter solving crimes with the aid of a British motorist. In April 1928 Fred Paul directed a six-episode series starring himself and H. Agar Lyons, *Dr Sing Fang Dramas*, for Pioneer. The final series film to be produced during the silent era was *Sexton Blake* (May 1928, six episodes) produced by British Filmcraft and starring Langhorne Burton. It was a detective series based on a character who had already appeared in a couple of short films.[11]

Narrational Strategies

Early American semi-serials such as *What Happened to Mary?* can be seen to function both as short and long narratives in that they tell a series of self-contained mini-narratives linked by an over-arching premise and concluding in the final episode. With the evolution of the true serial and the development of the cliff-hanger, the serial moved closer to the long narrative in that the individual episodes lack closure and are only minimally intelligible without reference to the other episodes. Taken as a whole, these serials offer a series of narrative climaxes and complications leading to a final resolution, a structure that is of course quite similar to a feature length narrative. Nevertheless there are fundamental differences between the classical narrative that became standardized by 1917 and the narrative structure of the serial. Whereas classical narratives generally progress in a linear fashion towards a clearly defined goal, embellished by a series of complicating actions which serve to postpone narrative resolution, Vicki Callahan sees serials as a never-ending loop in which every time the hero(ine) achieves his or her goal he or she is thwarted, only to pursue that same goal again.[12] For Ben Singer, this cyclical structure is a central premise, an excuse to offer a series of sensational thrills to the audience.[13]

The early British series, although they lack a continuing serial narrative and cliff-hanger endings, offer a series of recurrent situations so similar to one another as to create a repetitious structure that echoes Callahan's narrative loop. In more than half of the episodes of the *Lieutenant Rose* series, for example, there is a threat from an un-identified group of foreign spies or anarchists, and every episode sees them defeated, usually shelled by Rose's plane or ship. Each episode sets up an unspecific, ill-defined threat, then resolves it, only for an all but identical threat to reappear in the next episode. In over half of the episodes Rose is captured by the villains and is then either rescued or escapes, only to be recaptured in the next episode. Over half of the episodes involve either Rose or the villains donning disguises in order to achieve their goal. This repetition of generic narrative situations, with such minimal variation, is typical of both true serials and series films and is evidence that the two share an underlying sensationalist aesthetic, as described by Singer.

By the mid-teens these repetitious narratives began to resemble more closely true serial narratives. Rachael Low describes *The Adventures of Dick Turpin* as 'not so much complete stories as one long, meandering series of incidents in the famous highwayman's life. Their undoubted appeal lay neither in the stories nor in the acting . . . [but] was a question of swashbuckling adventures at breakneck pace . . .'[14] The *Ultus* films featured a master criminal who escaped at the end of each episode and was seen heading to a new adventure, clearly indicating a point of potential continuity with subsequent episodes (as one *Bioscope* reviewer states, 'the indefinite fate of the central figure leads us to hope that the last of his adventures has not yet been revealed').[15] The release of *Boy Scouts Be Prepared* offered a true serial narrative, to be followed by *The Great London Mystery*, of which *Bioscope* states, 'the plot is [no] more far-fetched than that of the ordinary serial. It is, as a matter of fact, built on strictly conventional lines. That each episode leaves the hero and heroine in horrible circumstances goes without saying.'[16]

Later British series utilize different strategies. In adapting the stories of Sir Arthur Conan Doyle and Sax Rohmer these films reject the serial narrative and repetitious, cyclical narrative structures in favour of more complex tools of narration typical of the mystery and detective genres. *The Dying Detective* from Stoll's *Adventures of Sherlock Holmes* series, for instance, features examples of flashbacks (explaining how the villain poisoned Holmes), mentally subjective sequences (where Holmes imagines how the victim may have contracted Asiatic flu) and restrictive narration (where a crucial character substitution occurs within the frame but is obscured from the audience's view by a car). Given that the focus of these stories is on the investigative logic Holmes employs, it is the narrative's manipulation of information (or focalization, to borrow narratology's term) that is the structuring principle of these films. The sensationalism of the serial narratives remains, however; unlike in Conan Doyle's stories, where Holmes is altogether a more rational, intellectual figure, Eille Norwood's Holmes is frequently seen brandishing revolvers, engineering dramatic escapes and the like. To quote a contemporary review: 'They are of a lurid, melodramatic kind and quite likely to be popular with devotees of the ordinary serial. The attraction is not at all similar to that of the printed stories.'[17]

The Aesthetic Uncertainty of the Serial

There is an argument to be made that this shift in the narrational strategies adopted by British sequential series reflects the gradual transition from a cinema of attractions to a cinema of narrative integration. American serials have been described as 'a hangover from the nickelodeon era' and the type of situations that the *Lieutenant Rose* and *Lieutenant Daring* films offer certainly have much in common with earlier films offering the pleasure of spectacle with a minimum of narrativization.[18] Vicki Callahan talks about an 'aesthetic of un-certainty' arising from the contradictory impulses towards spectacle and narrative, which characterizes the films of Feuillade, and which derives in part from the logistics of the serial narrative. A similar case could be made about the early British series.[19]

Lieutenant Daring Quells A Rebellion, for example, ostensibly tells of a group of anarchists in the West Indies who attempt to extinguish a lighthouse in order to signal the start of a general rebellion, only to be thwarted by Daring. This information is not fed gradually to the audience through unfolding narrative situations and character interaction but is given by two inter-titles at the very beginning of the film. Even the film's title is in itself a summary of the narrative. The film then proceeds to show two duels, a chase sequence, a capture and an escape, which are largely redundant in narrative terms and exist as pure spectacle. That the narrative is rudimentary and almost identical to the subsequent *Lieutenant Daring and the Plans of the Minefield* and countless other episodes simply underlines the point.

Another interesting device in the context of this aesthetic uncertainty is the use of the emblematic shot. This device was typical of much early film (most famously in Edwin S. Porter's *The Great Train Robbery*, 1903) whereby a single shot, separate from the main narrative, could be assembled by the exhibitor at the beginning, middle or end of the film according to his or her wishes. *The Exploits of Three-Fingered Kate* features a single shot of Kate thrusting her three fingers towards the camera; it is a clear case of interpellation more widely associated with the cinema of attractions than the cinema of narrative integration. Clearly this shot, common to every episode, helps to build up a sense of Kate's identity and creates a sense of continuity between the episodes. The *Lieutenant Daring* films also end with shots of the protagonist that appear to be extraneous to the rest of the narrative and (if less explicitly) directly address the audience. John Hawkridge notes that this practice was typical of the B&C series and he explains it in terms of a 'generic code', which is clearly consistent with the aim of creating a recognizable character within a generically branded product as demonstrated by these early series.[20] It remains to be seen if this practice of the emblematic shot was used more widely in other early British series, although I have as yet found no evidence to suggest that it was.

Distribution and Exhibition

Serials can also be seen as symptomatic of a transitional moment in the way in which they were distributed and exhibited. Serials were often billed as feature attractions, centre-pieces in a variety format program, and the fact that the serial as a whole ran for a considerable length of time allowed for extensive advertising in posters, magazines and the like. As the feature-length film became more widespread, serials continued to serve at least two crucial functions: they could be shown in smaller cinemas that couldn't afford feature-length films as a feature attraction, or they could be shown as a supporting feature before the main film. A regular release schedule has traditionally been seen as crucial to the success of the serial formula because the audience had to be aware of when the next instalment was due for release and, in the case of cliff-hangers, remember the ending of the previous episode. However it is worth noting that Feuillade's *Fantomas* (1913) and *Les Vampires* (1915) were distributed erratically with anything between one and four months elapsing between episodes and it was not until *Barabas* (1920) that he utilized a regular weekly release schedule.[21] A similar pattern is true of the early British series: Clarendon released sixteen episodes of *Lieutenant Rose* over forty-nine months, with anything between one and six months between episodes; B&C released thirteen *Lieutenant Daring* films over thirty-one months, with gaps of one to four months between episodes; Gaumont-Victory released four *Ultus* films over fifteen months with a four to six month gap between episodes.[22] The individual episodes were clearly filmed on separate occasions without a coherent plan for the duration or direction of the series at the time of its inception. By the 1920s, however, British series had begun to follow the American logic. For example the three series of *The Adventures of Sherlock Holmes* films were filmed together over three consecutive years, clearly following a pre-determined plan dictating the number of episodes and their sequence. Although I have been unable to locate release dates for all the individual episodes, given that each series numbers fifteen episodes, it would seem fair to suggest that they were released at the rate of one episode every three to four weeks at the very least, if not one episode weekly. As the *Bioscope* clearly demonstrates, the true serials like *Boy Scouts Be Prepared* exhibit the characteristic one episode per week schedule.[23]

As far as tie-ins are concerned, this is a practice that doesn't appear to have been widely exploited in the British cinema of the time, despite the flourishing penny dreadful serial literature of Victorian Britain. Many series exploited popular contemporary literature: besides the Conan Doyle and Sax Rohmer adaptations, *Leaves of my Life* adapted Ernest Haigh's *Secrets of Scotland Yard* stories, for example, while *Ultus the Man from the Dead* was also published in novelized form. However these series were not linked with the publications in order to gain the mutual benefits of their American counterparts. The only exception was *Don Q*, which was tied to Pearson's magazine serial by Hesketh Pritchard.[24]

The sequential series of the 1910s probably flourished, like the American serials, not in the picture palaces but rather in the remaining

Plate 17. Frame still from *Ultus and the Grey Lady* (Pearson, 1916),
featuring Aurele Sydney as Ultus

penny gaffs or smaller regional theatres; *Kinematograph Weekly*, for
instance, refers in condescending tones to 'kinemas where such serials
are appreciated'.[25] Given the short running time of these films (very
few exceed one reel), it is likely that they formed part of a varied
programme and were not promoted as feature attractions in themselves, a hypothesis that is supported by the scarcity of advertising for
these films in the contemporary trade press. It was not until the mid-
to late 1910s when the average programme had shifted to incorporate
'one long feature, one slightly shorter exclusive and perhaps one
short film' that longer series films like *Ultus* could be advertised as
main attractions.[26] It is interesting to note that the *Ultus* films were
distributed differently in America, with each film being split into two
two-reel episodes, thus making the series into seven two-reel episodes,
a format more typical of the American serial market.[27] The later series
of the 1920s, given their short length (two reels) in comparison with
the established norm, were probably, like their American counterparts,
programmed as supporting features or in older, regional cinemas as the
feature within a variety programme.

Genre

Like the American serial, the British series of the 1910s fall broadly into the crime or action/adventure genre. The action/adventure films, such as *Lieutenant Rose, Lieutenant Daring* and *Boy Scouts Be Prepared*, are characterized by disguises, chases, kidnappings and escapes and pit their hero against a foreign threat, while the crime films, such as *The Exploits of Three-Fingered Kate, Ultus* and *Don Q*, feature a master criminal who commits a new crime in each episode and eludes the policeman who is pursuing him or her. From 1921 onwards, however, the genre shifts almost exclusively to the detective format, featuring a brilliant private investigator or policeman solving a series of mysteries. This was possibly due to concerns expressed about crime films in the National Council of Public Morals report in 1917;[28] interestingly, that same year saw the character of Ultus inexplicably switch from being a criminal to operating on the other side of the law. These genres offered a perfect opportunity to provide the requisite sensational thrills and capitalized on prevalent trends in 'Blood and Thunder' sensationalist literature as well as the popularity of authors like Conan Doyle.

Ben Singer, drawing on the writings of Ferdinand Tonnies, interprets serials as representative of prevailing social anxieties and transformations, such as the fear of modernity and the impact of the First World War.[29] Unlike many of their American counterparts, the British series did not incorporate plots set against the background of the First World War (with the notable exception of *Boy Scouts Be Prepared*). However many of the pre-war series did exploit current xenophobic anxieties: certainly the *Lieutenant Daring* and *Lieutenant Rose* films, with their plots to assassinate royalty, and their spies, anarchists and exotic but threateningly 'other' foreigners, reflect not only an imperialist mentality but also fears about the changes that the early twentieth century was bringing.

Another important context in which to understand the British series is that of parody. As Hawkridge notes, *The Exploits of Three-Fingered Kate*, with the figure of the bumbling Sheerluck, can be seen as a direct parody of *Nick Carter—Le Roi des Détectives* (Éclair 1908).[30] There are also links with the comic film here too, as not only did the series parody popular cinematic trends but they also became the object of parody themselves: Fred Evans produced a number of *Lieutenant Pimple* films, for example.

Accounting for the Relative Lack of British Serials

Although some British series exploited elements of the American serial's success including sensationalist narratives, regular distribution patterns, magazine tie-ins and cliff-hanger narratives, no single series exploited all of these elements systematically in the way that the American industry did for many years. There is little evidence to explain the reasons behind this although a number of hypotheses can be safely proposed.

Rachael Low claims that the reason why British film didn't exploit the sensationalist narratives popular at the time was that it aimed very early on for sophistication and respectability.[31] Even so, while there was undoubtedly a trend in British cinema of the 1910s towards a culturally respectable cinema aimed at the audiences of the picture palaces (exemplified by much of Hepworth's work, for instance), there was also a concurrent trend offering a popular cinema to what was probably the largely working-class audience, which also constituted the American serial's principal audience (exemplified by Fred Evans's *Pimple* films). Furthermore, as I have already shown, several of the early British series offered exactly the kind of sensationalist narratives that the American serials did, and clearly did not embody a 'premature sophistication of the cinema'.[32]

Another explanation for the lack of true serials is that the formula became established in American cinema in 1914 when Britain became involved in the First World War, production declined and film imports (particularly from France and America, the two countries specializing in serials) increased dramatically.[33] Furthermore, given the economic state of the British industry during this period and the fact that the production of serials required a larger expenditure of money and a greater total footage than the average feature, it is not surprising that the serial format seemed unattractive.[34]

Conclusions

Clearly a comprehensive account of British series and serials remains to be written; a systematic analysis of the trade press needs to be undertaken and, above all, a large number of missing films need to be found and made available for study. Nevertheless several conclusions can be drawn from my brief discussion. First, there was an extensive production of sequential series in Britain that are worthy of study. Second, the presence of so many differing forms of serial narratives demands that the serial formula (in America as well as Britain) be analysed within the wider context of sequential series production. Third, the range of different strategies employed by these films shows that series and serials emerged for a number of reasons and certainly served functions other than simply helping to bridge the gap between short and feature-length films.

Several conclusions can also be drawn about the characteristics of the sequential series produced in Britain. The series of the 1910s correspond more closely to the serial formula in terms of narrational strategies (sensationalist narratives, aesthetic uncertainty), while the series of the 1920s owe more to the serial's distribution patterns (regular, weekly distribution dates). Few of these sequential series exploited all of these elements to the same degree as their American counterparts, and this perhaps partially explains their neglect by film historians.

Notes

1. Anthony Slide, *Early American Cinema* (New York: Zwemmer-Barnes, 1970), p. 158.
2. Karlton Lahue, *Continued Next Week: A History of the Moving Picture Serial* (Norman: University of Oklahoma Press, 1964), p. xvii.
3. Raymond William Stedman, *The Serials: Suspense and Drama by Instalment* (Norman: University of Oklahoma Press, 1977), p. 7.
4. For a discussion of the *Pimple* series, see Michael Hammond, '"Cultivating Pimple": Performance Traditions and the Film Comedy of Fred and Joe Evans,' in Alan Burton and Laraine Porter, eds, *Pimple, Pranks and Pratfalls: British Film Comedy before 1930* (Trowbridge: Flicks Books, 2000), pp. 58–68.
5. All the subsequent information on titles, dates, plot synopses, etc. has been collated from Denis Gifford, *The British Film Catalogue 1895–1970 —A Reference Guide* (Newton Abbot: David & Charles, 1973–1986) and the British Film Institute's SIFT database.
6. Jane Bryan, *The Exploitation of Elaine: the Serial Queen Melodrama and the American Girl* (unpublished MA dissertation, University of East Anglia, 2000), p. 43; on the depiction of the New Woman in serials, see Ben Singer, 'Female Power in the Serial Queen Melodrama,' in Richard Abel, ed., *Silent Film* (New Jersey: Rutgers, 1996), pp. 163–93.
7. *Lieutenant Daring RN and the Water Rats* and *Lieutenant Daring RN* respectively.
8. Rachael Low, *The History of the British Film, 1914–1918* (London: George Allen and Unwin, 1950), p. 90.
9. Indeed it is the only one to be extensively advertised in *Bioscope*. The final

episode, *Ultus and the Three-Button Mystery*, even gets a double-page advert and full page review (*Bioscope*, 17 May 1917, vol. 35, no. 551, pp. 402–4).

10. *Bioscope*, 25 November 1920, vol. 45, no. 737, p. 80.
11. *Sexton Blake* (Oct 1909) and *Sexton Blake v Baron Kettler* (April 1912).
12. Vicki Callahan, 'Detailing the Impossible,' in *Sight and Sound*, April 1999, vol. 9, no. 4, pp. 28–30.
13. See Ben Singer, 'Serials,' in Geoffrey Nowell-Smith, ed., *The Oxford History of World Cinema* (Oxford: Oxford University Press, 1996), p. 109.
14. Rachael Low, *The History of the British Film, 1906–1914* (London: George Allen and Unwin, 1949), p. 201.
15. *Bioscope*, 17 May 1917, vol. 35, no. 553, p. 606.
16. Ibid., 25 November 1920, vol. 45, no. 737, p. 80.
17. *Kinematograph Weekly*, 10 March 1921, no. 724, p. 81.
18. Singer, 'Serials,' p. 105.
19. Callahan, 'Detailing the Impossible,' p. 28.
20. John Hawkridge, 'British Cinema from Hepworth to Hitchcock,' in Nowell-Smith, ed., *The Oxford History of World Cinema*, p. 132.
21. See the 19th Pordenone Silent Film Festival Catalogue (14–21 October 2000) for full details of release dates for Feuillade's serials.
22. All data has been calculated from the release dates for the individual episodes given in Gifford, *The British Film Catalogue*.
23. *Bioscope*, September–October 1917, vol. 37, nos 571–6.
24. Low, *The History of the British Film, 1906–1914*, p. 97.
25. *Kinematograph Weekly*, 10 March 1921, no. 724, p. 81.
26. Low, *The History of the British Film, 1914–1918*, p. 28.
27. See references in Gifford, *The British Film Catalogue*.
28. National Council of Public Morals, *The Cinema: Its Present Position and Future Possibilities* (London: Williams and Norgate, 1917).
29. See Ben Singer, 'Serial Melodrama and Narrative *Gesellschaft*,' in *The Velvet Light Trap*, no. 37, Spring 1996, pp. 78–80.
30. Hawkridge, 'British Cinema from Hepworth to Hitchcock,' p. 132.
31. See p. 176.
32. Low, *The History of the British Film, 1914–1918*, p. 176.
33. Ibid., p. 40.
34. Lahue, *Continued Next Week*, p. 98.

10

The Spice of the Perfect Programme
The Weekly Magazine Film during the Silent Period

Jenny Hammerton

> Far from seeking an opiate, there is a large body of people who
> want to know more about this crazy, chaotic world . . . Through
> the screen magazine, the thin end of the wedge of knowledge
> could be given to the waiting audiences . . . [However] Its
> constant seeking after the odd and the curious satisfies the
> unintelligent lust for curiosity but achieves nothing.[1]

So complained D.F. Taylor in the *Cinema Quarterly* in the early
1930s—and it was by no means unusual for the weekly magazine film
to be criticized for its frivolousness and lack of depth. But it must have
been a format valued by exhibitors and audiences since virtually all
cinemas in Britain showed these short films as part of their full
supporting programmes during the silent period. In this chapter I will
seek to reclaim this almost forgotten film format as a highly revealing
and historically valuable non-narrative entertainment.

The short weekly films under discussion here were variously known
as 'screen magazines' and 'cinemagazines', although they were occasionally also referred to under the wider banner of 'interest films'. For
the purposes of this chapter they will be referred to as 'cinemagazines'
unless given another name by contemporary sources. I will begin by
describing the basic format of the cinemagazine and looking at how it
was exhibited. I will then go on to examine the typical subject matter

of the cinemagazine and how it was presented to audiences. Finally, I will consider the relationship of the cinemagazine to earlier forms of screen presentation.

The Cinemagazine Format and Exhibition Conditions

> . . . a very large proportion of the population, however much they may enjoy a novel, like to be able to entertain themselves with magazines and newspapers. As a parallel, the same people, regular kinema goers though they may be, definitely demand and appreciate the shorter items.[2]

During the late 1910s and 1920s cinemagoers could expect to see a plethora of short items before settling down for the main feature. Cinemagazines were part of this experience in Britain from 1918 when Pathé released the first issue of the long-running weekly *Pathé Pictorial*. Other British cinemagazines appearing in the silent era include *Eve's Film Review*, *Gaumont Mirror*, *British Screen Tatler*, *Ideal Cinemagazine*, *Whirlpool of War* and *Around the Town*.[3]

The cinemagazine was similar to the newsreel in format. It usually ran for around ten minutes with several separate items within each 'magazine'. These items were not linked by theme or story line but were self-contained entities. The unwritten motto of the cinemagazine was 'variety is the spice of life', and items as diverse as fashion parades, animals performing tricks and demonstrations of household gadgets might be contained in the same issue.

The newsreel was seen as more 'topical' than the cinemagazine. News items were more time-bound than cinemagazine films, turnover was faster and newsreels were produced twice a week to match the practice of programme changes in the cinema during the silent period. Cinemagazines by contrast were produced weekly. Newsreels had a long life in the silent era, showing for three or four days at each cinema; each reel would circulate for several weeks, with cinema proprietors paying less for the newsreel as it became progressively older. The cinemagazine had an even longer life. Cinemagazine items did not age as swiftly as those of the newsreels; they did not feature subject matter which would date them such as state occasions or celebrations. The distribution of cinemagazines was thus a much more leisurely affair. A gentleman who wrote to Pathé in October 1928 asking when he might be able to see an item in which he had appeared was informed that the *Pathé Pictorial* cinemagazine which contained it would be shown for three days at the following cinemas in his local Bristol area:

Triangle	November 5, 6 and 7
Globe	January 25, 26 and 27
Vandyke	February 11, 12 and 13
North Bath Cinema	February 14, 15 and 16[4]

Cinema programmes would usually include a combination of newsreel and cinemagazine items. Some cinemas would show reels from a variety of sources. The Piccadilly Cinema in Manchester, for example, included two cinemagazines and a newsreel in its supporting programme of 1923 (*The Gaumont Graphic*, *Eve's Film Review* and *Topical Budget*), each from a different supplier.[5] The Thatched Picture House in Norwich had both Pathé's silent cinemagazine offerings (*Eve's Film Review* and *Pathé Pictorial*) on the bill in the mid-1920s,[6] which would have pleased Pathé who promoted the reels thus: 'Eve [is] . . . a fitting companion to its Monday release partner—the Pictorial.'[7]

As part of an oral history project investigating cinema-going in the 1930s, Denis Houlston recounted his memories of the 'full supporting programme'.

> . . . looking back at the programmes, there again . . . you got such a load of little bits, you got a big film but then there were all the little bits and I estimate, lookin back, you used to get about seven different shawrt films to, to boost the programme. So [pause] if you didn't liike any of them you didn't suffer very long because they wouldn't be on for very long![8]

Although the main feature would be the biggest drawing factor for cinema patrons at this time, contemporary evidence suggests that other items within the full supporting programme were also enjoyed. In a Sidney Bernstein questionnaire of 1927 it was reported that, 'In reply to the question "Do you like 'News' pictures?", 82¼ per cent of the male patrons voted yes while 87¾ of the female patrons returned the same answer'.[9] The establishment in the mid-1930s of newsreel cinemas that showed shorts and cinemagazines as well as newsreels indicates that these peripheral forms of entertainment were indeed enjoyed. Mr Houlston's recollections confirm the appeal of this sort of material:

Ah mean this is your only way of seeing things happening, the Launching of a Thing, or a crash, or Aa think the Hindenburg went up in flames in those days, Aa might be wrong, and you got the newsreel and that it was really something to see but em nowadays you see it all on television you're blasé so. But Pathé, Pathé news also used to run short films about quarter of an hour or something like that of music-hall acts, a bit of entertainment. You might get a couple in that time and we liked those because you got clowns and eh unicyclists and jugglers which we enjoyed. Aa mean today they wouldn't be of interest. They're all blasé today.[10]

Topicality versus Frivolity

> With regard to the criteria used for differentiating between newsreel and cinemagazine, the basic one is that the newsreel carried 'hard news', while the cinemagazine was more like a colour supplement to today's Sunday newspaper.[11]

Whilst recognizing that the boundaries of the newsreel and the cinemagazine are somewhat blurred, the film trade and commentators of the time clearly saw them as different. To define a cinemagazine as different to a newsreel involves making two distinctions, one concerning content, the other style of presentation. The choice of subject matter of the newsreel revolved around notions of what was 'newsworthy', although, by virtue of its production and exhibition practices, the moving picture newsreel could scarcely match the print newspaper for speed of reporting. The tardiness of some of its items would have been tolerated for the extra dimension of being able to see the news *move*, and later having sound and moving images together. However, what was considered newsworthy for the moving picture newsreel was not necessarily the same as for the news that one would find in a newspaper. As one commentator observed, 'The news obligation is happily trivial. If the newsreels had to cover the news, they would be full of charts on taxes and reports on crop yields. No-one goes to the theatre to get news.'[12] The newsreel was thus limited by the peculiarities of the medium. It could never be just a filmed version of newspaper stories; it had to find its own filmically interesting subjects. Usually these subjects involved movement, the very essence of the 'moving picture' experience. Thus the docking of ships, grand parades and army manoeuvres were the kinds of event favoured by the silent newsreel. The motto of *Eve's Film Review* was 'Fashion, Fun and Fancy', which gives a good idea of the content of cinemagazines in general. The cinemagazine could be seen as more frivolous than the newsreel, with typical subjects including unusual people, clothes, hobbies and travel items. The filmmakers of these short entertainments were engaged in 'searching crazily for the strange and curious'[13] and they purported to offer a glimpse into the many peculiarities of life.

The subject matter of the newsreel was usually presented as 'serious'. A respectful, sombre, impartial tone of reporting was called for, and was achieved through intertitles in silent newsreels. With the cinemagazine the tone of reporting was much less deferential and more often than not commentaries were jokey and intimate. An intertitle in a *Topical Budget* newsreel item covering the funeral of Queen Alexandra in November 1924 illustrates the general tone of address of the newsreel: 'In London the people crowned her death with their grief and the heavens sent her a white shroud.'[14] By comparison, an *Eve's Film Review* item instructing women how to apply false eyelashes has an intertitle typical of the cinemagazine's witty banter: 'Her eyes swept the floor—They could have swept a park had they been aided by this latest beauty fad.'[15] While the newsreel was largely seen as an information source for male cinemagoers, from the general subject matter and from asides in intertitles it is fair to assume that the cinemagazine was addressing itself rather more to the female audience. *Eve's Film Review*, for instance, proclaimed itself to be 'for women' and concentrated on fashion and beauty items.

The distinction between the content and tone of address of cinemagazines and newsreels was not always clear-cut. Both formats strayed across the boundaries from time to time, the newsreel more so than the cinemagazine. The supposedly serious newsreels of the time often carried items which were not time-specific and which contrasted in tone with the seriousness of other items, with titles such as *Musical Dog* (1929), *Wrestling with a Lion* (1930) and *Santa Claus Without His Whiskers* (1921).[16]

It could be that sometimes the subjects that usually fell into the loose newsreel category of 'hard news' were scarce, or it could be that the production company felt that a less serious item would 'lighten' the tone. Peter Baechlin and Maurice Muller-Strauss propose three main categories for newsreel subjects: sudden events of immediate interest; scheduled events; and items of a general interest not necessarily connected with topical affairs. The latter items were those dealing with local customs and traditions, pictures of bathing beauties and 'pin-up girls', religious or traditional festivals . . . in short, all those items which editors keep in reserve for the 'dull' weeks when there is a shortage of items of the first and second categories.[17]

Thus a *Topical Budget* newsreel which featured the launch of the *HMS Nelson* and the destruction of the Shenandoah could also feature 'Amesbury's prettiest girl, Miss Margery Waller' and 'the dog show at Brighton'.[18] It is interesting to note that the items of general interest listed by Baechlin and Muller-Strauss are a fairly accurate guide to the type of subject favoured by the cinemagazine.

The tradition of ending a television news bulletin with a jokey or upbeat story was set in place by early cinema newsreels, as this review of *Gaumont Graphic* issue number 1,815 illustrates:

> The Prince of Wales and 11,000 British pilgrims pay silent homage to our dead at the Menin Gate ceremony at Ypres, and we are shown the impressive two minute silence which marked the solemn occasion . . . A huge fire of six great oil tanks on Wood River, Illinois, and jockeys on the Spree, a diversion on Berlin's river, which brings the issue to an amusing conclusion.[19]

Some critics disagreed with this mixing of tones, one contemporary writer expressing his views thus: 'There should, of course, be a mutual understanding that both types of film must remember their respective places, for this broadening of the field of the newsreel is tending to undermine the interest film.'[20] The cinemagazine was rather more constant in avoiding the serious topics and tone favoured by the newsreel; however we cannot dismiss the form as consisting entirely of 'Fashion, Fun and Fancy'.

A Serious Side to the Cinemagazine?

The editor of *Pathé Pictorial* and *Eve's Film Review* wrote in a press release in 1928:

> We realise our primary business is to entertain, amuse and interest our audiences—though, if at the same time anyone wishes to learn anything new from the pictures (and all of us are able to) he or she is very welcome.[21]

This statement underlines the tension at the heart of the cinemagazine. On the one hand, it had to have the potential to entertain, otherwise the cinema owner would not hire it. On the other hand, many felt that it should educate and inform its audiences at the same time. A comparison with the aims and achievements of the British documentary movement is revealing. This movement is popularly believed to have begun in the late 1920s with the John Grierson school. It is worth remembering, however, that the cinemagazine had been a forum for short, informative films of everyday life since the late 1910s.[22]

Pathé Pictorial had two mottoes in the 1920s, 'Pathé Pictorial puts the World Before You' and 'To See Much is to Learn Much'. Such sentiments were typical of the cinemagazine and its efforts to show audiences the wonders of the world around them. Since it existed outside the exigencies of narrative justification, it was in a unique position whereby almost anything could be shown, and one does get the feeling that 'all human life is here'. The cinemagazine also reached far wider audiences than any of the documentaries made by Grierson and his colleagues.

Writing in 1932, Andrew Buchanan, producer of the *Ideal Cinemagazine*, uses terms that quite explicitly bring to mind the concerns of the 1930s documentarists:

> The fact that the interest reel is non-fictional is its greatest advantage over the dramatic feature. It can bring to the screen places near and far, industries, sports, clothes, everything which constitutes Life, without straining to find a reason for doing so.[23]

For those more closely associated with the documentary movement, however, the cinemagazine failed to make the most of its didactic and edificatory potential. Writing in *Cinema Quarterly*, a magazine with close links to the documentary movement, D.F. Taylor launched an assault on the cinemagazine for its insistence on 'a low form of entertainment', characterized by 'a dash of industry, a dash of beauteous countryside, two dashes of fashion and a lacing of cabaret to give the reel a kick'.[24] He wanted the producers of cinemagazines to place a much greater emphasis on educating and informing their audiences:

> through the magazine, we have an aid to a socially conscious cinema. It has a journalistic format, and as such it is of value. We

want to elevate it from the ranks of 'Tit-Bits'; we want to make it a weekly review of the world.[25]

What is evident in Taylor's argument is a familiar suspicion of both popular culture and feminine culture. While the cinemagazine might not have dealt with such issues as social problems, slums and unemployment, this did not mean it was divorced from the process of educating and informing. Many *Eve's Film Review* items, for instance, document the reality of women's lives with a didactic seriousness. For example, many of the items showing women at work eschew the usual humorous titles and merely document the tasks performed. *Flower Girls of Lincolnshire* (1929) shows women picking, bunching and packing daffodils. *Light on Turkish Delight* (1924) documents women working in a sweet factory. Home sewing tips are given in *Odds and Ends* (date unknown, early 1920s).[26] Handy housekeeping advice is found in items such as *Eve's Home Hint—A Silver Cleaning Tip* (1921), techniques for making things for the home are demonstrated in *Sealing-wax Stunts* (1930) and timesaving devices are demonstrated in *Gadgets!* (1929). The idea of the cinemagazine as a 'window on the world' is also apparent in items about women in other countries such as: *Fishergirls of Ostend* (date unknown, 1920s), *The Bride of the Black Forest* (1929) and *Miss Japan Takes Up Billiards* (1929). As an accompaniment to the feature, which often portrayed a fantasy life out of reach of most of the cinema audience, the cinemagazine could offer a slice of comparative reality and could educate and enlighten as well as entertain.

Cinemagazines and the 'Cinema of Attractions'

The cinemagazine has a strong relationship with the earlier mode of filmic representation identified by Tom Gunning as the 'cinema of attractions'.[27] His findings are important when we look at the cinemagazine as a screened entertainment that existed outside the conventions of the narrative film. Gunning offers a way of approaching early film that does not see it as merely the forerunner of a purer, more systematic mode of representation that emerged with the dominance of the narrative film and continuity editing. He draws attention to elements of early film representation that are not precursors to what has come to be known as 'classical cinema'. He also claims that with the burgeoning of narrative that began around 1906–7 the cinema of attractions was forced to go 'underground' into certain avant-garde practices and as a component of narrative films such as the musical. It is my contention, however, that elements of the cinema of attractions remained highly visible within the 'full supporting programme' and, in particular, within the cinemagazine.

(i) Showing rather than telling
Cinemagazine items are firmly based on the cinema of attractions' predilection for showing rather than telling. This is a non-narrative form where rather than being told a story, we are shown something: a scenic view, the latest fashion in footwear or a four-year-old child driving a car in the streets of Paris. These items are presented as glimpses of the many facets of human experience.

The cinemagazine fashion item illustrates very well Gunning's notion of the supply of pleasure through spectacle that characterizes the cinema of attractions. It is ostensibly the clothes that are shown to the audience in these short fashion parades, although the women who model the clothes are also on display. Other items that do not centre around clothes also feature elements of spectacle such as the *Eve's Film Review* items that feature sportswomen and that focus on the beauty of movement. The woman's body as spectacle is emphasized in a *Bioscope* review of *Eve's Film Review* issue 375: 'the camera interview is with Misses Russell, Bengleburg, Rennie and Vandegoes, with slow motion pictures of the grace and precision these Empire Eves employ in swimming.'[28]

(ii) Direct address to the audience
Gunning also identifies in the cinema of attractions a particular relationship to the audience that differs from that of the classical mode of representation. This is typified by 'the recurring look at the camera by actors'.[29] Gunning observes that this look became taboo within the dominant mode of representation, only occurring now and again in moments of excess in the musical or in comic asides to camera. But the look at the camera is also a feature of the cinemagazine and newsreel. Although in the newsreel the look is usually naive (a person who notices the camera, for example), within the cinemagazine it is more often a 'knowing' look, an exhibitionist look. It is an address to the spectator that says, 'look at me—I am showing you something'. These looks occur in abundance in the cinemagazine, especially among the fashion display items. In an *Eve's Film Review* item entitled *Hair Fashions* (*c.*1921), a woman poses with a feather fan looking seductively at the camera and by implication at the audience [see Plate 18]. As

Plate 18. 'Hair Fashions', from *Eve's Film Review* (Pathé, 1921)—the direct look at the camera

Gunning observes, the acknowledgement of the spectator as voyeur in this form of direct address can often give these moving images an intense erotic power.[30]

(iii) The cinematic apparatus itself as an attraction
Gunning notes how, in the early days of cinema, the machinery of cinema was in itself an attraction. Audiences would come to see developments in technology rather than to view specific films. It seems to me that the cinemagazine provided a forum outside of the main feature film where experiments with the medium could continue to take place. Of *Pathé Pictorial* and *Pathétone Weekly* (a sound cinemagazine which began in 1930), an uncredited author writes:

> every camera development and novelty may be said at one time or other to have originated in various forms through the medium of these weeklies. The cartoon vogue, slow motion, stop motion, colour sections, reverse photography, multiple exposure novelties, sporting series, fashion and all forms of industrial and scientific progress have been featured.[31]

Although one might challenge the idea that some of these innovations actually originated within the cinemagazine (recall the trick photography of Georges Méliès, for example), it is true to say that they continued to be used in the cinemagazine rather than disappearing from the screen altogether. *Eve's Film Review* items such as *The Lens Liar* (*c.*1921) foregrounded the possibilities of the cinematic medium through a demonstration of various camera tricks. *The Keep Fit Brigade* (1927) used optical printing to superimpose a group of women over a shot of a man with his arm outstretched making it seem as though they were dancing on his arm. Slow-motion photography was used in many dance, sport and 'girls at play' items. The cinemagazine might in this sense be thought of as the research and development section of the film industry. With no narrative restrictions or diegetic effect to maintain, such self-conscious devices were totally acceptable and the cinemagazine became the site of playful experimentation.

(iv) The concept of variety—a series of discrete attractions
The early, short films that Gunning speaks of in terms of the cinema of attractions found their niche within the variety programmes of vaudeville, music hall and fairgrounds, in which a trick film may have been shown between a farce and an actuality. The cinemagazine too finds itself sandwiched between other items on the cinema programme including newsreels, cartoons, adverts, serials, short features and the main feature. The cinemagazine is thus one among the many attractions of the cinemagoing experience of the late 1910s onwards.

There is also variety within the cinemagazine itself. In fact, variety could be thought of as the *modus operandi* of the cinemagazine. Unconnected items are shown side by side without any attempt to link them together and can be understood without reference to their neighbours.

Conclusion

The cinemagazine was a form within which elements of the cinema of attractions survived and flourished. It could deal with a much wider range of subject matter and use more experimental techniques than the narrative film with its striving for 'realism'. The form seemed to scoop up all those bits and piece that early filmmakers relished, but which had been gradually pushed to the edges of the main feature: travel items, semi-pornographic displays of the female body, music hall acts and so on. Although these aspects were often made a part of feature films of the time, the narrative might strain to incorporate them. In the cinemagazine, these attractions were there to entertain and sometimes to inform without any justification or attempts to weave the spectacle into a narrative. Using techniques that had disappeared from the narrative film, the cinemagazine often foregrounded the process of filmmaking resulting in an interactive relationship with its audience.

As a filmic entity that exists outside the conventions and boundaries of the narrative form, the cinemagazine is a rich and fertile source of enlightenment as well as entertainment. A surprising number of these films still exist (around 2,400 individual silent cinemagazine items survive at British Pathe, for example). The cinemagazine offers a fascinating insight into 'real life' through its documentary style. We can learn a great deal about how life was lived in the past and can discern much about the way non-narrative films were constructed before what became known as the British documentary movement came into being. Far from being an 'opiate for the people' the cinemagazine is a complex and fascinating format worthy of a great deal of further investigation.

Notes

1. D.F. Taylor, 'Screen Magazines,' *Cinema Quarterly*, Winter 1933–4, p. 93.
2. Anon., 'Hints to the Programme Builder,' *Kinematograph Weekly*, 28 March 1926, Newsreels and Shorts Supplement, p. 3.
3. The British Universities Film and Video Council publish a chronological guide to newsreels and cinemagazines produced in Britain up to 1990. Published in the form of a poster, the guide was one of my main sources of information about cinemagazines produced during the silent era. For a more detailed survey of *Eve's Film Review*, see Jenny Hammerton, *For Ladies Only? Eve's Film Review: Pathé Cinemagazine, 1921–33*, Hastings: The Projection Box, 2001.
4. Letter in the *Pathé Pictorial* and *Eve's Film Review* correspondence file in the British Pathe archives.
5. Details from a programme for the Piccadilly Cinema, Manchester, 2 April 1923, from the file 'Cinema Ephemera: Regions/Manchester Piccadilly Picture Theatre', Special Collections, British Film Institute National Library.
6. Advertisements for this cinema in the *Eastern Daily Press* regularly mentioned cinemagazines as well as the main feature during October 1925.
7. 'Just "Pic and Eve" by Editor Watts,' press release in the *Pathé Pictorial*

and *Eve's Film Review* correspondence file. This press release is a fascinating insight into the aims of the creator of these cinemagazines; it was written in response to a memo dated 24 October 1928 from a Mr Judge of First National Pathé Limited asking Mr Watts to write an article on the production policy of the two cinemagazines. Some of the material in this press release was used in a much later article, 'World's Best Variety Talent in Pathe Periodicals,' *Kinematograph Weekly*, 14 November 1935, p. 25.

8. Extract from transcript T95-18 quoted in Annette Kuhn, 'Memories of Cinema-going in the 1930s,' *Journal of Popular British Cinema*, Issue 2, 1999, p. 102. The transcriptions attempt to convey a sense of the interviewees' voices so regional pronunciations are spelt phonetically.

9. Anon., *Bioscope*, 4 August 1927, p. 20. (It seems that the question 'Do you like "News" pictures?' would have referred to cinemagazines and short 'interest' films as well, since all the other questions related to the feature film.)

10. Extract from transcript T95-18 quoted in Kuhn, 'Memories of Cinema-going in the 1930s,' p. 102.

11. James Ballantyne of the British Universities Film and Video Council, in a letter to the author, 20 December 1993.

12. *Motion Picture Herald*, 26 May 1945, quoted in Peter Baechlin and Maurice Muller-Strauss, *Newsreels Across the World* (Paris: United Nations, 1952), p. 30.

13. Taylor, 'Screen Magazines,' p. 93.

14. Quoted in Luke McKernan, *Topical Budget: The Great British News Film* (London: British Film Institute, 1992), p. 121.

15. *Eve's Film Review* item entitled *Eyelashes While You Wait* (1930).

16. *Musical Dog—British Movietone News*, 2 December 1929; *Wrestling with a Lion—British Movietone News*, 27 March 1930; and *Santa Claus Without His Whiskers—Topical Budget*, 15 September 1921.

17. Baechlin and Muller-Strauss, *Newsreels Across the World*, p. 19.

18. *Topical Budget* issue 732 reviewed in Anon., 'The Week's Short Stuff,' *Kinematograph Weekly*, 10 September 1925, p. 29.

19. Anon. 'Short Features,' *Bioscope*, 15 August 1928, p. 40.

20. Andrew Buchanan, *Films, The Way of the Cinema* (London: Pitman, 1932), p. 197. Buchanan was the producer of the *Ideal Cinemagazine* which ran from 1926 to 1938.

21. From 'Just "Pic and Eve" by Editor Watts,' p. 1.

22. An interesting link between the 'serious' documentary makers and the 'non-serious' cinemagazine makers can be seen in a letter in the Pathé correspondence file from Frederick Watts to Major Creighton of the Empire Marketing Board. An extract reads: 'Very many thanks for your kind remarks regarding our work for you. We are pleased to hear it has proved so satisfactory. I trust to have the pleasure of doing more work for

you in the near future, which you may rest assured will have my personal attention.' The letter is dated 30 October 1929 so it seems that the Empire Marketing Board used the same team that made the 'frivolous' cinemagazine to make films for propaganda purposes before establishing their own documentary filmmaking department.

23. Buchanan, *Films, The Way of the Cinema*, p. 187.
24. Taylor, 'Screen Magazines,' p. 93.
25. Ibid.
26. Usually cinemagazine items can be dated by issue numbers or accompanying paperwork. Sometimes stock marks are used to date films (in these cases the abbreviation c. is used). In some cases there are no discernible stock marks.
27. Tom Gunning, 'The Cinema of Attractions: Early Film, its Spectator and the Avant-Garde,' in Thomas Elsaesser with Adam Barker, ed., *Early Cinema: Space, Frame, Narrative* (London: British Film Institute, 1990), pp. 56–62.
28. Anon., 'Short Features,' p. 40.
29. Gunning, 'The Cinema of Attractions,' p. 57.
30. Tom Gunning, 'An Unseen Energy Swallows Space: The Space in Early Film and its Relation to American Avant-Garde Film,' in John L. Fell, ed., *Film Before Griffith* (Los Angeles: University of California Press, 1983), p. 359.
31. Anon., 'World's Best Variety Talent in Pathe Pictorials', *Kinematograph Weekly*, 14 November 1935, p. 25.

11

Shakespeare's Country
The National Poet, English Identity and British Silent Cinema

Roberta E. Pearson

Shakespeare and Stratford's Dominant Image

In 1926 British cinema audiences were treated to *Shakespeare's Country*, an episode in the series *Wonderful Britain* (a Harry B. Parkinson Production for British Screen Classics). The film begins with an intertitle: 'Shakespeare found success in London—but his heart, from his earliest days, was in his native Warwickshire. In the little village of Wilmcote, lived Mary Arden his mother.' We see an exterior of a stone house, followed by a dissolve to a gate in a stone wall, then another intertitle: 'And in the country around Stratford on Avon there breathes the very spirit of the Bard.' A shot of a bridge over the river Avon is followed by a shot from one of the riverbanks. The rest of the film consists of similarly pretty 'chocolate box' shots of an old-fashioned, cosy England composed of thatched houses, cottage gardens and half-timbered buildings. I will argue that this travelogue, together with several other contemporary travelogues as well as newsreels about Shakespeare and Stratford, forms part of the 1920s discourse about the national poet and English national identity. These films show that Shakespeare is not for all time but for an age, his image constantly reconfigured to suit the needs of specific historical periods, as I have already illustrated in my work on Shakespeare and the American silent cinema.[1]

To confirm my argument, I shall relate these films to the period's dominant image of Shakespeare as seen in Shakespeare biographies and criticisms, as well as travel books. I focus on travelogues and newsreels, rather than, with one exception, the period's fiction films (adaptations or reworkings of the plays). I do this for two reasons. First, non-fiction cinema receives far less attention than fiction films. Second, more people may actually have seen these films than the fictional ones. They formed a regular component of the weekly cinema programme, and the travelogues, though not the newsreels, which might date, tended to remain in circulation for quite some time.

Like *Shakespeare's Country*, much Shakespearean commentary from the turn of the twentieth century to the inter-war years connected Shakespeare's heart with the heart of England in Stratford and the surrounding Warwickshire countryside. William James Rolfe claimed in 1897 that 'the county of Warwick was called the heart of England as long ago as the time of Shakespeare'.[2] In 1911, Reginald R. Buckley wrote that Shakespeare 'was an Englishman to the core, born in the heart of England, and living in the hearts of Englishmen'.[3] The same year, the reigning poet laureate, John Masefield, claimed that 'Shakespeare's heart always turned for quiet happiness to the country where he lived as a boy'.[4] And this country epitomized the ideal of a pleasant, timeless, rural England. In a copiously illustrated book about Shakespeare and Stratford, Emma Marshall described the surroundings in which the poet spent his boyhood:

> We may trace his footsteps in Warwickshire in the very heart of Old England . . . The flowers still grow in the shady lanes and hedges with which he makes his plays fragrant . . . The country is still peaceful with far-stretching woods and slow streams, and tall trees; while in flower-strewn meadows the meek-eyed cows stand knee-deep in buttercups and daisies.[5]

Although Shakespeare left his village in the heart of England to seek fame and fortune in the southern metropolis, period writers often saw Stratford as having a far more profound influence upon Shakespeare than London. In *Shakespeare's Avon*, Ernest Walls asserted that the poet

> came back in middle age to his home town and settled down . . . just as if London, the Globe Theatre, the Court, the plays and the sonnets had never been . . . The study of Shakespeare involves in no small measure the study of Stratford. If ever that great heart is unlocked it is here that the key will be found.[6]

People had been seeking the key to Shakespeare's heart in Stratford since the middle of the previous century. Actor David Garrick's 1769 Shakespeare Jubilee was the first event to celebrate the poet's birthplace, but in the nineteenth century, concomitant with the forging of nationalism and the invention of tradition discussed by such scholars as Benedict Anderson and Eric Hobsbawm, Stratford claimed an increasingly prominent place in the national psyche and the tourist circuit.[7] After a fund drive headed by Charles Dickens the Shakespeare birthplace house was purchased for the nation in 1847. Only a year later, travel writer William Howitt suggested that 'Stratford appears now to live on the fame of Shakespeare. You see mementoes of the great native poet wherever you turn.'[8] In 1860 the opening of a branch railway line increased Stratford tourism to such an extent that the tercentennial jubilee of 1864 attracted an estimated thirty thousand visitors. The Shakespeare Memorial Theatre, largely funded by the Flowers family of brewery fame, opened in 1877, beginning a run of summer Shakespeare festivals that continues to this day. The Shakespeare Birthplace Trust, headed by Oxford Professor of English and Shakespearean scholar Sidney Lee, was established by Act of Parliament in 1891 and the Trust purchased Anne Hathaway's cottage in 1892. By 1910 the Shakespeare Memorial Theatre offered one five-week Spring Season and one three-week Summer Season. In 1919 the Shakespeare Memorial National Theatre Committee helped to fund the establishment of the first permanent repertory company at the Memorial Theatre which would eventually evolve into the Royal Shakespeare Company (RSC). When the 1877 theatre burned down in 1926, a national competition was held for a design and the new theatre, which opened in 1932, is still in use by the RSC.[9] In the Stratford of the inter-war years, as in the Stratford of 1848, you could see mementoes of the great native poet wherever you turned.[10]

Stratford's emergence as a requisite stop on the tourist circuit and the Shakespearean Canterbury can be readily explained in terms of the attractions it offered. By 1877 tourists could not only visit the Shakespeare birthplace, Anne Hathaway's cottage and several other Shakespeare monuments, but also see plays at the Shakespeare Memorial Theatre. By contrast, London, the site of Shakespeare's professional life and theatrical triumphs, offered little if anything to tourists eager for material artefacts. The Globe Theatre, together with all the other unworthy scaffolds on which the players of Elizabethan and Restoration England had enacted the poet's work, had long disappeared. No theatre in the country's capital regularly staged

Shakespeare's plays, which, in fact, constituted a relatively small proportion of the city's theatrical offerings. Bankside, in Shakespeare's day the home of thieves, prostitutes and bear baiting as well as the city's theatres, remained a rather insalubrious neighbourhood until the late twentieth century when the opening of the new Shakespeare's Globe and other attractions began its transformation into a tourist venue. The British Museum, with its collection of First Folios, Quartos and other documents, was the sole place in London to bask in the poet's aura.[11] But the rejection of London and the exaltation of Stratford and the countryside with which the films under consideration accord had ideological as well as pragmatic motivations. The films' construction of Shakespeare as a country gentleman, divorced from the religious, economic and political upheaval of a newly modern London and safely ensconced in the heart of a traditional Merrie England, related directly to the image of the English countryside so central to the period's concept of English national identity, an image promulgated as well by much British silent cinema. Before turning to a discussion of several films, then, it is necessary to sketch the connections between English national identity, the English countryside, Shakespeare and the English silent cinema.

In *English Culture and the Decline of the Industrial Spirit*, Martin J. Wiener argues that 'the increasingly dominant image of the nation' circulating during the nineteenth and twentieth centuries rejected industry and the cities in favour of a 'myth of an England essentially rural and essentially unchanging [that] appealed across political lines both to Conservatives and Imperialists, and to anti-Imperialists, Liberals, and Radicals.'[12] This myth became especially attractive after the First World War, when 'fascination with old country life, real or imagined, spread throughout the middle class . . .'[13] Such a retrograde vision perfectly suited a populace seeking solace in the face of the period's social upheavals—labour unrest, economic depression, post-war trauma. And the vision was located not simply in the past but in the imagery of a specific region: the English South, with its thatched cottages, rose gardens, half-timbered buildings and gently rolling hills scattered with fluffy white sheep, all of which Stratford and its environs epitomized. By contrast, London, with its dense fogs, crowded streets and the supposedly stunted and unhealthy denizens of its slums, epitomized all the evils of modernity.

Reginald R. Buckley's 1911 book, *The Shakespeare Revival and the Stratford-Upon-Avon Movement*, for example, argued that art could no longer flourish in the nation's cities: 'The habitual amusement of our deformed and defiled cities no longer is pleasurable to normal people.'[14] Buckley was appropriating Shakespeare for the revival of 'folk' studies, local archaeology and county history which, according to Robert Colls, 'fixed the nation on populist lines of race, language, and tradition . . . not according to what its people were doing (or might do) but according what they had been and were . . . (and could not be any other).'[15] Buckley dubbed Shakespeare 'the standard-bearer of the race through the ages' and argued that 'because all the arts seem to have come together in Shakespeare . . . he is to be taken as the very centre of the Merrie England Movement'.[16] Central to this Movement was the 'campaign against the unloveliness of modern life' with which Buckley contrasted the 'life and beauty' that lived 'in the Festival town on the Avon'.[17] In that Festival town on the Avon, wrote Mary Neal in an essay on 'Folk Art' in the same book,

> on a summer's day, with the Theatre doors open on to the river, radiant in sunshine, and with its pollard willows making a delicate green shadow, and with one's ears full of the rhythm of Shakespeare's verse, one might well be back in the days when men saw in all beauty . . . some symbol of the gods they worshipped. And there is no jar between the play inside its walls and the surroundings in which one can walk between the acts and after the play is over, all is so different from the crowded city street into which so many theatres open in other places. Here all is peaceful and idyllic, and helpful to the best understanding of our national drama.[18]

Travelogues and Newsreels

As I stated at the outset, the vision of Stratford constructed by Neal and other writers strongly accords with that constructed in the period's newsreels and travelogues. Take, for example, H.V. Morton's meditation on the English countryside, *In Search of England*, which Martin J. Wiener tells us was the most successful of a series of post-war books on the same theme. Morton devotes a chapter to Stratford that not only accords with the dominant discourse outlined above, but also in parts bears a strong resemblance to a 1925 Hepworth Manufacturing Company travelogue, *Stratford on Avon*.[19] On first driving through the town in his motorcar, the author was dismayed by signs of modernity and even Americanization, changes that would have appalled anyone taking Stratford as the heart of Merrie England. Stratford contained 'a perfect death-rattle of motor traffic', 'a rash of trippers', and 'chars-a-banc from everywhere . . . piled up in the square'. Perhaps most shocking of all was the fact that 'this town is the very heart of the core of the American's England', 'full of long-legged girls from America, and sallow fathers and spectacled mothers' and Yankee tourists crass enough to ask, 'Say, guide . . . is it known how much Shakespeare made out of his plays?'[20]

Yet two places in Stratford remained the same, unsullied by trippers, or Americans or commerce, unchanged since the days when the Swan of Avon himself had roamed among them.

> One was a mossy seat on the high wall of Holy Trinity churchyard overlooking the Avon. This is . . . one of the supremely English views. It seems as you sit there with the willows dipping to the river, beyond, on the opposite bank, great freckled meadows, and in the air the sound of water rushing past the old mill, that all the beauty and peace of the Warwickshire countryside have been packed into one riverscape. And the woods by the river, they, too are unchanged . . . And this is the place where you will meet Shakespeare . . . It was evening when I went there on a real pilgrimage, and it seemed that Oberon and Titania had just hidden behind the great trees; that Mustard-Seed and Peas-Blossom had withdrawn into their acorn cups at the sound of footsteps.[21]

Morton's musings in the Holy Trinity Churchyard and the woods by the Avon strongly parallel the conclusion of the Hepworth *Stratford on Avon*. The travelogue's final shots contain a sequence in the Holy Trinity Churchyard, as the camera pans slowly right over the gravestones. An intertitle says, 'And when night has drawn her curtain, one can picture the characters created by Shakespeare hovering near his immortal spirit'. The following shot shows superimposed ghostly figures: an old man and a young man (Polonius and Hamlet?) and then a woman standing next to a man who gestures to the heavens. The travelogue's and Morton's similar situating of Shakespeare's immortal spirit in Stratford most likely results not from the writer's having seen the film but from the two texts' conformance to the period's dominant image of the national poet. But the travelogue conforms as well to the themes of Englishness, heritage and the countryside prevalent in much 1920s cinema.

As both Andrew Higson and Kenton Bamford have shown, due partly to the need for product differentiation from the American cinema and partly to cultural fears about Americanization, the English cinema of the 1920s seemed obsessed with Englishness.[22] This obsession resulted in the production of heritage films that focused on the past rather than the present—on the English countryside, English country houses and aristocratic characters, the films constructing England as an old country of fields, hills and hedges rather than a modern country of cities and industrialization. Contemporary evidence shows that those in the film industry perceived a great desire amongst audiences for such a Merrie England. According to the critic Iris Barry, one director from the period suggested that, 'if you really wanted to tickle your audience, really get them, you needed to do two things, and two things only. You had to give them sheep. And you had to give them running water.'[23] A book on the cinema advised that cheap and effective themes were 'children and dumb animals, the countryside and the sea.'[24] The most important of the British newsreel producers, *Topical Budget*, also promulgated Englishness through its annual coverage of events associated with English institutions: church, state, sport, Oxbridge and Shakespeare. For example, every April *Topical Budget* filmed newsreel segments on the Boat Race, the Blessing of the Palms ceremony at Westminster Cathedral, the FA Cup Final, Maundy Monday and, most importantly for our purposes, the Shakespeare birthday celebrations at Stratford.[25] The National Film and Television Archives (NFTVA) hold viewing copies of three *Topical Budget* newsreels devoted to Shakespeare: two cover the annual Stratford birthday celebrations—*Soviet's Salute to Shakespeare!* (1926) and *To Shakespeare's Memory* (1927)—while the third concerns the burning down of the Shakespeare Memorial Theatre in 1926. The archive also contains viewing copies of the *Pathe Gazette*'s *The Shakespeare Memorial Theatre Foundation Stone Laying at Stratford on Avon on July 2nd, 1929* and the *Gaumont Graphic* sound newsreel *Shakespeare's Birthday* (1930). These newsreels resulted as much from the film companies' needs to film regularly scheduled events as from the centrality of Shakespeare to English national identity, and they focus more on the great and the good gathered in the poet's honour than on Stratford itself. But the NFTVA also holds non-topical travelogues not limited to a week's distribution that do focus on Stratford, portraying the town in ways that correspond with the period's Shakespearean commentary, Stratford travel writing and heritage cinema.[26]

One of the most interesting of these is the Gaumont Film Company's 1922 *Around The Town, Series 110*. The first title reads 'Shakespeare revisits Stratford on Avon' and is followed by a figure of a man in Elizabethan costume (doublet, hose and ruffed collar). The second reads 'Members of the Will Shakespeare Company paid a visit to Stratford on Avon where they went over some of the scenes of the play'. Then we see Shakespeare walk in from the rear of the next shot, sit on a stone bench and assume a melancholy pose, in the background a half-timbered house, probably Shakespeare's birthplace. The film seems to be a staging of scenes from Clemence Dane's 1921 play *Will Shakespeare: An Invention in Four Acts*,[27] since it seems reasonable to conclude that the Will Shakespeare Company that visited Stratford in 1922 is the same company that had been performing the Dane play in the West End since 1921. And if this is indeed the case, then the choice of Stratford as location and the selection of the play's opening scenes for re-enactment provide support for my hypothesis concerning the centrality of Stratford to the period's dominant image of Shakespeare. Unlike many of the factual and even fictional intertexts of the period, Dane's play deals primarily with Shakespeare's London life, rather than his Stratford years. At the play's start, actor-manager Philip Henslowe lures the young Shakespeare away from Anne Hathaway and Stratford to fame and fortune in London. Shakespeare initially expresses some doubt about the great city, as in the following dialogue.

> Henslowe: Is not Thames broader than Avon?
> Shakespeare: Muddier.
> Henslowe: But a magical water to hasten the moult, to wash white a young swan's feathers.
> Shakespeare: Or black, Mephisto!

The contrast between the broad and muddy Thames, capable of blacking the young Swan of Avon's feathers, and the narrower, clearer Avon, metonomyically catches the period's contrasting images of Stratford and London. But in the play, Shakespeare departs for the big city, abandoning his pregnant wife and returning only upon the death of his child. The newsreel stages only those scenes set in Stratford, presenting the town as a series of touristic postcards: the afore-mentioned scene in front of the birthplace; Shakespeare saying goodbye to his wife in front of 'the famous 300 years old cottage of Anne Hathaway'; a long shot of Shakespeare and Henslowe walking across a famous old bridge over the Avon. The remainder of the play's scenes, set amidst the theatres and taverns of a tumultuous Bankside, would not have accorded nearly so well with the Merrie England, country gentleman Shakespeare of the period or with heritage cinema. But the play itself, which seems to have been a commercial success judging by the newsreel's re-enactment of key scenes, does provide a rare counterbalance to the dominance of Stratford in Shakespeare's contemporary image, as if the London stage was attempting to reclaim one of its own.

Of the other three travelogues available for viewing at the NFTVA, one, *Shakespeare Land*, produced by Kineto Ltd in 1910, dates from before the First World War. The film features the heritage sites of Warwickshire. Kenilworth Castle is shown as a glorious, gothic pile with arched mullioned windows intact in the ruined walls, surrounded by grazing sheep. Guys Cliff Mill in Warwick is first seen in long shot from across a river. Clearly, the film's director held to the view that cinema audiences loved sheep and running water. In Stratford, the film gives us the requisite tourist sites: Anne Hathaway's cottage; Holy Trinity Church; Shakespeare's birthplace; the King Edward VI Grammar School the poet attended; and the Shakespeare Memorial Theatre. The film ends with more water and more sheep, a tracking shot of the Avon showing the woolly animals grazing on its banks. The other two travelogues, from the 1920s, are Stratford pilgrimages, showing the Shakespearean shrines by now familiar to generations of British and American tourists. The Hepworth *Stratford on Avon* begins with a long shot of the town, the river and the Holy Trinity spire visible in the distance, the instantly identifiable scene reproduced in countless commodified views. The following intertitle makes the standard claim for the importance of Stratford to the poet's work: 'The River Avon . . . Inspiration of Artist and Poet . . . on whose banks nestles the home of the Greatest Poet, William Shakespeare.' Then follows a surprisingly lengthy tracking shot of the Avon from a boat, much like the phantom rides popular earlier in the cinema's history. The film continues with the requisite shots of the birthplace, the Grammar School, Anne Hathaway's cottage, the Memorial Theatre and streets lined with half-timbered buildings, and ends with a sequence including the superimposed figures in Holy Trinity Church-yard discussed above. The third of the travelogues is the *Shakespeare's Country* from 1926 with which I began this chapter. Like the others, the film dwells on thatched cottages, half-timbered houses and the usual tourist venues—Anne Hathaway's cottage ('famous throughout the world'), the Grammar School (where the young are 'schooled in the lore of *Pericles, King Lear, King John* and *Richard the Third*') and so on. As well as showing the typical Stratford and environs scenes, the film stresses antiquity, stability and continuity with the past. Inside Anne Hathaway's cottage 'all is snug and warm and secure against the worst of Tempests'. The Old Red Horse Inn has hosted Shakespearean pilgrims for the past century, including the ubiquitous Americans, among them, Washington Irving, the writer. Sydney Court dates back to 1500 and Tudor House to 1460, while the Guild Chapel is 'venerable in age'. Social relations, too, remain unchanged from those of Shakespeare's plays. 'At the Shakespeare Hotel errant husbands may wistfully discuss the Taming of the Shrew' for the hotel is 'an ideal place in which to quaff, and smoke and gossip and make Much Ado About Nothing'.

Two other newsreels in the NFTVA's collection relate only to Shakespeare and not to Stratford, but they too attest to the imbrication of the national poet, English identity and a backward-looking vision of the English countryside. The lengthy reel *Education Week—Newcastle on Tyne* (1911) appears to be one of a series of films made to publicize the efforts of local educational authorities and shows classroom activities at all levels within the Newcastle schools. In one sequence, students of about age 11, dressed in Elizabethan costuming that from its professional appearance may have been provided by the filmmakers, perform a scene from Shakespeare in an outdoor setting. Several of the performers gather around a cooking pot over a fire, while two more enter from screen right, one supporting the other. When the two have entered, another of the students then appears to deliver a speech. The textual evidence would suggest that the students are performing Act 2, Scene 7 from *As You Like It*, in which the clown Jaques delivers the famous Seven Ages of Man speech. Despite the fact that Newcastle was one of the country's most important industrial cities, its students must go to the countryside to perform a Shakespearean scene that is itself set in a forest. No attempt here at updating Shakespeare to make him relevant to the students' contemporary concerns. The second non-Stratford newsreel is *Twelfth Night* (Gaumont Graphic, 1916), in which 'the inmates of the Bournbrook Military Hospital enjoy an open air performance of Shakespeare's comedy'. The patients sit in the hospital's pleasant, garden-like grounds watching the actors perform what appears to be Act 2, Scene 3 of the play, in which Malvolio reproaches the carousing Sir Toby, Sir Andrew and Feste. The national poet's work, performed in a setting reminiscent of the English countryside, serves as a tonic for convalescent soldiers, physically traumatized while serving their country in the Great War. This brief newsreel presages the uses that would be made of Shakespeare during the traumatic interwar years, when much of the nation turned to the past to forget its present.

Old Bill Through the Ages

The final film that I wish to discuss is not a newsreel or travelogue but a fiction feature, *Old Bill Through the Ages* (Ideal Films, Thomas Bentley, 1924), based upon the well-known war cartoons of Captain Bruce Bairnsfather, who wrote the script. In the film, the titular character, private soldier Old Bill, enjoys a rich meal of tinned lobster and falls asleep over a copy of *The History of England from Norman Times*. He dreams an anachronistic *Black Adder* history featuring sequences in which he becomes William the Conqueror, a feudal baron and a courtier of Good Queen Bess sent to bring Shakespeare from Stratford to London. As with the films discussed above, the film attests to the strong relationship between a backward-looking vision of English national identity and the national poet. Alun Howkins describes the emergence of a sense of national identity predicated upon an idealized view of rural England. 'Central to this ideal were the ideas of continuity, of community or harmony, and above all a special kind of classlessness.'[28] Old Bill begins with a description of what it takes to be the men at the centre of this idea of continuity, community and a special kind of classlessness. The first set of titles states:

> There is an heroic figure symbolic of the average Briton, symbolic of the average everyday man who catches his train and does his job, loves his wife and spanks his children, symbolic too with his modest heroisms and good humoured patience of the real stuff, both warp and weft, of which the gorgeous tapestry of our History has been woven through the centuries.

The background changes to show a Union Flag with the superimposed title, 'The Great War was the last proof of his sterling qualities.' The title then fades into a mid-shot of a steel-helmeted, fag-smoking Tommy. Another title follows. 'But the Great War proved that there were millions like him.'

The notion of an Englishness vested in 'ruralism and the South Country' became especially salient, Howkins asserts, for the young officers on the Western Front, giving them a

> model society—an organic and natural society of ranks, and of

inequality in an economic and social sense, but one based on trust, obligation and even love—the relationship between the 'good Squire' and the 'honest peasant.' It was a model that admirably suited the relationship between the young infantry Subaltern and the sixty or so men under his command.[29]

This feudal relationship is clearly that enjoyed between the typical private Old Bill and his progenitor, Captain Bairnsfather, referred to in an intertitle as 'the father of that great Bairn Old Bill'. It is Bairnsfather's gift of tinned luxuries that precipitates Old Bill's dream and his stolen book that provides its content. Shakespeare too provided a model of proper social order in the trenches of the Western Front, as the lower ranks continued to behave in the time-honoured fashion of their forebears, grumbling but nonetheless performing their duty, just as did Old Bill. Literary critic Arthur Quiller Couch asserted during the war that English patriotism drew upon the spirit of Merrie England, residing in the 'cheerful irony of the English private soldier'.[30] The aptly named Shakespearean scholar Walter Raleigh asserted that this 'cheerful irony' could be traced to the Bard himself. 'The wit of our trenches, especially perhaps among the Cockney and South Country regiments, is pure Shakespeare'.[31] How appropriate then, that the great Bairn Old Bill, whose dialogue intertitles identify him as probably hailing from London or the South, dreamt of Shakespeare as a result of a meal and a book provided by his 'father' Captain Bairnsfather.

While the ideological positioning of *Old Bill Through the Ages* corresponds with that of the films discussed above, the film treats Shakespeare less than deferentially, the comedy deriving in part from forcibly inflicting the chaos of the twentieth century upon the strongly established connections between Shakespeare, the countryside and the past. In the film's Shakespeare sequence, Queen Elizabeth 'great in Literature no less than Arms . . . sends Old Bill to summon Master William Shakespeare to beguile her court'. In the next shot Old Bill, dressed in Elizabethan garb, runs down a modern roadway, past a signpost indicating the routes to Stratford and to London. The film cuts to a shot of Shakespeare (iconically correct in wide white collar and cuffs, moustache and goatee) who sits in a wood-panelled study, his right hand holding a book, his left hand propping up his head. Here we have the scholarly aesthete safe in his seventeenth-century country retreat, but he must soon contend with the twentieth century as personified by Old Bill. The film returns to Bill as he runs after and then boards a modern bus for Stratford. An accident violently precipitates him into the kitchen of Shakespeare's home, where he asks an outraged Anne Hathaway in his best Cockney, 'Is Mr. Shakespeare at 'ome?' When the poet sees the destruction wrought by the soldier, he exclaims to his wife, 'Why, oh, why did you let that air raid policy lapse?' Shakespeare then helps his wife clean up with a manually operated vacuum cleaner. More anachronisms follow. When Shakespeare hands Old Bill a copy of *Venus and Adonis*, the soldier remarks 'This one's barred the public libraries. It's got an A certificate.' At Elizabeth's court, Old Bill instructs Shakespeare to tell them 'that one about Richard III—the dirty dog wot done in them two Barnardo boys in the Tower'. When Shakespeare begins to recite *Romeo and Juliet* with the declamatory poses of the nineteenth-century actor, Bill in a cutaway points to his head in the classic 'he's nuts' gesture. Finally, Bill inflicts the ultimate indignity upon Shakespeare by blowing him up with a Mills bomb. In the Shakespeare sequence the 'cheerful irony of the English private soldier', Shakespeare-inspired though it may be, gets the better of the revered national poet, wrested from the countryside and the past. The inclusion of Shakespeare in Old Bill's dreamt pageant of the nation's history reaffirms the poet's centrality to the period's concept of national identity, but the film shows that the poet was not always accorded the reverence displayed in the newsreels and travelogues discussed earlier. While I have for good reason focused on non-fiction film in this essay, it would be well worth while examining other fiction films in light of my hypothesis concerning Shakespeare's ideological positioning in the British silent cinema.

Notes

1. See William Uricchio and Roberta E. Pearson, *Reframing Culture: The Case of the Vitagraph Quality Films* (Princeton: Princeton University Press, 1993).
2. William James Rolfe, *Shakespeare, The Boy* (London: Chatto and Windus, 1897), p. 3.
3. Reginald R. Buckley, *The Shakespeare Revival and the Stratford–Upon–Avon Movement* (London: George Allen & Sons, 1911), p. 108.
4. John Masefield, *William Shakespeare* (London: Oxford University Press, 1911), p. 65.
5. Emma Marshall, *Shakespeare and His Birthplace* (London: Ernest Nister, no date but circa 1900), n.p.

6. Ernest Walls, *Shakespeare's Avon* (Bristol: J.W. Arrowsmith Ltd, 1935), p. 147.
7. See Eric Hobsbawm and Terence Ranger, eds, *The Invention of Tradition* (Cambridge: Cambridge University Press, 1983); and Benedict Anderson, *Imagined Communities: Reflections on the Origin and Spread of Nationalism* (London: Verso, 1983).
8. William Howitt, *Visits to Remarkable Places* (London: Longmans, Green, and Co., 1888, condensed version of two-volume work originally issued in 1848), p. 37.
9. Some of this information can be found in Gary Taylor, *Reinventing Shakespeare: A Cultural History from the Restoration to the Present* (London: The Hogarth Press, 1990). The rest I have gathered from a variety of nineteenth- and early twentieth-century sources, since, surprisingly, there seems to be no published history of the Stratford/Shakespeare connection.
10. For information on the current Stratford tourist scene see Barbara Hodgdon, *The Shakespeare Trade* (Philadelphia: University of Pennsylvania Press, 1998).
11. Stratford itself barely acknowledged that its favourite son had lived and worked in the metropolis. The 1925 *Catalogue of the Books, Manuscripts, Works of Art, Antiquities and Relics Exhibited in Shakespeare's Birthplace* contains a myriad of documents and artefacts from Shakespeare's Stratford days, but only two items related to London and the Globe; an imaginary picture of the interior of the Globe from a painting by George Pycroft and 'A View of London as Shakespeare knew it,' a reproduction of the famous 1616 view of London by C.J. Visscher. Frederick C. Wellstood, *Catalogue of the Books, Manuscripts, Works of Art, Antiquities and Relics Exhibited in Shakespeare's Birthplace* (London: Oxford University Press, 1925), p. 20.
12. Martin J. Wiener, *English Culture and the Decline of the Industrial Spirit, 1850–1980* (Cambridge: Cambridge University Press, 1981), pp. 1, 5.
13. Ibid., p. 6.
14. Buckley, *The Shakespeare Revival*, p. 181.
15. Robert Colls, 'Englishness and Political Culture,' in Robert Colls and Philip Dodd, eds, *Englishness: Politics and Culture 1880–1920* (London: Croom Helm, 1986), p. 47.
16. Buckley, *The Shakespeare Revival*, pp. 42, 65.
17. Ibid., pp. xi, 118.
18. Mary Neal, 'Folk Art,' in Buckley, *The Shakespeare Revival*, p. 191.
19. Wiener, *English Culture and the Decline of the Industrial Spirit*, p. 7.
20. H.V. Morton, *In Search of England* (London: Methuen and Co. Ltd, 1927), pp. 210–13.
21. Ibid., pp. 212–13.
22. See Andrew Higson, *Waving the Flag: Constructing a National Cinema in*

Britain (Oxford: Clarendon Press, 1995) and Kenton Bamford, *Distorted Images: British National Identity and Film in the 1920s* (London: I.B. Tauris Publishers, 1999).

23. Iris Barry, *Let's Go to the Pictures* (London: Chatto and Windus, 1926), pp. 240–1, quoted in Bamford, *Distorted Images*, p. 10.

24. Kenelm Foss, *Cinema, A Practical Course* (London: Standard Art Book Co., 1920), p. 20, quoted in Bamford, *Distorted Images*, p. 10.

25. Luke McKernan, *Topical Budget: The Great British News Film* (London: BFI Publishing, 1992), p. 70.

26. For a full list of viewing and archive copies of Shakespeare related newsreels in the NFTVA, see Olwen Terris and Luke McKernan, eds, *Walking Shadows: Shakespeare in the National Film Archive* (London: British Film Institute, 1994).

27. Clemence Dane, *Will Shakespeare: An Invention in Four Acts* (London: William Heinemann, 1921). Luke McKernan informs me that many of the films in the 'Around the Town' series were indeed devoted to contemporary West End plays.

28. Alun Howkins, 'The Discovery of Rural England,' in Colls and Dodd, p. 75.

29. Ibid., p. 80.

30. Arthur Quiller Couch, *Studies in Literature* (London: Cambridge University Press, 1918), p. 294, quoted in Peter Brooker and Peter Widdowson, 'A Literature of Their Own,' in Colls and Dodd, p. 117.

31. Walter Raleigh, *Shakespeare and England* (London: British Academy Annual Lecture, 1918), p. 5, quoted in Brooker and Widdowson, 'A Literature of Their Own,' p. 117.

12

Representing 'African Life'
From Ethnographic Exhibitions to *Nionga* and *Stampede*

Emma Sandon

> The Poly has been making box-office successes of these films to the extent of record runs . . . This is proof to the world that in London alone exists a large white public interested in the life of his coloured brethren.[1]

So enthused Hay Chowl about films of 'ethnographic' interest in a special issue of *Close Up*[2] dedicated to promoting 'Negro Art for the Cinema'. Two of the films successfully screened by the Polytechnic Theatre on Regent Street in central London were British travel films: *Nionga* (Stoll, 1925), made by missionaries in central Africa,[3] and *Stampede* (British Instructional, 1929), made by adventurers Major C. and Stella Court Treatt in southern Sudan.[4] Both films were shot on location using indigenous performers, and claim to show 'native life'. According to Chowl, *Nionga* moved beyond the 'picturesque' to deal with the 'delicate fabric of humanity', yet

> the dramatic moulding was never obtrusive enough to parody the natives' psychology and rob us of their naivete and simple charm which has always drawn us to these films as a relief from the sexual saturation of the white man's drama.[5]

Stampede was also praised in the pages of *Close Up* for its documentation of 'African life'.

Close Up was not the only journal to promote the films. On its theatrical release four years earlier, *Nionga* was described by *Bioscope*, a trade paper, as 'a great improvement upon the conventional patchwork travel productions'; the reviewer evidently enjoyed the portrayals of 'natives', noting that 'the heroine is a comely and charming little person, and among the players of minor roles are many striking native types'.[6] *Kinematograph Weekly*, the other key trade paper of the period, judged the film to be well made, with excellent camerawork and good curiosity and novelty value, giving 'a vivid insight to the customs, rites and superstitions of primitive Central African tribes of the Tanganyika and Congo districts'.[7] Following its launch, introduced by the Court Treatts, in January 1930 at the London Hippodrome, *Stampede* received the following review from *Bioscope*: 'The photography is excellent and the editing and continuity of the film makes it a subject which should prove of unusual interest. The female interest is capably sustained by a charming dusky maiden.'[8] *The Times* pointed out that '*Stampede* is to be enjoyed and remembered not as a love story or a morality play, but as a film in which animals not men, however brilliantly and unconsciously they acted, were the real heroes'.[9] Clearly the films appealed on their release through their exotic subject matter, their location shooting and their aesthetic accomplishments.

These contemporary reviews do not sit comfortably beside retrospective assessments of *Nionga* and *Stampede*. Historians have approached the two films through a comparison with better-known north American ethnographic films of the period, such as *Nanook of the North* (Flaherty, 1922) and *Grass* (Cooper and Schoedsack, 1925), films which pioneered subjective and participant observation aesthetics. In this context, the British films are usually considered inauthentic and more like fiction than non-fiction.[10] The argument I am making in this paper is that to understand their appeal at the time it is necessary to look at them in relation to earlier cultural practices in Britain, both filmic and non-filmic. Whilst neither of the two films can be viewed today as lost masterpieces of 1920s British cinema, they reveal the extent to which their filmmakers drew on the existing aesthetics of live ethnographic representations and displays and early actuality films through their combination of dramatized re-enactment, performance and what we would now call documentary. The films can be seen as adaptations of the kinds of representations of 'African life' seen by British visitors to colonial and missionary exhibitions, live theatre performances and museum displays during the late nineteenth century and early twentieth century. These practices were taken up in photography, lantern slides and early film, especially in the form of travelogues and re-enactment actualities, and eventually found their way into these British travel films. Narratives of 'the everyday life of African tribes and peoples' were familiar to audiences in Britain and in London in particular. The novelty of the films was in how these narratives of racial difference were presented and the fact that they were shot on location in Africa.

Nionga

Nionga, at 5,000 feet, runs for just over an hour. The story is a melodrama about how superstitious beliefs can bring death, war and unhappiness to 'primitive' peoples in Africa. This Christian morality tale, based loosely on the story of Adam and Eve's fall from paradise, is interwoven with extensive footage of village life and natural landscape, scenes of comic relief and exotic performances. Focusing on a young couple, Nionga and Masari of the 'Molungo'[11] tribe, who are betrothed to be married, the film depicts their downfall when they seek fortune and happiness through consulting the witchdoctor, Katoto. Katoto, seizing the opportunity to revenge himself on 'Kimana' villagers who discredited him, tells the couple that, in order to secure their happiness for the future, Masari should lead an attack on the tribe. Masari, thus tricked, sets fire to the Kimana village but is killed when they retaliate. Nionga is sacrificed by her father, the Chief Kaieye, to appease the spirits and to restore peace.

Apart from the Christian structure of the story, the mode of address of the film is constructed within an evolutionary discourse. One of the appeals of this story is its presentation of 'African life' as a 'primitive' existence in contrast to the 'civilized' world of the film's audience. This effect is achieved formally on a number of levels. *Nionga* uses a range of stylistic forms and strategies of address drawn from early travelogues, scenics, live performance, comic drama and the direct address of the fairground entertainer. As Miriam Hansen has pointed out, this kind of composite film, which mixes documentary and comic dramatic styles within an overall narrative format, allows for a diversity of viewer interests rather than attempting to absorb the viewer through action alone.[12]

The film opens with titles that draw on the manner of a fairground entertainer:

Our patrons must not look for the skill and artistry of the well
known film stars in this drama of the crude life of simple people.
Some idea of the difficulties overcome in producing *Nionga*
may be realized when it is known that rehearsals alone occupied
three years! *Nionga* was made in the almost unexplored Lake
Tanganyika district in Central Africa. The players were until
recently cannibals and are still unfettered, cruel and warlike.

Such expository titling directly addresses the spectator throughout the
film with humorous comments on the activities presented, very much
in the style of live narration in early cinema;[13] dialogue is only briefly
introduced in intertitles on a couple of occasions. Comic relief is also
provided through vaudeville dramatic techniques that audiences would
have been familiar with, such as the use of stereotypical characters like
Katoto who directly engages with the audience like a villain in a
pantomime.

The film positions the spectator as a traveller at the beginning of the
film, in the tradition of scenics and travelogues, through the use of the
'phantom ride' device, a moving viewpoint which has its antecedent in
popular fairground entertainments. The spectator travels in a boat
down river to what an intertitle describes as the 'heart of Africa'. The
'phantom' shots and closed-down lens suggest that the protagonists
and the activities shown are seen from the narrational point of view of
the traveller/spectator, who will 'glimpse into the minds of savages', as
the opening titles promise. During the ride, the camera captures
panoramic scenes of nature such as the 'Victoria Nyanza Falls'[14] and
other waterfalls, people and villages on the river banks, and men in
boats, until we reach the village. Once in the village the style of filming
changes. These scenes are shot in tableau style involving frontal
display.[15] This presentational conception of space and address—found
in theatrical staging, magic lantern shows, cartoons and postcards—
offers an observational viewpoint that does not introduce the spectator
into the narrative space of the characters.[16] The film is shot in natural
light; the camerawork is generally static, like still photography, with
wide shots filmed from waist height; although occasionally the camera
pans to follow characters. People are often framed showing the entire
body, while the villagers are grouped face to the camera, as if for a
photographic portrait. Each scene presents aspects of everyday life,
such as social relationships, meals, fishing and hunting, craft making,
sporting activities and celebrations. For example, the men of the
'Molungo' tribe are shown melting iron to make spear heads and then

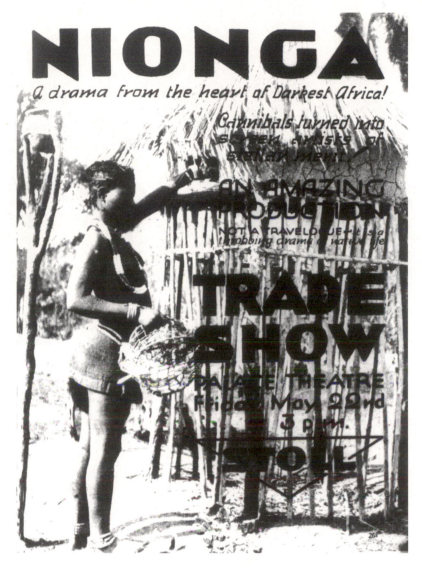

Plate 19.   Advertisement for *Nionga* (Stoll, 1925)

engaged in archery practice; the 'Luama' men are shown bringing in a fishing catch and the women scaling and drying the fish [see Plate 20]. The sets, costumes and furniture in the shape of leopard skins, carved seats and drums, all give the air of an 'authentic' Africa. From the evidence of *Bioscope's* advice to exhibitors on the release of *Nionga* —'special attention should be paid to the musical setting which should

Plate 20.   The 'Luama' tribe fishing: *Nionga* (Stoll, 1925)

be of a wild and barbaric nature'—music probably added to the
exoticism of the viewing experience.[17]

Through the titles, visual puns and jokes, the 'primitive' activities
presented in the film are compared to those of 'modern' life. Some of
these comparisons are humorous, identificatory and empathic, whilst
others are judgemental and distance the spectator. All seem designed
to make the spectator feel superior. The opening shots of the film,
for example, introduce Chief Kaieye presiding over a dispute over
bride-price, and the titles make a joke about wives and what they are
worth. The footage of Maca, the 'Luama' chief, sitting outside the huts
having a meal with his family, who eat with their hands and share their
food from a bowl, is accompanied by the title 'Dinner is informal!'
The practice of decorative art, scarification, is explained by the title
'insensible to pain the girls adorn their backs with curious designs'.
When Masari is chased and his pursuers see his footprint in the dust, a
joking reference is made to Robinson Crusoe. These familiar imperial
images play on evolutionary notions of the scientific lineage from apes
to man.

Plate 21. The 'Dance of the Fetishes': *Nionga* (Stoll, 1925)

Ethnography was one of the ways in which naked bodies could be viewed without moral censure in Britain and *Nionga's* presentation of people with little clothing is often intended to be erotic. For example, on several occasions when the women are shown with naked breasts, the titles make overt reference to their sexual desirability. The footage of dancing, in the staging of the 'Dance of the Fetishes', the male warrior displays and the female 'saribanda' dance, provides the opportunity to show lengthy sequences of exotic spectacle for the audience [see Plate 21].

Stampede

Stampede, at 7,200 feet, runs for about an hour and three quarters.[18] It opens with titles that suggest a narrative of destiny and natural selection: 'Here we show you the adventures of a wandering tribe in the African forests. In their battles with fire, famine and beasts of prey you may perhaps see a symbol of Man's eternal struggle of existence.'

The film's portrayal of 'native life' is adapted from that familiar genre of the popular romantic adventure story, the 'Arabic tale'. It tells the story of Boru, who is adopted into the 'Habbania' tribe after his mother is killed by a lion, to grow up with the Sheikh's son, Nikitu. The two friends are secret rivals for the love of Loweno, a young girl they both befriend. Nikitu by right of birth seems destined to marry Loweno. When the tribe is forced by drought to migrate across the desert to a more fertile place, however, destiny intervenes and Nikitu and his father are killed in a forest fire. Boru, naturally selected through his bravery and leadership, becomes Sheikh of the tribe and is able to marry Loweno. The Darwinian logic of the tale is symbolized throughout the film through the theme of hunting. The men hunt for food and for survival and there is footage of a snake hunt, a lion hunt and an elephant hunt.

Formally, *Stampede* is much closer than *Nionga* to classical narrative cinema. The use of point of view shots and shot/reverse shot structures encourage identification with the characters within the narrative. Much of the narration is carried visually, while the titles are usually used to convey dialogue. The footage of the journey across the desert is clearly motivated by the actions of the protagonists. There is often close framing, which increases spectator involvement with the action, and some scenes use inter-cutting and parallel editing to increase the suspense and action of the film. Music and sound effects, according to *The Times*, were also carefully integrated through synchronization.[19]

At the same time, like so many travelogues, interest films and cinemagazines of the period, *Stampede* also uses devices that derive from the early cinema of attractions. There are extended sequences of scenics in which people, wildlife and the environment are portrayed. There are trick images and stunts such as a shot of a snake about to drop from a tree onto a baby, a shot when Boru runs through the forest fire and a shot of a mirage, an example of a scientific 'wonder of nature' or of the 'magic' of photography. There is a comic sequence when two men engage in a tug-of-war over a donkey in a slapstick style and there is a lot of footage of performances such as horse racing and dancing, shots and scenes which are not integrated into the narrative. Tom Gunning has pointed out how certain early cinema devices have persisted in avant-garde practices, and certainly some of the editing of *Stampede* is experimental and can be seen to have been influenced by avant-garde and modernist practices in European filmmaking of the time. One dancing sequence, for instance, builds up in rhythm from slow to frenzied dancing, with footage of women in a trance-like state inter-cut with that of a male piper rolling on the floor. In a similar vein, the comparison between the 'primitive' life of the people and

Plate 22.   Native life as exotic: *Stampede* (Court Treatt, 1929)

animal life is made not through titling this time, but through a montage of visuals. For example, at the beginning of the film Boru is being carried by his mother and the scene is inter-cut with images of a monkey and its baby. As Hansen has noted, parallelism in early film enabled a conceptual or moral point to be made and implied a different form of spectatorship to that encouraged by parallel editing in classical film.[20]

Like *Nionga*, *Stampede* also portrays 'native life' as exotic and exciting, and the filmmakers evidently cast performers they thought audiences would find attractive.[21] At the same time, and again like *Nionga*, *Stampede* retains a strong moralistic and evolutionist perspective in the construction of its narratives of 'primitive' man.

The Tradition of Ethnographic Exhibitions

As Ella Shohat and Robert Stam have observed, the visualization of other cultures in cinema had its social origins in the world fairs of the late nineteenth and early twentieth centuries.[22] *Nionga* and *Stampede* were produced at a time when live ethnographic narratives and performances in large exhibition spaces in London and other cities of Britain were just coming to an end. *Nionga* was released in 1925, the year of the British Empire Exhibition at Wembley, one of the last exhibitions to have peoples from the colonized regions of Africa and other parts of the world presenting their 'native life' to audiences. These live representations of 'African life' had been a very popular element of Victorian and Edwardian leisure, particularly from the 1890s onwards, at the height of imperialism when Britain had acquired territories in the African continent. The forms these representations of other cultures took combined those found in theatrical shows and museum displays.

Indigenous people had been employed to stage dramas of 'native life' in museums and colonial and imperial exhibitions since the 1850s. These performances often combined staged re-creations of weddings, funerals, hunts, wars and religious rituals involving dancing, alongside re-enactments of everyday activities such as cooking and craft making. Barbara Kirshenblatt-Gimblett, in her study of museum displays, cites the example of Charles Dickens writing in 1847 about the bushmen who were presented at the Egyptian Hall, William Bullock's museum in London, acting out aspects of hunting scenes.[23] Another newspaper report she quotes is from 1852, of an African display at St George's Gallery at Hyde Park Corner, which created a whole drama of 'Caffre life' including meals, a witchfinding meeting, a wedding, a hunt and battles between rival tribes performed by Zulus from Natal.[24] The representation of 'African life' in *Nionga* and *Stampede* bears a close resemblance to these live performances. *Nionga* shows the everyday life of the village, in scenes of a proposed marriage, a marriage dispute, a visit to the witchdoctor, meals, sporting activities, crafts and fishing. *Stampede* covers less in the way of everyday activities, but the theme of hunting is central to its story of the life of the 'tribe' of the Sudan.

Whilst museum displays focused more on representing the 'everyday life' of other cultures, theatres tended to concentrate on performance-based aspects of 'native life', and in London theatres and music halls we can find many examples of shows of dancing combined with re-enactments of battles. At the London Hippodrome in 1905 Batwa Pygmies, brought to England by the explorer and hunter Lt Col. J. Harrison, were featured for a season.[25] This was a venue owned by Stoll, who later produced *Nionga*; it was at the same venue that *Stampede* had its West End opening in 1929. At the Olympia Earls Court, re-enactments of the Matabele wars were performed in 1899 in an immensely popular show, *Savage South Africa*, by a troupe of performers shipped over from South Africa; the show was later transformed for the Greater British Exhibition.[26]

These live performances had a direct influence on early film practice in that film companies often recorded live events. The Warwick Film Company is reported to have filmed sections of *Savage South Africa*, and there are other examples of performances like this being filmed by commercial companies.[27] In keeping with this tradition *Nionga* and *Stampede* both include long sequences of staged performances and dancing. It is not just in the filming of existing events but in the idea of 'staging' real events for the camera that we can trace the influence of live theatrical displays on films. As Hansen points out, many actualities involved 'dramatic re-enactments of current events [that] were considered legitimate'.[28] Drawing on the theatrical tradition of staging re-enactments of colonial wars, the Hove filmmaker James Williamson, for instance, filmed local reconstructions of battle scenes reported in the press at the turn of the century.[29] The staged battle scene inserted into the narrative of *Nionga* can therefore be seen as a continuation of a strategy used in early actualities.

The colonial and international exhibitions created some of the most spectacular ethnographic displays through the combination of both museum practices and theatrical performances. The parallels we can draw between these shows and the way in which the films stage 'native life' are striking. A key aspect of the exhibition experience was the notion of travel, which is central to the experience of spectatorship in *Nionga* and implied in *Stampede*. Exhibitions created this travel experience by building different 'villages' in the halls for visitors to walk around; in the larger exhibitions there were even trains and other forms of transport to take passengers around the sites.[30] The reconstructions of 'native' villages were large enough to allow indigenous performers to act out quotidian activities as well as stage re-enactments of colonial wars. In some of the exhibitions, between fifty and two hundred people lived in the villages, where they were given raw materials to build houses and foodstuffs to prepare, and they were called on to perform rituals and special activities at particular times. For the Greater British Exhibition in 1899, for instance, about two hundred Zulus were brought over with their families and visitors paid to visit their kraal. At the Franco-British Exhibition in 1908 the French section presented Senegalese in a village, and in 1911 the Coronation Exhibition represented people from East and West Africa and included a Somali village, whose contingent performed war dances and demonstrated fighting techniques. Both *Nionga* and *Stampede* used village sets on location to stage their 'dramas of native life'. Although much of *Nionga* was filmed in existing villages, a set is used in one scene, while a complete village was built for *Stampede*.[31]

The producers of both the exhibitions and the two films were concerned to promote the realism of their representations. The reference to real people rather than professional actors found in the films' opening titles reproduces similar claims to those made in the literature and promotional materials for the exhibitions. In both we find the use of props and costumes to authenticate 'African life', although the use of artefacts was often not indigenous to the culture portrayed. The exhibitions were keen to distinguish their displays from theatrical shows, as Annie Coombes found in the literature of the French Exhibition at Earls Court in 1890. The exhibitors described their act by a Somali Arab troupe as a 'life picture' and the programme assured the audience that what was being presented was not a mere imitation or a 'show' but an illustration of 'Life in Africa'.[32]

Earlier, I distinguished between *Nionga* and *Stampede* in terms of their modes of narration and address and again we can find a parallel with the exhibitions. Coombes draws attention to important distinctions between the purpose and appeal of colonial exhibitions and missionary projects. The colonial exhibitions presented a different image of Africa and Africans to that of the missionary societies. They were organized by entrepreneurs, were trade orientated and attracted millions of visitors. They were more concerned with creating narrative coherence in their exhibition spaces than with the authentic representation of the cultures they were exhibiting. Often the material artefacts they displayed were included for their dramatic and spectacular impact and they staged more performances and re-enactments of wars than the missionary exhibitions. They appropriated aspects of popular colonial fiction to set their visitors up as adventurers, travellers and explorers. The missionary exhibitions on the other hand were aimed at raising financial and moral support from lower- and middle-class congregations and were targeted especially at women and children. Attendances at their exhibitions, which often ran over a period of months, were still large but more in the hundreds of thousands. The missionaries who organized these events were usually evangelical[33] and their exhibitions were sensationalist and endorsed an evolutionary perspective. Yet missionaries were also regarded as serious ethnographers and their collections were seen as credible by experts, collectors and academics. The missionary shows attempted to give more emphasis to presenting Africans as skilled artisans, as in the Africa and the East Exhibition in 1909, where African participants in the village were seen practising crafts and household activities. The missionary groups, with support from prominent members of the Liberal Party, were keen to emphasize their humanitarian purpose in serving imperial interests, while the colonial exhibitions were a pure celebration of imperial rule.

If we look again at the two films, we can see that *Nionga*, made by missionaries, mixes its melodramatic narrative of superstition, witch-craft and human sacrifice with a considerable amount of footage devoted to presenting the everyday life and activities of the tribes. The casting of Katoto, the witchdoctor, as a comic villain, takes the edge off a moralistic tale and the film appeals to the audience to take pity on the 'savages' who know no better and are indeed capable of redemp-tion. *Stampede* on the other hand is more sensationalist and less interested in portraying the cultural aspects of the society. Based on a popular colonial fiction model, its themes are adventure, conquest and action and it involves more romanticism and sexual voyeurism. Its action scenes are more typical of the physical shows of strength that were common in colonial exhibitions. Its narrative gives more room to fate and destiny, rather than appealing to human intervention in the name of 'God'. In *Stampede* it is natural events, such as famine and drought, that cause the migration of the tribe and it is the fittest who survive. Education, ethics and moral choices do not have a role to play in its sub-text.

This difference in moral tone was picked up by some film critics, although their comments were couched in terms of authenticity rather than ethics. *Stampede* received some dismissive reviews from American film critics on its release; the *New York Times* found it 'lacking spontaneity and truth', whilst *Variety* described the narrative as telling of 'the tough times folks in Sudan have chasing waterholes'.[34] *Nionga* as far as I know did not receive any negative reviews. This reflected the increased concerns of American critics with the 'authenticity' of representations of 'native life' in the late 1920s, stemming from a preference for the more subjective aesthetics of emerging American documentary as well as reflecting a shift in attitudes towards racial difference, which were not immediately evident in Britain.

The Consolidation of Documentary Aesthetics

These two relatively modest colonial travel films of the 1920s can be seen as indicative of four important trends in film history. First, they demonstrate the extent to which film routinely draws on pre-existing cultural practices. Second, they show that the longer films of the 1920s were very often little more than compilations of strategies and subject matter drawn from earlier short films, held together by a more or less coherent narrative framework. Or, to put it another way, they underline the fact that the feature film still retained strong elements of the cinema of attractions. Third, both *Nionga* and *Stampede* illustrate the shift from the dominance of non-fiction or actuality filmmaking in the early period to the dominance of narrative cinema in the classical period. Fourth, and somewhat paradoxically, these films also point to the consolidation of a distinctive European documentary film practice that runs in parallel with the narrative feature film.

Nionga's use of tableau staging and framing situates it in relation to a European rather than American documentary tradition. Noël Burch, for instance, has argued that the tableau framing of early Lumière films was bound up with a quasi-scientific attempt to capture a moment as in a still photographic view.[35] Charles Musser also traces the lineage of documentary and by implication ethnographic narratives to photography, via lantern slides. His example is that of Robert Flaherty, who used slides to lecture on Eskimo life before moving to film with *Nanook of the North*.[36] However Musser's account of the development of documentary practices favours those films which show the new 'mode of perception' implied by the subjective aesthetics of participant observation. Such an account overlooks the emergence of broader documentary practices, especially in Britain, which adopted a less subjective and more distant observational gaze at the documentary subject.[37]

Nionga and *Stampede* both adopt this quasi-scientific aesthetic in their attempt to retain a distant observational rather than subjective viewpoint. These 'objective' stylistic devices draw both on the engagement with artefacts found in photography and early actuality films and on live representations in museums and exhibitions. Films used by scientists and anthropologists in the observation of 'native types' adopted a presentational style in order to imply an evidential purpose. Felix Louis Renault, for instance, used film as a record at the 1895 Exposition Ethnographique de l'Afrique Occidental,[38] while A.C. Haddon took film equipment on the Cambridge anthropological expedition to the Torres Straits in the South Pacific in 1898, from which he brought back footage of performance and quotidian activities. There are several other ways in which the more distanced observational spectatorship evident in the films was similar to the viewpoint encouraged in museums and exhibitions. Framing and staging are important but so also are the comparative structures both films use, which are similar to the comparative structures embedded in museum and exhibition display practices. Such structures are designed through their portrayals of primitive life to show evidence of the different stages of evolutionary development between races of man and between man and animals and they create the effect of comparing the modern to the perceived pre-modern.[39] Rather than seeing *Nionga*'s and *Stampede*'s objective aesthetics as evidence of an anachronistic and unimaginative British attachment to 'primitive' modes of production, as Low argues,[40] it makes more sense to see the films as examples of attempts to retain a 'scientific' method in filmmaking, a method which became incorporated into documentary aesthetics, and which brought with it specific moral and ethical effects.

Notes

1. Hay Chowl, 'London and the Negro Film,' *Close Up*, vol. 5, no. 2, August 1929, p. 128.
2. *Close Up*, founded in 1927, was one of the first critical journals on film in Europe. For further details, see Jamie Sexton's chapter 18 in this volume.
3. The film is in the National Film and Television Archive (NFTVA), London. It was probably made by evangelist missionaries; the London Missionary Society and Church Missionary Society were active in Central Africa, though *Bioscope*, 28 January 1926, p. 72, suggests that it was made by Jesuits.
4. An incomplete copy of the film is held in the NFTVA.
5. Chowl, 'London and the Negro Film,' p. 127.
6. *Bioscope*, 18 June 1925, p. 35.
7. *Kinematograph Weekly*, 28 May 1925, p. 56.
8. *Bioscope*, 22 January 1930, p. 29.
9. *The Times*, 25 February 1930, p. 10.
10. See Rachael Low, *The History of British Film, 1918–1929* (London: Allen and Unwin, 1971), pp. 289–90, and *The History of the British Film 1929–1939, Films of Comment and Persuasion of the 1930s* (London: Allen and Unwin, 1979), pp. 70–1; and Paul Rotha, *Documentary* (London: Faber, 1936), p. 81.
11. The names of the tribes and protagonists in this film are not authentic.

12. Miriam Hansen, *Babel and Babylon: Spectatorship in American Silent Film* (Cambridge, Massachusetts and London: Harvard University Press, 1991), p. 48.

13. See Charles Musser, 'The Travel Genre in 1903–4: Moving Towards Fictional Narrative,' in Thomas Elsaesser with Adam Barker, ed., *Early Cinema: Space, Frame, Narrative* (London: BFI, 1990), p. 123.

14. This titling confuses Lake Victoria Nyanza with the Victoria Falls.

15. See Noël Burch, *Life to those Shadows*, translated and edited by Ben Brewster (London: BFI, 1990); and Tom Gunning, 'The Cinema of Attractions: Early Film, its Spectator and the Avant-Garde,' in Elsaesser, ed., *Early Cinema*.

16. Hansen, *Babel and Babylon*, p. 35.

17. *Bioscope*, 28 January 1926, p. 72.

18. There are forty minutes of viewable material. Other sections of the film can be seen in Bruce Connor's *A Movie* (1960), for which he used 'found' footage from a print of *Stampede*. The Court Treatts also produced another film from the footage they shot in the Sudan, *Stark Nature* (Pro Patria, 1930), and Stella Court Treatt published two books, *Sudan Sand* (London: Harrap, 1930), an account of the filming and *Stampede* (London: Hutchinson, 1930), a novel from which it is possible to construct the plot of the missing sections.

19. *The Times*, 8 January 1930, p. 10.

20. Hansen, *Babel and Babylon*, p. 137.

21. Court Treatt, *Sudan Sand*, p. 80.

22. Shohat and Stam, *Unthinking Eurocentrism, Multiculturalism and the Media* (London: Routledge, 1994), p. 106; see also Fahimah Tobing Rony, *The Third Eye* (Durham and London: Duke University Press, 1996), p. 36.

23. Kirshenblatt-Gimblett, 'Objects of Ethnography,' in Ivor Karp and S. Levine, eds, *Exhibiting Cultures, The Poetics and Politics of Museum Display* (Washington, DC: Smithsonian Institute, 1991), p. 405.

24. Ibid.

25. Brian V. Street, 'British Popular Anthropology: Exhibiting and Photographing the Other,' in Elizabeth Edwards, ed., *Anthropology and Photography* (New Haven and London: Yale, in association with the Royal Anthropological Institute, 1992), p. 126.

26. See Ben Shepard, 'Showbiz Imperialism: The Case of Peter Lobengula,' in John Mackenzie, ed., *Imperialism and Popular Culture* (Manchester: Manchester University Press, 1986).

27. Andrew D. Roberts, 'Films on Africa in British Archives,' paper presented to the *Images et Colonies Magreb Noire au regard du cinema colonial 1895–1962* conference in Paris, 1994), p. 1. See also his 'Africa on Film to 1940,' in *History in Africa 14* (Wisconsin: Madison, 1987), pp. 189–227; and Emil De Brigard, 'The History of Ethnographic Film,' in

Paul Hockings, ed., *Principles of Visual Anthropology* (The Hague: Mouton Publishers, 1975), p. 18; and John Barnes, *The Beginnings of Cinema in England, 1894–1901: Volume Five, 1900* (Exeter: University of Exeter Press, 1997), p. 271.

28. Hansen, *Babel and Babylon*, p. 31.
29. See Martin Sopocy, *James Williamson: Studies of a Pioneer of the Film Narrative* (London: Associated University Presses, Inc., 1998), pp. 39–45; and Eric Barnouw, *Documentary* (Oxford: Oxford University Press, 1993), p. 24.
30. Annie Coombes, *Reinventing Africa. Museums, Material Culture and Popular Imagination in Late Victorian and Edwardian England* (New Haven and London: Yale, 1994), p. 31.
31. Court Treatt, *Sudan Sand*, p. 78.
32. Coombes, *Reinventing Africa*, p. 86.
33. The Church Missionary Society organized 'Africa and the East' exhibitions in 1909, 1913 and 1922 and the London Missionary Society an exhibition on the Orient in London in 1908.
34. Quoted in Kenneth Cameron, *Africa on Film* (New York: Continuum, 1994), pp. 50 and 207.
35. Burch, *Life to those Shadows*, p. 18.
36. Charles Musser, 'Documentary,' in Geoffrey Nowell-Smith, ed., *The Oxford History of World Cinema* (Oxford: Oxford University Press, 1996), p. 88; Hansen, *Babel and Babylon*, p. 42.
37. See Andrew Higson, ' "Britain's Outstanding Contribution to the Film": The Documentary-Realist Tradition,' in Charles Barr, ed., *All Our Yesterdays: 90 Years of British Cinema* (London: BFI, 1986).
38. See Tobing Rony, *The Third Eye*, pp. 21–43, for a discussion of the problems of talking about these early scientific films as records.
39. See Mark Sandberg, 'Effigy and Narrative: Looking into the Nineteenth Century Folk Museum,' in Leo Charney and Vanessa R. Schwartz, eds, *Cinema and the Invention of Modern Life* (London, Berkeley and Los Angeles: University of California Press, 1995), p. 349.
40. Low, *The History of British Film, 1918–1929* p. 290.

13

Distant Trumpets
The Score to *The Flag Lieutenant* and
Music of the British Silent Cinema

Neil Brand

The World of the Music

Thanks to a chance discovery in a pile of oratorios and operettas in a
second-hand shop in London, we now possess a copy of the only score
known to survive for a British feature film of the 1920s (see Plate 23).[1]
The film in question is Maurice Elvey's box-office hit of 1926, *The
Flag Lieutenant*. The score, put together by Albert Cazabon, provides
us with a window on to a distant and much-misunderstood world. It is
a commonplace to note that silent cinema wasn't actually experienced
in silence, that at virtually all film shows, from very early on, there
would have been some form of musical accompaniment, whether a
single pianist, a small band or a full orchestra. But there is as yet no
adequate history of musical accompaniment for silent films in Britain.
Silent film accompaniment is by its nature mercurial, transitory and
difficult to discuss as a whole because the very term is a catch-all for a
wealth of musical methodology. Even those of us privileged to see
a fine silent film restored and working with a modern audience nurse a
suspicion that the reputation of the music of the time would be more
difficult to salvage. Very little in the way of historical record survives of
performances or 'ear-witness' accounts. Scores are helpful but tell us
nothing of the abilities of the bands called upon to perform them and
the experience of one cinemagoer of the period will be utterly different

Plate 23.   Front cover of music score for *The Flag Lieutenant* (Elvey, 1926)

to another according to the venues they attended and their own taste in musical performance.

> Quite recently I was at a popular West End kinema renowned for its musical entertainment . . . I was thinking how excellent was the orchestral accompaniment when a lady behind me remarked how poor she thought the music to be; she said she didn't notice it! I thought this a very great compliment to the capable musical director . . . the music was *so good* that my neighbour was only subconscious of it . . .[2]

The quotation is from Gilbert R. Stevens' column 'Picture Music', which appeared regularly in *Kinematograph Weekly* in the 1910s and 1920s. His voice is authoritative, elitist and uncompromising concerning the highs and lows of silent musical accompaniment, yet overall his view of the potential for the cinema orchestra aims high. He is on conversational terms with the leading musical directors of the day (mostly London-based) and often sings the praises of Albert Marchbanks of the Tower Cinema, Peckham, or Louis Levy at the New Gallery Kinema in the West End; he celebrates and decries good and bad accompaniments and suggests newly published music in every column. He is a very useful touchstone, for when investigating music of the period we can find small significant details and try to apply them to the cinemagoing experience as a whole, but for every description of an inappropriate accompaniment or bad musicianship there will be a corresponding paean of praise for a job magnificently done or a band that is the best in the region. Forming a convincing overview is dependent on documents that suggest at least some consensus regarding a desirable standard of silent film accompaniment. The musical pages of *Kinematograph Weekly* give us the observer's consensus, while the *Flag Lieutenant* score, to my mind, gives us the musician's and film producer's.

According to Rachael Low, by 1914 the average number of cinemas in Britain's major cities was fifty-four (Manchester had 111) and with that kind of competition a cinema would not last long that did not have at least an adequate provision for music, probably more than just a piano.[3] The British silent cinema was born in the country's music halls (the first theatre in the country devoted entirely to cinema was the Balham Empire, which played movies exclusively through the summer of 1907) and the basic theatre facilities fitted both forms of entertainment. The band was already ensconced in the pit, used to playing a large number of musical pieces with quick changes of pace and key; the audience, flocking to early film at music hall prices, was used to the orchestra playing a major part in the proceedings—and the dynamics barely changed until the arrival of sound. From 1895 to 1927 one finds good and bad comments in equal measure heaped on the music. It becomes clear that although the practicalities of accompanying silent films could become more sophisticated the overall quality of music throughout the country barely evolved at all. The first *Kinematograph Weekly* of 1920 notes that '. . . 1919 has been an annus mirabilis for the kinema industry . . . the solitary pianist is not so frequently encountered as was the case 12 months ago; he is now aided by strings, woodwind or brass . . .'[4] (Ironically this observation brings a letter the following week claiming that a piano is more flexible than an orchestra and therefore to be preferred.) The article goes on to welcome the settlement of a musicians' dispute:

> the exhibitors have at last realised that the position of musical director is one of dignity and responsibility, and that the kinema musician is most certainly worthy of his hire . . . only the threat of a strike by the musicians brought home to many exhibitors the fact that the music is as essential a part of the entertainment as are the pictures.

The Kinema Musician and the Musical Director

What were these responsibilities that the musician had so dutifully to fulfil? Not just playing the notes, that's for sure. In the course of an evening's entertainment in even the small cinemas in the mid-1920s, a musician could expect to be playing for four to six hours. Breaks were allowed but often the film breaks were filled with musical interludes, so musicians' breaks were taken during the 'less important' films, such as the newsreel, played in silence or accompanied by the deputizing pianist or organist, an excellent way of breaking in new pianists. Indeed the newsreels were so hot off the press that no preparation would really be possible, so one assumes a healthy amount of improvization on march themes and exotic locations. When the musicians were playing they were usually reading music, sometimes, though not often, a score especially compiled for the film. This would take rehearsal, but rehearsal time was restricted to one play-through on the afternoon of a new feature. More likely the musicians would be playing music they knew very well, compiled by their own musical director (MD) who

MUSICAL SUGGESTIONS
FOR
"STAGE STRUCK"

Theme   -   -   -   -   " Want a Little Lovin' "   -   -   *Davis* (Lawrence Wright)
2/4 moderato

No.		Title or Action.	Tempo.	Selection.
1.		Open	Tragic maestoso, 4/4 andante maestoso	Drama Overture—Mouton (Piena)
2.	T.	The crowned heads of Europe	Light classy inter., 3/4 allegretto	Coquette—Arensky (Lafleur)
3.	T.	Rivals who come to scoff	Majestic march, 4/4 marziale	Processional—Savino (Lafleur)
4.	T.	Power and wealth for the choosing	Dramatic operatic, 2/4 moderato	Manon Lescaut—Puccini (Ricordi)
5.	T.	Wait!	Operatic Oriental, majestic, 12/8 allegro maestoso	Herodiade—Massenet (Lafleur)
6.	A.	Fade-in waitress with tray	Light inter., 4/4 fox-trot	She was just a Sailor's Sweetheart—Burke (Francis, Day & Hunter)
7.	A.	Crowd of men rush in	Light allegro, 2/4 vivo	Rush Hours—Sanders (Lafleur)
8.	T.	Mr., I wouldn't lose them beads	THEME	
9	T.	Here, mouse, chaperone this griddle	Light allegro inter., 2/4 vivo allegro	Mirth and Merriment—Delille (Lafleur)
10.	T.	A hungry mob	Repeat	Rush Hours
11.	T.	All Jenny's ambitions	THEME	
12.	T.	Orme in his room	Light eccentric, 4/4 quick walking pace	The Hustler—Srawley (Lafleur)
13.	A.	Orme leaves Jenny	Light inter., 4/4 allegretto	Merry Pranks—Rapee-Axt (Francis, Day & Hunter)
14.	A.	Insert—typed letter	Light characteristic operatic, 2/4 marcia	I want to be a Prima Donna, from " The Enchantress "—Herbert (Schotts)
15.	T.	For forty summers	Light eccentric, 4/4 moderato	The Show-Off—Sanders (Lafleur)
16.	T.	While Orme was looking over	Light operatic, 4/4 allegro moderato	If I were on the Stage, from " Mlle. Modiste "—Herbert (Schotts)
17.	T.	Insert—" He tells you he is leaving "	Light pathetic burlesque, 4/4 moderato burlesque	Hearts and Flowers—Tobani (Hawkes)
18.	A.	Jenny sees shirt burning	Sentimental popular, 3/4 valse lento	Honest and Truly—Rose (Francis, Day & Hunter)
19.	T.	Orme's shirt had cost	THEME	
20.	A.	Orme enters	Repeat	The Hustler
21.	A.	Actress enters restaurant	Light inter., 4/4 allegro	Vanity Caprice—Jackson (Lafleur)
22.	T.	Jenny pulls Orme's tie off	Light popular, 4/4 moderato	Jealous—Little (Feldman)
23.	T.	Sorry I kept you waiting	Light popular, 4/4 moderato	Cecelia—Ruby (Francis, Day & Hunter)
24.	T.	Do you know what that means?	Sentimental popular, 4/4 moderato	You're just a Flower from an Old Bouquet—Denni (Francis, Day & Hunter)
25.	T.	All's fair in love and war	Light inter., 4/4 allegro moderato	Dainty Blossoms—Hahn (Lafleur)
26.	T.	On the day of the Martinsville picnic	Light inter., 2/4 allegretto	Fireflies—Savino (Lafleur)
27.	A.	Steam whistle seen blowing	Light inter., 2/4 allegretto	Rural Flirts—Bradford (Lafleur)
28.	A.	Jenny left alone	Light popular, 4/4 moderato	My Sweetie Turned Me Down—Kahn (Francis, Day & Hunter)
29.	A.	Band starts playing	Light characteristic march, 2/4 allegro moderato	March No. 1, from " Yankianna Suite "—Thurban (Boosey)
30.	A.	Jenny hands drum stick to Buck	Light burlesque, 4/4 moderato	I ain't got Nobody—Graham (Feldman)
31.	T.	The next day all Martinsville	Light allegro, 2/4 allegro	Gossip—Borch (Lafleur)
32.	A.	Orme and Jenny together	Light popular, 4/4 jazz	Cheatin' on Me—Pollack (Lawrence Wright)
33.	T.	Saturday night	Light bright, 2/4 allegro	Merriment—Kempinski (Lafleur)
34.	A.	Orme enters box	Repeat.	The Hustler
35.	A.	Curtain rises	Chord in F, then segue	
35a.		Segue	Light characteristic, 2/4 march time	Ole South—Zamecnik (Keith Prowse)
36.	T.	Introducing the Lady Champion	Light march, 4/4 marcia	The Amazon March—Zamecnik (Keith Prowse)
37.	A.	Bell rings—fight starts	Light popular, 4/4 moderato	Oh, Me! Oh, My!—Youmans (Chappell)
38.	A.	Lady Champion knocked out	Light one-step, 2/4 allegro	Ouch—Kaufman (Francis, Day & Hunter)
39.	A.	Jenny thrown out of door	Pathetic melody, 3/4 adagio	Forsaken—Koschat (Schotts)
40.	T.	She jumped in the river	Dramatic allegro, 4/4 allegro giusto	Hurry, No. 87—Berge (Lafleur)
41.	T.	What did you do it for	Repeat	You're just a Flower from an Old Bouquet
42.	T.	Waldo Buck's prayer was	Light sentimental, popular 4/4 moderato TILL END.	The Love Nest—Hirsch (Chappell)

Plate 24. 'Musical Suggestions for *Stage Struck*'

knew the strengths and weaknesses of his team and the likes and dislikes of his audience. This would allow the band to 'relax' into playing piece after piece from a repertoire they knew and enjoyed and within which they could quickly move around. I suspect it also gave the audience a reassuring sense of security watching a picture of life in a possibly alien environment whilst listening and possibly singing along to music that was as familiar as their own front doors. As the 1920s progressed so did the film producer's involvement with the music ('the producer can render still more valuable help by employing a capable musical director to draw up a synopsis while the actual production is taking place'[5]). Increasingly, the MD was likely to have been issued with a cue sheet by the distributor, a breakdown of the film and musical suggestions for the mood changes (see Plate 24) but the final choice was down to him. The layout of an orchestra pit is such that most musicians, in order to face the pianist/conductor, would be facing away from the screen; the cueing of each instrument and the points at which music and tempi change would therefore have been signalled to musicians who could not see the film and had to rely on the MD to make those changes cleanly. Thus it was entirely the MD's fault if the music didn't synchronize.

The MD would have received some help with synchronization. A slow fade or iris out on screen might signal a change, for instance, but these are usually only at the end of sequences. A tight band that had frequently played together (a fortnight at six nights a week would do!) could quickly replay twenty bars of music or make a cut to the next piece. If all went wrong a soloist could improvise until the band was ready (indeed the organ or piano was used specifically to take over the music and allow the orchestra a break during the running of the feature). In a large number of houses there was even a rudimentary communication system between the musical director and the projection box. This would consist of a buzzer and bell or light system by which the MD could have the film speeded up or (more likely) slowed down to allow the band to re-synchronize. In the major houses with a thirty-piece orchestra such an arrangement would be vital, and one can see it as a small touch of imperialism over the film by the music—if the music was perfect at a certain tempo, the film would have to be flexible! The speed change seems to have been something of a double-edged sword for MDs of the period:

> The practice pursued by many managers of causing a film to be
> run through at an increased rate is one which causes much

tribulation to the musical director and one which it is highly desirable should be discontinued. I realize that an extra ten minutes or quarter of an hour may make a considerable difference to the pay-box receipts but it is fair neither to the audience nor to the musicians—and these latter have certainly sufficient troubles as it is.[6]

In both large and small orchestras it was the job of the percussionist to provide effects, although these exercised the editor of the *Kinematograph Weekly* music page more than any other aspect of film accompaniment. It must have been tempting to make a silent film into a sound film by adding bells ('like that employed by the muffin man'), horses' hooves ('even though the horses were obviously running on grass!'), sea sounds ('when one considers the sheer volume of music inspired by the sea') and so forth. Gilbert Stevens was clearly not alone in finding such effects distasteful:

we see the person knocking on the door or pressing the bulb of the car-horn; must our musical sense be jarred by use of effects in these cases? . . . they have rightly come to be regarded as both antiquated and offensive . . .[7]

Whether lulled or affronted by the music on offer, the majority of audiences would, one hopes, have been held in the thrall that silent film uniquely generates when music and image are working harmoniously. As the audience leaves at the end of the performance they are prepared already for the next exciting feature and they will come back to that film theatre rather than any other partly because they know what they will get musically. One can imagine that even in the worst musical circumstances, like the supporters of a permanently third division football team or a dire local amateur dramatics society, the audience is loyal to their local kinema. Even the most hopeless band in the smallest cinema is theirs, their small connection with the glamour of Hollywood, in which the greengrocer's daughter and the man who teaches piano to their children unite to help Douglas Fairbanks down that mast, Harold Lloyd up that clock and Lillian Gish to find true happiness.

The Flag Lieutenant and Albert Cazabon, the Musical Director's Musical Director

So where does the *Flag Lieutenant* score fit into this diverse world? Was it a major work of silent film music? Would it have warmed the heart of Gilbert R. Stevens? To discover that we must find out more about the film itself and about the author of its score. First, the film. A 'boy's own' naval drama, *The Flag Lieutenant* was one of the most successful British films of 1926–27, directed by Maurice Elvey, one of the leading British filmmakers of the period; it was also a very effective star vehicle for Henry Edwards.[8] It was adapted from a 1908 play, which had two very successful pre-war runs at the Haymarket. A first film version appeared in 1919, while a sequel to the Elvey version was released in 1928 (*Further Adventures of the Flag Lieutenant*), with Edwards again in the starring role. He returned one more time, as both star and director, for a sound version in 1933. Clearly, the story struck a chord with contemporary British audiences.

By comparison with the big Hollywood studio films of the period, the 1926 version of *The Flag Lieutenant* was not a major production, but it was a solid and well-made one nonetheless. For the Review Editor of *Kinematograph Weekly*, that was one of its great strengths,

> for it is not necessarily the big super picture that is best for the exhibitor or public, and a steady flow of first class pictures is much more desirable from every point of view than the occasional heralding of a lavish and expensive production.[9]

This 'excellent naval melodrama', 'a real credit to British screen art', was admired at its trade show for its 'well-told and interesting story', its 'clean, virile entertainment, with naval and fight thrills to suit the most sophisticated', and its 'fine settings on both sea and land'.[10] It was a film 'to stir the emotion and patriotism of every class of audience' (or as *Variety* put it, it was 'well seasoned with propaganda for king and empire').[11]

To appreciate the qualities of the film's score, which I will examine shortly, it is necessary to know something of the story the music must help to bring to life. The film opens at sea, with a regatta and rowing race taking place near the British naval flagship. A ball is held on board the flagship after the sporting events have finished and we are introduced to all the major characters. In particular, we meet our hero, Dicky Lascelles, his close friend Thesiger, their Admiral, and Sybil, the

Admiral's daughter, whom Dicky is wooing. Let the words of a contemporary plot synopsis take up the story:

> Richard Lascelles, D.S.O., R.N., and Major Thesiger are called away during a ball on the flagship for a landing party to rescue a beleaguered garrison; to Thesiger, an elderly man, this means his first real chance. After fighting their way into the fort, means of communication are destroyed, and Thesiger, putting on a dead native's clothes, starts to climb out to signal the destroyer. He is shot through the head [in fact the bullet only grazes him] and Lascelles takes his place, does the job successfully, and saves the garrison. Thesiger is acclaimed the hero; his memory having gone he thinks he achieved the task, and only the doctor and Lascelles know the truth. Lascelles insists on the deception remaining undiscovered. Returning to the fleet, Lascelles' actions during the siege are called into account, but finally the Lieutenant who heard the shouted message recognizes Lascelles' voice, and his reputation is cleared. Thesiger is kept in ignorance with his new honours, and marries a widow who has been in instrumental in learning the truth, while Lascelles marries the admiral's daughter, who has believed in him all through.[12]

For a film advertised as 'The British Film Masterpiece of All Time' and already heralded at its trade show as a potential box-office winner, one would expect a prestige score, perhaps even a specially composed one. That would require a composer or musical director of distinction and Albert Cazabon was such an MD.[13] He studied at the Guildhall with Holst (among others) and first toured Europe as a virtuoso violinist to great acclaim. Between 1902 and 1927, as resident musical director for several London theatres and the Royal Shakespeare Theatre in Stratford, he was responsible for at least seventy productions including premieres of *Little Lord Fauntleroy*, *Goodbye Mr Chips* and *Pygmalion*. One presumes he also oversaw the compilation of movie scores from that time but I can find evidence of only one, the full score to *The Flag Lieutenant*. In 1927 (possibly having seen the writing on the wall for silent pictures) he took up a new position as resident composer at the Prince of Wales theatre, Sydney, Australia, and did not return for ten years. He went on to broadcast regularly on the BBC as a violinist and bandleader and continued to write incidental music for the theatre and humorous pieces for the orchestra. In terms of a prestige production like *The Flag Lieutenant*, Cazabon can be described at the very least as a safe pair of hands.

The *Flag Lieutenant* Score

The score that survives is a unique copy of a piano-conductor score; in other words, it contains all the notes necessary to play the piano part and lead in other instruments. This does mean, however, that there are some bars that are blank because they cue music for other instruments for which we do not have the score. As the piano was expected to lead both dynamically and melodically, however, most of the tunes are recognizable, even if it is impossible to put a name to them without considerable knowledge of the sound of the popular tunes of the day. The title page of the score carries the information 'Compiled by Albert Cazabon. As played at the Gala Performance before their majesties the King and Queen. Supplied by the Motion Picture Music Company of Denman St. London W1' (see Plate 23). This then is as 'prestige' as a British picture could get and Cazabon's compilation is a textbook example of movie music scoring by a thoroughgoing professional, even though he personally wrote almost none of it. The score consists of 110 pieces of widely varying length with each piece introduced by its on-screen cue and its copyright holder (although not its author) named at the final bar. Each piece is written in a key that bears some resemblance to its predecessor's key (mostly F, B flat and E flat, easy keys for playing and transcribing). After the pre-titles march, 'Rule Britannia' makes a not unexpected appearance followed by a sprightly tune (known to contemporary audiences in all probability) and then the 'Sailor's Hornpipe', covering the footage of the regatta and rowing-boat race, which is missing from the surviving print in the National Film and Television Archive. There are notes regarding Syren [*sic*] effects for the signal of the winning boat, which would have been for the sort of orchestral spot-effect so detested by Gilbert Stevens, then a slow, grand theme for the introduction of the Admiral, which becomes his leitmotif for every subsequent appearance in the film.

The early scenes mostly introduce the characters and feature the ball on board ship at which the characters are seen determinedly dancing the Charleston or waiting to be invited to. For reasons best known to Cazabon the score features a pleasant but slightly old-fashioned-sounding Foxtrot at this point. Possibly it was thought that the Charleston was beneath the dignity of their Majesties or possibly it was too expensive to clear the necessary rights. The music used consists of a very catchy dance tune, which I suspect was intended to rise in popularity because of its connection with the film. No doubt Sylvester Music, the rights holders, were delighted. Throughout this section comes a medley of 'naval' pieces, including 'Dear Old Pals' and 'All the Nice Girls Love a Sailor', as well as the start of a beautiful love theme for Dick and Sybil which, whilst keeping the melody intact, allows the orchestration and harmony to change according to how things are going for their relationship. This, I suspect, is Cazabon's greatest gift, that of arranging the evolution of leitmotifs throughout the progress of a film so that the music matches the imagery. It is not quite the skilled creativity of a composer at work but it would have required a very gifted arranger both to decide on the dramatic content of a film's thematic material and to rework the music to run alongside it without losing the melodic through-line that the audience will recognize.

On average there is a screen cue every minute or so in the score to help with synchronization, although the dances are allowed time to play without being hurried on by the plot, again allowing the music to be properly heard. Towards the end of the long dance sequence there is a standby cue, warning of the approach of the end of the scene and the last eight bars of music. At this point the MD has a chance to put a wayward accompaniment back on track, if necessary by a brutal cutting of all sound and preparation for the title 'An Outpost'.

With the abrupt shift to the desert fortress we are away from musical high-jinks and into a more impressionist landscape in which lowering strings and an insistent tambourine warn of imminent danger. As the rifles fire, the score erupts into a furioso in classic style, possibly a piece of classical music. The Admiral is notified, his theme returns, unaltered, and at the intriguing screen cue 'Deck—Blue Film', a reference to an (as yet) undiscovered tinting in the original print, the snare-drummer plays a roll and the trumpet gives the accurate bugle call for 'alarm', bringing the ship's company on deck at the double. The military music, particularly bugle calls, would have to have been accurate throughout, not only because of the Royal connection with the navy but because an audience watching *The Flag Lieutenant* only eight years after the armistice was likely to have heard the real thing. As the company embarks to save the beleaguered garrison, the score swings in with the opening of Elgar's 'Pomp and Circumstance' march, though stopping short of going on into the 'Land of Hope and Glory' section, possibly aware that the audience could burst into song. As the British forces move off to battle, the on-screen bandmaster signals his drummer and the live band plays them on their way with one final burst of 'Rule Britannia'.

The action scenes are very impressive, as is the music that accompanies them, the sort of furioso fireworks that would become the norm in later sound war films. Big gun and rifle effects are added, a merry jig is played as the Arabs run away (somewhat confusing to modern ears) and the whole sequence would have been a nightmare to synchronize for a musical director trying to maintain order in the pit. A segue cue comes on the instruction 'as men kneel', which is a detail all too easily missed, although bugle calls help to break up the orchestral pieces and allow the band to 'regroup' (see Plate 25). On the firing of a cannon we have the first piece by Cazabon himself, a climbing chord motif followed by impressionist shellburst effects on cymbal and bass drum, then a second piece of molto mysterioso tremolo violins to cover the plan to get a message out of the fort (see Plate 26). The music generally builds to a pitch of suspense up to Thesiger's shooting, at which three more bars of Cazabon give us the musical equivalent of Thesiger's body hitting the ground. Lively, upbeat music takes over as Dicky takes his place. In the central scene of the film, Dicky shouts to the man on board ship who will eventually recognize his voice and disprove his cowardice. Cazabon again gives us a closely timed musical equivalent of real sound, Lascelle's voice being replaced by a trumpet call (including a build-up in volume to make the officer hear), followed by a triumphant major chord as the message gets through. A slow, tremolo rendition of 'Dear Old Pals' greets the return of the wounded soldiers (a distinct reference back to the Great War), the aeroplanes roar to the rescue, complete with orchestral effects, and the Union Jack flies over the fort to the strain of 'Three Cheers for the Red White and Blue'.

The formal regimental scenes that follow are scored with due deference to the traditions of the navy. From 'Hearts of Oak', through 'The Boys of the Old Brigade', to a long drum roll under 'Gentlemen, the King', the music plays the whole regimental dinner with dignity and informs those scenes with a sense of honour and patriotism which resonate even today. As we see the ladies in their separate room we hear the strains of 'For He's a Jolly Good Fellow' from the banquet next door, and Thesiger rises to give his speech to a suitably hesitant minuet. The choruses of Jolly Good Fellow are literally cut short as Thesiger mentions Dicky Lascelles, the orchestra brutally silenced on that title to be replaced by four bars of non-specific but certainly doom-laden timpani. Sybil and Dicky's love theme resurfaces gallantly as she tries to defend her betrothed but now Cazabon sets it in a minor key. The music plucks at the heartstrings in the subsequent scene including a lamenting andante by Cazabon, which represents the profundity of Lascelles's devotion to his friend. As we arrive at the

Plates 25(above) and 26 (opposite). Pages from the music score
for *The Flag Lieutenant* (Elvey, 1926)

Plate 26.

celebration for the King's birthday, a Cazabon fanfare of three-part brass becomes a cheeky variation on the sailor's hornpipe, before the woodwind and brass impersonate a concertina being played (with a stern order for silence from the piano) and the orchestra launches into light, upbeat music for the final scene. Lascelles's shout is repeated exactly in the orchestra, the similarity of the voice to the ship's officer being in no doubt musically, and the ladies' realization of the real truth is represented with an accelerando, building in volume to an outburst of musical fireworks and flowing lines on the piano. A grandioso finale is rounded off with the National Anthem (synchronized on-screen but the traditional end to public performances) and a final triumphal 'Rule Britannia' to send the audience on its way, finishing on the end title.

Some Conclusions

To my mind, the *Flag Lieutenant* score is not a masterpiece but is fascinating for that very reason. It represents professional musicianship in its working clothes, not its Sunday best. This score, to me, represents the attainable aspirations of thousands of unknown pit bands who, given the job of compiling the score for themselves, would almost certainly come up with a similar approach to the material if not the sophistication of technique. It is a score compiled with a flair for the theatrical, a shrewd eye on the patriotism of the film and the audience for whom it was intended and an educated taste in music. Gilbert Stevens was, I'm sure, entranced, but would have hated the effects.

> The amazingly rapid strides towards perfection which Kinema music has made during the past few years causes me to wonder what the kinema orchestra of the 1930s will be like. There can be no doubt but that the solitary pianist will be as extinct as the dodo . . . the super-kinemas with their orchestras of from seventy-five to a hundred and twenty players, will provide not only musical settings to the film, but will render classical compositions between the pictures. The music to every film will be composed by an expert and breaks will be unknown, as, I hope, will be 'effects'. Every orchestra will be provided with a music library and it has even been suggested that the kinema musician will come to be regarded as a musician and not as a man hired to make a noise for so many hours at a wage less than that of a dock labourer.[14]

Stevens got his wish some three or four years early, once the organ had been added to the musical ensemble to fill out the sound and give variety to the 'one man band', once titbits of information on possible ways to synchronize sound on to film had been thrown up and dismissed, once cue sheets were the norm and filmmakers began to insert visual cues into their films (Von Stroheim in particular), thereby giving MDs the most direct instructions for musical requirements. But the very musical diversity that was both the blessing and the curse of silent cinema brought about the complete demise of the art form. Hollywood producers, led by Fox and Warners, were struggling to perfect a film/sound system in order to standardize the music. The content of a film could be wildly altered from venue to venue at the whim of a less discerning MD or a moribund orchestra, and the final goal had to be to bring the same score to every venue, played to perfection. The Vitaphone shorts were nearly all musical, the Los Angeles Philharmonic Orchestra in particular sounding ravishing. That they could sound equally ravishing in Salford was at the back of every distributor's, MD's and cinema owner's mind. When the crunch came, it was swift and merciless. The number of musicians in the UK put out of work at the coming of sound is anybody's guess, but in America it was close on 55,000. With them went an expertise, a professionalism and a musicality that was irreplaceable.

In March 1928, the *Musical Mirror* published an article entitled 'The Cinema Pianist—How To Become One'. The final paragraph reads

'If a person has an artistic temperament of high quality, also the ability to teach or otherwise earn money, he had better leave the cinema alone. But for others who have no choice, or who are not so highly developed musically or temperamentally, the cinema offers as many opportunities as any other branch of the musical profession.[15]

That viewpoint had about another six months to remain valid. It is not hard to see why cinema musicians were so derided but I find it harder to understand why so little is written about the music, why film reviews took no account of the music, why trade shows were usually played silent and why almost nothing in the way of British cinema music has survived. The chance discovery of the score to *The Flag Lieutenant* has at least given one of the old masters a chance to be heard and, through the pages of his score, speak for the best of a generation.

Notes

1. I am indebted to Geoff Brown, film and music critic for *The Times*, who found the score and subsequently passed it on to me. I am currently in the process of preparing a musical accompaniment, based on the score, for the National Film and Television Archive's print of the film. My thanks to Bryony Dixon for making the print available.
2. Gilbert R. Stevens, 'Picture Music,' *Kinematograph Weekly*, 8 January 1920, supplement, p. xvii.
3. Rachael Low, *The History of British Film, 1906–1914* (London: George Allen and Unwin, 1949), p. 50.
4. Gilbert R. Stevens, 'Picture Music,' *Kinematograph Weekly*, 1 January 1920, supplement, p. xvii.
5. Ibid.
6. Ibid., 26 August 1920, supplement, p. xv.
7. Ibid., 19 February 1920, supplement, p. xv.
8. I am grateful to Andrew Higson for providing background details on the film.
9. Lionel Collier, 'Trade Shows Surveyed,' *Kinematograph Weekly*, 4 November 1926, p. 70.
10. Anon., 'New Films at a Glance,' *Kinematograph Weekly*, 4 November 1926, p. 71; Anon., '*The Flag Lieutenant*,' *Kinematograph Weekly*, 4 November 1926, p. 74; Anon., '*The Flag Lieutenant*,' *Bioscope*, 4 November 1926, p. 52; Collier, 'Trade Shows Surveyed,' p. 70.
11. Anon., '*The Flag Lieutenant*,' *Bioscope*, p. 52; 'Sid.,' '*The Flag Lieutenant*,' *Variety*, 6 July 1927 (page number not known).
12. Anon., '*The Flag Lieutenant*,' *Kinematograph Weekly*, p. 74.
13. I am grateful to Janice Healey and David Robinson for providing me with Cazabon's biographical details.
14. Gilbert R. Stevens, 'Picture Music,' *Kinematograph Weekly*, 29 July 1920, supplement, p. xv.
15. S. Turnbull, 'The Cinema Pianist—How To Become One,' *Musical Mirror*, March 1928, p. 65 (my thanks to Nick Hiley for providing this reference).

SECTION D

The Feature Film at Home and Abroad
Mainstream Cinema from the End of the First World War to the Coming of Sound

14

Writing Screen Plays
Stannard and Hitchcock

Charles Barr

Cut from a peacock, spreading its feathers, to a leader in military uniform. Cut from a man in solitary confinement to images of nature and freedom in the world outside, then back to the prison cell. These will be recognized at once as two of the most celebrated instances of Soviet montage. Eisenstein in *October* (1927) uses the peacock to ridicule the pretensions of Kerensky, enemy of the Revolution. Pudovkin in *Mother* (1926), in a scene where his imprisoned hero Pavel is told he is being released, uses images of the natural world to convey emotions that would otherwise be hard to express filmically: 'The photographing of a face lighting up with joy would have been flat and void of effect.'[1] Among the images cut in are birds and a laughing child. This kind of montage practice, and the texts in which Pudovkin and Eisenstein expounded it, quickly became central to the development of a coherent theory of film, and the two scenes are cited in turn in publications with such definitive titles as *The Art of the Film* (1948), *The Technique of Film Editing* (1953), and *The Cinema as Art* (1965).[2]

One of those who felt the early impact of Soviet montage, from the films and from the writings, and perhaps from the authors themselves when they visited London to lecture, was, of course, Alfred Hitchcock, who had entered the British film industry in 1919 and whose first films as director were released in 1926. To the end of his life, Hitchcock would affirm his allegiance to the principles of montage and to the ideas of, especially, Pudovkin.[3] This fits in with what is still the dominant account of his early career: that his distinctive form of cinema came together through the successive and cumulative influences of Hollywood narrative, German composition, and Soviet montage, each of which gave him something he manifestly could not have picked up from the impoverished British cinema context within which he would continue working up to 1939.

Let us go back, though, to the peacock and the prisoner. Cut, this time, from the peacock not to Kerensky but to the German Kaiser: the context is a British film of 1918, a biopic of *Nelson*, told in flashback from the present day. And the man in solitary confinement is, this time, not Pavel the revolutionary but the central figure of John Galsworthy's play *Justice*, adapted for cinema by the British company Ideal in 1917. Reviewing it, the leading trade paper the *Kinematograph and Lantern Weekly* (hereinafter *Kine Weekly*) singled out for special praise 'the sudden flash from the horrors of solitary confinement to a vision of freedom. This latter is presented by a view of a lovely garden in which a youth is joyously chasing a care-free maiden.'[4] The film itself is not known to survive, but in an article for the same paper two weeks earlier the scenario writer had given more details:

> In order that you may more fully realise the horrors of solitary confinement I have shown a wild bird at liberty soaring upwards into the sky; the mental agony of the guilty is contrasted by the mental innocence of children playing in the sunshine.[5]

Though the context is slightly different, there being no joyful expectation of release, the scene in its concept, and in details like bird and child, clearly has an affinity with Pudovkin's.

Do we then need to rewrite cinema history, to show Eisenstein and Pudovkin picking up some of their best ideas, without acknowledgement, from unfashionable British sources? Maybe not, but these two startling anticipations at least demonstrate that some British filmmakers were, many years earlier, thinking in imaginative montage terms, even if their ideas may not have been realized on screen with anything like the force of the contemporary films of D.W. Griffith, or of the later Soviet ones. And it doesn't seem so implausible to trace a link between these flurries of montage experimentation and the young Hitchcock, who, unlike Pudovkin and Eisenstein, was in London at the time: in his late teens, not yet working in films, but already a keen playgoer, filmgoer, and reader of the trade papers. His biographers tell us that he did this reading because of his interest in American and

CINEMA
PRACTICAL COURSE IN
CINEMA ACTING

IN TEN COMPLETE LESSONS
by
MARY PICKFORD
CHARLIE CHAPLIN
KENELM FOSS
AURELE SYDNEY
. . TOM MIX . .
ELIOT STANNARD
STEWART ROME
JOSE COLLINS
VIOLET HOPSON
GLADYS BROCKWELL

LESSON SIX

National Business and Personal Efficiency
Department of
The Standard Art Book Co., Ltd.,
2, BRAMHAM GARDENS, S.W.5.

MR. ELIOT STANNARD
The well-known Scenario Writer

Plate 27. The title pages from Eliot Stannard, 'Writing Screen Plays,'
Lesson Six in the series *Cinema—in Ten Complete Lessons*
(London: Standard Art Book Company, 1920)

Continental films; but he could very easily have seen the Galsworthy play, read about the adaptation in *Kine Weekly*, and watched the film with interest—he did, after all, repeatedly cite Galsworthy as an enduring influence, and was to direct a film version of *The Skin Game* in 1931.[6]

This might still add up to no more than speculation, were it not for one very material connection. The screenwriter of both *Justice* and *Nelson* is Eliot Stannard. On Hitchcock's first nine films as director, released between 1926 and 1929, the single credited screenwriter, other than, on two occasions, Hitchcock himself, is the same Eliot Stannard; he has solo credit on seven out of the nine, and a shared credit on *Champagne*, and his name is absent only from *The Ring*, to which he is known, however, to have made some kind of contribution as well. When Hitchcock left Gainsborough, after the first five films, to take up a more lucrative contract with British International Pictures, he had made a point of taking his screenwriter with him.[7]

Despite this intensive association with the most studied figure in cinema history at the formative stage of his career, Stannard has been not so much neglected by critics as written out of film history altogether; he features in no standard works of reference, and is unmentioned in the bulk of the critical literature on Hitchcock, including even Tom Ryall's *Alfred Hitchcock and the British Cinema*, a book whose purpose is not textual analysis nor the celebration of an *auteur* but, precisely, the placing of the man and his work within their cultural and film-industry context.[8] It does this effectively as far as it goes, but the blind spot about writers is strange, or it would be if there were not so many precedents for it. In my own recent book *English Hitchcock* I discuss this neglect further, and make a first attempt to rectify it by collecting some data about Stannard and suggesting how he may have contributed to the early films, and thus to the shaping of the phenomenon that Hitchcock has come to constitute.[9] Although the book quotes from a pamphlet published by Stannard in 1920, referred to below, I was not then familiar with the amount of material he had also written, at around the same period, for *Kine Weekly*.

Stannard on Cinema

These trade-paper writings are significant in several ways. They demonstrate the high status of Stannard within the industry; indeed some of them are based on, or refer to, lectures given at the invitation of professional bodies.[10] They suggest that the construction, both overall and in terms of montage effects, of the films of that period on which he is credited came primarily from him as screenwriter rather than from the director. And the range and prominence of the articles increases the likelihood that Hitchcock became familiar at an impressionable age with Stannard's name and ideas. In addition to many one-off contributions, he supplied a series of five weekly articles in summer 1918 on 'The Art of Kinematography'. Pending any further happy discoveries, these add up to one of the two sustained testaments about his craft that we have from him, the other being his pamphlet, divided similarly into five chapters, on 'Writing Screen Plays', issued in 1920 as part of an instruction manual about the cinema by various hands.[11] Whether or not Hitchcock actually read and pondered these items as they came out—and, given his already developed interests, it is not hard to imagine him doing so—they provide fascinating evidence about the man he was to collaborate with so productively a few years later.

Born in 1888, Stannard seems to have entered films in 1914 by writing, and acting in, the adaptation of a story by his mother, a prolific popular novelist who wrote under the name of John Strange Winter. From that point, he put all of his energies into the film business. The 1920 pamphlet starts by 'Introducing the Author':

> After a short career as journalist and writer of fiction, Eliot Stannard entered the film industry and passing through various stages as actor, stage-manager, art-expert, film-cutter and producer, he acquired a complete mastery of screen-technic [sic] and then devoted himself exclusively to writing scenarios . . .[12]

This is not unlike the apprenticeship Hitchcock was himself about to embark on: he went from title designer to art-director to scenarist before becoming a specialist in production (i.e. direction), and incidentally married a scenarist and ex-cutter in Alma Reville. Stannard repeatedly emphasizes the way all the skills of filmmaking interlock, or at least ought to. The third of the five *Kine Weekly* articles, 'The Unseen', insists on the proper valuing and integrating of all the contributory skills from editing to props to processing, and argues presciently—in a period long before extended credit titles, and before unionization—for all technicians to be listed in the equivalent of a theatre programme:

> This method would be instructive to the discerning buyer or renter. Furthermore, such booklets would prove immensely useful to the unseen workers, and would establish a record of their work and be a guide to film manufacturers with whom they sought employment.[13]

In a lecture in 1921 to the Kine-Cameramen's Society he envisages 'a kind of trinity composed of the producer, scenario-writer, and cameraman . . . the cameraman would become a creative artist working in collaboration with his two *confreres*'.[14] 'Film production involves a collaborative integration of skills, and the product itself should be formed out of an appropriate integration of compositional principles drawn from literature, drama, painting, music, psychology.'[15] A comparable principle of integration is at work in Stannard's model of the organically constructed scenario. He begins by describing the most common failings of the scripts that have passed before him as a scenario editor:

They were nearly all composed of a series of exciting incidents and nothing else; melodramatic, improbable and often impossible situations followed each other in bewildering rapidity, but I sought in vain for any central motive or theme upon which the stories *should* have been constructed. A successful film-play depends as much upon the soundness of its central theme as a stage play or novel, and that theme must never be lost sight of by the Scenario-writer, *for every scene which does not bear upon it is a blemish to the Scenario.*[16]

This passage is of particular interest for the way it evokes first the tendency in Hitchcock that his later writing collaborators, from Charles Bennett to Ernest Lehman, would often complain of—that of suggesting a variety of vivid scenes or 'touches' without having much sense of how they might be fitted into a narrative—and then the ideal of tight construction at which he frequently said he aimed, and for which he required the services of, to use Bennett's term, a 'constructionist'.[17] Stannard would become the first in a succession of them.

Within the overall model of unity, the two specific principles that come across most strongly are those of symbolism and of time-management. The 1920 manual contains a brilliantly lucid exercise based on this situation: 'Let us suppose a child is suddenly taken ill and, while the distracted mother watches over the invalid, the father rushes off for the doctor.'[18] The ponderousness of a representation tied to real time is contrasted with the manipulation of time and audience response made possible by judicious editing, laid out at the scenario stage. Key terms in the exposition are 'cross-cutting', 'suspense', and 'time-anxiety'. Though this is not one of the places where he names him, the analysis surely owes something to the example of Griffith, whose methods were an acknowledged inspiration to Hitchcock, as to Eisenstein, Pudovkin, and many others; the point is that, some years before any of these were active as theorists or filmmakers, Stannard is showing and promulgating his grasp of the same key principles.

As for symbolism, this is the title of the first of the five *Kine Weekly* articles on 'The Art of Kinematography', and he foregrounds it from time to time elsewhere. On the one hand, the word refers to obviously 'symbolic' interpolated material such as the peacock intercut with the Kaiser, and the series of images of freedom intercut with the prisoner in his cell; this scene from *Justice* is the main one Stannard uses for his exposition of the concept, rather in the way Pudovkin will later write about the corresponding scene from *Mother*. But the term also seems to encompass devices that we would now call metonymic—the showing of a part or a detail to represent the whole—and indeed to cover more various forms of concisely expressive image.

> It is ... the scenario-writer's business to hand the producer a script so carefully constructed and so minutely pruned of all that is superfluous that he can obtain the greatest number of symbolic impressions with the least amount of film-footage.[19]

If the term *montage* had by then been current in discourse about film, one feels he might have appropriated it.

Before Hitchcock

The fifth and final chapter of the 1920 pamphlet begins with these lines (again saying producer when Hollywood would by now have said director):

> Scenario-writers should become as intimately acquainted as possible with Producers. If you can find one whose temperament is in harmony with your own, then write exclusively for that one man; for your joint work should express all that is best in each of you. To like a Producer personally is not, of course, enough. You must also admire his work and his methods, as he must admire and understand your scenarios.[20]

Stannard could already, in 1920, look back on one sustained collaboration. Between 1914 and 1929, he wrote at least ninety silent films; this is a conservative figure, based mainly on credits assembled by Rachael Low and Denis Gifford, and some estimates go higher.[21] Of the first block of around thirty-five, up to late 1918, twenty-four are directed by Maurice Elvey, including both *Justice* and the last of their films together, *Nelson*. Most of them are adaptations from stage or novel, and Low refers disparagingly to the pair of them 'busily turning everything into the same formula stuff'.[22]

It is hard to know quite how to take this comment. Low was such a pioneer, and dealt so painstakingly and so authoritatively with the unexplored field of British silent cinema, that her judgements deserve respect; but it is not clear how many of the Stannard-Elvey films she had been able to see. Moreover, she was writing in 1971, well before the growth of systematic attention to early cinema that the FIAF conference of 1978 can be seen as having inaugurated, and before the systematic mapping of the evolution of the 'classical' norms by writers like the Bordwell-Staiger-Thompson team.[23] But it is quite possible that, if we could now summon up all the films for viewing, they would seem disappointingly stodgy, rather than some heady blend of Griffith and Pudovkin. We might then, with the benefit of hindsight, want to see Stannard as having been held back by a pedestrian director, or by a regressive environment. Or, and I prefer this, we can envisage him working out various models and ideas, at a hectic pace and by trial and error, at a period of rapid change in the industry and in the medium. He starts, on this reading, by going along with the prevailing approach to adaptation as, in his own words of 1917, a crude kind of 'cut and slash trade', and produces scripts that are turned into visual digests, a succession of 'scenes from' the original.[24] As a number of revisionist historians have argued, such a system is not necessarily to be despised. Andrew Higson sees the careful representation, in tableau style, of scenes from English novels and plays or from English history, using 'heritage' architecture and landscapes, as a legitimate way of marking out a path for a British national cinema, one that is distinct from the Hollywood model that was becoming established, and it is significant that one of his prime examples is the final Stannard-Elvey collaboration, *Nelson*.[25] It would certainly be interesting to be able to look at their preceding films and interrogate them in this light. But my sense is that both Stannard and Elvey, unlike the older Cecil Hepworth, were starting, by the time the collaboration ended, to move away from this model towards a more flexible system, one closer to the internationally influential models that we associate respectively with 'classical Hollywood' and with European modernism. This is suggested by the montage tropes that were already, as we have seen, entering the films, as well as by Stannard's own writings; he refers to the 'cut and slash trade' only in order to argue the necessity of moving on from it. It should be noted, too, that a number of Elvey's post-Stannard silent films have recently been revived, and attracted new attention from critics and historians.[26]

In the early 1920s, Stannard's main directorial associate is A.V. Bramble; the tentative figures are twelve films directed by him, out of a succession of thirty scripts in three years. Pending, again, the emergence of more evidence from the archives, one might envisage this as a period of marking time for Stannard, involving an intermittent collaboration with a journeyman director who does not stretch him or do justice to his scripts; but it is always possible that the prolific

Bramble, like the prolific Elvey, is a candidate for rediscovery. He is remembered by history mainly for his director's credit on Anthony Asquith's highly accomplished and inventive first film, *Shooting Stars*, and we take it for granted that he was simply an experienced professional who had a consultative role and allowed his name to be foregrounded, in order to satisfy the money-men, while Asquith really did it all; but maybe it is more complex than that. In any case, after this period of writing for him and various others, and for a variety of companies, Stannard moves across to Gainsborough and teams up with the young Alfred Hitchcock.

Writing for Hitchcock

Rachael Low claims that the low valuation of the script was 'a great weakness in the British industry' across this whole decade. Citing Stannard by name, alongside Kenelm Foss, she offers this summary: 'The professionals turned up in company after company, 'knowing their craft' and imposing their second-rate conception of what a film should be on one new hopeful director after another'.[27] So here is another new hopeful director, descended upon by the experienced professional writer. Are we to see Hitchcock as having to struggle against Stannard's irredeemably second-rate conceptions? If he did so, the quality of the films indicates a degree of success; but in that case, why stick with the same writer for so long? Low simply doesn't address this remarkable anomaly.

I have already quoted Stannard's lines of 1920: 'If you can find [a director] whose temperament is in harmony with your own, then write exclusively for that one man; for your joint work should express all that is best in each of you.' Surely this is a far more convincing explanation of what now happens. The fact that Hitchcock's debut film *The Pleasure Garden* is also Stannard's first Gainsborough credit suggests that he may have been brought to the studio specifically to work with him, whether at Hitchcock's own instigation or that of Michael Balcon; neither the Hitchcock nor the Balcon archives, unfortunately, contain much material that relates to these early years. Contractually, Stannard needs to write for others too; but of his last fourteen silent scripts, Hitchcock still directs eight—the figures become fifteen and nine if one includes *The Ring*, which doesn't actually name Stannard on the credits. Switching to the reverse angle: of Hitchcock's nine silents, eight are written by Stannard; or, counting *The Ring*, all nine.

It is an extraordinarily rich series of films, solidly constructed and inventively realized; in the space of this chapter, I can't do much more than refer the reader to my detailed account of them in *English Hitchcock*.[28] Whatever frustrations Stannard may have encountered in writing for others, or, conversely, whatever achievements may remain to be discovered from among his work with the likes of Elvey or Bramble or Thomas Bentley, these films provide consummate fulfilment of the ideas he had earlier been expounding about construction, time-management, and symbolism. His screenplay for *The Farmer's Wife* (1928), for instance, is a model of intelligent adaptation, combining boldness with sympathetic fidelity; it reworks the play's 'backstory' in a new opening section, compresses the time-scale, and cuts out a number of minor characters. All the films, *The Lodger* included, have this same quality of concentration, of being constructed, as the 1920 pamphlet insists, around a 'central theme' and story-line. Several of them, from *The Pleasure Garden* onward, likewise follow that manual in including judicious passages of cross-cutting between different locations. And they are self-evidently rich in the varieties of 'symbolism' that for Stannard was, as we have seen, a key term.

After Hitchcock

The fifth and last of Stannard's *Kine Weekly* articles in 1918, 'What of the Future?', ends with these playful words:

> It is a dangerous and hazardous pastime attempting to gaze into the future, and so I will conclude by making one prophecy which is sure of fulfilment, and unhesitatingly predict that nothing will ever persuade Eliot Stannard to disappear from the kinematograph industry.[29]

In the event, he was to disappear from it while still in his early forties—persuaded, it seems, not by a change of heart, nor by better offers from elsewhere, but by the brutal fact of becoming unemployable. The same article had begun by addressing the possibility of 'speaking pictures', which were in 1918, as on so many occasions prior to *The Jazz Singer*, rumoured to be imminent, a prospect Stannard deplores: 'The whole theory of kinematography is against [this] innovation . . .' His response foreshadows the reservations widely expressed a decade later by many critics, by Eisenstein and his colleagues, and by Hitchcock himself, who in the 1960s was still expressing regret, to Truffaut, for what had been lost: 'the silent pictures were the purest form of cinema . . . It seems unfortunate that with the arrival of sound the motion picture, overnight, assumed a theatrical form.'[30] One of the objections voiced by Stannard in 1918 is, likewise, that the change would 'require the work of polished play-wrights, who, for the sake of euphuism, would revert to the rules of the theatre to the detriment of film technique'. When the move to synchronized films became unstoppable, he may have been too obstinate, or too demoralized, to struggle to adjust to the new situation in the manner that Hitchcock did—especially after the link between them had, in circumstances about which we can only conjecture, been broken.

After *The Manxman*, only six screen credits for him are on record. Two of the films, *The American Prisoner* and *The Hate Ship*, were made in 1929 in the familiar surroundings of BIP's Elstree, around the same time that Hitchcock was shooting *Blackmail* there; they seem, likewise, to have involved a hasty adjustment to the new technology, but achieved nothing of *Blackmail*'s commercial and critical success. Stannard was evidently one of the silent film specialists, alongside a mass of actors and musicians, whose contracts were at this time dropped. He is credited on four sound films, the last of them released early in 1933: long-forgotten 'quota quickies', made for four different companies. Most of what happened between then and his unremarked death in London in 1944 is, at present, a mystery. In *English Hitchcock* I quote a story told by Sidney Gilliat, to the effect that Stannard was rumoured to have had a wartime job in a vehicle licensing department, and to have systematically sabotaged the filing system before walking out.[31] Since then, Gavin Lambert has published his own memory of him in the year of his death: when Lambert began his first humble film-industry job, writing two-minute film commercials, he found himself working alongside the 55-year-old Stannard, who spoke bitterly of how his contribution to Hitchcock's early films had been ignored.[32] Perhaps he had come back to films after an absence; perhaps the vehicle licensing story is apocryphal, and he had simply been working away for years in this kind of anonymity, rather as Cecil Hepworth did when his own feature-film career collapsed in the 1920s.

These things happen—think of the inactivity of Griffith between 1930 and his death in 1948. But neither Griffith nor Hepworth disappeared from view, or had the work of their productive years forgotten, as Stannard did so comprehensively. His misfortune was to carry a triple handicap: he was British, he was a screenwriter, and he began his career at the wrong time, in the dark ages of British cinema which critics and historians have been slow to illuminate.

All this scholarly argument can no doubt be developed further, with the help of additional archival viewings and trade-paper research, but I will end by proposing a dramatization. *Stannard and Hitchcock*: an archetypal story of the younger man who learns from and uses the older man, and then moves on. It has overtones of Prince Hal and Falstaff, and of Orson Welles and Herman Mankiewicz. Told in flashback from 1944, when Hitchcock's latest Hollywood triumph is in the cinemas and Stannard is dying in obscurity, it builds up a parallel narrative between the busy writer, full of ideas but never fully satisfied with the results, and the canny, ambitious beginner who soaks up impressions and ideas, as Jane Sloan puts it, like a sponge.[33] He reads Stannard, keeps his eye on him, and, when the time comes, draws heavily on his skills. Stannard in turn is thrilled at the way his ideas are at last being properly realized on screen, but also, increasingly, anxious, since the younger man is getting all the publicity, and growing more assured, and, it seems, impatient, planning new moves. And then the synchronized sound film, so often rumoured, actually arrives, and the fallout from this gives the drama the kind of Act Three climax that Hitchcock always liked his writers to provide.

If properly researched, and written by a dramatist with a feeling for film history, this could become a story not just of two men and a betrayal, but of core developments in British cinema; and it could be more effective than any work of academic criticism in suggesting how much, after all, the great man owed to his writers, and to the British film industry out of which he emerged.

Notes

I am especially grateful to Jon Burrows for locating, and copying for me, the majority of the *Kine Weekly* items referred to.

1. V.I. Pudovkin, *On Film Technique* (London: Victor Gollancz, 1929), p. 27.
2. Ernest Lindgren, *The Art of the Film* (London: Allen & Unwin, 1948), pp. 83ff.; Karel Reisz, *The Technique of Film Editing* (London and New York: Focal Press, 1953), pp. 26ff.; Ralph Stephenson and J.R. Debrix, *The Film as Art* (Harmondsworth: Penguin, 1965), p. 131, and plate 29 (the peacock).
3. An editorial note to *On Film Technique* indicates that part of the text had

been delivered as a lecture to the Film Society in London in February 1929. Pudovkin's translator and friend, Ivor Montagu, was a founder of that Society, and had begun the first of two periods of collaboration with Hitchcock by helping with the editing and titling of *The Lodger* (1926). Hitchcock talks about the influence of Pudovkin in, for instance, chapter 11 of François Truffaut, *Hitchcock* (revised edition, New York: Simon and Shuster, 1985; first published in French in 1966, and in English in 1968).

4. W. De-W, 'The Triumph of "Justice",' *Kine Weekly*, 26 July 1917, p. 79.

5. Eliot Stannard, 'The Use of Symbols in Scenarios,' *Kine Weekly*, 12 July 1917, p. 108.

6. For Hitchcock's reading of the trade papers, see Donald Spoto, *The Life of Alfred Hitchcock: The Dark Side of Genius* (London: Collins, 1983), pp. 38ff. For his acknowledgement of Galsworthy's influence, see the 1950 interview by David Brady, reprinted in Sidney Gottlieb, ed., *Hitchcock on Hitchcock* (London: Faber and Faber, 1995).

7. John Russell Taylor, in the authorized biography *Hitch: The Life and Work of Alfred Hitchcock* (London: Faber and Faber, 1978), p. 89, indicates that Hitchcock 'brought [Stannard] with him' when he moved to BIP and that Stannard worked on the script for *The Ring*, despite his absence from the credits. See also note 31, below.

8. Tom Ryall, *Alfred Hitchcock and the British Cinema* (London: Croom Helm, 1986).

9. Charles Barr, *English Hitchcock* (Moffat, Scotland: Cameron and Hollis, 1999).

10. 'Eliot Stannard at the S.P.T. [Stoll Picture Theatres] Club,' *Kine Weekly*, 18 April 1918; 'Eliot Stannard on the Cameraman and the Scenario Writer,' account of lecture to the Kine-Cameramen's Society, *Kine Weekly* 17 February 1921, supplement, p. xx.

11. Eliot Stannard, 'Symbolism,' *Kine Weekly*, 23 May 1918, p. 76; 'The British Film Actor,' 30 May, p. 79; 'The Unseen,' 6 June, p. 97; 'The Life of a Film,' 13 June, p. 81; 'What of the Future?,' 20 June, p. 87. Eliot Stannard, 'Writing Screen Plays,' Lesson Six in the series *Cinema—in Ten Complete Lessons* (London: Standard Art Book Company, 1920).

12. Stannard, 'Writing Screen Plays,' p. 3.

13. Stannard, 'The Unseen,' p. 97.

14. 'Eliot Stannard on the Cameraman and the Scenario Writer,' p. xx.

15. Stannard, 'Writing Screen Plays,' *passim*.

16. Ibid., pp. 8ff.

17. Charles Bennett interviewed in Pat McGilligan, ed., *Backstory: Interviews with Screenwriters of Hollywood's Golden Age* (Berkeley: University of California Press, 1986).

18. Stannard, 'Writing Screen Plays,' pp. 16ff.

19. *Kine Weekly*, 23 May 1918, p. 76.

20. Stannard, 'Writing Screen Plays,' p. 24.
21. Rachael Low, *The History of the British Film, 1914–1918* (London: Allen and Unwin, 1950); Low, *The History of the British Film, 1918–1929* (London: Allen and Unwin, 1971); Denis Gifford: *The British Film Catalogue 1895–1970, A Guide to Entertainment Films* (Newton Abbot: David & Charles, 1973). Low omits his name from her credits for *Justice*, signalling the film as simply being adapted from Galsworthy; the *Kine Weekly* coverage establishes his responsibility for the scenario, and this is unlikely to be the only such gap in Low's records. In addition to his own scripts, Stannard evidently worked on a wide range of films as scenario editor and as 'script doctor', as described by Sidney Gilliat in his memories of working for BIP in the 1920s: 'The only resident British writer I can remember was Eliot Stannard, a great character. He seemed to be writing or rewriting everything. If something went wrong on a picture, Stannard was called up—like Shakespeare would have been—and asked to come in and pep up the scene a bit.' Gilliat, interviewed by Kevin Macdonald in John Boorman and Walter Donohoe, eds, *Projections 2* (London: Faber and Faber, 1993), p. 123.
22. Low, *The History of the British Film, 1914–1918*, p. 240.
23. On the influence of the 1978 FIAF event, see for instance Thomas Elsaesser with Adam Barker, eds, *Early Cinema: Space, Frame, Narrative* (London: BFI, 1990); on 'classicism', see David Bordwell, Janet Staiger and Kristin Thompson, *The Classical Hollywood Cinema: Film Style and Mode of Production to 1960* (London: Routledge & Kegan Paul, 1985).
24. Stannard, 'The Use of Symbols in Scenarios,' *Kine Weekly*, 12 July 1917, p. 108.
25. See Andrew Higson, *Waving the Flag: Constructing a National Cinema in Britain* (Oxford: Clarendon Press, 1995), pp. 26ff.; also Higson, 'The Victorious Re-cycling of National History: *Nelson*,' in Karel Dibbets and Bert Hogenkamp, eds, *Film and the First World War* (Amsterdam: Amsterdam University Press, 1995).
26. An Elvey retrospective was shown at the annual silent film festival in Pordenone, Italy, in 1997; it is discussed by Ian Christie in 'Mystery Men: Two Challenges to Film History,' *Film Studies*, issue 1, Spring 1999, pp. 78–80; see also David Berry and Simon Horrocks, eds, *David Lloyd George: the Movie Mystery* (Cardiff: University of Wales Press, 1998), a series of essays about a rediscovered but never released Elvey film of 1918.
27. Low, *The History of the British Film, 1914–1918*, p. 241.
28. Barr, *English Hitchcock*, pp. 27–57.
29. *Kine Weekly*, 20 June 1918, p. 87.
30. Truffaut, *Hitchcock*, p. 61.

31. Barr, *English Hitchcock*, p. 26, quoting Gilliat's unpublished memoirs (in private hands).
32. In view of his absence from the credits of *The Ring*, it is interesting that this is the film that Lambert recalls Stannard mentioning: 'at least fifty per cent of the *most important* ideas were mine.' Gavin Lambert, *About Lindsay Anderson: a Memoir* (London: Faber and Faber, 2000), p. 35.
33. Jane Sloan, *Alfred Hitchcock, A Filmography and Bibliography* (Berkeley: University of California Press, 1995), p. 37.

15

H.G. Wells and British Silent Cinema
The War of the Worlds

Sylvia Hardy

Prose Fiction and British Cinema in the 1920s

The title of this chapter is in a sense misleading because I shall not be writing about H.G. Wells's famous scientific romance *The War of the Worlds*, published in 1898, nor about the film which was eventually made of the book by Byron Haskin in 1953. The conflict I want to consider is not between humans and Martians but the one that has existed between the 'worlds' of literature and film from the very beginning of cinema. Wells's involvement with British cinema made a unique contribution to this particular war of the worlds. This is partly because his work has been filmed so extensively.[1] But it is also because his writings both reflect and have contributed to the changes which have taken place over the decades in the way film makes use of and sees itself as relating to prose fiction.

Herbert George Wells's emergence as a writer coincided with the beginnings of film. His first book, *The Time Machine*, was published in 1895, the year of the Lumières' presentation in Paris, and its popular success brought him into contact with Robert William Paul, one of the pioneers of British film. Paul arranged to meet Wells to discuss patenting his plans for a machine which, through a combination of mechanical devices and the projection of 'animated photographs' would persuade audiences that they were travelling through time, into the past or the future.[2] Nothing came of the idea, and Wells later claimed that he had forgotten all about it.[3] Replying to a letter from Terry

Ramsaye in 1924, Wells denied that he had been aware of any relation between his early fiction and the motion picture film, but Ramsaye remained unconvinced. In *A Million and One Nights* he writes: 'It would seem pretty definite that the *Time Traveller* was all eyes and the story all motion picture.'[4] What is more, Ramsaye claims, had Wells chosen at that stage of his career to give his attention to the motion picture rather than to the printed page, 'he might have set the screen's progress forward many a year'.[5]

From the outset, then, Wells's position as a writer had affinities with the burgeoning British film industry. As Roy Armes, amongst others, points out, the cinema did not arrive when it did by chance, and social and demographic changes towards the end of the nineteenth century played an important part: 'From the beginning films were entertainment artefacts made by bourgeois manufacturers for the urban working classes who were just starting to find their voice.'[6] The rapid and revolutionary changes taking place in the literary world in that period were part of the same process, and Wells was one of the first really successful writers to emerge from an impoverished lower-middle-class background. Ill-educated,[7] never fully accepted by the literary elite, Wells was well aware that he owed his good fortune to the growth of a vast new readership within the urban working class and the subsequent demand for fiction of all sorts. Just as the new film industry at this period made 'great efforts to achieve a gloss of respectability and live down its origins as a popular art of the fairgrounds',[8] so the literary world had also undergone its own tensions and readjustments. The closing decades of the nineteenth century saw an explosion of a new kind of journalism. Wells identified himself with popular culture, telling Henry James that he would rather be called a journalist than an 'Artist', deliberately associating himself, as Peter Keating points out, 'with what he knew James would regard as one of the most corrupting forces of modern life'.[9]

Wells's willingness to embrace the new medium of film relates partly to his enthusiasm for science and for the future. Thus, while many literary figures in the 1920s and 1930s regarded the cinema with distaste, even fear—Q.D. Leavis, for instance, associated film with day-dreaming, drug-taking and masturbation[10]—Wells extolled film as the art form of the future. He also took a cheerfully iconoclastic approach to literary pretensions, welcoming cinema's ability to reach large, non-middle-class audiences and relishing the discomfiture of his more traditional colleagues in the face of mass culture. In the late 1920s he wrote that:

> It has been interesting to watch the elegant and dignified traditions of the world of literature and cultivated appreciation, under the stresses and thrusts produced by the development of rapid photography during the past half century.[11]

Forming links with an already established art form has always been a way of attaining artistic respectability. Just as in the 1880s Henry James promoted the novel as a serious art form by linking it with the then more prestigious art of painting, so film, once it was established as primarily a narrative form, turned to literature.[12] This, of course, was not only for purposes of prestige but also because existing novels and plays provided ready-made and already popular stories and characters. Wells made fun of the studios' avidity for source texts. 'The industry clamoured for stories,' he wrote,

> and its chief anxiety was that the supply of 'stories' might come to an end. It bought right and left; it bought high and low; it was so opulent it could buy with its eyes shut. It did. Its methods were simple and direct. It took all the stories it could get, and changed all that were not absolutely intractable into one old, old story, with variations of costume, scenery and social position.[13]

Wells's comments on the cinema's passion for stories were written in 1928, by which time he had already sold the film-rights to a number of his books. Alan Wykes claims that the first to reach the screen was *The Invisible Man*, filmed in 1909 by Charles Pathé at Vincennes with the title of *L'Invisible Voleur*.[14] Not much is known about the film, but judging from the stills that have survived,[15] it appears to have treated the story primarily as an opportunity for trick photography. Wells's first major contract was with the British Gaumont Company. *The Times*, announcing this on 10 January 1914, pointed out that although the terms of the contract were not new, they showed a new trend. While a good plot is essential for film-manufacturers, said the article, 'its value is also greatly enhanced if there is associated with the production the name of a famous author'.[16] Film-writing was clearly very much on Wells's mind later that same January when he wrote from Russia to his mistress, Rebecca West, who was expecting his baby. In the course of giving her instructions about finding a house in Wales where she would be able to spend her pregnancy discreetly, Wells writes:

You are Mrs West, I am Mr West. Write and arrange that you are to stay at Llandudno until your baby is born. Mr West is in the cinematograph business and he has to write things. He wants a quiet room to work in and has to have a separate bedroom.[17]

At the beginning of 1913 Wells agreed to sell the film-rights to *The Invisible Man* and *The First Men in the Moon*. A large number of production companies showed interest, but, in the words of Wells's agent, 'they all declare that the books we have offered from you would be too expensive to produce'.[18] The cost and technical difficulties of producing the special effects required by science fiction may explain why British Gaumont—who purchased the rights to *The First Men in the Moon* at the end of that year—did not begin filming until the end of the war. The film was released in 1919. Then came three Stoll productions in the space of two years, *Kipps* (1921), *The Wheels of Chance* (1922), and *The Passionate Friends* (1922). Brian McFarlane estimates that in 1922, 23 per cent of the year's total output of seventy British feature films was based on novels,[19] and there were particular reasons why the early 1920s marked a peak period for film literary adaptation in British studios. There was a strong desire to promote the British film industry,[20] and, as an article in *Bioscope* makes clear, one way of furthering this aim was through films which 'show Britain as it has been pictured by its own great writers'.[21] In 1922, Stoll Film Productions launched a new programme, Stoll's Eminent Authors Series, which comprised eleven screenplays, 'stories that carry the name of a famous author behind every one of them'.[22]

One of these authors was H.G. Wells. Although Wells had been a popular writer since 1895, by 1922 he had acquired considerable prestige. Not only was he an established author of serious novels as well as scientific romances, he was also the acclaimed author of *The Outline of History*, a project which had brought him a vast new readership.[23] Even allowing for journalistic hyperbole, *Kinematograph Weekly*'s claim that 'Mr Wells is one of the biggest forces in the world today, a literary giant, and his admirers are legion'[24] was not only good publicity, it was not far from the truth.

Adaptations: *Kipps* and *The Passionate Friends*

The most substantial adaptations of Wells's work in the silent period were Harold Shaw's version of *Kipps* and Maurice Elvey's *The Passionate Friends*. Wells's 1905 novel, *Kipps*, which tells the story of an apprentice draper, Artie Kipps, who comes into a fortune and attempts to enter genteel society, soon became a best-seller and to date has never been out of print. *The Passionate Friends*, on the other hand, which depicts a doomed love affair between a politician, Stephen Stratton, and Lady Mary Christian and their confrontation with her husband, Justin, was never one of Wells's most popular novels and is now virtually unread.

No filmic adaptation can reproduce exactly what is achieved in a novel because film and prose fiction employ different signification systems. The decisions about story, characterization and *mise en scène* made in these two films thus throw an interesting light on the approach of British directors to literary texts at this period, particularly their expectations of their audiences. Wells declared *The Passionate Friends* to be a novel of ideas, and *Kipps*, he felt, was not only a comedy but also 'the complete study of a life in relation to England's social conditions'.[25] Both films, however, either play down or leave out altogether the political and social comment so prominent in the novels, and although there is no reason why any adaptation should adhere rigidly to its source-text, these changes affect the way the films deal with time, story and subjectivity.

Shaw's *Kipps*, like the book, depicts the stages of its hero's development in linear fashion, with the addition of a brief flashback sequence showing his childhood relations with Sid and Ann Pornick. Although the film is in one sense faithful to Wells's novel—the reviewer in the *Bioscope* calls it 'an unusually faithful transcription from book to screen'[26]—it does leave out the one explicitly ideological part of the book, the scene in which Kipps listens open-mouthed to the Socialist opinions of Sid Pornick's lodger, Masterman. This is an important omission because there is now no adequate explanation for Kipps' new-found militancy on his return to Folkestone. Presumably the filmmakers were concerned with audience appeal—Masterman's tirade is both didactic and controversial—but as one contemporary reviewer puts it: 'the whole of one aspect of the novel, the most seriously important aspect, has been dropped completely . . . the ethics and social lesson of the original story have been eviscerated.'[27]

The problem is that both *Kipps* and *The Passionate Friends* are novels that depend to a large extent on the narrative voice for their satirical effect. In *Kipps*, of course, some of the social satire is built into the events of the story itself—the Anagram Tea, for instance, or the debacle of Kipps' dinner in the London hotel—which the film reproduces faithfully; the copious expository intertitles also often echo the tones of the novel's kindly but ironic omniscient narrator. A typical example is the title which accompanies Kipps's early experiences at the draper's: 'In the indentures that bound Kipps to Mr Shalford for seven long years there were vague stipulations about teaching him the whole art and mystery of the trade.' This incorporates several of the ironic, mock-heroic phrases that characterize the novel's narration.

The material of *The Passionate Friends* presents the adapter with greater difficulties because it takes the form of a letter from Stephen Stratton to his son in which he describes the love affair but gives equal weight to his own development and political ideas. Elvey's film as a whole fails to find an adequate substitute for Stratton's first-person commentary, although the opening shots are promising because they foreground, in visual terms, the issues of class and political privilege central to the book. The first of the film's titles—'Lady Mary Christian's world . . .'—is followed by a lengthy long shot of an imposing stately home viewed from the garden. Then there is a close shot of two men, who are looking intently at the group of fashionably dressed people clustered around Lady Mary Christian; one says: 'As a Labour man, I consider it disastrous that political power depends on the patronage exercised by the people of Lady Mary's world.' But these radical issues are not followed up, the unnamed Socialist does not appear again, and the social chasm which divides Stratton and Mary—which is central to the plot of the novel—is scarcely touched on in the subsequent scenes.[28]

Elvey's film also simplifies the convoluted chronology of the novel, shortening the twenty-five year time-span of the story to two years—presumably in order to clarify the plot for the audience; but this still leaves periods where very little happens that can be represented visually since the focus is on the emotions and psychology of the characters rather than their actions. Wells sends his hero off to the Boer War after Mary's marriage. The film, instead, offers lengthy shots of Steven Stratton suffering—lying on the sofa, smoking moodily, walking by the river, gazing at Mary's photograph—scenes which are introduced by titles such as: 'And in the weeks that followed, Steven, overwhelmed by the turmoil of life, paid no heed to his work', 'The old longing . . .', 'The depths of despair' and so on.

The film does come to life again in the confrontation scene when Justin discovers his wife in Steven's arms, and even more effectively in a later sequence which depicts the lovers' accidental meeting at a hotel in France. In the novel, Stratton and Mary, who have sworn never to meet again, spend the night in adjoining rooms but are unaware of the fact until the morning; in the film Elvey contrives a connecting door between their rooms, which enables him to show the maid listening at the outer door. It also gives a considerable erotic charge to the scene, which alternates shots of Stratton's and Mary's anguished faces on either side of the door with extreme close-ups of the bolt and Mary's hand hovering over it. The connecting door is an interesting change because when he was writing *The Passionate Friends* in 1912 Wells was in the middle of an affair with the novelist, Elizabeth von Arnim, spending the summer with her in Switzerland and helping her superintend the building of a chalet. In the *Postscript* to his 1934 autobiography, Wells tells of how they arranged for a secret door 'which always moved on well-oiled castors' between von Arnim's bedroom and the visitor's room where he stayed. 'We said "Goodnight" in the passage to each other and whatever guests were with us,' he adds, 'and there was no subsequent creaking in the passage or any opening or shutting of doors.'[29] Since the *Postscript* was not published until 1984, it would seem that the film's scriptwriter, Leslie Howard Gordon, had either heard rumours or was remarkably prescient.

It would be interesting to know what Wells thought about this scene in *The Passionate Friends*. Indeed, it would be interesting to know what he thought about any of the films that were made of his work during the silent period. With the exception of one visit to the Savoy Hotel, where he watched the filming of the dinner-party scene in *Kipps*—an incident which was widely reported, probably because it was so rare[30]—Wells kept his distance from the productions themselves. He did attend a private showing of *Kipps* in 1921 where Stoll Productions had arranged a meeting with Charlie Chaplin. Chaplin did not like the film and said so—he pointed to 'faulty photography' and occasionally 'bad direction'[31]—but, as he later recorded, his companion remained silent. 'Wells's attitude to movies was an affected tolerance,' Chaplin writes, '"There is no such thing as a bad film," he said "the fact that they move is wonderful!"'[32] It seems likely that Wells's non committal attitude was governed by good manners; he had after all agreed to sell his work to film companies and, as he comments in *The King Who Was a King*, 'It would be ungracious to complain'.[33]

H.G. Wells's Direct Involvement with British Silent Cinema

Whatever his opinion of the adaptations which British studios had made of his work Wells made no secret of the fact that he considered

1920s films in general to be shallow and hackneyed. In 1923, for instance, in a contribution to a symposium on the novelist and the film, he attacked the commercialism of British studios, describing 'cinema people' as 'utterly damned fools, beneath the level of a decent man's attention'.[34] In 1936, looking back on this period, he declared: 'I wouldn't then associate myself with any of the big film companies because I did not consider their work particularly edifying.'[35] The introductory chapter to *The King Who Was a King* makes it clear that Wells's major objection to what he calls 'crude, shallow trade movies'[36] is their naivety and conventionality. Wells believed that the novelist should be a teacher as well as storyteller and entertainer and he extended this notion to film. To date, he complained, filmmakers had not attempted to explore the vast potential of their medium because they were content to take the easy way and to rely wholly on 'variations which do not innovate' of the same old story.[37]

Interestingly, Wells puts much of the blame on 'the war of the worlds', the absence of rapport between filmmakers and established writers such as himself who, he argues, had been reluctant to engage with the new medium and to explore new modes of expression. In 1914 *The Times* had expressed the hope that Mr Wells would write stories 'especially for cinematograph productions' but Wells did not begin to explore the techniques of scenario writing until 1927, when a producer called Edward Godal approached him with plans for a film to be called *The Peace of the World*, a title Wells had already used for a series of newspaper articles,[38] and which was bound to appeal to him because it related to his idea of a World State.[39] When Godal went bankrupt, Wells regained the rights, rewrote and retitled the piece and in 1929 published it in book form as *The King Who Was a King: the Book of the Film*. Since the scenario was never filmed, its only interest today is what it tells us about Wells's idea of film at this period and the extent to which the script fails to live up to the strictures set out in the introduction. His avowed aim had been to avoid a conventional story and to do without what he calls 'a normal love interest',[40] but what the script offers is a Ruritanian romance structured around very familiar plot devices: a hero of royal descent reluctantly assuming the throne from a sense of duty; a villain next in line who seeks to depose him; a beautiful princess with whom he falls in love, and so on. The script direction for the final scene, which shows King Paul piloting an aeroplane with Princess Helen standing behind him, reads: 'They are flying towards the audience. They are Man the Maker and Woman the Protector and Sustainer. The music throbs to a climax.'[41] This sounds

Plate 28.   Production still from *Bluebottles* (Montagu/Wells, 1928), featuring Elsa Lanchester

more like the ending of a conventional woman's picture than the political statement Wells intended.

In the same year he was revising *The Peace of the World*, Wells was persuaded to make a direct contribution to British cinema, partly to further the career of his second son, Frank, who was then working with Ivor Montagu and Adrian Brunel in their editing company. An American backer had offered to finance three short comedy films if Wells would provide the stories. Wells agreed, the only proviso being that Elsa Lanchester, then a rising actress, should be given the leading roles. Montagu found it difficult to get the synopses from Wells, who was heavily engaged with his latest novel. In the end, he travelled overnight to Wells's Paris flat and, he records, stood over him.

> while in his dressing gown, he wrote down 'Bluebottles'. The other two, 'Daydreams' and 'The Tonic' were even more difficult but I dug my heels in. Finally they emerged as about a paragraph each and I flew back triumphant to London on the afternoon plane.[42]

The films were shot in the old Gainsborough studio in Islington and completed by December 1928, but they were held up by the distributors, Ideal Pictures, for nearly a year. Montagu blames this delay for their failure at the box-office: 'Conception occurred in a world of silent films,' he writes, 'Parturition in a world already invaded by sound . . .'[43]

In *Bluebottles*, Lanchester plays a servant girl who picks up a police-whistle lying on the pavement, blows it, and ends up capturing a gang of thieves. *Daydreams* presents her fantasies of marrying a French count, being abducted by a Rajah and then shipwrecked, eventually emerging as 'the most popular widow in Europe'. In *The Tonic* she plays an inept servant who is sent by her grasping employers to a rich aunt in the hope that she will mix up the medicines and kill the old lady. From today's perspective, *Bluebottles* and *Daydreams* are engaging, fast moving and very funny—largely because of the performance of Lanchester, who Wells believed had 'Chaplinesque' qualities.[44] (Charles Laughton, Lanchester's husband, also appeared in all three films.) Although the films were financed and promoted on the strength of H.G. Wells's name, it seems clear that his brief synopses were interpreted and expanded by Montagu and Frank Wells. Montagu, who directed the films, recalls that at the Islington studio 'we were desperately working on H.G.'s scraps of paper, trying to think up visual jokes and turn them into scripts'.[45] Frank's unpublished typewritten script for *Bluebottles*, which corresponds in every detail to the finished film, includes 222 scenes (shots), each with a heading which specifies the setting, time of day, type of shot and whether it is interior or exterior. His father's would-be silent film scenario, in contrast, *The*

King Who Was a King, reads more like a novel, with long, descriptive passages and the dialogue titles picked out in italics.

Thus, although it is difficult to make comparisons between the fast-moving and visually innovative Frank Wells/Ivor Montagu films and H.G. Wells's unfilmed script, one enormous contrast is evident in the scenarios themselves. The twenty-minute long *Bluebottles* has two expository intertitles and only eight dialogue titles; the first part of *The King Who Was a King*, which would occupy roughly the same amount of screen-time, includes sixty-two expository titles (many of them lengthy) and a staggering 211 dialogue titles, plus a vast number of inserts of various kinds: posters, news bills, banners, telegrams and so on. If we accept that intertitles perform the function of a narrator in silent films,[46] it is clear that Wells found it impossible to step aside from the role and think visually; as author he must direct the spectator's attention, and his medium is words, not pictures. The issue of sub-titles was in any case a controversial one in the 1920s. In the main, it was felt that films should tell their stories through visual images wherever possible. 'When is a motion picture not a picture?' asked a writer in the *Bioscope*. 'The answer is when it is a collection of sub-titles.'[47] Film critics then and since have also tended to extol as 'pure' cinema films with few or no titles, possibly as a way of stressing film's independence from literature.

Wells presents a paradox in his relation to the worlds of literature and film during the silent period. Seen from one perspective he was a writer whose work not only lent itself to brilliant cinematic effects but often anticipated them; from another he appears as a would-be film-writer unable to write effective screenplays. Nonetheless, Wells's enthusiasm for the potential of cinema was unbounded. He was a founder member of the Film Society in 1925[48] and remained a member for the fourteen years of its existence, never deviating from his belief that film was the art form of the future. As he wrote in 1929:

> Behind the first cheap triumphs of the film today rise the possibility of a spectacle-music-drama, greater, more beautiful and intellectually deeper and richer than any artistic form humanity has hitherto achieved.[49]

Notes

1. To date, thirteen of Well's major fictions have been filmed, some of them more than once (there have been two versions each of *The Passionate Friends* and *Kipps*, and three of *The Island of Dr Moreau*).

2. 'An Interview with Robert William Paul,' *Era*, 25 April 1896.

3. H.G. Wells, *The King Who Was a King: The Book of a Film* (London: Ernest Benn, 1929), p. 10.

4. Terry Ramsaye, *A Million and One Nights* (New York: Simon and Schuster 1986; first published 1926), p. 154.

5. Ibid., p. 162.

6. Roy Armes, *A Critical History of the British Cinema* (London: Secker and Warburg, 1978), pp. 16–17.

7. Although he achieved an honours degree in Biology from London University and eventually became a Doctor of Science, Wells's haphazard education was not regarded as acceptable by the literary establishment of his period.

8. Armes, *A Critical History of the British Cinema*, p. 33.

9. Peter Keating, *The Haunted Study: A Social History of the English Novel 1875–1914* (London: Fontana Press, 1991; first published 1989), p. 294.

10. Q.D. Leavis, *Fiction and the Reading Public* (London: Bellew Publishing, 1978; first published 1932), pp. 54–5, 165.

11. Wells, *The King Who Was a King*, p. 8.

12. Brian McFarlane, 'A Literary Cinema? British Films and British Novels,' in Charles Barr, ed., *All Our Yesterdays* (London: BFI Publishing, 1992), p. 121.

13. Wells, *The King Who Was a King*, p. 11.

14. Alan Wykes, *H.G. Wells in the Cinema* (London: Jupiter, 1977), pp. 28–9.

15. It is possible that *L'Invisible Voleur* had few links with *The Invisible Man*. There is no record of a contract with the Pathé Company, and in 1913 Wells's agent was attempting to sell the film rights of *The Invisible Man* to a number of production companies. A 1933 memorandum, showing which of Wells's film rights had been sold, begins with the 1913 sale of *The First Men in the Moon* to Gaumont and ends with the sale of 'all motion picture, broadcasting and television rights' in *The Invisible Man* to Universal Pictures, 1931 (unpublished letter to A.S. Watts, 9 February 1933, Wells Archive, University of Illinois at Urbana, USA).

16. *The Times*, 10 January 1914.

17. David C. Smith, *The Correspondence of H.G. Wells* (London: Pickering and Chatto, 1998, vol. 2), p. 363.

18. Unpublished letter, Curtis Brown to Wells, 5 June 1913 (Wells Archive).

19. McFarlane, 'A Literary Cinema? British Films and British Novels,' p. 121.

20. See for instance *Kinematograph Weekly*, 6 January 1921, p. 102.

21. 'Filming English Literature: A Real Attempt to Interpret Britain on the

World Screens—Wilfred Noy's Production of "The Lady Clare",'
Bioscope, 30 October 1919, p. 59.

22. *Kinematograph Weekly*, 5 January 1922, p. 89.

23. *Photoplay* announced in July 1922 that D.W. Griffith was visiting Britain in order to discuss with H.G. Wells a project for filming *The Outline of History*—'In seventy-two reels!'—which not surprisingly never saw the light of day (*Photoplay*, July 1922, p. 58). Kevin Brownlow believes that this was never intended as a serious suggestion: 'announcements like this were designed to keep G.'s name in the public eye rather than to confirm his new projects' (letter to the author, 28 October 1996).

24. *Kinematograph Weekly*, 5 January 1922, p. 89.

25. From a letter to Well's agent, J.B. Pinker, quoted in Norman and Jeanne Mackenzie, *The Time Traveller: The Life of H.G. Wells* (London: Weidenfeld and Nicolson, 1974), p. 192.

26. *Bioscope*, 27 January 1921, p. 62.

27. *Kinematograph Weekly*, 27 January 1921, pp. 69–70.

28. Interestingly the class aspect was picked up by American reviewers who reacted against the film's aristocratic setting. The *New York Times* dismissed *The Passionate Friends* (retitled *One Woman's Story* in the USA) as 'sedulously dull, with the iron hand of British breeding shackling its content'. Quoted in Wykes, *H.G. Wells in the Cinema*, p. 58.

29. G.P. Wells, ed., *H.G. Wells in Love: Postscript to An Experiment in Autobiography* (London: Faber, 1984), p. 88.

30. See e.g. *Bioscope*, 11 November 1920, p. 51; *Stoll's Editorial News*, 8 September 1921, pp. iv-viii.

31. Charles Chaplin, *My Wonderful Visit* (London: Hurst and Blocket, 1922), p. 142. Chaplin does not give us his reactions to the portrayal of Wells's 'little man' in the film, which in several scenes shows a figure whose clothes, stick and stance bear a close resemblance to Chaplin's tramp.

32. Charles Chaplin, *My Autobiography* (London: Bodley Head, 1964), p. 295. The autobiography was written forty years after Chaplin's first meeting with Wells, which is recorded in more detail in his 1922 memoir, but here too the only thing he noted about Wells's response to the film was the writer's concern for the feelings of 'the boy', George K. Arthur, who played Artie Kipps. *My Wonderful Visit*, pp. 142–3.

33. Wells, *The King Who Was a King*, p. 11. There is no doubt that by the end of the 1920s Wells had benefitted considerably from the silent cinema. In addition to his English contracts, in 1919 Wells received an offer from Samuel Goldwyn: a contract for a five-year film option at £1,000 per work, with the guarantee of at least £2,000 a year. By 1933, according to one biographer, Wells had received £6,750 and $10,000 from British and American production companies; David C. Smith, *H.G. Wells: Desperately Mortal* (London: Yale University Press, 1986), pp. 322–3.

34. 'The Novelist and the Film,' *John o'London's*, 4 August 1923, p. 578.

35. 'I Wrote this Film for Your Enjoyment, says H.G. Wells,' *Film Weekly*, 29 February 1936, p. 8.
36. Wells, *The King Who Was a King*, p. 15.
37. Ibid., p. 12.
38. Rachael Low, *The History of British Film, 1918–1929* (London: George Allen and Unwin, 1971), p. 199.
39. Plans for the film went ahead rapidly, but by December 1927 Wells's son Frank was indicating that Godal International Company was in financial trouble. Godal, he wrote, had 'a stranglehold on the story' and had already signed up stars, cameraman and director but had not raised the money to pay them (unpublished letter dated 6 December, Wells Archive).
40. Wells's, *The King Who Was a King*, p. 31.
41. Ibid., pp. 243–4.
42. Ivor Montagu, *With Eisenstein in Hollywood* (London: Lawrence and Wishart, 1968), p. 19.
43. Ibid., p. 23. Simon Rowson, managing director of Ideal Films, wanted to issue *Bluebottles, Daydreams* and *The Tonic* as sound films, but in a letter dated 3 July 1929, Montagu told him: 'I know that Mr Wells is not pleased at the idea of the delay which means that his motive in giving us the stories which in part were to give a 'leg-up' to those engaged in the pictures by bringing them (particularly Elsa) to public attention largely misfires' (Ivor Montagu Special Collection, British Film Institute National Library). For further discussion of Montagu, and the three films, see the chapters elsewhere in this volume by Gerry Turvey and Jamie Sexton.
44. *Film Weekly*, 29 February 1936, p. 8.
45. Montagu, *With Eisenstein in Hollywood*, p. 20.
46. Celestino Deleyto, 'Focalisation in Film Narrative,' in Susana Onega and José Ángel Garcia Landa, eds, *Narratology: An Introduction* (London: Longman, 1996), p. 218.
47. 'Matters of Moment,' *Bioscope*, 15 January 1920, p. 23.
48. In 1925, Wells received a letter from Iris Barry inviting him to become an 'original member' of the Film Society. She was writing, she claimed, because Ivor Montagu was in Russia, and Wells had 'charmingly promised' to be a member (unpublished letter, undated, Wells Archive).
49. Wells, *The King Who Was a King*, p. 17.

16

War-Torn Dionysus
The Silent Passion of Ivor Novello

Michael Williams

Born in Cardiff in 1893, David Ivor Davies, better known as Ivor Novello, would become the jewel in the crown of Gainsborough Studios and, indeed, of British film in the 1920s. He starred in some twenty-two films between 1919 and 1934, of which, remarkably, eighteen are known to be extant. Novello was *the* British star of the 1920s, collaborating with a series of celebrated directors such as Graham Cutts, Adrian Brunel and Maurice Elvey. Most famously, a young and relatively unknown director named Alfred Hitchcock grudgingly worked with the matinée idol for two films, *The Lodger* (1926) and *Downhill* (1927).[1] As I have noted elsewhere, despite recent efforts to restore his (famously elegant) profile to the canon of British film history, Novello remains curiously overlooked.[2]

The film career of the British star began, ironically, with two films produced on French soil for the esteemed French director Louis Mercanton, *The Call of the Blood* (*L'appel du sang*, 1919) and *Miarka: Daughter of the Bear* (*Miarka, Fille de L'Ourse*, 1920). By the time Novello's first British feature, *Carnival* (Harley Knoles, 1921), was released in 1921 and as a 'British masterpiece', the actor's place was assured in what *Picturegoer* termed 'the front rank of British movie stars'.[3] At the end of 1924 he was the only British star to figure in a popularity contest run by the same magazine.[4] The next few years, despite an abortive seven-film contract with legendary director D.W. Griffith in America (resulting in only one film, *The White Rose*, 1924), were truly halcyon days for Novello. The wrong note sounded by

Plate 29. Production still from *The Rat* (Cutts, 1925),
featuring Ivor Novello as The Rat

Griffith's melodrama was swiftly modulated by the enormous success
of *The Rat* (Graham Cutts, 1925), the first of the star's ten features for
Gainsborough. Based on Novello's own stage play, which had been a
smash-hit in the West End the previous year, the film concerned the
louche adventures of the titular 'Rat', an Apache of the Parisian
underworld. The Rat attempts to clear the name of his young friend
Odile, who has been assaulted by the villainous 'ex' of a glamorous
courtesan with whom he has become involved. The film was so
successful that two sequels were made, again starring Novello. Another
critically acclaimed hit for Novello was Hitchcock's *The Lodger: A Tale
of the London Fog*. Set amid the clandestine intrigue evoked by the
full title, Novello plays the eponymous stranger who stays at the
Bloomsbury lodging-house of the Bunting family, only to be suspected
of being the notorious murderer called 'The Avenger', to whom he
bears an uncanny resemblance. *The Bioscope* thought it probably 'the
finest British production ever made'.[5]
By 1927, Novello's position at the heart of British film production

had been fully consolidated. This was made abundantly clear in *Bioscope*'s 'British Film Number' in June 1927, when film critic Iris Barry bemoaned the fact that 'our producers have only two stars—the now inactive Miss Balfour and Mr. Novello—to share among them- selves'.[6] A readers' poll conducted by the *Film Weekly* in 1929 came to similar conclusions, with Novello and Betty Balfour topping the bill.[7] Perhaps the strongest testament to Novello's importance for British film production is provided by the star's great friend and producer at Gainsborough Studios, Michael Balcon:

> The years 1914–1918 were catastrophic for the British film industry: they brought it to a virtual standstill and stopped nearly all technical progress . . . Novello was an invaluable ambassador for British films at a time of difficulty when ambassadors were few and far between.[8]

Given the fervency of Balcon's flag-waving, it appears that Novello was somehow uniquely endowed with enough cinematic *gravitas* to enter an international market so well guarded by his American rivals Ramon Novarro and Rudolph Valentino.[9]

Perhaps it is no accident that such a task fell to a figure so closely associated with upholding British national identity since 1915. This chapter will show how Novello's star persona as an icon of both beauty and horror drew upon his pre-existing celebrity as the composer of one of the most popular songs of the First World War, 'Keep the Home Fires Burning'. Moreover, Novello's brand of classical, luminous male beauty precipitated a fascinatingly oblique mode of reference to the war when Novello was reconstructed as a film star for popular consump- tion. This image of Novello comes through most clearly in the pages of *Picture Show*, where, perhaps in deference to the singularity of Novello's national star status, the star was promoted as not only a matinée idol, but something of a post-war hero. While such publica- tions cannot offer a direct insight into how audiences thought or felt about Novello, they can throw light on the ways in which his audiences were constructed to appreciate their star as a culturally specific, in- tertextual construct. It is these issues that I explore in the pages that follow.

Richard Dyer argues that the 'charismatic appeal' of stars is 'effective especially when the social order is uncertain, unstable and ambiguous and when the charismatic figure or group offers a value, order or stability to counterpoise this'.[10] Such figures can be perceived as either 'heroically living out the tensions or painfully exposing them'.[11] Such tensions, both heroic and painful, seem deeply rooted in Novello's cultural appeal at a time of great social transition, Novello's first film having appeared only a year after the end of the First World War. Following Dyer's argument, I will suggest that a dramatic tension arises between Novello's radiant, 'classical' form of male beauty and a counter-image of the terrible and agonized.

Apollo and Dionysus

There are few more eloquent evocations to the dual persona suggested above than a preview of two forthcoming Novello films in a 1926 edition of *Picture Show*. *The Lodger* was screened to the press in parallel with *The Triumph of the Rat* (Graham Cutts, 1926), the first sequel to the 1925 film, as if to invite comparisons between them while cashing in on Novello's success. Edith Nepean constructs this striking eulogy to the contemporary attraction of the star in her weekly column 'Round the British Studios':

> If there is one thing that Ivor Novello hates about himself it is his own good looks. He once showed me a terrible photograph of himself—his face begrimed, his hair dishevelled, a terrible agonized expression blotting out his usual calm, classic features. 'There, I like that,' he declared earnestly. There are times when handsomeness hurts. That is when a man has enormous talent and ability like Ivor Novello. He is a big enough artiste to 'get over' if he were an ugly man, instead of an Adonis!
>
> . . . Graham Cutts has never produced anything so fine, and many successes are already to his credit, than *The Triumph of the Rat*. Ivor Novello's down and out scenes are remarkable, his entire physique is a bitter revelation of debased despair, and we are left chilled, wanting more—a happy ending, a kiss from Madeleine . . . . And *The Lodger* is full of gripping mystery. Ivor restrained, a haunting picture . . .[12]

This description encapsulates Novello's stardom as it was presented in the popular press of the 1920s. His handsomeness was fundamental, there was simply no getting away from it, no sooner is his name invoked than we are witness to a plethora of swooning testaments to those ubiquitous 'classic features'. Yet there is often the hint of something else underscoring them. While his clean, fresh looks inspire reference to Adonis, if they should become begrimed and dishevelled, then that, as I hope to demonstrate, is the stuff of Greek tragedy. It is as if Novello's perennial, idealized good looks were merely an emotive trigger to another, less palatable but totally irresistible image, as suggested in the *Bioscope*'s review of Novello's performance as the Lodger: 'He conveys admirably the impression of a horror-haunted man. Even in lighter moments, when he is making love to the girl, one can see the suggestion of horror still in his eyes. His best performance to date.'[13]

To help elaborate this fascinating binary image, a somewhat surprising guide can be found in Friedrich Nietzsche's discussion of Greek drama. In *The Birth of Tragedy*, Nietzsche explored the nature of an ancient Greek society whose people, he argues, 'knew and felt the fears and horrors of existence'.[14] Nietzsche's task was not to directly scrutinize such horrors, but to examine the artistic mechanisms that respond to them, and thus account for the simultaneity of beauty and brutality in society.[15] He conceptualized this binary of 'beauty' and 'horror' in the mythical figures of Apollo and Dionysus. On one side stands Apollo, 'etymologically "the shining one," the deity of light', whose qualities are sculptural and abstinent. On the other is the war-like Dionysus, who is dissonant, orgiastic and indulgent.[16] The crucial part of Nietzsche's theocracy is that Apollo and Dionysus are united through artistic expression: a 'taming of horror through art,' as the beauty of the Apolline both lightens and enlightens the 'horrors of existence.'[17] Here too, one might argue, is the dual persona of Novello: the youthful, romantic composer who promised us the 'silver lining through the dark cloud shining' with 'Home Fires' in 1915, and the violent, sexually ambivalent 'Rat' in 1925, both personas framed against the 'horrors' of the first 'modern' war.

Novello, I suggest, literally *embodies* Nietzsche's theocracy; as *Picture Show* asserts, 'his entire physique is a bitter revelation of debased despair'. This appears to be exactly the Dionysian quality described by Nietzsche, with symptoms of the 'terrible' and the 'agonised' expressed through those 'calm, classic features'. This conception of Novello's star image thus suggests that it was anything but a cathartic, glowing placebo that could help anyone forget the problems of the outside world. This silver lining was inseparable from its cloud. Thus it was, perhaps, the receptivity of early twentieth-century poets such as Rupert Brooke to Nietzsche's mythic legacy, combined with the 1920s preoccupation with all things classical, that informs Nepean's tribute to Novello in *Picture Show*. Moreover, such eclectic acts of appropriation coincide with what Jay Winter terms a 'search for appropriate languages of mourning' in the wake of the First World War.[18]

Taking Winter's cue, it is tempting to read Novello's persona as typical of those post-war cultural products that Winter and others see as revealing the impact of the war in their form and content.[19] Many people in the 1920s seem to have shared the sense of abiding horror that the *Bioscope* perceived in the Novello's performance in *The Lodger*. As one writer put it, 'the war's baneful influence controlled still our thoughts and acts, directly or indirectly'.[20] Film was perhaps uniquely endowed as a medium through which to relive the events of the recent past, Jay Winter going so far as to suggest that cinema-going could function on a level of seance, where 'millions could half dream of the war, its supernatural aura, and of course the men who had fallen'.[21] While I do not wish to argue for a psychic, 'mirror' model of cinema, I would suggest that the war is present *implicitly* in much of Novello's work. With the composition of 'Home Fires', Novello indelibly associated his own identity with that of Britain; as Novello biographer W. Macqueen-Pope put it, 'war made Ivor Novello'.[22] Novello's fans, furthermore, reading fan magazines in the 1920s, were never allowed to forget it.

'Baneful Influence' or 'Inspiration'?

Picture Show, for instance, reminded its readers in 1921 that 'it is estimated that every officer and every man has at one time or other sang that song [*sic*]'.[23] Indeed, Hannen Swaffer, writing for *London Calling* in 1929, relates that Novello's music was considered such a 'work of national importance' for the war effort that its composer was dispatched to Sweden for a three-month propaganda tour in 1918, to counteract a similar tour (with a similar song) by the German conductor Nikisch.[24]

Ten years after the song was first heard, Part 6 of *Picture Show*'s epic biography of the star, 'Life, Romance of Ivor Novello' (attributed to the pen of Novello himself), proudly heralded 'The War—"Keep the Home Fires Burning"'.[25] Here, Novello recalled his war experience through the song, which he confessed caused more letters to be sent to him 'than anything I have ever had to do with', suggesting that the horrors of the war were also rather inspiring:

> I came back to England [from America] in the winter of 1913 and went on with my composing. And then, a year afterwards, you know all too well what happened. The War came!
>
> In a moment we were pitched into a different world. Everything seemed to stop or turn upside down. Those first few months, however, were full of inspiration for me so far as my music was concerned.[26]

After describing the 'hundreds of thousands' of people singing the song in front of Buckingham Palace on Armistice Day, its composer concludes that it was 'the best thing that has happened in my life, because it was a significant thing. It had to do with big issues, and I am proud that I had this connection with them.'[27]

By thus reasserting the war credentials of this 'Composer, Stage and Screen Star', *Picture Show*'s retrospective marks a consolidation of Novello's public identity in preparation for the launch of his first film for Gainsborough, *The Rat*. Part of this project, silent film being a visual medium, was to give this post-war identity a 'face' befitting its nature, assimilating the strong thread of poetic, classical and frankly florid adjectives that had been accumulating in press reviews since the star's first appearance in 1919. Here, I suggest, another inspiring figure of the war is brought into covert play. 1915 was not only the year in which Novello became a 'war' composer, it was also the year in which 'war poet' Rupert Brooke met his death near Gallipoli and became in the popular consciousness 'one of the first modern icons of beauty'.[28]

No reference to Brooke is deemed complete without quotation from Frances Cornford's 1905 description of the poet as a 'young Apollo . . . dreaming on the verge of strife', which has come to encapsulate perfectly the mythology surrounding that 'young Apollo' lost to the Great War, along with the generation that he posthumously symbolized.[29] Brooke and Novello were continually evoked with the same mellifluous vocabulary even, as in the case of their obituaries, soliciting exact repetitions of phrasing in deference to their classic symmetry of mind and body. Novello was promoted in 1923 as no less than 'England's Apollo', an exquisite symbol of the youthful, classical and national.[30] Thus through the persona of Novello, I suggest, we can apprehend a kind of figurative re-embodiment of Brooke. Consider, for example, the way Novello's features are rendered as if a work of (Apolline) classical sculpture by Sydney Carroll in 1934:

> Observe that magnificent head, with its coal-black hair swung from a forehead shaped as a sculptor might have loved to form it. That profile approximating to nobility denoting command in every part; that determined chin; those large and luminous eyes, such as Dante might have had—these surely cannot belong to a mere mummer? Surely some Greek statue of a young, athletic poet has been brought to life?[31]

Does the eulogized persona of Brooke 'live on', in some ingenious way, in the popular persona of Novello, whom *Picturegoer* described in 1923 as the 'handsome youth' with 'classic charm to his features'?[32] Perhaps this sentiment is echoed by the very first intertitle that described the composer to his new screen audience in *The Call of the Blood*, where, only months after the Armistice, Novello is simply introduced as 'the very embodiment of youth'.

'The "War" Note'

The Call of the Blood was just the first of many Novello films dealing with themes of suffering, death, resurrection and return, with varying degrees of opacity. Novello was, in effect, typecast into a role that portrayed him as the tortured outcast, forever on the brink of physical and mental breakdown, often dwelling on the very periphery of society.

It is the implicit reference to the war and its after-effects that typifies Novello's films, however. The 'suggestion of horror' in such roles as the Rat and the Lodger reaffirms the assertion by Anton Kaes, discussing Weimar film, that recent history 'had lasting repercussions which imprinted themselves even in those cultural productions . . . that do not overtly deal with the war'.[33] Nepean expressed this sub-text to her readers in 1924 as 'the war touch' or '"war" note' (the latter perhaps more appropriate for the composer), which she observes both on stage and on film. Nepean is struck by the 'the popularity of plays that possessed the "war" note, not as a principal theme . . . but as a 'note' of terrific passion, a gleam that showed its sinister or heroic qualities in the moulding of human desires'.[34] Such 'sinister' or 'heroic' gleams could easily be ascribed to *The Rat*, too, certainly a film of terrific passion, which Cutts directed the following year; its two leads, as an early intertitle claims, being 'like driftwood on life's ocean', subject to a fate beyond their control. Moreover, the film is not only set in France, but dug beneath it, for it is in 'The White Coffin', a violent and labyrinthine art-deco catacomb, that we discover the Rat's lair.

The territorial struggle of life and death, framed by the architecture of this truly underworld setting, is a spectacle of the 'terrific passion' cited by Nepean, with that added element of mortal danger. The adrenaline that moves the body to fight is transformed into nervous, sexual energy; as Vera Brittain puts it in her *Testament of Youth*, 'the war generation was forcibly coming back to life, but continued to be possessed by the desperate feeling that life was short'.[35] In *The Rat*, to cite two tag-lines recommended by the press book for the film, 'All the romance of Europe's gayest city' is at once 'A great love realised under the shadow of the guillotine'.[36]

If we examine the press book, as well as the twelve-part serialization of the film in the pages of *Picture Show*, the closet-identity of the Rat as a kind of war-torn Dionysus becomes apparent. The conclusion to Part One of the magazine serial, when the Rat is first introduced, is, like the ending of the film itself, with Novello on his knees, extra-ordinarily bitter-sweet:

> There on the platform, and looking down into the hall was a youth of very striking appearance . . . His head was the head of a Greek god, and he was startlingly handsome.
>   But his smooth black hair and his burning black eyes rendered more striking the pallor of his face, and in those eyes there was an expression of profound mournfulness and disillusion, while his shapely mouth was curved in a half-contemptuous sneer as though he had already found life bitter to the taste.[37]

The tone of *Picture Show*'s fictional account of Novello's post-war characterization is strongly reminiscent of Brittain's melancholy evocation of the distracted youth of the 1920s, a resemblance which only grew stronger as the serial developed.

In another episode, evocatively titled 'The wounded Rat crawls home', the Rat appears at Odile's door as a 'ghastly white face streaked with blood', a countenance that prefigures that of Novello at Mrs Bunting's door a year later in *The Lodger*, equally the 'pale and drawn' figure described by the *New York Times*, and the 'horror-haunted man' perceived by the *Bioscope*.[38] Both the *Picture Show* serialization and the press book enable a reading of Novello in the *Rat* films as a man who suffers violent swings of temperament, going from brutal violence to extreme passivity and inertia and recalling symptoms that engage with contemporary perceptions of war neurosis. The Rat's distress is precipitated by not only his guilt at having killed Odile's assailant,

Herman Stetz, but also his acceptance that she take the blame for the murder in an effort to save him. The Rat is said to reel around 'like a drunken man', and to have nightmares; he is said to have 'tossed around feverishly on the bed in an agony of despair, and in the brief intervals when he lost consciousness, he was tortured by hideous visions'; he is, in fact, 'almost a raving lunatic'. In short, 'the past came back to him'.[39]

These delusions occur in the film version too. In a scene near the end of the final reel, Novello is thrown violently on to the floor of his flat by two gendarmes, who are swiftly dismissed by Mère Colline (who runs the White Coffin), who rushes to the assistance of the collapsed, inert, Rat. As she helps him over to his bed, the camera tracks in, emphasizing her role as both mother and nurse in a two-shot. He then appears to hallucinate, exclaiming 'There! Didn't you hear her voice—she wants me' and 'Killing a flower—nobody wants common flowers', a somewhat ambiguous metaphor, presumable referring to the fragility of youth and innocence (the poppy symbol springs to mind), to which Mère Colline can only roll her eyes in resignation. Novello loses consciousness, which he seems to do in the majority of his films, as Mère Colline lays him down to rest, stroking his hair gently to complete a genuinely poignant scene. It's worth noting that this maternal role is played by Marie Ault, that perennial 'mother figure' of 1920s British cinema, who would play 'mother' (Mrs Bunting) in *The Lodger*, too, which also finds the stricken Novello, after another shock, being nursed in the arms of her daughter, Daisy (June), the one person who believes in the Lodger's innocence.

In being offered as publicity material for the press, it seems clear that this reading of Novello was privileged by the studio as one of the ideal ways in which to consume its star. It is striking that such psychological ambivalence occurs as protracted periods of inertia and nervous collapse punctuating a generally violent and aggressive plot. This suggests that *The Rat* as a whole might be read in terms of the kind of ironic, mythical reworking of the war that Paul Fussell finds so typical of post-war cultural production.[40] Thus all that we need to know about Herman Stetz is that, in the dubious words of one magazine, he is 'a villain, the German name is a sure indication of that'.[41] The moral ambivalence of the Rat's violent conduct was perhaps indicative of the difficulty of readjustment after the war, a point raised by the *Daily Mail* in 1926, discussing a court case involving the petty crime of a disturbed veteran who 'could not control himself'; 'Invalid or Criminal?' the headline asked.[42]

Of course, the degree of correspondence between Novello's symptomatology and the 'actual' symptoms of 'war neurosis,' 'neurasthenia' or 'shell-shock,' the various nervous conditions that have since been assimilated into the umbrella term Post Traumatic Stress Disorder (PTSD), is a matter of contention.[43] However, I would argue that as symbolic symptoms of the kind of vague neurosis that Vera Brittain alludes to, Novello's nervous simulacra do, to some extent, emulate the kind of hysterical effects popularly associated with such disorders. Elaine Showalter argues that 'hysteria is a mimetic disorder; it mimics culturally permissible expressions of distress'.[44] This enables us to define Novello's bouts of something akin to shell-shock as a 'cultural symptom' of the mid-1920s, an acceptable, or at least diagnosable, expression of his historically-specific condition; sanctioned histrionics, one might say. (In 1925, a study had revealed that up to 60 per cent of veterans were 'still affected by varying degrees of nervous anxiety'.[45])

Recalling Dyer's discussion of 'charisma', Novello's charismatic distress, like that of Valentino, perhaps, lay in the way he embodied both the nervous and the sexual tensions of his day. It is notable that the stresses of post-war masculinity personified by Valentino were also indirectly linked to the war by the press. The infamous 'Pink Powder Puff' article in the *Chicago Tribune* in 1926, which attacked the 'beautiful' Valentino for being exactly that, or rather, 'effeminate', concludes with this astonishing rhetorical question: 'Is this degeneration into effeminacy a cognate reaction with pacifism and the virilities of the war?'[46] There is evidence, however, that measures were taken to keep the 'war touch' and particularly any sexual implications, strictly implicit.

'Youth and Vigour'

In the sequence from *The Lodger* referred to above, a handcuffed Novello, wrongly pursued by the authorities who suspect him of multiple murder, is cared for by Daisy, who guides him to a local pub in search of brandy. The Lodger, his immobile arms concealed under his cape, is eyed up cautiously by the clientele; one of them, an older man, asks: 'lost his arms, has he, dearie?' As Jessica Tipping observes of this scene, 'while not explicitly signifying a body ravaged by the wounds of war, the Lodger's body certainly serves as an implicit signifier of this'.[47] Indeed, with some 41,000 amputations during the war, and another 272,000 servicemen with serious limb injuries, such afflictions were a common sight in the 1920s.[48] This oblique reference to the war would have been much more explicit, however, had the original intertitle remained: 'Pore thing! Lost 'is 'ands in the war'. Moreover, an examination of *The Lodger* editor Ivor Montagu's work-in-progress notes on the film's intertitles reveals some sexual innuendo regarding the Lodger and the war experience. The next, again deleted, title would have read: 'Rough luck, miss, 'aving to do your own cuddling', or, in an alternative version, 'Bet yer don't get many cuddles from him'.[49]

The work undertaken on the titles indicates the extent to which this 'war touch' pervades Novello's films in this period, as well as the very limit to which the 'war touch' can be taken without rupturing the narrative of the film text entirely, suggesting a different film, with different characters. In Wilfred Owen's poem 'Disabled', an ex-soldier finds himself perceived, due to the ambiguous extent of his injuries, as lacking virility or as impotent with regard to women.[50] Novello's situation is not so very different. The physical impairment simulated by the star combined with the distinct absence of, let's say, heterosexual *gravitas* to the star's manner, all serve, rather disingenuously, to re-affirm the prejudice articulated by the *Tribune* that one is either the war-like Dionysus or the 'abstinent', 'effeminate' Apollo. The reduction of the number of titles in the film, for which Montagu is widely celebrated, only serves to demonstrate how unnecessary it was to make the war reference explicit. It was enough that Novello's persona could gently connote both the desire of or for rarefied youth and the despair of a physical Otherness realized through the slippage of his own ambivalent connotations of war and sexuality. The 'war touch' appears to become wildly problematic if made explicit; its power, it seems, lies in its being 'unspeakable'. Novello can only embody both the desirable matinée idol and a terrible anxiety if his connotations are kept diffuse and abstract, or on a 'poetic' level, perhaps.

In conclusion, I would suggest that the 'war touch' is an abiding gleam in the work of Novello, shaping his body to the extent that he stands as an ambiguous polysemic composite, simultaneously, recalling Nepean's and Dyer's terms, the 'calm, classic' hero and the 'bitter revelation' that exposes 'debased despair'. Thus, at the end of *The Lodger*, in a version of a scene that reoccurs in the majority of his silent films, we see Novello lying unconscious on a hospital bed, an intertitle informing us that Novello has 'suffered a severe nervous strain'. We can rest assured, however, that, as the physician says, 'his youth and vigour will pull him through'. Each of these scenes marks a resurrection, as this surrogate Dionysus is restored to life once more, serving us the formula that *Picture Show* told us we needed in the 1920s: a 'haunting picture', as Nepean put it, with, perhaps, an equally haunted star.

Notes

1. *Downhill*, like *The Rat*, was based on a play written by Novello and Constance Collier under the pseudonym David L'Estrange. A further two films starring Novello were adapted from his own plays, *Symphony in Two Flats* (Gareth Gundry, 1930) and *I Lived With You* (Maurice Elvey, 1933).

2. See Lawrence Napper and Michael Williams, 'The Curious Appeal of Ivor Novello,' in Bruce Babington, ed., *British Stars and Stardom: from Alma Taylor to Sean Connery* (University of Manchester Press, 2001), for a discussion of Novello's film career; and Michael Williams, 'A Sequestered Poodle-faker: Droll, Camp and Ivor Novello,' in Alan Burton and Laraine Porter, eds, *Pimple, Pranks and Pratfalls: British Film Comedy before 1930* (Trowbridge: Flicks Books, 2000), for more discussion of Novello's critical neglect and how that relates to the definition of 'Camp'.

3. *Picture Show*, 26 March 1921, p. 17; *Picturegoer*, September 1921, p. 14.

4. *Picturegoer*, December 1924, p. 32.

5. *Bioscope*, 16 September 1926, p. 39.

6. Ibid., 16 June 1927, p. 50. See also Geoffrey Macnab, 'The Not-So-Roaring 20s: Ivor Novello and Betty Balfour,' in Macnab, *Searching for Stars* (London and New York: Cassell, 2000), pp. 34–58.

7. *Film Weekly*, 14 January 1929, p. 5.

8. Michael Balcon, 'Man of the Theatre, and Screen: Novello the Ambassador of the British Film,' *Daily Film Renter*, 7 May 1951, p. 7.

9. Novarro and Valentino were actually Mexican and Italian respectively.

10. Richard Dyer, 'Charisma,' in Christine Gledhill, ed., *Stardom: Industry of Desire* (London: Routledge, 1991), p. 58.

11. Ibid., p. 59.

12. *Picture Show*, 13 November 1926, p. 13.

13. *Bioscope*, 16 September 1926, p. 39.

14. Nietzsche, *The Birth of Tragedy* (London: Penguin, 1993; first published 1871), p. 22.

15. Ibid., p. 22.

16. Ibid., p. 16.

17. Ibid., p. 40.

18. Jay Winter, *Sites of Memory, Sites of Mourning: The Great War in European Cultural History* (Cambridge: Cambridge University Press 1995), pp. 7–8.

19. See Winter, *Sites of Memory*; Paul Fussell, *The Great War and Modern Memory* (New York and London: Oxford University Press, 1975); Joanna Bourke, *Dismembering the Male: Men's Bodies, Britain and the Great War*

(London: Reaktion Books, 1996); and Anton Kaes, *M* (London: BFI, 1999).

20. Stanley Casson, *Steady Drummer* (London: G. Bell and Sons, 1935), pp. 269–70, quoted in Fussell, *Modern Memory*, p. 325.

21. Winter, *Sites of Memory*, p. 138.

22. W. Macqueen-Pope, *Ivor—The Story of an Achievement* (London: Hutchinson, 1951), p. 55.

23. *The Musical Courier*, 24 February 1916 (unpaginated and unattributed cutting, Theatre Museum Library, London); *Picture Show*, 22 January 1921, p. 10.

24. Hannen Swaffer, *London Calling*, 19 January 1929, p. 13.

25. *Picture Show*, 9 May 1925, p. 18.

26. Ibid.

27. Ibid.

28. Paul Delany, *The Neo-Pagans: Friendship and Love in the Rupert Brooke Circle* (London: Macmillan, 1987), p. 174.

29. Cited in Michael Hastings, *Rupert Brooke: The Handsomest Young Man in England* (London: Michael Joseph, 1967), p. 18.

30. *Picture Show*, 9 February 1924, p. 6. The title 'England's Apollo' is used to promote Novello in an advertisement for *The Man Without Desire* (Adrian Brunel, 1923).

31. Sydney W. Carroll, 'Ivor Novello: A Versatile Talent,' in *Daily Telegraph*, 8 November 1934 (unpaginated cutting, Theatre Museum Library).

32. *Picturegoer*, May 1923, p. 11.

33. Anton Kaes, 'The Cold Gaze: Notes on Mobilization and Modernity,' in *New German Critique*, Spring/Summer 1993, issue 59, p. 117.

34. *Picture Show*, 28 June 1924, p. 20.

35. Vera Brittain, *Testament of Youth: An Autobiographical Study of the Years 1900–1925* (London: Virago, 1983), p. 498.

36. Large press book for the 1925 Gainsborough production *The Rat* (Theatre Museum Library).

37. *Picture Show*, 13 February 1926, p. 13.

38. 'Ivor Novello in Lurid Film,' *New York Times*, 1 June 1928, p. 27; *Bioscope*, 16 September 1926, p. 39.

39. *Picture Show*, 3 April 1926, p. 6; 10 April 1926, pp. 7 and 6.

40. See Fussell, *Modern Memory*.

41. *Everyman*, 27 June 1924 (Novello Collection, Box 7, 'Press Cuttings 1924–1925,' Theatre Museum Store, Blythe House, Olympia, London).

42. 'Invalid or Criminal?—Medical Problems of an Ex-Soldier,' *Daily Mail*, 20 January 1926, p. 6.

43. See Cathy Caruth, ed., *Trauma: Explorations in Memory* (Baltimore and London: The John Hopkins Univeristy Press, 1995).

44. Elaine Showalter, *Hystories, Hysterical Epidemics and Mass Culture* (London: Picador. 1997), pp. 9 and 15.

45. Chris Feudtner, 'Minds the Dead Have Ravaged,' in *History of Science*, vol. 31, pt. 4, 1993, p. 377, quoted in Anthony Babington, *Shell Shock: A History of the Changing Attitudes to War Neurosis* (London: Leo Cooper, 1997), p. 122.
46. Anon., 'Pink Powder Puffs,' *Chicago Tribune*, 19 July 1926, p. 10.
47. Jessica Tipping, 'Exploring The Implicit War/Post-War Subtext of *The Lodger*,' unpublished MA Film Studies essay, University of East Anglia, 1997.
48. Joanna Bourke, *Dismembering the Male: Men's Bodies, Britain and the Great War* (London: Reaktion Books, 1996), p. 33; statistics from G. Howson, ed., *Handbook for the Limbless* (London: Disabled Society, 1922), p. xii.
49. Ivor Montagu Collection, Item 18—'Lodger Titles,' Special Collections, British Film Institute National Library, London.
50. Wilfred Owen, 'Disabled,' in John Silkin, ed., *The Penguin Book of First World War Poetry* (London: Penguin, 1981), pp. 184–5. Interestingly, in *The Man Without Desire* (Adrian Brunel, 1923), Novello reawakens from a death-like state to discover that he is impotent.

17

Tackling the Big Boy of Empire
British Film in Australia, 1918–1931

Mike Walsh

Cinema has always been an international business, yet national cinema formations are all too rarely understood in that context. This chapter looks at the distribution of British films in Australia between the end of the First World War and the conversion to sound. It thus looks at what should have been one of the British film industry's key export markets, given the professed importance of imperial trade to the British economy. In fact, the fortunes of British film exports to Australia in this period fluctuated significantly. This was partly because of developments within the British film industry itself, and partly because of developments in the Australian film industry. But there are two other key issues to take into account. The first is the domination of the major American distributors, which inevitably had a marked effect on the place of British films in Australia. The second is Australia's changing and contested sense of its own cultural identity and how Britain, British culture and British economic ties might figure in relation to this identity. This too had a marked impact on Australian receptiveness towards British films by the trade, by audiences and within broader political debates. The idea of 'British Film' (as distinct from British films) thus played a key role in debates about the development of Australian economic and cultural life in this period.

In the aftermath of the First World War, British exports contracted sharply due to a decrease in investment capital, the rising competitiveness of other manufacturing nations (primarily the United States), and increasing protectionism in Europe. In response, Britain attempted to use its Empire as an economic bloc that could hedge the erosion of its international position. The tensions that this situation created were felt throughout the 1920s, as instanced by Britain's attempts to maintain sterling against the American-backed gold standard. Australia was a major arena for this struggle between Empire loyalism and the commercial modernity of an increased American presence. British investment in Australian manufacturing at this time was strategically aimed at preventing American investment from extending its foot-hold.[1] The rising influence of American commodities and business practices in Australia rendered problematic not only the economic ascendancy of British capital, but also the legitimization of an elite whose authority was based on British cultural models absorbed into Australian society. Motion pictures provided a spectacularly visible field in which these social conflicts could be played out.[2] As in Britain, the overwhelming bulk of the films screened in Australia were American. In 1925, 3 per cent of the feature films imported into Australia were British in origin, as opposed to 93 per cent from the USA.[3] The film exhibition industry, as one of the most visible exponents of American cultural commodities, was vulnerable to a range of oppositional pressures: from xenophobic nationalists, Empire loyalists, anti-Americanists and proponents of a local production industry, as well as those conservative pressure groups inclined to be suspicious of the social influences of films of any national origin. The coalescence of these pressures following the Imperial Conference in London in 1926 contributed to the formation of a Royal Commission into the Australian film industry in 1927–8. This was a major (though anti-climactic) event in the Australian film industry, with terms of reference which included the investigation of charges of collusion to exclude British and Australian films, and the investigation of the commercial and social consequences of Hollywood domination.

Such developments raise important questions about the cultural politics of both Britain and Australia. The film industry provides a strong sense of the relational matrix within which national identity was constantly resituated and debated. The idea that films represented a new force that might alter existing national and social frameworks was a significant feature of contemporary debates about the film industry. Foremost among these was the debate about the extent to which Australia's British heritage was being Americanized by Hollywood.

Empire Loyalty and Americanization

Within established institutions such as the parliament, the mainstream press and prominent pressure groups such as returned soldiers' associations and conservative women's groups, there was no serious doubt that Australian identity should be seen as deriving from Britishness. Australians claimed British citizenship for themselves, travelled abroad on British passports and volunteered in large numbers to fight in British wars. One recent history of Australian nationalism has stressed the connection to the British Empire as a major unifying factor in the Australian colonies, capable of transcending intercolonial and then interstate rivalries. This connection was arguably more effective than attempts to unify the nation around the dispersed geographical space of the Australian continent.[4] The link to British heritage as a source of racial unity, forming an exclusionary basis for Australian nationalism ('White Australia') was also a major part of the politics of both the right and the left.

This British link was not easily challenged, and even forces within the film industry which might have had material reasons to see Australia distance itself from its British origins attempted to appropriate the connection wherever possible. *Everyones*, Australia's main film trade paper, defended the dominance of American films by arguing:

> It is a notable fact that of the twenty-five millions of pounds invested in the exhibiting business in this country EVERY PENNY IS BRITISH—sufficient evidence that the oft-repeated canard of 'the foreign domination of the Australian film business' is a myth.[5]

Even American distributors bought into this discourse when, in 1921, Paramount ran an advertisement for its British productions:

> Britons to the backbone
> Aussies to the core
> We want British Pictures
> Give us more and more.[6]

While Britain may have functioned as a source of legitimation for Australian institutions and exclusionary racial identity, the relationship was not without its problems. One way round this was to make a distinction between Britishness and Englishness. Britishness was used to connote positive values of heritage and identity. The term English-ness, on the other hand, allowed colonial subjects to express frustration in their dealings with a British government and British institutions whose interests were often at odds with those of Australasians. The distinction can be seen clearly in a statement by John Fuller, a New Zealand exhibitor, who complained that: 'We are to encourage British films, while at the same time England is encouraging foreign [Argentinian] meat and wool.'[7] *Everyones* argued against a British film quota in similar terms: 'This quota is presented to us as an Empire inspiration. Rot! It's something so one-sidedly English that Australian sentiment recoils.'[8]

In its most common usage, Britishness was used to differentiate Australia from Asia and hence to justify restrictive immigration practices. Within cultural debate about the film industry, however, Australian Britishness was generally constructed in opposition to Americanization. A handful of examples will suffice to demonstrate the point, but they were abundant in the press of the day. One Federal parliamentarian, citing the scandals coming out of Hollywood in 1922, claimed that: 'It is time that we as Australians turned our faces towards London instead of Los Angeles.'[9] In 1924, the ex-premier of New South Wales and founder of the Nationalist Party, W.A. Holman, warned of Australians 'turn(ing) away from British models towards American' and of 'a danger of the Australian mentality becoming Americanized'.[10] The 1925 Tariff Board enquiry into the film duty saw a prominent state parliamentarian and newspaper proprietor accusing American films of 'prostituting our language and destroying our ideals'.[11]

Ironically, the Australian federal constitution had been drafted with an eye to the American system, and it was common for those in public life to ponder Australia's chances of following the path of the USA to become a future world power. Even so, anti-Americanism had become an endemic force in Australian political discourse by the 1920s.[12] In part, this was because it was such a flexible sentiment. It could be appropriated by the political right as a form of Empire loyalty or a general reaction against modernity, but also by the political left as opposition to capitalist expansion. The recent experiences of the First World War had sharpened these antagonisms to an ally who had come late to the fight. In 1923, the general manager of United Artists' Australian subsidiary reported to his head office in New York:

It must be thoroughly appreciated that (with a few exceptions, of course) Australasians do not like American things or American ways; they only tolerate our pictures because at present they cannot be replaced. The daily papers continually adversely criticize American ways and things in general . . . The writer several times while viewing American weeklies that showed scenes from the American Army or Navy has heard persons in the audience cry out 'Who won the war'.[13]

While the vehemence of this report might be attributed to a mid-westerner suddenly finding himself a long way from home, anti-American and pro-American sentiments could be rapidly mobilized as domestic and international agendas changed. In 1924, Stanley Bruce, the Australian Prime Minister, used a film industry luncheon given by a visiting Motion Picture Producers and Distributors of America (MPPDA) representative to declare pointedly that if Britain would not give Australia the trade support to which it felt entitled, Australia must turn elsewhere.[14] By 1929, however, under the rising pressures of mercantilism, Bruce referred to:

a danger facing us; and that danger is from America. She is going to start flooding the world in the next few years, and it will be a disastrous flood in all countries. I believe there will be no better way of tackling this problem and benefiting the secondary industries of Australia than by saying that we will give to Britain the market which we do not want ourselves, and keep out the other fellow.[15]

The perceived movement in Australian public life from a British orientation to an American one was often exemplified by comparisons between British royalty and American movie stars. Two quotes from *Everyones* demonstrate the way these broadly social conflicts were played out around the cinema:

I've only ever seen three moving pictures in my life but I could tell the names and recognize the faces of hundreds of the artists who appear on the screen, and I know their personal histories and domestic affairs as well as mother knows those of the Royal Family.

Today the Prince of Wales is the most popular man in Sydney but Eugene O'Brien runs him a close second; and if there is a flapper

in this city who is not head over heels in love with him I have yet
to find her.[16]

The first quote is attributed to a young woman from a country town
while the second is an editorial comment, also centring on young
women. In both, American film stars have usurped the British royal
family as figures of fame, respect and affection, driving a wedge
between old and young, the (male) world of traditional social authority
and a newer social order which is consistently represented as more
vulnerable and impressionable and is made up primarily of women.
Another reference in *Everyones* to 'the flappers whose jobs are in
Sydney but whose hearts are in Los Angeles' is exemplary of this.[17]
Flappers were constantly invoked as figures who combined Americanization, femininity and modernity. We will see that a standard trope in
these debates was to line up national differences with hierarchies of
sexual difference.

   The political currency of anti-Americanism provides a good example
of a dislocation of interests between those of the state and those of the
market, as the Australian cinema industry had progressively organized
itself around the accommodation of American distribution. With the
expansion of direct distribution by American companies in the 1920s,
the Australian cinema industry centralized its capital investment in
exhibition and geared itself to a high volume turnover of films. The
system relied upon American distributors to supply that volume of
films. Given that the local industry had strong structural reasons for
preferring an unhindered (and minimally taxed) supply of American
films over calls for Empire preference or tariff discrimination, British
heritage had to be accepted and finessed. An *Everyones* editorial
in 1925 began by disputing that there was a specifically Australian
national culture, attempting to reinstate the limits of cultural ex-
clusivity along linguistic and then racial lines rather than national ones:

> What peculiar national sentiment has Australia that is not
> possessed by any other country in the British Empire, or indeed
> by any English-speaking peoples? Pride of race is probably the
> fundamental. And seeing that most of the Anglo-Saxon races have
> sprung from the same stock, this gives us a sort of neutral basis to
> work upon.[18]

The balancing act attempted here appeals to an exclusionary sense of Australian cultural identity; certainly it avoids the American industry's rhetoric of a cosmopolitanism which can efface any sense of cultural difference;[19] but it also tries to establish racial grounds for admitting Americans as culturally similar. In 1924, an MPPDA representative visiting Australia adopted a similar strategy in speaking of 'the mighty power for good in this world which exists in the close unity of two great branches of the white race—the British Empire and the United States of America'.[20]

Some exhibitors and their trade press allies argued for the commonality of Australian and American cultural identity as youthful and virile in opposition to a Britain seen as old, maternal and often effeminate. *Everyones* took great pleasure in reprinting *Kinematograph Weekly*'s attack on British films as written by 'precious young men of the Chelsea type'.[21] One prominent Australian exhibitor, Stanley Wright, argued that:

> America is a young country and Australia is a young country and the outcome is that the Americans have produced sparkling stories that have appealed to the Australians, and the Australian public has responded by expressing a preference for American made films.[22]

He concluded that Australians required 'spirited and virile' pictures that the British couldn't make.[23] As we have already seen, both sides in this debate took recourse to analogies of age and particularly gender. The importance of this operation lay in maintaining one's own position as masculine, while imputing femininity to the national influence that is to be rejected or denigrated. One Hollywood trade paper, the *Film Mercury*, describing anti-British sentiment in Australia, mixed its gender metaphors furiously in maintaining this balance between three competing national groups:

> Although the influence of the mother country, fostered by titled resident governors, has successfully kept the big boy of the Empire [Australia] free from foreign exploitation it has never meant much to the man in the street. While Australia, like a fractious child, sulkily threw the calculating parent occasional filial favours in the form of preferential tariffs and what-not, Colonial eyes strained eastward, fascinated with the spectacle of Fords and fox-trots. Enjoying utter social isolation, adolescent Australia was ripe for seduction by the first of the older civilizations who made

overtures. And it was Hollywood who swept her off her feet with a deluge of nebulous fairy tales. Romance, as Lasky and Laemmle sees, prevailed over its less ardent rival, the culture of Europe.[24]

The Three Phases of British Film

Thus far it might be argued that none of this is particularly specific to Australia. In a perverse way, Australian exhibition's domination by American films only shows its continuing reliance on British models. This is not a line I want to argue, however. The temptation is to view Australian cultural life as a periphery moving between two centres; as acted upon, rather than having any agency of its own; as involving only the options of sulky big boy of Empire or distracted Sydney flapper. It is when we study the conditions under which British films actually reached Australian screens between the end of the First World War and the conversion to sound that we have to take into account the priorities of local interests and institutions in shaping the possibilities for British films. During this period there were three distinct phases, or regimes, under which British films were distributed in Australia.

Phase One: 1918–1928

The first phase extended from the end of the War up to the beginning of 1928. During this phase, British films were marginal to the interests of the Australian film industry, which was reorganising its profit centres around the expansion of exhibition. This involved a necessary downgrading of local distribution as American companies moved in, a change from leasing theatres into building and owning large, first-run theatres, and the consolidation of suburban theatres into circuits. As far as production was concerned, this generated two imperatives. First, there was a need for high budget 'specials' such as *The Ten Commandments* (De Mille, 1923) and *The Covered Wagon* (Cruze, 1923) which could fill new movie palaces for long-run periods. Second, a high volume of films was needed so that 52-week packages could be used for block-booking circuits. British films offered neither of the advantages of scale or supply and hence were relegated to marginal distributors such as Australasian Films, the distribution arm of the dominant exhibition circuit, Union Theatres. In the early 1920s Australasian held the rights to Hepworth, Alliance, Stoll, and Welsh Pearson.[25] In 1924, Australasian distributed only nine British films out of a total of twenty-five British features imported.[26] By 1927 the number of British imports had risen only marginally to thirty-nine out of 715, or 5.5 per cent of total imports.[27]

Pressure for British films had gathered political momentum following the Imperial Conference of November 1926, which included general recommendations for Empire preference schemes and more effective customs duties, as well as turning its attention specifically to film with calls for a ban on blind- and block-booking. At this point, the major American distributors began to engage in token distribution of British and Australian films. The most prominent example was Paramount's distribution of *The Flag Lieutenant* (Elvey, 1926), undertaken during the Royal Commission into the Australian film industry in 1927–8.[28] This was a far cry from wider responsiveness to British production. American distributors produced a volume of film geared at satisfying their own domestic market. In smaller foreign markets—most notably Britain itself—the problem of American distributors was that there were too many films, and the last thing they needed were additional sources of supply. United Artists' (UA) Australian subsidiary took the same position as other American distributors in actively resisting the introduction of British films into Australia. In November 1927, its manager reported happily on the lacklustre showing of *The Flag Lieutenant*, commenting that:

> This practical evidence of the inferiority of English pictures as compared to the American product will be of great benefit to the American Distributors, inasmuch as the Royal Commission . . . will undoubtedly believe that the preponderance of evidence that has been given demonstrating the inferiority of the average English picture is more than borne out by actual hard box office figures.[29]

Hollywood, ever willing to explore workable compromises, was attempting to arrive at a reconciliation of the industrial needs of the exhibition industry with broader cultural and state pressures. Within the space of a year, the same UA manager explained to New York that UA's *Sorrell and Son* had been popular in Australia because of its English subject matter. He noted, 'English life and the history of an Englishman has a particular appeal in this country'.[30] UA's advertising campaign for Douglas Fairbanks's *Robin Hood* had already attempted to sell the film by emphasizing the Britishness of its subject matter. An advertisement for the film in Australia stressed that given 'Douglas Fairbanks' great friendship for all things that are British, I feel that this enormous investment in a subject laid in the old chivalrous days of our Forefathers is a fine compliment indeed'.[31] This reflected the standard view within the mainstream of the American film industry that the national origin of production and national referentiality could be prised apart, and that Americans were better at portraying Britishness than the British. It was also especially frustrating for British producers. A British report on Australia notes that *The Ten Commandments* (De Mille, 1923), *Beau Geste* (Brenon, 1926) and *Sorrell and Son* (Brenon, 1927) had all featured 'British stories, British stars and British sentiment—but [were all] made in America'. The report continues:

> There is little evidence in Australia of any demand for moving pictures different from the usual run of American feature films. This may be because the practical monopoly enjoyed by American films has not afforded much opportunity for the cultivation of a taste for anything else. There appears to be little appreciation for films of artistic and kinematographic merit.[32]

It may well have been the case that American film versions of British-ness were preferred because they offered a compromise. They could satisfy Australians' sense of their social traditions without actually bringing them into close contact with the British (or, to use the connotations I introduced earlier, with the English) and the class-bound attitudes which some Australians associated with their former colonial masters. American films may well have been better British films than the British could make in offering Australia a mediated, distanced version of a mother culture which Australian nationalism simultaneously reacted against and imitated.

Phase Two: 1928–1930

The second phase in the distribution of British films was a short-lived one corresponding with the British production bubble of 1927–8, a production boost built around the initial impact of the Cinematograph Films Act. As much as the Films Act altered the landscape for the production of British films, it did little or nothing for the development of an international distribution network, at least as far as Australia was concerned. While the unchecked cultural effects of American films on Empire subjects were repeatedly cited in the debates over the Films Act, the British industry continued to rely on a pre-war model of

international distribution, in which territorial rights were sold from London to local agents. In 1928, the *Daily Film Renter* complained of the paltry offers of £150–200 per film for Australian rights to British films in spite of Australian protestations of loyalty at Imperial Conferences.[33] This ignored the fact that, at this time, the Australian distribution sector was overwhelmingly in the hands of the vertically integrated Americans.

Two Australian distribution companies began to gear themselves up for the distribution of British films. These were British Dominions Films (BDF) and Cinema Art Films (CAF). While the former was established with the express purpose of distributing British films, CAF had functioned in the margins of commercial distribution for some time, acting primarily as an agent for Ufa. Both of these distributors quickly armed themselves with distribution agreements with British producers. BDF held the rights to Gaumont British, Herbert Wilcox's B&D, New Era and Gainsborough, while CAF distributed British International films. Given that its sole *raison d'être* was the distribution of British films, BDF's methods were aggressively nationalistic. It advertised itself as 'the only 100% British organization in Australia,' as 'John Bull's answer to Uncle Sam' and as issuing an 'amazing challenge to American Film Domination'.[34] It also associated itself with heavily masculine imagery: John Bull, the British bulldog, and Lord Nelson.[35] CAF, on the other hand, trying to balance the distribution of British International and Ufa, aimed at a version of cosmopolitanism that minimized national difference. Its managing director announced that 'the trend towards the internationalisation of the screen is so pronounced that within a few years I doubt whether we will be able to distinguish the country of origin of any film'.[36]

In 1926 British films constituted 3 per cent of all feature films imported into Australia. This figure rose to 5 per cent in 1927, then 12 per cent in 1928 before falling back to 7 per cent in 1929. The increased production of British films and the availability of new avenues of distribution at this time only go part of the way to explaining the increased prominence of British films in Australia. A more important factor was the struggle between the two major exhibition circuits, Union Theatres (UT) and Hoyts, which provided the motivation for their exhibition of British films. In 1928, Walter Marks, the Chairman of the Royal Commission, recommended that British producers should make the most of the exhibition struggle raging between UT and Hoyts rather than wait for an Empire quota.[37] Midway through 1928, UT had attempted to force the capitulation of

Hoyts by signing exclusive first-run arrangements with all the major American distributors. Hoyts was forced to look towards Britain as the only alternative source of supply. They quickly concluded an output arrangement with BDF, to which UT responded by signing a first-run deal with CAF. The managing director of Hoyts told British reporters:

> Truth is the film war is the greatest thing that ever happened for British distributors. But for the fact they couldn't get American pictures, Hoyts wouldn't have been so keen to buy English product; by doing so, Hoyts forced Union Theatres into more or less a political situation. Union Theatres had to purchase English pictures also. Together they opened up the whole first-run proposition for England—and first-runs, commanded as they are by two powerful circuits, are the toughest nut any new distributor has to crack.[38]

The political situation referred to by Griffith involved Hoyts, from its stronghold in Melbourne, encouraging a series of articles in the *Melbourne Age*, and the *Argus*, reviving the political issue of Americanization.

Phase Three: Into the 1930s

The second phase was quickly brought to an end by the introduction of sound, which stifled supply from Britain by bursting the production bubble and caused the unravelling of the first-run agreements between American distributors and UT in Australia.[39] It took until 1930 for British films to begin to recover. The British proportion of feature films imported into Australia rose from 9 per cent in 1930 to 20 per cent in 1931 to stabilize at 23 per cent in 1932 and 1933.[40] This third phase, however, was based on another reconfiguration of distribution and exhibition in Australia: a return to vertical integration on the part of Australia's major exhibitor, UT. Throughout the 1920s, UT's distribution arm, Australasian Films, had dwindled in importance. UT withdrew entirely from distribution in 1928, divesting Australasian Films, which became Greater Australasian Films, whose major business was as the local distribution agency for Columbia. Sound strengthened the position of the American distributors (who moved aggressively from flat-rate to percentage booking to cash in on the popularity of sound films), while the Depression brought about the end of the theatre-building boom. In this context, distribution re-emerged as a potential profit centre for Australian companies, and British films became the central alternative on which to base any new distributor. In 1930, UT reversed their earlier policy and decided to re-enter the distribution business. Australasian Films was reconstituted as Union Theatres Film Exchange and took over the distribution of British International from CAF, which quickly collapsed.[41]

Throughout the 1920s, the large Australian exhibition circuits had defended themselves against charges of anti-British collusion by noting that the British had failed to set up their own distribution and marketing in Australia. Now it was the failure of British producers to set up their own international distribution that made their films attractive to UT as it looked to re-establish itself in distribution in opposition to the American distributors. This opposition took on an increased urgency following the pooling of UT's and Hoyts's film-buying as a response to the Depression, a move that was eventually formalized into a temporary merger, the General Theatres Corporation (GTC). The move from bitter competition to co-operation between the major exhibition circuits displaced conflict on to the relations with American distributors, leading to a 'Film War' against the Americans in 1934. This transformation is most obvious in the public statements of Stuart Doyle, the General Manager of UT/GTC, who had led film industry opposition to anti-Americanism at the time of the Royal Commission. At the 1934 New South Wales Government Inquiry into the Film Industry, Doyle laid the ills of Australian exhibition at the feet of American distributors.[42]

With the increased distribution of British films, claims that local companies had engaged in a conspiracy to exclude Empire production could no longer be sustained, though now claims of an ongoing conspiracy shifted terrain and were directed to the issue of censor-ship.[43] By 1930, the influence of the distributors behind British films had grown to such an extent, given their ability to mobilize public sentiment and political pressure, that British unhappiness with Australian censorship was aired prominently and compromise quickly effected through minor cuts ordered by the Appeals Board. By August 1930, British films occupied three of Sydney's seven long-run theatres and the box office for *Atlantic* (Dupont, 1929) was on a par with Warner's *The Singing Fool* (Bacon, 1928).[44] *Everyones* summed up the situation as one in which 'people are thinking, talking and seeing British films'.[45]

There was a palpable sense of relief in the way that the Australian industry could celebrate its embrace of British films, as they settled into a healthily marginal position in Australian exhibition. From the viewpoint of the Australian cinema industry, British films performed a number of functions. Most importantly, they reconciled the economic interests of the market with the cultural pressures brought to bear in the broader political sphere. Actual British films came to fill the position marked out in advance for 'British Film'. They also crucially provided Australian companies with a way to re-enter film distribution at a time when the interests of local exhibitors and American distributors had begun to diverge. Australian popular culture and cultural identity inevitably involve some degree of negotiation of influences from other nations such as the USA and Britain. What my analysis shows is that these negotiations were grounded in material as well as ideological practice, and that the interests of Australian institutions provide a crucial determinant in this process.

Notes

1. Peter Cochrane, *Industrialization and Dependence: Australia's Road to Economic Development 1870–1939* (St Lucia: University of Queensland Press, 1980), p. 43.
2. Victoria de Grazia adopts a similar line in her analysis of the influences of American films in Europe. De Grazia, 'Mass Culture and Sovereignty: The American Challenge to European Cinemas, 1920–1960,' *Journal of Modern History*, vol. 61, no. 1, March 1989, pp. 53–87.
3. Commonwealth Film Censorship, 'Report on the Work for the Year 1926,' *Commonwealth Parliamentary Papers*, vol. 72, 1926–28, p. 745.
4. W.G. McMinn, *Nationalism and Federation in Australia* (Melbourne: Oxford University Press, 1994).
5. *Everyones*, 18 December 1929, p. 7.
6. Ibid., 10 August 1921, p. 17.
7. Ibid., 11 July 1928, p. 6.
8. Ibid., 19 September 1928, p. 4.
9. Ibid., 24 September 1924, p. 5.
10. Ibid., 3 September 1924, p. 11.
11. Ibid., 12 August 1925, p. 5.
12. Roger and Philip Bell, *Implicated: The United States in Australia* (Melbourne: Oxford University Press, 1993).
13. Cresson E. Smith to Hiram Abrams, 18 October 1923, O'Brien Legal Files Box 55, Folder 10, United Artists Collection, Wisconsin Centre for Film and Theatre Research, Madison (hereafter 'O'Brien').
14. *Exhibitor*, 7 May 1924, p. 6.
15. *Everyones*, 3 July 1929, p. 4.
16. Ibid., 16 June 1920, p. 10 and 23 June 1920, p. 9.

17. Ibid., 16 February 1921, p. 12.

18. Ibid., 7 October 1925, p. 4.

19. I have explored the cosmopolitan attitude of American producers, and British responses to it, in Walsh, 'Fighting the American Invasion with Cricket, Roses and Marmalade for Breakfast,' *Velvet Light Trap*, vol. 40, Fall 1997, pp. 4–17.

20. *Everyones*, 16 April 1924, p. 5.

21. Ibid., 13 February 1929, p. 4.

22. Ibid., 5 August 1925, p. 8.

23. Ibid., 15 July 1925, p. 24.

24. Ibid., 27 August 1930, p. 34.

25. Ibid., 12 October 1921, p. 10, and 14 December 1921, pp. 22–3.

26. Ibid., 5 August 1925, p. 5.

27. US Department of Commerce, Bureau of Foreign and Domestic Commerce, 'Motion Pictures in Australia and New Zealand,' Trade Information Bulletin, 608, 1929, p. 2.

28. Paramount also distributed Raymond Longford's *The Dinkum Bloke* (1923) and the *Know Your Own Country* series of informational shorts (which began in 1925), as well as *The Life of Jack Hobbs* (1925) in an attempt to conciliate Empire sentiment. *Everyones*, 9 September 1925, p. 15.

29. Doyle to Kelly, 10 November 1927, O' Brien 56/10. *The Flag Lieutenant* ran for six weeks at the Capitol in Melbourne, resulting in a loss of £4,000 against its minimum rental guarantees. (Undated report, entitled 'Australia. Cinematograph Films,' in the Michael Balcon Collection, British Film Institute, p. 38).

30. Doyle to Kelly, 'General Report for Month Ending 3rd March 1928,' 14 March 1928, O'Brien 56/1.

31. *Everyones*, 26 September 1923, p. 2.

32. 'Australia. Cinematograph Films,' p. 28.

33. *Everyones*, 6 June 1928, p. 10.

34. Ibid., 11 April 1928, p. 29, 1 August 1928, p. 17 and 27 March 1929, p. 16.

35. Ibid., 20 June 1928, p. 27 and 8 August 1928, p. 34.

36. Ibid., 29 August 1928, p. 8.

37. Ibid., 31 November 1928, p. 10.

38. Ibid., 31 October 1928, p. 25. See also ibid., 12 December 1928, p. 139.

39. Michael Walsh, 'The Years of Living Dangerously: Sound Comes to Australia,' in Deb Verhoeven ed., *Twin Peeks* (Melbourne: Damned Publishing, 1999), pp. 69–83.

40. Commonwealth Film Censorship, 'Report on the Work for the Year 1934,' Australian Customs Department Library.

41. *Everyones*, 7 May 1930, p. 7.

42. John Tulloch, *Australian Cinema: Industry, Narrative and Meaning* (Sydney: Unwin and Allen, 1982), p. 67.

43. I have described this in detail in Walsh, 'The Empire of the Censors: Film Censorship and the Dominions,' *Journal of Popular British Cinema*, no. 4, 2000, pp. 45–58.

44. *Everyones*, 23 July 1930, p. 35 and 6 August 1930, p. 23.

45. Ibid., 6 August 1930, p. 23.

SECTION E

Taking the Cinema Seriously
The Emergence of an Intellectual Film Culture in the 1920s

18

The Film Society and the Creation of an Alternative Film Culture in Britain in the 1920s

Jamie Sexton

In the early 1920s a growing number of intellectuals in Britain became fascinated by film's potential as a new and unique art form. They were interested in the cinema as a modern, international phenomenon, which led them to reject the dominant tendencies of mainstream film culture in Britain. First, they rejected the view of cinema as mass entertainment; for them cinema was primarily an art form, not a commodity. Second, they rejected the hitherto dominant form by which cinema was justified as art: in nationalist terms, which saw film as an extension of 'middlebrow' theatre and literature.[1] I regard those intellectuals who were interested in the cinema as a modern, aesthetic and international phenomenon as constituting the basis of what became an 'alternative' cultural movement; in 1925 they firmly established themselves on the cultural map by forming the Film Society.

The Film Society was chiefly an exhibition outlet at which, once a month, members could watch a wide selection of films from a variety of countries. It catered for those who wanted to see films that were not otherwise available for viewing in Britain. The Society has been seen as an important landmark in British cinema for the way in which it both established a tradition of independent exhibition and influenced British intellectual film culture in general.[2]

In this chapter, I will focus on the Film Society as a central component of alternative film culture in Britain during the 1920s, noting in particular the range of films that it showed and the critical practice that it helped establish. I will look at some of the reasons for the critical and aesthetic predilections detectable within the Society's programmes and programme notes, and at how these predilections may have influenced film production in Britain.[3] Although the Society was principally an exhibition outlet, its rules and constitution stated that it aimed 'to introduce films of artistic, technical and educational interest, and to encourage the study of cinematography, and to assist such experiments as may help the technical advance of film production'.[4] Thus whilst it was primarily a site in which international 'advances' could be consumed, it hoped that these could feed back into native production and therefore rejuvenate British filmmaking. To this end, the Society offered cut-price membership for film technicians.

The Emergence of an Alternative Film Culture

In the early 1920s an alternative film culture was beginning take root in Britain. In newspapers and the trade press sporadic articles focused on film in a serious and detailed manner. On the whole, though, film was still treated primarily as an entertainment in the trade papers, whilst in newspapers it received scant attention in relation to other arts. As a contributor to the *Bioscope* wrote in 1924:

> New plays receive serious criticism, despite the probability that not 10 per cent of the paper's readers will ever have the opportunity or desire to see them. Even the art galleries have their share of attention. But the new films are dismissed in half a dozen inches of space, containing merely the barest details, not always accurate, of the week's releases.[5]

A cursory look through a range of newspapers will confirm that coverage of film was far outweighed by coverage of arts such as literature, theatre or music. This was understandable to some extent, considering the status of other arts in comparison to the relatively new art of film. Even so, cinema was now in its fourth decade, and in France, for example, it had been receiving serious attention as an art form since around 1915.[6]

Whilst cinephilia was slower to develop in Britain there were sporadic developments that can be seen as the beginnings of an alternative film culture. Universities became a focus for aesthetes to share their passion for cinema through the formation of film clubs:[7] Ivor Montagu, for instance, saw *The Cabinet of Dr Caligari* (Wiene, 1919) whilst at Cambridge, when he also began to write film criticism for university magazines.[8] Outside the universities, Adrian Brunel had attempted to form a Cinemagoers League in 1920 in order to make articulate the demands of 'a new and more discriminating public',[9] while the Cinema Art Group of the Faculty of Arts had been formed in 1923 'to give practical support for films of outstanding merit' and 'to influence the public to appreciate the cinema as an art medium'.[10] Even a few commercial cinemas—such as the New Gallery and the Marble Arch Pavilion—showed an occasional (non-British) European film in the early 1920s.[11] By 1925 *The Times* was publishing a regular feature on the art of film ('Film World'), Iris Barry was writing a regular film column in the *Daily Mail*, and Ivor Montagu was writing on film for the *Observer*.[12]

The Film Society, which can be seen as the first systematic manifestation of this emergent alternative film culture, was a non-profit organization that showed a monthly programme of films to paying members. It was set up by Montagu and actor Hugh Miller, who came up with the idea when returning from a visit to German film studios. They loosely based it upon the Stage Society, a theatrical establishment that staged plays ignored within commercial circles;[13] Montagu has also cited French ciné-culture as a significant influence.[14] Adrian Brunel, Iris Barry, journalist Walter Mycroft, exhibitor Sidney Bernstein, and sculptor Frank Dobson became council members of the Society, which involved organizing activities, getting hold of films and putting together programmes. Other founding members of the Society included Anthony Asquith, Michael Balcon, John Gielgud, biologist Julian Huxley, Ivor Novello, George Pearson and theatre director John Strachey.

Running on a non-profit basis, the Society still had to cover its expenses in order to survive. Income was needed in order to offset the considerable costs involved in its running and was chiefly gained through membership subscription. Its expenses included theatre rental, payment for staff, lighting and an orchestra at each performance, titling of films, customs duties and entertainment tax. Performances were held once a month, with a break for summer. The main venue for performances was the New Gallery in Regent Street, but other venues included the Tivoli, the Astoria and the New Victoria, which were often obtained free of charge.

The Society obtained films on an *ad hoc* basis, through contacts that its members had built up. Since there was no independent distribution company handling the right range of films at the time, each council member would travel abroad whenever possible to visit companies, directors or like-minded organizations, thereby establishing a network of informal international connections. The Society's closest links were with representatives of the Film Arts Guild in New York and the Vieux Colombier in Paris.[15]

The Society's membership rates were expensive and beyond the range of the average citizen's income. As a members-only, class-demarcated organization, the Society's adversaries often charged it with elitism. This charge was not without reason, but it did ignore the fact that such status was necessary in order for the Society to operate in an often hostile climate. It could not, for instance, be sure about the extent of interest in 'alternative' films, so it would have been a con-siderable financial risk for it to operate as a public, commercial cinema. More importantly, as a members-only society it was allowed to show films unclassified by the British Board of Film Censors (necessary in that many of the films it wanted to show had not been classified), so long as permission was granted by the London County Council (LCC). The LCC did grant permission as long as its screenings remained private and for a restricted audience; even so, it remained wary of the Society and some of the films shown had to be cut.[16]

Programmes

The Society's programmes usually consisted of four or five films of diverse scope and varied length. The first programme, held on 25 October 1925 at the New Gallery, was as follows:

- 2.30 p.m., *Opera 2, 3, and 4* (1923–5), short films by German engraver and lithographer Walter Ruttman, which the programme notes described as 'studies in pattern, with drum accompaniment'.[17] These were part of the Society's 'absolute films' series, which comprised short abstract films, usually by independent artists experimenting with the formal aspects of the film medium.
- 2.50 p.m., *How Broncho Billy Left Bear Country* (1912), an old two-reel American western produced by the Essanay company and starring G.M. Anderson. This was part of the Society's 'resurrection' series.
- 3.00 p.m., *Typical Budget* (1925), a British burlesque film directed by Film Society council member Adrian Brunel and produced by

Gainsborough pictures. This was part of a series of films and was exclusive in that it had yet to be trade-shown or released.

- 3.15 p.m., *Waxworks* (1924), which was the main feature. This was a German film (now regarded as a classic 'Expressionist' text), directed by Paul Leni, produced by Wilking Film, and starring Emil Jannings and Conradt Veidt. It had not at that time been purchased in Britain for film exhibition.
- 4.35 p.m., *Champion Charlie* (1916), an early Chaplin short.

This programme was representative of the main trend in programming: an eclectic range of films including an abstract film, a revival, a burlesque and a feature-length narrative. The Society usually showed three or four shorts accompanied by a main feature and showed a wide range of films in terms of both generic and national categories. Amongst other types of films it screened were travel films, sport films, educational films, documentaries, scientific films and cartoons. It showed films from a number of mostly European countries, but also showed many American films and some films from China, Japan, Mexico and South Africa. The Society also showed clips for technical study and hosted lectures on the art of filmmaking. For example, in its forty-fourth performance (11 January 1931) it showed a demonstration of new colour processes; in its forty-fifth performance (8 February 1931), it showed clips of two Hitchcock films—*The Lodger* (1926) and *The Skin Game* (1931)—for technical study; its most famous lectures were given by Pudovkin (February 1929) and Eisenstein (November 1929). The Society even ran a film production course led by Hans Richter, which resulted in an unreleased film, *Everyday* (1929).

The eclecticism of the Society's screenings reflected a desire to counter the restricted programmes of mainstream British cinemas and present a much wider range of films it considered important, especially films perceived as aesthetically innovative. Although the programmes were eclectic and members' tastes were not homogeneous, there were evident trends that reflected general predilections. During its first five years these were, first, an admiration for German films that were often 'expressionist' or psychological in tone;[18] second, in the later 1920s, a privileging of Soviet 'montage' films; and third, an interest in avant-garde shorts, most of which were from France and Germany.

In the mid-1920s, films such as *The Cabinet of Dr Caligari* were viewed by intellectual aesthetes as the pinnacle of film art; other German films shown and admired at the Society included *Waxworks* (Leni, 1924), *Raskolnikov* (Wiene, 1923), the psychological realist films of Pabst and the more abstract films made by Hans Richter and Walter Ruttman. Though 'expressionist' films were not always seen as masterpieces, the impressive and unconventional use of design and lighting within these films was often mentioned in the programme notes.

The preference for German films can be understood in several ways. One of the most obvious is that these were the films that were being shown internationally by other intellectual film groups with which the Society had connections. As noted above, the Society built up connections with similar organizations around the world in order to exchange films and advice, and these organizations undoubtedly influenced each other to some extent. This does not explain the aesthetic appeal of such films, however. A key factor in this respect was that, in order to locate the vanguard of cinematic art, the Society felt they had to look beyond America, which represented the commercial 'norm' and which provided the majority of films that played in commercial British cinemas. It was Germany that came to represent the alternative paradigm of excellence, with a small group of 'artistic' films sharing an identifiably coherent and 'advanced' aesthetic and consciously targeted at an international, cultured market.[19] These stylistic attributes were seen as a striking alternative to the films that constituted 'mass entertainment'; their fantastical and exaggerated qualities represented a radical trend in cinema that appealed directly to the intellect.

'Expressionist' films, however, stemmed from a theatrical lineage, which was just the kind of association that British aesthetes were trying to sever. This suggests their denial of the theatrical and literary heritage was overstated. Many of the German films they admired were marked by their stage influences, most notably the avant-garde techniques of theatrical producer Max Reinhardt.[20] Such theatrical influence was acceptable due to its avant-garde lineage, its internationalism, and its primarily visual nature. The theatrical and literary influences that were attacked were those associated with mediocrity, nationalism and wordiness. In addition, whilst many German films did borrow from other art forms, they also flaunted their 'cinematic specificity' through advanced special effects and fluid camera work.[21]

As overt antipathy to theatrical and literary values intensified, however, many protagonists within minority film culture became enamoured with the school of Soviet montage, most particularly the work of Eisenstein and Pudovkin. These films seemed so fresh to British aesthetes that they soon relinquished adherence to the German films, which appeared static and antiquated by comparison. A particular group of Soviet films were therefore singled out for their dynamism; in particular, of course, the manner by which they constructed their films around montage—seen as a uniquely cinematic technique—was much admired. Their extensive use of location shooting also further distinguished them from theatrical 'staginess'. The fact that some of the filmmakers—Eisenstein in particular—were also engaged in complex theoretical discussions of their work further justified the intellectual defence of film as a new, advanced art form.

The Establishment of a Critical Discourse

In addition to showing films, the Society also engaged in a form of critical discourse through its detailed programme notes. These notes provided an important and influential discursive contribution to an inter-war tradition of alternative film aesthetics. Other important contributions to this tradition include the journals *Close Up* (1927–33), *Cinema Quarterly* (1932–36) and *Film Art* (first published as Film, 1933–7); and books such as Iris Barry's *Let's Go to the Movies* (1926), Eric Elliot's *Anatomy of Motion Picture Art* (1928), Ernest Betts' *Heraclitus, or the Future of Film* (1928) and Paul Rotha's *The Film Till Now* (1930).[22]

The programme notes were written by Ivor Montagu for most of the 1920s,[23] and came in the form of a four-page leaflet, which included credits for the films being shown. For short films the notes varied in length from about twenty words to two hundred; for features they were substantially longer. They encompassed a range of topics, including print information, production details and categorization. Three characteristics of these notes were dominant features of alternative discourse. First, the notion of formal balance: for a film to be a great work, it had not only to innovate and experiment, but also to incorporate such manoeuvres into a coherent structural whole. Second, there was the privileging of the director as the creative intelligence guiding every aspect of the film, expressing him- or herself cinematically. Third, great importance was placed upon a work of cinematic art containing a dual structure: a 'surface' appearance and a 'deeper' meaning and, by extension, concrete and abstract levels. When all of these features were combined in a single film, it was hailed as a work of genius, as was the case with, say, Eisenstein's *October* (1928) or *The Cabinet of Dr Caligari*.

This manner of judging films aesthetically was a way of elevating the artistic status of film as a unique and modern art form. Paradoxically, such appreciation can be traced back to more traditional aesthetic paradigms. The notion of harmony and balance, for example, can be found in much humanist thought, itself a revival of Hellenic aesthetics.[24] The Society was 'modern' in the sense that its members saw cinema as a new, unique art form that should constantly innovate through progression; yet they relied on traditional aesthetic notions to validate this art form. 'Good cinema' was a mixture of the modern and the traditional: new innovative techniques and radical moments wrapped in more familiar notions of artistic vision, balance and coherency. The Society thus relied upon literary and dramatic concepts when they approached film. Such reliance—which seems inoffensive today—could not be admitted at a time when intellectuals were struggling to distance film from other arts.

Such a strategy was typical of the way in which the Society dissimulated important features of its aesthetic outlook. Thus despite the attention placed upon formal matters, content was important, even if not explicitly so. Within much alternative criticism importance was placed upon how themes and details were translated cinematically, thus shifting the importance of a film from its source material to its cinematic articulation. This was a tactic employed to encourage respect for the unique properties of the medium. But in so doing, aesthetes underplayed the important role content played in their artistic preferences. If one looks at the Film Society programmes, for example, it is evident that there is a tendency to overlook popular melodramas or historical costume dramas. Undoubtedly, aesthetes negatively evaluated the generic themes of these films, but such automatic distaste towards content went against 'cinematic' appraisal and was never boldly admitted.

Alternative Film Production

Alongside developments in alternative exhibition and critical writing about cinema as an art form, several films were also made, perhaps more than has generally been acknowledged. The critical debates of the period inevitably affected the types of films that were made and the aesthetic strategies adopted.

Adrian Brunel, for instance, made a number of what he called 'ultra-cheap experiments in cinematography' during an uncertain period in his career as a director of commercial feature films.[25] The first two—*Crossing the Great Sagrada* (1924) and *Pathetic Gazette* (1924) —were made independently; the next five—*Battling Bruisers, The Blunderland of Big Game, So This Is Jollygood, Cut It Out* and *Typical*

Plate 31.   Frame still from *C.O.D.—A Mellow Drama*
(Dickinson *et al.*, 1929)

parody as criticism

Budget (all 1925)—were made for Gainsborough.[26] Most of the films satirized aspects of the British film industry. *Crossing the Great Sagrada*, for instance, sent up the imperial pretensions of the 'expedition' film, the title a punning reference to *Crossing the Great Sahara*, which was shown in the British Films Week in February 1924; *Pathetic Gazette* and *Typical Budget* parodied newsreels such as *Pathé Gazette* and *Topical Budget*; *Cut It Out* lampooned the strict, Victorian prudishness that characterized censorship within Britain in the mid-1920s; and *So This is Jollygood* mocked the way British films were made, especially their feeble attempts to imitate American films. It is noteworthy that these films were littered with intertitles: on the one hand this was an effect of a tight budget, on the other hand it satirized the perception that British films over-used titles, which were felt to hinder a purely visual film form.

The tendency to deconstruct reflected not only on British cinema but also other filmic traditions. In *Battling Bruisers*, for instance, Brunel parodied Soviet montage styles, whilst Oswell Blakeston—a contributing editor of *Close Up*—made a short film entitled *I Do Like to be Beside the Seaside* (1928), which parodied a variety of 'artistic' styles. There was a tendency in this period for alternative cinéastes to deconstruct existing styles, even those that they most admired. This suggests that there was an extensive awareness of how a style could congeal into mechanical formula. It is therefore no surprise that

299

alternative criticism often disapproved of those British films that did attempt to incorporate styles associated with other movements. Even films that treated experimentation seriously, as a means to convey visual information relevant to the unfolding plot, were marked by a light-hearted, parodic tone. Thus the films made by Ivor Montagu, Frank Wells and his father, H.G. Wells, for their independent production company Angle Pictures in 1928 were burlesques: *Bluebottles, Daydreams* and *The Tonic* (all 1928). In a similar vein, *C.O.D.—A Mellow Drama* (Dickinson et al., 1929)—a short experiment made by Stoll technicians while their studio was being converted for sound— exaggerated German expressionist codes.

Although these films were inevitably related to the outlooks and concerns of alternative film culture, they did not fit into the more serious paradigms of its discourse. Their preoccupation with debunking and satirizing did not really constitute a serious 'artistic vision'; neither did they appear as deep, complex, formally balanced texts. Although they were shown within the eclectic and pluralistic frameworks of British film societies, they were never seen as great artistic works.

In contrast to this deconstructive strain in alternative film culture, several other films can be seen as attempting to reconstruct a specifically British mode of alternative filmmaking. It is true that the alternative culture disseminated and promoted international films and ideas, but this fact been overplayed in the past. Anne Friedberg, for example, has argued that *Close Up*'s major role was in translating international ideas.[27] British alternative culture framed these ideas in a specific manner, however, and it was the merging of international styles in a 'distinctively British' manner that eventually paved the way for a native, alternative film movement.

An alternative, *modern* type of content, placing itself against a perceived 'pre-modern' vision of society characteristic of mainstream British cinema was an important element in the construction of an authorized, alternative British movement. This was rarely acknowledged as such in critical writings in the 1920s, however, partly because of the emphasis in alternative culture on form over content and partly because an antipathy towards patriotic discourses led to a reluctance in promoting 'specifically' British qualities. Yet several films did incorporate international influences with more recognizably 'British' qualities in the 1920s. These films focused upon what were perceived as modern aspects of British society and attempted to represent excluded segments of contemporary society. One of the key representational strategies would become the depiction of the working classes, who were seen as a repressed absence in British films. In Brunel's *Cut it Out*, for instance, there is a scene that parodies the prevailing ideology of British filmmaking. A film crew begin to shoot in a pastoral location, but on spotting an anomalous factory-type building pumping out smoke they are warned by the censor: 'be careful or I'll cut it out.' The implication was that the British film industry was welded to a nostalgic vision of Britain, unwilling to face up to the realities of urban modernity.

Reaction to such content was also evident in the Montagu-Wells collaborations, which merged deconstructive and reconstructive strategies. For example, *Bluebottles* is the comic story of a lower-class woman (Elsa Lanchester) who becomes unwittingly mixed up in a police fiasco. The film in a sense looks back to the first ten years of British cinema, both in its slapstick moments and because this was a period when the lower classes were more widely represented, if only negatively and for comic effect. This looking back is also blended with more contemporary aspects, such as the use of experimental techniques, as though acknowledging its cinematic literacy.

Yet it was in the commercial sphere that 'modern' content was most consistently blended with international influence, especially in the films of Alfred Hitchcock and Anthony Asquith. Hitchcock's internationalist influence has been much noted, especially in *The Lodger* (1926); Tom Ryall, for example, cites the influence of German expressionism in the lighting, Soviet montage in the editing, and the French avant-garde in its formal experimentation.[28] This is correct, but Hitchcock also focused, in part, on the ordinary lives of British people. Metaphorically the film can be read as an encounter between Britishness and internationalism. The plain, realistic scenes of the Buntings are interrupted by the exaggerated and expressionist internationalism of Novello's Lodger. The distrust of him can be seen as symbolic of patriots' distrust of internationalist incorporation. Yet the film goes on to show that internationalism and Britishness can co-exist: the Lodger (internationalism) is vindicated at the film's conclusion. In *Underground* (1928), Asquith portrayed ordinary British people (a shop worker, a subway worker and an electrician) within a specifically modern locus of urban Britain (the underground), and spun a psychological thriller around it, which utilized the 'expressionist' technique of chiaroscuro lighting. It is no surprise that Asquith and Hitchcock were both members of the Film Society, whilst Montagu carried out significant post-production work on *The Lodger*.

Critical writing did begin slowly to absorb the fact that some British films incorporated international styles but at the same time differentiated themselves from the films they took inspiration from. Robert Herring thus wrote that *Underground* was not only formally impressive, but also made a good attempt to 'use and realise London'.[29] Along with other writers such as Hugh Castle and Ralph Bond, he began to pay more serious attention to British films as distinct artworks in their own right within the pages of *Close Up*. This was partly because many amateur films of the period were seen as adopting Soviet-influenced methods of quick cutting in uninspired ways.

Thus by 1929, the critical writing that had influenced production was in turn being influenced by some of the films that had been made and began to appeal for an alternative, specifically national film move-ment which was nevertheless alert to international innovations. It was therefore within a particularly receptive environment that the founding text of the documentary movement, John Grierson's *Drifters* (1929), was released. This film focused on overlooked aspects of the British environment but also drew on international influences, such as Soviet montage. The film was carefully structured and both appealed to the need for formal balance and contained concrete and abstract levels of articulation. Grierson also stressed its creative, formal attributes in order to distinguish it from the newsreel film.[30]

In the first half of the 1930s the more formal side of the documen-tary movement was championed by both *Film Art* and *Cinema Quarterly* as an advanced mode of native filmmaking, which blended educational and 'realist' aspects with formal and poetic elements. The movement also appealed to both apolitical formalists on the one hand, and the new strain of workers' film societies on the other, who rejected excessive formalism in favour of trying to get across a political message through content alone. Both these strains were directly influenced by the milieu of the Film Society and their respective differences were not as great as they sometimes made out. Grierson, Montagu and Kenneth Macpherson, editor of *Close Up*, were all members of the Federation of Workers' Film Societies, but were also heavily involved in the running of either the Film Society or *Close Up*, the two organs most consistently attacked for being interested in formal rather than political concerns. It wasn't until the latter part of the 1930s that realist content became dominant and directly opposed formal experiment, which was seen as inherently decadent. Until then, there was a vital strain of formal experiment: Len Lye, Norman McLaren and Oswell Blakeston all made films that explored extremely abstract cinematic territory. These films represent a different tradition of native, alternative filmmaking, in which subject matter was less important as a concrete reference point; sadly, I do not have the space to examine them here.

Conclusion

The Film Society was a vital element of alternative British film culture in the 1920s. It not only helped to build an alternative exhibition network but also played an important part in the development of alternative criticism and production, both independent and commercial. Although I have only been able to sketch the connections between these different spheres of activity, it is important to recognize the extent to which they were interdependent.[31] The Film Society's critical discourse and its choice of films had a significant influence upon films made in Britain, but there were also some tensions between alternative production, exhibition and critical practices. Alternative criticism was sensitive towards the faults of British films in terms of both mimicking international styles and failing to construct a serious mode of British cinema. This was reflected in many independent films that were caught between parody and seriousness. Such a contradictory aesthetic meant that these films lacked the balance and coherence privileged within alternative critical discourses and were therefore largely overlooked within this alternative film culture. A more serious mode of internationally influenced cinema did emerge within the commercial environment, but it was only towards the end of the 1920s that criticism, influenced by production, began to call for a serious form of distinctively British, alternative filmmaking. By this time, however, antipathy towards the commercial cinema was growing and it was eventually the documentary movement that became privileged within such critical frameworks.

Notes

1. This type of patriotic promotion of 'artistic' British films was represented by the British National Film Weeks. The first of these (February 1924) was dominated by costume dramas. For an advertisement for the first film week, see the *Sunday Pictorial*, 3 February 1924.
2. See Jen Samson, 'The Film Society,' and Charles Barr, 'Introduction: Schizophrenia and Amnesia,' both in Barr, ed., *All Our Yesterdays: 90 Years of British Cinema* (London: BFI, 1992); Phillip Kemp, 'Not For Peckham: Michael Balcon and Gainsborough's International Trajectory in the 1920s,' in Pam Cook, ed., *Gainsborough Pictures* (London: Cassell,

1997); Andrew Higson, *Waving the Flag: Constructing a National Cinema in Britain* (Oxford: Clarendon Press, 1995); and Tom Ryall, *Alfred Hitchcock and the British Cinema* (London: Athlone Press, 1996).

3. Much of the information on the Film Society has been drawn from the Film Society Special Collection, held at the British Film Institute National Library.

4. 'Constitution and Rules of the Film Society Limited,' item 2, the Film Society Special Collection.

5. Imogen, 'Film and the Press,' *Bioscope*, 14 August 1924, p. 27.

6. See Richard Abel, *French Film Theory and Criticism: 1907–1936, Vol. 1: 1907–1929* (Princeton: Princeton University Press, 1988).

7. Rachael Low, *The History of the British Film, 1918–1929* (London: George Allen and Unwin, 1971), p. 34.

8. Alan Lovell, Sam Rohdie and Peter Wollen, 'Interview with Ivor Montagu,' *Screen*, vol. 13, no. 3, 1992, p. 72.

9. Low, *The History of the British Film*, p. 33.

10. *Bioscope*, 18 October 1923, p. 54.

11. Low, *The History of the British Film*, p. 34.

12. On Barry's and Montagu's critical practice in the 1920s, see the chapters by Haidee Wasson and Gerry Turvey elsewhere in this volume.

13. For more details on the Stage Society see Clifford Bax, 'The Stage Society: A Retrospect and an Appeal,' *London Mercury* (vol. 21, no. 21, November 1929), pp. 38–45.

14. Ivor Montagu, 'The Film Society, London,' *Cinema Quarterly*, vol. 1, no. 2, Winter 1932, pp. 42–6.

15. See 'Correspondence With New York Film Organisations,' item 33, the Film Society Special Collection.

16. For example, it had to cut some scenes from *The Cabinet of Dr Caligari*, which was shown in the sixth programme (14 March 1926). See Ivor Montagu, *The Youngest Son: Autobiographical Sketches* (London: Lawrence and Wishart), pp. 323–4.

17. Programme notes for performance 1 (25 October 1925), item 5, the Film Society Special Collection.

18. Although the term 'expressionist' is problematic, it was used in contemporary reviews internationally. See Kristin Thompson, 'Dr Caligari at the Folies-Bergère,' in Mike Budd, ed., *The Cabinet of Dr Caligari: Texts, Contexts, Histories* (New Brunswick: Rutgers University Press, 1990), pp. 127–36.

19. See Thomas Elsaesser, *Weimar Cinema and After: Germany's Historical Imaginary* (London: Routledge, 2000), pp. 18–61, and Sabine Hake, *Cinema's Third Machine: Writing on Film in Germany 1907–1933* (Lincoln: University of Nebraska Press, 1993), p. 113.

20. Reinhardt used spotlights and a revolving stage to 'revolutionize' the theatre; he was said to be extremely visual (rather than dialogue-based),

and was influenced by industrialization. Many of the early Ufa directors, including Lubitsch and Murnau, worked with him. See Klaus Kreimeier, *The Ufa Story: A History of Germany's Greatest Film Company 1928–1945* (New York: Hill and Wang, 1996), p. 61.

21. Elsaesser, *Weimar Cinema*, pp. 62–6.
22. Iris Barry, *Let's Go to the Movies* (New York: Arno Press, 1972), Eric Elliot, *Anatomy of Motion Picture Art* (London: POOL, 1928), Ernest Betts, *Heraclitus, or the Future of Film* (London: Kegan Paul, 1928), Paul Rotha, *The Film Till Now* (London: Vision Press, 1963).
23. Ivor Montagu, 'Old Man's Mumble,' *Sight and Sound*, vol. 44, no. 4, Autumn 1975, p. 224. Thorold Dickinson and Sidney Cole wrote most of the subsequent notes.
24. See Tony Davies, *Humanism* (London: Routledge, 1997), pp. 10–13.
25. See Adrian Brunel, 'Experiments in Ultra-Cheap Cinematography,' *Close Up*, vol. 3, no. 4, October 1928, pp. 43–6. For a fuller account of these films, see my 'Parody on the Fringes: Adrian Brunel, Minority Film Culture and the Art of Deconstruction,' in Alan Burton and Laraine Porter, eds, *Pimple, Pranks and Pratfalls: British Film Comedy Before 1930* (Trowbridge: Flicks, 2000).
26. Brunel, 'Experiments in Ultra-Cheap Cinematography'.
27. Anne Friedberg, *Writing About Cinema: 'Close Up' 1927–1933*, unpublished Ph.D. thesis, University Microfilms International: University of New York, 1984, p. 181.
28. Ryall, *Alfred Hitchcock and the British Cinema*, pp. 24–6.
29. Robert Herring, 'The Movies,' *London Mercury*, vol. 19, no. 111, January 1929, p. 316.
30. See, for example, John Grierson, 'Documentary (1),' *Cinema Quarterly*, no. 2, Winter 1932, and 'Documentary (2),' *Cinema Quarterly*, vol. 1, no. 3, Spring 1933.
31. For a fuller account of the interconnections between exhibition, critical discourse and production within British alternative film culture, see my Ph.D. thesis, 'The Emergence of an Alternative British Film Culture in Inter-War Period,' University of East Anglia, 2001).

19

Towards a Critical Practice
Ivor Montagu and British Film Culture in the 1920s

Gerry Turvey

Ivor Montagu played a key role in the development of British film culture over several decades and yet, while his name may be readily recognized, the full extent of his activities in the British cinema is probably still not fully appreciated. These activities began in the second half of the 1920s and rapidly took on considerable significance. My chapter will outline the range of projects he helped initiate in this period and then focus on his early attempts to generate a critical practice.

Montagu, who was still only 25 in 1929, characterized his family as 'plutocratic but not aristocratic';[1] nevertheless, he became a militant socialist. Further, just as he became a political activist, so the role he created for himself in the film world could be seen as that of a 'cinema activist' operating on several fronts. When Montagu got involved in British film production in the mid-1920s after leaving Cambridge University, the industry was at its lowest ebb. From 1925 onwards, he participated in attempts both to regenerate production and to extend the boundaries of tolerance in the existing, primarily commercial, film culture. This was the period when the 'old guard' of production—such as Cecil Hepworth—went out of business and new, more modern companies and producers—such as Michael Balcon—were emerging. Montagu attempted to bring fresh ideas to these latter through the Film Society, his writing and, later, his sponsorship of Vsevelod

Pudovkin. Beyond this, he participated in several attempts to change the terms of the culture in which the industry was embedded, not only through the work of the Film Society and his critical activities but also through his challenge to the British Board of Film Censors (BBFC).

While Montagu made a significant individual contribution to these areas, his activities were also carried out in association with a number of groups, organizations and sympathetic friends so that he was operating as part of an identifiable cultural formation which was young, primarily male, mostly university-educated and from upper- or middle-class backgrounds. This was an earlier generation than that of the better-known British documentary movement and one more closely associated with commercial feature films. Montagu's involvement began with his friendships at Cambridge with Ian Dalrymple and Angus MacPhail—both of whom were to become significant figures in the industry—and expanded to embrace such established industry personnel as the director Adrian Brunel and the young producer Michael Balcon.

The Variety of Montagu's Projects

Montagu is probably best known for his association with the Film Society, which opened in October 1925 and ceased operation in 1939. Although the Society is discussed in more detail in chapter 18 of this volume, it is worth noting that the idea for the Society came directly from Montagu when, returning from a visit to survey the German film industry in the autumn of 1924, he and the actor Hugh Miller discussed the formation of a society to show films which would adopt the model of the Stage Society. The latter had long been putting on Sunday performances to a subscription-paying membership of plays that commercial companies had declined or which the Lord Chamberlain—the theatre censor—had refused. Hence, the Film Society's own programme regularly stated that it had been 'founded in order that work of interest in the study of cinematography, and yet not easily accessible, might be made accessible to members'.[2] Once the Society was established, Montagu became its Chairman (until 1929), a Council member helping find suitable films and determine a season's programmes (for the duration) and, for the first four seasons, the writer of the Programme Notes issued at each performance. These latter formed an important component of his critical-theoretical project. More specifically, a prospectus issued at the foundation of the Society indicated that its intention was to offer 'films of intrinsic merit', both old and new, with a view to raising the 'standards of taste' for films and establishing a 'critical tradition'—something to which Montagu's film reviews were a further contribution. The Society also directly addressed itself to present and future personnel 'in the film trade itself', partly in the hope that standards of 'executive ability' might thereby be raised.[3] Thus, Montagu and the other Council members were instrumental in setting in process a broad programme in film education aimed, in particular, at stimulating the film industry. Hence, the choice of films was designed to enrich members' knowledge of world cinema and to introduce them to a broad spectrum of film techniques.

Montagu slipped into the industry itself in the autumn of 1925 as a result of his Film Society contacts with Adrian Brunel. Since 1923, the latter had run, in Montagu's words, 'a sort of film knacker's business—repair and rebeautifying of ravaged pictures'.[4] In August 1927 this became the firm of Brunel and Montagu Limited and, with their colleagues (who came to include Dalrymple and MacPhail), they provided a service to the film industry which generated a considerable volume of uncredited post-production work designed to improve already completed films. Montagu, for example, handled over 100 silent movies. The firm dealt with foreign imports, titling them, preparing them to pass the BBFC and making adjustments so they would appeal to British audiences. They edited and titled material for Film Society programmes. They were also regularly called in to enhance the quality of British-made films, often going into studios at short notice to exercise their remedial skills. Montagu himself provided a crucial creative input into Alfred Hitchcock's *The Lodger* for Balcon in the summer of 1926. Brunel's own directorial experience and the activities of his firm convinced him that 'Editing is the basis of film craft'[5] and this became the lesson he passed on to the young men for whom he was providing a basic training in film. In its turn, such practical work and collective learning fed into the ideas Montagu was introducing into his reviewing. It later made him receptive to Soviet ideas regarding the importance of montage.

Furthermore, several of the men trained at Brunel and Montagu came to enjoy a close relation with Balcon's Gainsborough Pictures. Brunel went there to direct, Dalrymple to edit and MacPhail to write. Montagu found himself taken on to supervise both scripts and editing in December 1926. As he recalled: 'I found myself with a sort of roving authority over an embryo script department (days) and editing department (nights as well).'[6] This was followed in 1927 by his

Plate 32. Production still from *Bluebottles* (Montagu/Wells, 1928)

move into direction. At Gainsborough's Islington studio, he made three comedy shorts, including *Bluebottles*—using personnel from Brunel and Montagu—for a company he set up with Brunel, Charles Laughton and Laughton's wife, Elsa Lanchester, a personal friend who took the leading role in the films. Thus, Montagu had become directly involved in the revival of production in British popular commercial cinema of the late 1920s—a phenomenon he was also keen to encourage in his critical writing.

Montagu also played a prominent part in the challenge to censorship launched in the late 1920s. Britain's system of film censorship had finally been consolidated in 1924, when local authorities decided to accept BBFC rulings, but this 'settlement' was called into question by a series of controversies in 1928–9. Montagu had already had direct knowledge of the vagaries of the Board through his work at Brunel and Montagu and through the Film Society; in September 1929, his opposition to existing censorship practices resulted in his writing a widely distributed pamphlet, *The Political Censorship of Films*, which was accompanied by a campaign to get MPs to take up the issue of film censorship. He also delivered a speech on 'The Censorship of Sex in Films' to the London Congress of the radical World League for Sexual Reform.[7] The pamphlet condemned covert government involvement in film censorship and the speech the censor's sexual repressiveness.[8]

Montagu also deplored the absence of serious film criticism in the mid-1920s. In his autobiography, he recalled how

> [i]t was a grievance amongst us enthusiasts for film 'art' that the 'quality' press at that time in general ignored the cinema . . . and there was no counterweight to the cheap gossip and rehashed publicity material that so often masqueraded as film journalism.[9]

Consequently, he offered himself to the *Observer* as their first film critic—a position he occupied for the first five months of 1926. Already, in 1923–4, Dalrymple, MacPhail and he had introduced film reviews into *Granta*, the Cambridge student magazine. As I pointed out above, between 1925 and 1929, he also compiled the Programme Notes for the Film Society. In all this writing he was attempting to originate a critical practice and explore various promising theoretical positions.

Establishing a Reviewing Practice

The editing work undertaken at Brunel and Montagu seems to have made him particularly sensitive to issues of filmic construction and this concern was taken up in his reviews. Thus he recognized the narrative vocation of commercial feature films and proceeded to discuss matters of structure, pace and dramatic impact. For example, of the Valentino star vehicle *The Eagle* (Clarence Brown, 1925), he wrote: 'A fast, exciting, if hackneyed story is made dull, slow, inconsequent, and every dramatic situation is bungled, set out without being led up to cinematically'[10]—though he failed to clarify precisely how he was using the latter term. In another film, he found 'the development of the plot is primitive, many important incidents being passed over by a sub-title, and others not being worked up to a dramatic climax'.[11] Thus he found fault with films that evidenced too slow a pace, incoherent plot organization and a lack of effective dramatic climaxing. Conversely, his approval was directed to films that handled these issues more successfully.

Montagu's remedial work had made him acutely aware of the appropriate use of intertitles in silent films. He deplored ungrammatical, uninspired and redundant titles; thus, of one Seastrom film, he wrote:

> It is a brilliant production, whose only fault, a serious one, is bad titling and verbosity. Moods, emotional reactions, moral judgements which are clearly implied in the action and acting are none the less iterated by written words, presumably in the belief that cinema-goers are below normal level of intelligence, and will otherwise miss them.[12]

For him, the proper application of titles in silent films was one which would avoid redundancy, length, ugliness and poor use of language.

Montagu also commented on the contribution of performances to story development. Here, he was operating with the traditional aesthetic assumption that a part must be integral to the whole. So, he reproached Emil Jannings's performance in *Variety* (E.A. Dupont, 1925) because 'often he seems a pastiche of himself, and we often seem to be kept waiting for him to finish his dramatic little pieces before the general action is allowed to proceed'.[13] Similarly, in Hollywood, the 'shameless evil of the star system' was that—as one particular example showed—'every protagonist but Miss Swanson [the star], from her leading man . . . to the largest groups and crowds, play round and up to her'.[14]

Another focus in the reviews was a film's photography. In one it was rejected for being 'curiously flat throughout' and, in another, held to be 'obscure at the corners and like photogravure in the middle'.[15] More positively, photography might be 'exquisite' or 'beautifully clear' and, in one of Cecil B. De Mille's films, it was recommended for being 'soft and smooth, like an art portrait done by a firm of society photographers'.[16]

Finally, Montagu assigned responsibility for particular films to their directors. Hence a hierarchy emerged in his account where individuals were esteemed because of their ability to realize visually the dramatic narration he was encouraging. D.W. Griffith, Cecil B. De Mille, Charles Chaplin and Ernst Lubitsch were highly rated in American cinema whilst, in Britain, the young Hitchcock was recommended whereas Herbert Wilcox was deemed to have 'no feeling for the material he is handling'.[17] Montagu also revered contemporary German directors such as Paul Leni and Ludwig Berger until his enthusiasm migrated to Vsevelod Pudovkin and Sergei Eisenstein at the end of the decade.

Mapping Contemporary 'World' Cinema

Montagu's critical project offered a broad mapping and evaluation of contemporary 'world' cinema which drew heavily on the showings of the Film Society. In November 1925, he offered himself as one of those 'who believe that American films are the best in the world'[18] and, elsewhere, advocated the early work of Griffith, the films of Douglas Fairbanks, De Mille and Chaplin, the comedians developing out of the slapstick tradition and individual movies such as The Big Parade (King Vidor, 1926). The mid-1920s, of course, was a moment when British cinema screens were overwhelmed by Hollywood films but such willingness to embrace them and take them seriously by an upper-class intellectual like Montagu was an unprecedented move.

Montagu seems to have understood European films—especially those selected for the Society—in terms of their *difference* from American cinema. Within Europe, German cinema held the greatest interest before its decline in the later 1920s.[19] For him, the merits of mainstream American films was their sense of pace and space and their espousal of dramatic narrative, whereas the significant properties of German cinema in the early and mid-1920s were to be found in their architecture and decor, their stylized performances and the originality of their cinematography. The key German film—as it had been for his Cambridge friends—was *The Cabinet of Dr Caligari* (Robert Wiene, 1919) which he found 'remarkable for its *formalisation of gesture and scenery to accord with and enhance the moods and tempers of the picture*'.[20] Similarly, the qualities of *Waxworks* (Paul Leni, 1924) were 'partly architectural—*the sets and groupings* of Dr Leni are of great pictorial beauty—and partly in the *stylised acting* of the wax figures'.[21]

When discussing the French 'artistic' films that constituted a regular part of Film Society programmes, Montagu offered a perspective which drew cultural contrasts between national cinemas. Thus, whilst discussing Alberto Cavalcanti's *En Rade* (1928), he approvingly stated:

> It has been suggested . . . that the best virtues of any national film output are conditioned by the form of culture most living in its immediate traditional local influence. In the course of analysis it was cited the dramatic and acting qualities of a certain German school, influenced by stage tradition, and the compositional qualities of the work of the younger Frenchmen, influenced by nineteenth century painting. In this instance, at any rate (an attempt to create atmosphere without narrative) . . . the qualities are essentially those of almost static composition.[22]

In his comments on British film, he tried to be encouraging. Hence, in April 1928—and in contrast to his estimate of the current German situation—he was writing of a 'British Film Revival',[23] a claim which had some justification given the upsurge in production around the time of the 1927 Quota Act, a process in which he too was caught up. At the same time, he was not uncritical and identified a 'fundamental fault' in many British films.[24] Thus, Herbert Wilcox's *The Only Way* (1925) was 'stale, dead and unconvincing' because the direction meant it was 'made up of a series of sets and groups, each one of which [Wilcox] seems to feel quite statically and separately, like a theatre scene'.[25] By contrast, Alfred Hitchcock's first feature, *The Pleasure Garden* (1926), held considerable promise and, in his review, Montagu presciently identified those aspects of the newcomer's approach that were to typify his subsequent British films—his skill with film narrative, his London naturalism and the realism of his characterization.

The breadth of Montagu's enthusiasm for film extended to the emergent avant-garde and, when the Film Society programmed some of the abstract or 'absolute' films made in the 1920s, he described them for the readers of the newly established, intellectual film periodical *Close Up* in 1927:

> The basis of [Viking Eggeling's] work is line, and his patterns are mainly the varying positions on a two dimensional plane, the screen, of his one dimensional figures, in contradistinction to the patterns of [Walter] Ruttmann and [Hans] Richter which are usually flat two-dimensional forms moving in three dimensions. The screen is a blackboard to Eggeling and a window to Richter and Ruttmann.[26]

Intellectual Resources

It should not be assumed Montagu was a lone figure attempting to pioneer the analysis of film from scratch because there did exist a limited body of critical and theoretical writing he could turn to. As he later recalled, there was, in the mid-1920s, 'practically no serious writing on cinema except the very early Vachel Lindsay and Gilbert Seldes's essay on Chaplin in *The 7 Lively Arts*'.[27] Both texts were known to him and his Film Society colleagues and they not only helped form his early film-reviewing practice but also stimulated the cinephilia of his friends and gave direction to the Society's early programming strategies. Thus, until the latter part of 1928, when he became better acquainted with the ideas of the Soviet avant-garde, Montagu's thinking about cinema drew on American insights.

Lindsay's pathbreaking work, *The Art of the Moving Picture*, was first published in 1915 and then reissued for Montagu's generation in 1922. Seldes's *The 7 Lively Arts* was published in 1924. Both books were particularly likely to appeal to young, upper-class intellectuals discovering cinema and needing to justify their interest. Lindsay, whose background was in the study and teaching of art history, was quite explicit that his 'platform' was that the 'motion picture art is a great high art, not a process of commercial manufacture'.[28] Seldes, a book reviewer and drama critic, declared his theme was 'that entertainment of a high order existed in places not usually associated with Art, that the place where an object was to be seen or heard had no bearing on its merits'.[29] As a consequence, he found the book was enthusiastically read by young people and college students—that is, people like Montagu and his friends. Thus, Lindsay and Seldes provided an intellectual rationale for taking cinema seriously and a preliminary set of concepts and judgements with which to embark on film analysis.

Lindsay's book presented a threefold typology differentiating the 'Action Film' from the 'Intimate Film' and the 'Photoplay of Splendor'. Montagu seems not to have applied this classification directly but, I suspect, its intellectual self-consciousness and aesthetic rigour helped give him the confidence to examine film analytically and take the early American cinema seriously. In some places, Lindsay's influence is more directly apparent. For example, he had declared that the 'key words of the stage are passion and character; of the photoplay splendor and speed'.[30] Montagu, in one of his *Observer* reviews, advanced the parallel claim that American films 'possess a *cinematic sense of pace and space* that is in contrast with the often deliberateness [*sic*] of German and Swedish . . . films'.[31] Comparable comments are to be found in Seldes's own attempt to identify the 'correct principle of the aesthetics of the moving picture'.[32] This, he maintained, involved the 'two agencies' of movement and light and he claimed to count 'in movement everything of pace and in light everything which light can make visible to the eye'.[33] Elsewhere, Montagu expanded on the significance of space for film when he suggested:

> The *essential character* of a film play is use of space or the
> implication of space. In a theatre, the limitations of the stage

mean that everything of importance must take place in, or balanced about, its centre . . . In a cinema, space is unlimited . . . the field of vision may be made to move—the imminence of any one of a hundred possible devices keeps us constantly aware of space the whole time, of the geography of each situation.[34]

Before his encounter with theories of montage, Montagu thus adopted American ideas in which film's defining feature was its unique capacity to embrace space and movement.

For Lindsay, the Photoplay of Splendor, with its emphasis on landscape and the movement of crowds, was 'the equivalent of the epic'.[35] Following this, Montagu identified *The Big Parade* as a 'National Epic, condemning and glorifying a nation's part in the war'.[36] Similarly, when the Film Society showed *Charles XII* (John Brunius, 1925), he characterized it as 'a national epic, and the most ambitious film produced in Sweden' but admitted the Society had reduced its length by removing parts of a personal family story 'yet retaining all scenes portraying crowd movements and battles'—a procedure shifting it towards conformity with Lindsay's definition of the epic film and its turning away from the personal relationships of the Intimate Film.[37]

Beyond these direct borrowings, Lindsay's book appears to have underpinned the programming policies adopted by the Film Society. For example, one strand was their screening of 'resurrections' wherein, as Montagu explained to the *Observer*, they planned to revive old films from the 1905–15 period.[38] This, of course, was precisely the period Lindsay had been dealing with and his forceful defence of early American cinema would have recommended it to the Society's attention.

The intellectual position Seldes adopted may have had a more direct appeal than Lindsay to the iconoclastic impulses of Montagu and his friends for Seldes's aim was to promote the significance of popular culture in general and cinema in particular. In effect, he was conducting a polemic aimed at distinguishing between 'the great arts', 'the bogus arts' and 'the lively arts'. The latter ranged over popular song, comic strips, dancing, circus, vaudeville and films. Montagu, MacPhail and their friends shared such enthusiasms, especially those for cinema and music-hall; in particular, they enjoyed British comics such as Billy Bennett and the French clown, Grock. Seldes had also declared that 'we require arts which specifically refer to *our* moment, which create the image of *our* lives . . . [That is,] we require for nourishment something fresh and transient.'[39] For him, such nourishment could best be found in the 'ephemera' of the lively arts and so his book provided Montagu with a rationale for investigating and promoting popular film.

Writing on American cinema nine years after Lindsay's initial foray, Seldes sketched an account which described an early promise betrayed. His analysis therefore served to reinforce the respect Lindsay had accorded the films of the early period and to strengthen the retrospective emphasis in the Film Society's programming. It also gave orientation to much of Montagu's film critical activity. In 1915, Lindsay had rejected the 'irrelevant slap-stick work' used to fill cinema programmes[40] but, in 1924, Seldes was writing of how the 'drama film is almost always wrong, the slap-stick almost always right'.[41] Montagu's reviewing, confronted as it inevitably was by a preponderance of dramas, did not—like his mentor—reject them out of hand but he and his Film Society colleagues nevertheless espoused Seldes's enthusiasm for comic films. For Seldes, accepting slapstick had to do with recognizing film's defining characteristics and this issue offers further insight into the initial theoretical premises adopted by Montagu. Seldes claimed that the 'true elements in the cinema which, being *theoretically* sound, had a chance of practical success . . . [were] the spectacle (including the spectacular melodrama) and the grotesque comedy'.[42] He also proposed that Mack Sennett's work in the latter 'was doing with the instruments of the moving picture precisely those things which were best suited to it . . . [for] everything in slap-stick *is* cinematographic'.[43] By this, he meant that everything was 'done with the camera, through action presented to the eye'.[44]

Alongside their essential 'filmic-ness', slapstick and comic films had qualities that also made them a prime example of the lively arts. The *Granta* reviewers and Montagu took over this emphasis. The Film Society also took note and slapstick films appeared on its programmes from the outset. Thus, Montagu's very first programme note referred to Seldes's 'brilliant essay' on Chaplin and introduced *Champion Charlie* (1916) as coming from Chaplin's 'Essanay period' where 'he retained, almost unmodified, the original slapstick convention he had learnt under Mr Sennett at Keystone'.[45] The periodizing of Chaplin's work and his derivation from Sennett was taken directly from Seldes. The latter's sponsorship of slapstick may also have given added licence to the Society's programming of a number of short British 'burlesque' comedies, particularly those of Montagu's friend and partner, Adrian Brunel.

Montagu's *Observer* period coincided with the release of several new films from the comedians dealt with by Seldes and this allows a comparison of the two men's critical positions. For example, Seldes's 1924 judgement of Harold Lloyd was that he was 'a man of no tenderness, of no philosophy, the embodiment of American cheek and indefatigable energy. His movements are all direct, straight . . . [and] there is no poetry in him.'[46] There were elements of this characterization in Montagu's commentary of 1926 but the latter developed the analysis rather more deeply and pointed it up with reference to figures from both the major and the lively arts:

> Mr Lloyd's clown is never attractive in itself. He never forces one to feel with him. His separate misfortunes would be neither pitiful nor amusing but rather painful; to witness the incessant cruelty of the baiting reminds one disagreeably of Ben Jonson. But their succession, the swift vigour with which incident follows after incident, is quite irresistible . . . Mr Lloyd's misfortunes lose their naturalistic meaning of hurt, and the whole scene becomes invested with a dream-like sense of wonder. The nightmarish quality of his incompletely finished ballroom suit [in *College Days*] is worthy of [the clown] Fratellini.[47]

I suspect Montagu's critical writing on comic film achieved its analytical force because he was both building on and developing Seldes's ground-breaking commentary. For example, he could suggest a *development* within the whole comic tradition that seemed to elude the American:

> The wheel of American comedy has now turned completely round. In its birth days the hero was one who, by agility and finesse, inflicted blows and pains on an infinity of opponents stronger and larger than himself, only to be overwhelmed by failure in the final fade-out. But now each of the great comedians, who have emerged from that slapstick apprenticeship, Mr Keaton, Mr Lloyd, and Mr Chaplin, becomes the increasingly pitied and helplessly isolated butt, whose only wins are by some narrow accident or miracle. Alexander the Conqueror is becoming a melancholy clown.[48]

Ivor Montagu's attempt to promote an intellectually adventurous film culture in the 1920s had led him into an enthusiastic embrace of films from America, Europe and even Japan. His development of a critical practice had drawn on insights derived from work on commercial films at Brunel and Montagu, research and programming undertaken for the Film Society and ideas gleaned from Lindsay and Seldes. In fact, his writing about film can best be understood as his personal contribution to the elaboration of what David Bordwell, in his recent history of film style, has called the Basic Story, regarding the early history of film art, and the Standard Version, accounting for its stylistic evolution.[49] Like his contemporaries who were 'defining the seventh art' elsewhere in the 1920s, Montagu was working to set up a 'canon' of valued silent films and—following the received protocols of art history—to establish the idea of distinctive national cinemas and the significance of individual creators. In drawing on Lindsay and Seldes, he was also attempting to define those characteristics that would help distinguish film as a distinct means of artistic expression.

But then the cinema of the Soviet avant-garde captured his imagination. In the winter of 1925–6, after a short visit to the Soviet Union, he had written of the 'staginess' and 'clumsiness' of Russian films.[50] By 1928, however, he had become acquainted with films by Eisenstein and Pudovkin and with the latter's two theoretical handbooks. Thereafter, because of his political sympathies and his enthusiasm for the new films, he made himself the major conduit whereby Soviet films and montage principles might be introduced into British film culture. With Brunel, he began to import Soviet films into Britain. In late 1928 and 1929, he was instrumental in having films by Pudovkin and Eisenstein screened at the Film Society and, in 1929, he brought both men over to speak to Society members. Also, in 1928, he translated Pudovkin's writings on film technique into English. That text was to have a profound effect on filmmakers, film theorists and film culture over the next few years and inaugurated a new phase in Montagu's cinema activism.[51]

Notes

1. Adrian Brunel, *Nice Work* (London: Forbes Robertson, 1949), p. 127.
2. *The Film Society Programmes, 1925–1939*, Introduced by Dr George Amberg (New York: Arno Press, 1972), passim. Subsequent references to *Film Society Programmes* are to the specific programmes reprinted in this volume.
3. Document titled 'The Film Society,' in the Film Society Special Collection, held at the British Film Institute National Library.
4. 'Working with Hitchcock,' *Sight and Sound*, vol. 49, no. 3, Summer 1980.
5. Brunel, *Nice Work*, p. 117.

6. 'Michael Balcon, 1896–1977,' *Sight and Sound*, vol. 47, no. 1, Winter 1977–8, p. 12.

7. *The Political Censorship of Films* (London: Victor Gollancz, 1929); 'The Censorship of Sex in Films,' in Norman Haire, ed., *Sexual Reform Congress, London 1929: Proceedings of the Third Congress* (London: Kegan Paul, Trench, Trubner, 1930).

8. See my 'That Insatiable Body: Ivor Montagu's Confrontation with British Film Censorship,' *Journal of Popular British Cinema*, Issue 3, 2000.

9. *The Youngest Son: Autobiographical Sketches* (London: Lawrence and Wishart, 1970), p. 345.

10. *Observer*, 29 November 1925, p. 9.

11. Ibid., 28 February 1926, p. 17.

12. Ibid., 21 March 1926, p. 23.

13. Ibid., 18 April 1926, p. 5.

14. Ibid., 28 March 1926, p. 5.

15. Ibid., 3 January 1926, p. 15 and 14 February 1926, p. 16.

16. Ibid., 21 March 1926, p. 23; 11 April 1926, p. 5; 17 January 1926, p. 14.

17. Ibid., 14 February 1926, p. 16.

18. Ibid., 29 December 1925, p. 9.

19. *Film Society Programme*, vol. 3, no. 23, 1 April 1928, p. 91.

20. *Observer*, 21 March 1926, p. 23, my emphasis.

21. *Film Society Programme*, vol. 1, no. 1, 25 October 1925, p. 3, my emphases.

22. Ibid., vol. 4, no. 30, 10 March 1929, p. 118.

23. Ibid., vol. 3, no. 23, 1 April 1928, p. 90.

24. *Observer*, 14 February 1926, p. 16.

25. Ibid., 14 February 1926, p. 16.

26. *Close Up*, vol. 1, no. 6, December 1927, p. 80.

27. 'Old Man's Mumble,' *Sight and Sound*, vol. 44, no. 4, Autumn 1975, p. 221.

28. Vachel Lindsay, *The Art of the Moving Picture* (New York: The Macmillan Co., 1922; first published 1915), p. 17.

29. Gilbert Seldes, *The 7 Lively Arts* (New York: Sagmore Press Inc., 1957; first published 1924), p. 3.

30. Lindsay, *The Art of the Moving Picture*, p. 165, his emphases.

31. *Observer*, 29 November 1925, p. 9, my emphasis.

32. Seldes, *The 7 Lively Arts*, p. 285.

33. Ibid., pp. 276–7.

34. *Observer*, 14 February 1926, p. 16, my emphasis.

35. Lindsay, *The Art of the Moving Picture*, p. 80.

36. *Observer*, 30 May 1926, p. 22.

37. *Film Society Programme*, vol. 3, no. 24, 29 April 1928, p. 94.

38. 'The Film Society,' *Observer*, 20 September 1925, p. 9.

39. Seldes, *The 7 Lively Arts*, p. 293, my emphases.

40. Lindsay, *The Art of the Moving Picture*, p. 45.
41. Seldes, *The 7 Lively Arts*, p. 20.
42. Ibid., p. 16, my emphasis.
43. Ibid., p. 16, his emphasis.
44. Ibid., p. 28.
45. *Film Society Programme*, vol. 1, no. 1, 25 October 1925, p. 3.
46. Seldes, *The 7 Lively Arts*, p. 26.
47. *Observer*, 3 January 1926, p. 15.
48. Ibid., p. 15.
49. See chapter two of David Bordwell, *On the History of Film Style* (Harvard University Press, 1997). A key contemporary contribution to both the Basic Story and Standard Version was Paul Rotha's *The Film Till Now*, published in 1930 when he was 23 years old, and recognized as a founding text for British film culture. This book, however, is profoundly indebted to the programming policies of the Film Society and the intellectual resources made available by Montagu. For example, Rotha's listing of the 'various forms of cinema' and his outline of world cinema rely heavily on the films screened by the Society and the distinctions proposed in its programme notes. Furthermore, his discussion of 'The Development of the Film' draws, like Montagu, on Seldes's claim regarding the importance, for film, of light and movement, whilst his theatrical section depends on the Pudovkin texts Montagu had just translated.
50. *Observer*, 29 November 1925, p. 5 and 24 January 1926, p. 14.
51. V.I. Pudovkin, *Pudovkin on Film Technique: Three Essays and an Address*, translated and annotated by Ivor Montagu (London: Victor Gollancz, 1929).

20

Writing the Cinema into Daily Life
Iris Barry and the Emergence of British Film Criticism in the 1920s

Haidee Wasson

Iris Barry is perhaps best known as the influential first curator of the Film Library at the Museum of Modern Art, New York (MoMA), a post she held from 1935 to 1951. During this period, she also helped to found the International Federation of Film Archives, was involved early on with the film programme of the United Nations, and was the first American representative at the fledgling Cannes Film Festival in 1947. She authored several books, among them *Let's go to the Pictures* and *D.W. Griffith: American Film Master*.[1] During a time in which the phrase *film study* struck many as odd if not oxymoronic, Barry effectively advocated the creation of archives, educational programmes, and non-commercial exhibition circuits—spaces in which the significance of cinema as a modern medium would be explored and secured.

Born in 1895, Barry was in fact British, and in the 1920s served as a prominent film critic for the *Spectator* (1923–7) and the *Daily Mail* (1925–30); she was also a founding member of the Film Society (1925). As Rachael Low points out, this was the period in which 'people started treating film seriously in Britain'.[2] One manifestation of this 'seriousness' was the appearance of film writing in daily and weekly, local and national, specialist and mass circulation publications; another was the formation of film societies, clubs and libraries. As an important participant in these shifts, Barry helped establish infrastructures and discourses that have significantly influenced the way films are produced, distributed, exhibited and thought about, and that we now take for granted as basic elements of film culture.

In Britain, some of these institutions, such as the Film Society, reacted against the power exercised by state censorship and the film industry; others accommodated popular and middlebrow interests. Some did both. While Barry's participation in the Film Society has long identified her with 'minority' film culture, her criticism invites assessment of her place in mainstream film culture. Indeed, Barry's writing stands less as a precious outpost of bourgeois and specialized film activity and more as one example of a remarkable proliferation of discourses about cinema in 1920s Britain.

Barry's criticism is important for our understanding of this period for two reasons. First, hers was the most widely distributed film writing of its day. The *Daily Mail* was the highest circulating British newspaper in 1925, twice exceeding that of its closest competitor, the *Daily Mirror*.[3] At the same time, she also wrote for the more highbrow and limited circulation weekly magazine, the *Spectator*, ensuring that her prose reached not only the widest but the most diversified readership of its day. Second, Barry's writing raises historiographical questions about how to write about film's social, political and cultural significance. Until recently, histories of this period have emphasized three things. Some focus on the impoverished state of indigenous film production and the policy debates that ensued to redress this. Others focus on select *auteurs* such as Hitchcock. Still others focus on the development of 'minority' film cultures that emerged as critiques of mainstream film culture: the Film Society, Workers' Leagues and the modernist journal *Close Up*.[4] While such work has provided crucial insights into British film history it has also obscured the varied ways in which films— British or otherwise—were taken up in everyday life and in popular critical practices.

One example of the ways conventional histories have contributed to this elision is through the persistent use of the standard dichotomies familiar in so much film scholarship: high/low, art/commerce, American/international. Barry's writing, on the other hand, resonates with contemporaneous theoretical work on the cinema as well as with ordinary concerns about getting along with other moviegoers: 'No hats please!'[5] She discussed popular American cinema within the context of an unfolding international aesthetic project. Her tastes were eclectic, ranging from popular melodramas to science films and time-motion studies. In other words, her writing readily complicates the binaries often employed to understand the period.

To read Barry's writing, then, is to gain access to a somewhat different view of film's cultural status in the 1920s; it is to witness a prominent critic's efforts to articulate both the quotidian and the complex challenges posed by cinema. In what follows, I will explore how Barry balances critical modes with popular practices, and utopian ideas about film with the key debates that characterized film culture of the period. Three themes will be identified: first, the kind of medium film was conceived to be; second, the American presence in British film culture; and third, the recommended British response to that presence.

It is also worth noting in passing that two of the most prominent film critics of the period were women—Barry, and the better known C.A. Lejeune, who wrote for the *Observer*. The *Daily Mail* actively sought out female readers and was one of the first national papers to feature cinema regularly in its pages. Barry herself suggested in the pages of her book, *Let's Go to the Pictures*, that cinema's future resided predominantly with women who would serve as producers and as discriminating consumers. Interestingly, the early feminist meditations present in her book do not surface in her weekly writing.[6]

Taking Film Seriously

Barry was enthralled with the formal and functional possibilities of the cinema; its distinct and protean aesthetic was as exciting as its promise of eliminating national boundaries and transporting new kinds of visual knowledge everywhere. Its promise of global citizens, its mass popularity, as well as its contribution to the 'respectable' arts, were each seen as complementary and constitutive elements of cinema's larger whole. For Barry, cinema's hybridity—art, industry, information, daily experience, national form—was foundational and inescapable, something she embraced, not rejected.

As with any such writing, Barry's was informed by its cultural and institutional context. Unlike the comparatively unrestrained and polemical writing that appeared in now acclaimed journals such as *Close Up*, or the specialized notes that accompanied Film Society screenings, Barry's criticism was shaped by concerns that informed newspaper and periodical content: editorial influence, readership interest, advertising revenue, the tension between urban, regional and national concerns, publishing and distribution schedules and so on.

Writing weekly for two quite different publications, the sprawling nature of Barry's commentary is unsurprising. Rather than reasoned

323

and methodical critique of film form, content or function, it ranges from ruminations on the phantasmagoria of Hollywood's artifice to sober considerations of the problems facing British films. If there is a theme common to her work for both the *Spectator* and the *Daily Mail* it is the redemption of film as an expressive form and as a modern technological system. A key problem, she contended, was that the cinema suffered for too long under the weight of its benighted status as a mechanical art and as a popular entertainment—both attributes Barry refused to consider faults and preferred to see as merits. Summary judgements and prejudiced disposals based on the medium's accessibility and popularity were unacceptable to her. How then was she able to introduce her often populist concerns to the highbrow readers of the *Spectator*?

Writing for the *Spectator*: What Kind of Medium is Film?

When John Strachey hired Barry in 1923 to 'do something about the cinema', film became part of the *Spectator*'s editorial mission: 'to be a truthful and attractive record of all social movements, and of all that was accomplished in art, science, or literature.'[7] Significantly, Barry inherited a readership predisposed to discussions of poetry, literature, theatre and politics befitting a well-educated, socially respectable and highly literate cohort. The *Spectator*'s early acknowledgement of film as a noteworthy contemporary phenomenon supports observations made by Low and others that attending as well as discussing the cinema was slowly being accepted by a small group of reputable citizens.[8] This acceptance, however, was neither simple nor complete. Barry's writing also coincided with the increasing association of film, by a number of intellectuals, with an attack on traditional cultural values, which they saw as indicative of a broader social breakdown. Such associations emanated from the left and the right, casting film either as an affront to working-class literacy or as a challenge to the necessary and desirable cultural domination of the elite.[9] British censors also registered their mark. 'Taking film seriously' did not always produce the happy environment in which the cinema as a medium was vindicated as art or leisure; it also marked the wider contestation of cinema as a mass medium capable of moulding minds deemed weak and therefore vulnerable.

Barry herself was likely very familiar with the many forms of judgement against film then circulating, from high modernist to culturally reformist. From her earliest days in London, through introductions made by Ezra Pound, Barry was a regular of the Bloomsbury scene. Compounding her involvement with such moderns was her relationship with Wyndham Lewis, lasting several tumultuous years and yielding two children. Against the tide of her daily life, Barry's earliest writing for the *Spectator* addressed the pervasive tendency of the literary and cultural elite to further particular aesthetic and ideological positions against cinema without actually considering cinema at all. She argued persistently that the cinema embodied aesthetic achievement and possessed civic utility and was thus worthy of detailed analysis and discussion.

In the effort to prove that cinema was capable of aesthetic achievement, Barry elaborated the basic components of film art, tending towards characteristically highbrow concepts of formal distinctiveness and individual genius. To a contemporary reader, her strategies will seem familiar. Camera movement and the use of editing to manipulate space, evoke rhythm or create dramatic suspense were often celebrated. She argued that film was essentially a medium for telling stories through moving pictures,[10] as exemplified by her review of Ernst Lubitsch's *The Marriage Circle* (1924): 'Everything is visualized, all the comedy is in what the characters are seen or imagined to be thinking or feeling, in the interplay, never expressed in words, of wills and personalities.'[11] Also now familiar but at the time unconventional, was her celebration of 'genius' directors emerging from national art cinemas, situating cinematic accomplishment in singular animating personalities rather than more diffuse collaborative processes: Fritz Lang, Ernst Lubitsch, Karl Grüne, Robert Wiene, Victor Seastrom, Charlie Chaplin and D.W. Griffith.[12]

Importantly, Barry's writing extended beyond these now familiar tropes of intellectual film history. She also explored cinema's technological and democratic particularities, paying frequent homage to its informational capacities as well as its ability to offer the spectator new experiences of space and time. A telling example resides in Barry's efforts to free cinema from the constraints of the theatre. For her, the cinema possessed a scope that not only rivalled but far surpassed that of the theatre. She maintained that cinema 'alone can handle natural history, anthropology and travel' as well as more fully develop 'parable, fairystory, pageant, romance and character-study'.

> It has infinite variety of scene, endless angles of vision and focus, it can use for its own ends all the resources of landscape and architecture, and, very important indeed, it brings out an

enormous significance in natural objects. Chairs and tables, collar-studs, kitchenware and flowers take on a function which they have lost, except for young children, since animism was abandoned in the accumulating sophistications of 'progress.'[13]

Barry wrote of animated objects and of the 'infinite variety' of vision offered by the cinema, which she argued lent a clear expressive edge over the theatre. While the use of these qualities for developing fictional narratives was important, it was not their only significance. Natural history and travel films would benefit as much as parable and romance films. The fascination of visual information—animating the previously lifeless—worked in tandem with cinematic narratives. Each enhanced the value of the medium. Theatre did not stand a chance.

Barry's interest in what film made visible is further evident in her commentary on travel, nature and science films. The camera's slow-motion capacities held particular fascination for her.

> The Film Society recently showed one of these marvels of patience, *The Life of a Plant*, in which a nasturtium germinated, grew up, flowered, was cross-fertilized, languished, shot its seeds off and died in five minutes. Gigantic on the screen, this plant ceased to have any vegetable attributes and became the most temperamental of creatures, dashing itself about, waving its 'arms' like a prima donna in a rage.[14]

Like many others, including members of the surrealist and constructivist movement, Barry became enamoured with the protean, fantastical ability of the cinema to reconfigure the visual world by depicting otherwise abstract or invisible phenomena. Any object could take on renewed symbolic presence, greeting a malleability of form that went hand in hand with a new kind of knowledge made visible by moving photo-realistic images.

As well as slowing time and expanding space, the cinema could also accelerate time and minimize space, endowing the medium with the courage and cause of an explorer. According to Barry, the camera transported its audience, democratizing ocular discovery. Thus the travel film *The Epic of Everest*

> has magnificently that rare quality of communication through the visual sense which is one of the peculiar qualities of the cinema: it communicates an experience which almost none of us can ever have in fact. And it is good for human beings to see, as they do in

their hundreds of thousands daily, the appearance of the remoter places, whether they be untouched African forests, the island homes of Papua, or the ghastly face of the Black Country.[15]

For Barry, the cinema provided a privileged form of knowledge, which she rhetorically construed as transcendent of not only geographic space but also historical time and national psychology. Of the 'reasonably intelligent spectator', she remarked:

> He can see more clearly than if he were an actual spectator of race meetings, volcanic eruptions, eminent persons, and landscapes from California to Jerusalem. He can even see the past, whether it be the deeply moving past of reality as films like *Ypres* recreate it, or the romantic past of an historical piece like *Helen of Troy*. And if he be of a reflective mind he can learn as much of German, French, and American mentality as any other who has travelled widely.[16]

This ability to take spectators out of themselves and immerse them in faraway, unfamiliar places was for Barry the 'purest' and most 'plainly socially valuable' quality of the cinema: simplicity of form and clarity of thought combined with a myth of exploration and education. She ascribed these qualities not only to travel pictures and documentaries but also to farces (especially those of Chaplin and Keaton). These film forms, she suggested, sat at opposite ends of the film spectrum but shared this quality of simple beauty, clarity and therefore social value.[17]

Barry's celebration of American popular films deserves mention. Her unapologetic embrace of Chaplin, Fairbanks, Griffith, early animation, cowboy serials and slapstick, while reasonably familiar to the internationalist canon of film writing, must have appeared unusual to her readership. To assuage anxieties about such films, Barry couched her discussions in terms her readers might find more familiar. For instance, in championing Douglas Fairbanks, she likened his swashbuckling to the 'grace of ballet'. In favouring animation and slapstick, she dubbed Felix the Cat and Charlie Chaplin distinctly 'highbrow'. She loved Western serials, celebrating their 'great open spaces', proclaiming such 'horse operas' to be the best of American product.[18] Somewhat more polemical and agitating against the dominance of the established arts was her bold assertion that Chaplin's *Gold Rush* (1925), Fairbanks's *Don Q* (1925), and Griffith's *Sally of the Sawdust* (1925) represented more vitality 'than anything that the other arts are at the moment

Plate 33.   The painting 'Praxitella' (1920–21) by Wyndham Lewis

offering humanity'.[19] Barry's strategy was sometimes to familiarize but sometimes to confront.

For Barry, cinema was a polymorphous form with the promise of multiplying utility, presenting new configurations of aesthetics and knowledge. The implied audience was not irretrievably seduced by cinematic pleasure or duped by national ideologies, but was liberated and enlightened by the cinema. This utopian strand in Barry's writing demonstrates her euphoric fascination with film, and is as such typical of an important genre in the history of writing on film.

Writing for the *Daily Mail*

While the *Spectator*'s mandate granted Barry latitude to ruminate on the particularities of the cinematic image, the *Daily Mail* presented different working conditions. Founded in 1896, the *Daily Mail* was conceived as an inexpensive, accessible and national daily. It was designed to appeal to women as well as to working men by including articles on fashion, marriage, recipes and housekeeping. The strategy was extremely successful, attracting a wide range of readers. The largest portion of these readers were, however, solidly middle-class.[20] In accepting the *Daily Mail* post, Barry thus acquired an audience for her writing unprecedented in size and scope. Now she would have to balance the needs of a large, diverse and diffuse audience with her own sensibilities about film.

As well as inheriting a new readership, Barry was bequeathed a particular set of debates about British film. In the mid-1920s, domestic film production was in decline, despite a concurrent increase in distribution and exhibition circuits. The number of British films on British screens fell steadily, reaching 5 per cent in 1925, while the percentage of American films increased to approximately 85–90 per cent.[21] American practices of block-booking, underselling and high production and marketing budgets combined with the popularity of American films to expedite this imbalance. Film attendance was relatively healthy in Britain; film production was not.[22]

When Barry began writing for the *Daily Mail* in 1925, it was widely acknowledged that the low status of the British film was a serious problem in need of a quick remedy. But there was little agreement as to how to rectify such a complex set of cultural, commercial and political problems. Many constituencies staked out a place in the murky terrain. Importantly, the *Daily Mail*'s editorial pages represented one of the more extreme and persistent of these constituencies, often reducing the role of British exhibitors, distributors, producers and audiences to the victims of an overt act of domination orchestrated by the American film industry and government. Indeed, during the 1920s, the paper's wide readership supplied Lord Rothermere, figurehead of the *Daily Mail*, with an audience for his increasingly anti-American, protectionist beliefs. The paper's editorials invoked inflammatory nationalist rhetoric in order to support a 'free trade' platform aimed at opening up markets within the British Empire but squeezing out (usually American) competitors. Film fell comfortably within this purview. It was argued that British films should be sent aggressively throughout the colonies and that the dominance of British screens by American films was as undesirable as American dominance by other means. The editorial stance of the *Daily Mail* resonated with the assertion, also evident in policy debates, that American cinema was a powerful and persuasive force, contaminating consumer habits as well as national ideologies. The problem of establishing a native film industry was clearly linked to general concerns about the economic autonomy of the nation as much as its cultural or spiritual well-being. While fostering native film production was a legitimate concern of policymakers and necessarily, in part, of British businessmen, it is important to note that such ideas about the nation and film often depended on concepts of British audiences that infantilized or completely disregarded them. The editorials either penned or sanctioned by Rothermere provide no exception.[23]

In both the *Spectator* and the *Daily Mail*, Barry addressed the state of the British film industry, as well as the place of American cinema within this. Surprisingly, her writing on this issue did not differ greatly between publications, suggesting that she and Rothermere must have more than occasionally disagreed. How she negotiated his nationalism must, unfortunately, be relegated to speculation. In extreme moments, however, some of her opinions did seem to resonate with his. For instance, she once declared that American films are on the whole 'deplorable, vulgar, sensational and even dismally stupid'.[24] Nevertheless, even as the great debate escalated, she also boldly claimed that 'we owe the present vitality of the cinema as a whole to the Americans . . . their best films are the best in the world'.[25]

Barry acknowledged the importance of a healthy British production base. Nevertheless, she was unafraid to polemicize against the rising tide of anti-American sentiment, claiming that as a pleasure-loving member of the public she could not be dragged by 'wild horses' to a British picture if an American picture could be seen instead.[26]

Concurrently, she also neatly rejected Hollywood's aggressive business practices as well as the bulk of formulaic and sometimes gaudy pictures that flooded British screens. She nevertheless eschewed extreme protectionist measures: 'Take away American films and you close the cinemas.'[27] She dismissed those who confused 'a few bad American films' with the output of an entire nation, let alone an entire medium. English literature, she pointed out, continued to garner respect despite the success of *penny horribles*.[28] Thus at times she rejected and at others she embraced nationalist rhetoric, yet she was steadfastly averse to the more conservative, anti-film and anti-populist elements of this rhetoric.

Perhaps more than any other aspect of the debate about British films, the public's pleasure was clearly, for Barry, a cause in need of an advocate. She argued against the fear-mongering inherent in contamination debates, acknowledging that audiences can actually think, disagree and dislike films for some reasons but like them for others: 'Yes, American films paint an idealized view of America but does it really affect us that much, since bad films also give us reason to reject or dislike America?'[29] In short, Barry saw America's domination of British screens as a highly problematic yet often pleasurable preoccupation; she liked some American films, but deplored others; she yearned for a superior British film but remained fascinated by America and Hollywood as cinematic spaces unto themselves.

Barry's anti-Americanism is best evidenced by her discussions of Cecil B. De Mille. At its worst, American cinema embodied opulent wealth, moral indulgences, stars but no actors, and spectacle without cleverness or reason. Thus she imagined De Mille directing *Ben Hur* (1925), standing behind camera, exclaiming through his megaphone: 'More money!! More money!!'[30] In a later article, titling him the 'Prince of Hollywood', she continued:

> He it is who chiefly specialises in the making of easily thrilling, inconsistent and expensive films which reveal a world where riches always spell vice and vulgarity, and which always appeal to the 'gallery' with their second-rate ideas about Socialism, or religion, or reincarnation or any other big theme which it happens to occur to Mr. DeMille to cheapen . . . All the DeMille pictures are brilliantly photographed. Technically they are far above the average. Spiritually they reek of the producer's subterranean—and, one fancies, over-heated and over-scented—boudoir.[31]

Even in her scathing criticism of De Mille's excesses, it is clear that Barry enjoyed her distaste too much to utterly dismiss the objects of it.

Barry travelled to Hollywood in October 1927. Exploring her ambivalence toward American film as well as her responsibilities to the readers of the *Daily Mail*, Barry wrote about the film capital from her experience of studio tours, evening parties and flaneurial wanderings. This yielded a series of articles with topics ranging from America's luxury picture palaces to Hollywood's 'English film colony'.[32] Barry expressed a muted fascination with Hollywood, pleasing fans hungry for news of the American film centre but filtering it through ambivalent, sometimes melancholy, prose. In one article, she wrote:

> There are tens of thousands of men and women registered as extra players: there are on an average two thousand of them employed every day. For the rest—managing ways and means, hope, starvation. Hollywood is all heartbreaks: but somehow in the smiling, haunted eyes of the men whom the tide of the Great War swept out here there is something other than heartbreak. There is a sermon for humanity, if they would read it.[33]

Barry observed former European military officers colliding with young starlet hopefuls. She did not interpret such scenes as depictions of exploited labour or suffering diasporas. Instead, she saw both a 'sermon' eulogizing the atrocities of war and the possibility of redemption, evident in the chaotic mix of nations that the cinema turned to relative harmony through the use of crowds choreographed as moving backdrops.

For Barry, Hollywood was not America, nor was it cinema. It was an uncanny, self-enclosed world of infinitely regressive likenesses, where everything she encountered it seemed she had seen 'somewhere, sometime' before, referring wistfully to films of which she had only vague recollections.[34] The celebrities and other industry members Barry observed were as self-absorbed as the film capital itself: 'Perhaps it is this which is the cause of the lack of proportion, even of common sense, in so many Hollywood films. They do not mirror life, but Hollywood's film world only.'[35] Considered in the context of her editor's policies, Barry's Hollywood seemed compelling, uncanny and, most importantly, unthreatening.

The British Film?

Barry's thoughts about American films should be situated within a generalized internationalism, manifest also in her Film Society activities. She made casual and frequent mention of film production in France and Germany, aware both of policy debates and of the aesthetic ferment underway. Importantly, she often used such examples to provide suggestions for addressing the problem facing British films, noting, for instance, that English artists had been much slower to give film its due than artists of neighbouring countries and that this, in part, contributed to the lack of British innovation.[36] (She often used the term 'English' interchangeably with the term 'British'.) Barry did not see the success of other national cinemas primarily as threatening. Rather, she considered such cinemas to provide the raw material necessary for expanding the appeal of British films. She identified the anti-American elements of the British industry as the most responsible for perpetuating British mediocrity and advocated drawing freely on all available cinematic traditions.[37] Such lessons were to be drawn both from the failures as well as the successes of these cinemas. For instance, she suggested that from German films 'we see how wise it is to use stories created specially for the screen and by contrast to avoid persistent morbidity and excessive length'. From America, we learn to avoid plots 'false to human experience', to eschew 'vulgar moralizing', and to resist substituting stars for actors.[38]

While Barry recognized that the domination of American films was a serious challenge to establishing a British industry and a 'properly' British film, she did not hesitate to identify domestic complicity in this. She blamed British distributors and exhibitors—happy with the comfortable profits they made exhibiting American films—as often as she identified an 'abysmal' lack of production talent.[39] On the whole, however, Barry should be read as an optimist. She constantly made recommendations for the kinds of films that might be made, and for the processes required to support those films, and was confident that British audiences would pull their weight by becoming more discriminating. She happily advocated what she believed to be the two primary qualities of popular cinema: 'One, which is narrative, answers the old demand: "Tell me a story." The other, melodrama, replies to the age-old query: "And what happened next?"'[40] She embraced the role of cinema as popular entertainment, arguing that in order to be successful films must appeal to the emotions.

For the kinema exists primarily to entertain. It does so best not when it clumsily attempts to uplift, but when deep emotions and stirring events of past or present take life on the screen, typified in the deeds of men and women from whom heroes and history alike are made. It is a nation's soul, which flowered so finely in men like Drake, Nelson, and Scott that can most finely inspire films. The dry bones can be left to the museums and libraries where they belong.[41]

She did not believe that British films should compete directly with Hollywood but that they should strive for a specificity that captured British as well as cinematic essence:

Our new films must be patently English [sic], introducing to the world the spirit as well as the appearance of life here, and showing for the first time normal existence, heightened by drama or comedy, and discovering to audiences for the first time railways, towns, factories, playing fields, schools, shops, horse-shows, and seaside resorts in England.[42]

Despite persistent complaint about British films, she wrote with hope about a select number of promising directors, favouring George Pearson, Maurice Elvey, Adrian Brunel and Alfred Hitchcock, while tolerating Graham Cutts, Walter Sumners and Manning Haynes.[43]

Conclusion

For Barry, the future of British cinema rested in somehow combining the grandeur of American and international cinematic innovation with the specificity of British life. She knew this was a complicated task and required not only support from industry and government but also a shift in consciousness regarding what the cinema could and should become. Achieving a properly British cinema would involve an ongoing dialogue whose resolution required industrial, state and public bodies to admit first of all the many ways in which cinema mattered; detailed discussion of why and how it mattered would need to follow. Her criticism stands as one example of these seemingly simple but then-novel assertions.

The cinema, Barry maintained, was a peculiar phenomenon: a machine art born of the industrial age, made great by the distinctly modern combination of technology, aesthetics, spectacle, industrialism and mass popularity. For this reason, it remained as much potential as it was a reality. Barry's criticism thus provides an interesting example of wishful cinematic thinking, partly grounded in the present and partly in the promise of what might be. Crucially, to take her critical writing seriously is to open up wider consideration of the discourses that set the terms by which film cultures have historically taken shape. Such widely distributed film writing should not be treated necessarily as a lesser discursive site than any other. Such writing not only helps us to characterize film culture of any given period but provides a constitutive site for the very terms by which filmgoers (as well as scholars) understand and shape film culture itself. In Barry's case, such consideration indicates a body of writing that combines an intellectual's cinephilia with a firm commitment to cinema's populist appeal, a rhetoric of technological utopianism with a steady dedication to the quotidian task of building institutions, and a clear desire to forge a British cinema while openly embracing the contradictions of loving and hating American cinema.

Notes

I would like to thank the generous research support of the Social Sciences and Humanities Research Council of Canada and the Centre for Research and Teaching on Women, McGill University.

1. *Let's Go to the Pictures* (London: Chatto and Windus, 1926); *D.W. Griffith: American Film Master* (New York: Museum of Modern Art, 1940).
2. Rachael Low, *The History of the British Film, 1918–1929* (London: George Allen and Unwin, 1970), p. 15.
3. Circulation figures for the *Daily Mail* were 1,743,000 per day, for the *Mirror* 964,000 per day. See Tom Jeffrey and Keith McClelland, 'A World Fit to Live in: *The Daily Mail* and the Middleclasses,' in James Curran, Anthony Smith and Pauline Wingate, eds, *Impacts and Influences: Essays on Media Power in the 20th Century* (London: Methuen, 1987), pp. 27–52.
4. See e.g. Julian Petley, 'Cinema and State,' in Charles Barr, ed., *All Our Yesterdays: 90 Years of British Cinema* (London: British Film Institute, 1986), pp. 31–46; James Donald, Anne Friedberg and Laura Marcus, eds, *Close Up, 1927–1933: Cinema and Modernism* (Princeton: Princeton University Press, 1998); Don Macpherson, ed., *Traditions of Independence: British Cinema in the Thirties* (London: British Film Institute, 1980); Margaret Dickinson and Sarah Street, *Cinema and State: The Film*

Industry and the Government 1927–84 (London: British Film Institute, 1985).

5. 'Kinema Manners,' *Daily Mail*, 23 February 1926, p. 8.
6. See Barry, *Let's Go to the Pictures*, pp. 60–6; 147–9; 176.
7. Quoted in William Beach Thomas, *The Story of the Spectator, 1828–1928* (Freeport, NY: Books for Libraries Press, 1928; rpt 1971), p. 5.
8. Low, *The History of the British Film*, p. 17.
9. See Peter Miles and Malcolm Smith, ' "The Embattled Minority": Theorists of the Elite,' in *Cinema, Literature and Society: Elite and Mass Culture in Interwar Britain* (London: Croom Helm, 1987), pp. 81–101.
10. Cf. David Bordwell, *On the History of Film Style* (Cambridge, MA: Harvard University Press, 1997), pp. 12–45.
11. Barry, 'The Cinema: Hope Fulfilled,' *Spectator*, 17 May 1924, p. 788.
12. Ibid.
13. Barry, 'The Cinema: A Comparison of Arts,' *Spectator*, 3 May 1924, p. 707.
14. Barry, 'The Cinema: Lesser Glories,' *Spectator*, 6 March 1926, p. 415.
15. Barry, 'The Cinema: "The Epic of Everest" at the Scala,' *Spectator*, 20 December 1924, p. 982.
16. Barry, 'The Lure of the Films,' *Daily Mail*, 9 October 1925, p. 8.
17. Barry, 'The Cinema: "The Epic of Everest" at the Scala,' p. 982. See also "The Cinema: Back to Simplicity," *Spectator*, 17 July 1926, p. 88, and 'The Lure of the Films,' p. 8.
18. Barry, 'The Cinema: Laughter Makers,' *Spectator*, 19 September 1925, p. 444. See also 'Cowboy Films for "Highbrows",' *Daily Mail*, 10 August 1927, p. 8, and 'Lesser Glories,' *Spectator*, 6 March 1926, p. 415.
19. Barry, 'The Laughter Makers,' p. 445.
20. See Jeffrey and McClelland, 'A World Fit to Live in,' pp. 27–52.
21. Dickinson and Street, *Cinema and State*, p. 5.
22. Ibid., pp. 5–33.
23. See for instance 'The Foreign Film and the English Soul: An Insidious Form of Attack,' *Daily Mail*, 16 April 1926, p. 8; 'Why We Must Have British Films,' *Daily Mail*, 16 December 1925, p. 8; 'The Film Dictators,' *Daily Mail*, 9 April 1925, p. 8; and 'The Cosmopolitan Film: Made in Germany for Britain,' *Daily Mail*, 2 April 1925, p. 8. For a general history of the paper and Rothermere's influence, see J.S. Taylor, *The Great Outsiders: Northcliffe, Rothermere and The Daily Mail* (London: Phoenix Giant, 1996).
24. Barry, 'The Cinema: Of British Films,' *Spectator*, 14 November 1925, p. 870.
25. Barry, 'The Cinema: American Prestige and British Films,' *Spectator*, 11 July 1925, p. 52.
26. Ibid., p. 52.
27. Ibid., p. 51.

28. Ibid., p. 51.
29. Ibid., p. 52.
30. Barry, 'The Cinema: Ben Hur at the Tivoli,' *Spectator*, 20 November 1926, p. 898.
31. Barry, 'The Prince of Hollywood,' *Daily Mail*, 23 March 1927, p. 10.
32. See Barry, 'American's Giant Cinema,' *Daily Mail*, 21 November 1927, p. 10; and 'Hollywood's English Colony,' *Daily Mail*, 18 November 1927, p. 10.
33. Barry, 'Pity the Extras of Hollywood,' *Daily Mail*, 1 November 1927, p. 10.
34. See especially 'An Outpost of Hollywood,' *Daily Mail*, 14 December 1927, p. 10.
35. Barry, 'Actors Who Dream of Films,' *Daily Mail*, 24 November 1927, p. 10.
36. Barry, 'The New Art,' *Daily Mail*, 15 April 1926, p. 8.
37. Barry, 'New Blood for British Films,' *Daily Mail*, 17 December 1925, p. 7.
38. Barry, 'Films the Public Want,' *Daily Mail*, 21 November 1925, p. 8.
39. See Barry, 'Films We Do Not Want,' *Daily Mail*, 21 September 1926, p. 8; 'The Curse of the Films,' *Daily Mail*, 14 November 1925, p. 8; 'What We Owe to the Kinema,' *Daily Mail*, 18 May 1926, p. 6.
40. Barry, 'Films the Public Want,' p. 8.
41. Barry, 'Nelson and Three Bad Men,' *Daily Mail*, 4 October 1926, p. 8.
42. Barry, 'Films We Do Not Want,' p. 8.
43. Barry, 'Do-Everything Film Makers,' *Daily Mail*, 22 February 1927, p. 17.

SECTION F

Bibliographical and Archival Resources

21

A Guide to Bibliographical and Archival Sources on British Cinema before the First World War

Stephen Bottomore

Key Bibliographical Sources

There is still no better introduction to the origins of British cinema than the first two volumes of Rachael Low's *The History of the British Film*, which offer an overview to 1914, covering the major sectors of the film industry, and key films, companies and personnel.[1] Though Low's first volume is rather thin on detail, this defect has now been rectified by the five volumes of John Barnes' history, covering the first half decade of British cinema. The sheer dynamism of this period was breathtaking, and Barnes describes in great detail the contributions of numerous individuals and companies.[2] Perhaps the central thrust of this history is technological development, so the rather different focus of a more recent book offers a fine complement: the British Mutoscope and Biograph Company was the biggest of the early British film companies, and in a recent study of this enterprise Richard Brown brings a business historical perspective, while Barry Anthony situates the company in the context of other entertainments of the period. Their first chapter is an excellent introduction to the economics of early British cinema, and should be read by anyone interested in this field. There is also an invaluable filmography of British Biograph with thematic indexes.[3]

The Brighton conference of 1978 led to great advances in our understanding of early film style, notably in British cinema, and this was consolidated by the work of Barry Salt. More radical views of early British film appear in Michael Chanan's *The Dream that Kicks* and in Noël Burch's chapters on the British pioneers in his *Life to Those Shadows*.[4] Ian Christie's *The Last Machine* offers an accessible way into various issues of early film.[5] *Cinema: the Beginnings and the Future* is a collection of essays which are not only informative about the early era, but also keep the reader aware of interesting connections with the modern media.[6] The Edwardian cinema in Britain is a somewhat neglected subject, and John Hawkridge has offered a brief but refreshing defence of this post-'pioneer' era.[7] Nicholas Hiley's remarkable research on early British cinema focuses on the social context of exhibition and production, but only a fraction of his work has yet been published.[8] In terms of reference works no one interested in British silent cinema would want to be without Denis Gifford's *British Film Catalogues*, which list all British fiction and non-fiction films from the earliest period up to the 1990s, while the *Who's Who of Victorian Cinema* includes many entries for British pioneers.[9]

For most research projects on British cinema in the period in question, one of the first ports of call should be the three key trade papers published at the time, the *Bioscope*, the *Kinematograph and Lantern Weekly* and the *Cinema. News and Property Gazette* (details of where these can be consulted are given below). These periodicals deal with all aspects of the film business and are an enormously rich and vital source of information. Several film-related books were also published in the early period. Two key works first published in the 1890s deal primarily with technical matters, Cecil Hepworth's *Animated Photography* and Henry Hopwood's *Living Pictures*. Later publications take on additionally the question of cinema's status as an aspiring art form, including Frederick Talbot's *Moving Pictures* (1912) and, perhaps the most fun, Harry Furniss' *Our Lady Cinema* (1914).[10] Another key publication was Colin Bennett's *Handbook of Kinematography* (1911), which aimed to provide a reference guide to all aspects of the film industry in Britain.[11] This is reprinted in Stephen Herbert's new three-volume *History of Early Film*, destined to be a major resource for those researching this period.[12] Herbert's *History* also contains reprints of various British catalogues from the 1900s, such as Charles Urban's June 1905 catalogue, several periodical articles, and such curios as Hardwicke Drummond Rawnsley's 1913 pamphlet, *The Child and The Cinematograph Show, and the Picture Postcard Evil . . . With A Note on the Cinematograph by the Headmaster of Eton*. The British Library has quite a few pamphlets in this vein, including

Montagu A. Pyke's *Focusing the Universe: a Defence of the Cinematograph* (1910). *In the Kingdom of the Shadows* is another charming collection of articles and illustrations from the early period, with a bias towards British sources.[13]

First-hand accounts are often the most readable, though they are sometimes unreliable; the autobiographies of George Pearson, entitled *Flashback*, and of Cecil Hepworth, *Came the Dawn*, are no exceptions, but are full of period atmosphere, from the early years of British cinema through the 1920s and beyond.[14] The memoirs of other British pioneers crop up sporadically in the trade press and elsewhere from the 1910s to the 1950s; the reminiscences of Colonel Bromhead, the head of British Gaumont, are especially detailed (and include contributions from several other pioneers).[15] John Bird's anecdotal *Cinema Parade* also contains much useful information.[16]

There were important connections between early film and other entertainments. Both *The Travelling Cinematograph Show* and *Fairground Art* deal with fairground cinema and are well produced with some fine photographs of bioscope shows, though more rigorous research on this subject may be found in Vanessa Toulmin's various articles.[17] The lantern was a crucial influence on early film, and the Magic Lantern Society's current project for a lantern encyclopaedia will add to the many other valuable resources they have produced over the years.[18]

In recent years various conferences have both reflected and stimulated interest in early British cinema. The proceedings of the cinema centenary conference in Bradford, *Celebrating 1895*, contain some fine essays on early cinema, including cinema in Britain.[19] Another post-conference publication is *Moving Performance*, which includes contributions about the arrival of cinema in Scotland and music hall's influence on early film.[20] Papers from the innovative 'Visual Delights' conference in Sheffield in 1999, devoted to early film and the nineteenth century image, have also been published.[21] The annual British Silent Cinema weekend in Nottingham has generated two excellent collections of published essays, one mainly on silent British comedy, the other mainly on performance in British Films. Both contain extracts from Gerry Turvey's pioneering work on British and Colonial.[22]

Important individuals in British early film are being researched. William Friese-Greene was the subject of Ray Allister's biography in the 1940s, but recent work by David Robinson and others on Greene and his predecessor, J.A.R. Rudge, is providing a more objective assessment.[23] A number of researchers including Hauke Lange-Fuchs, Alan Acres and Deac Rossell are investigating Birt Acres, perhaps a more important pioneer than has been realized.[24] As yet John Barnes remains the best source on Robert Paul, but Barnes's work on the Brighton pioneers Smith and Williamson is being augmented by Frank Gray and others.[25] I myself am researching a number of pioneers including Joseph Rosenthal, J. Gregory Mantle, Charles Rider Noble, and Frederick Burlingham, while Fred Lake is compiling detailed bibliographical information on Cecil Hepworth. Janice Headland is working on a list of all actors in British films from 1895 to 1932, often going back to primary sources to find accurate information.

Journals worth checking for articles on early British cinema include *Journal of Popular British Cinema*; the new *Film Studies*; the *Historical Journal of Film, Radio and Television*; and *Film History*. Several recent issues of the latter have covered early British film history, including articles on the work of important pioneers such as G.A. Smith and Mitchell and Kenyon.[26] The long-gone *Cinema Studies* of the 1960s published several articles on early British film.[27] British exhibition history is covered in *Mercia Bioscope*, while the organization Domitor with its *Bulletin* (and published bibliographies) deals with early film history in general. A new and important entrant to the field is likely to be *Living Pictures: the Journal of the Popular and Projected Image before 1914*.[28] Naturally the Internet is proving a handy source of information: sites for the National Fairground Archive and Charles Urban are excellent in themselves and offer useful links elsewhere.[29]

A few smaller publishing houses are especially focused on early film issues, including Flicks Books, John Libbey and Co., and The Projection Box. The latter has brought out books about the Kinora system, film pioneers Donisthorpe, Theodore Brown and producer Charles Urban and my own book on *The Titanic and the Silent Cinema*.[30] Forthcoming are the business records of exhibitor William D. Slade from 1897 (possibly the first film-show accounts in the world).

Many studies of regional British film history are in whole or in part devoted to the early period. For the northern half of England these include useful works on cinema in Yorkshire, the Black Country, Gateshead, Swadlincote, Manchester, Birmingham, Market Harborough, and Leicester.[31] For the southern part of England some of the better publications deal with East Anglia, Oxford, Lewisham, and Walthamstow.[32] While Dave Berry has investigated early Welsh film, too little has yet been published on the early era in Scotland or Ireland.[33]

A Guide to Further Resources

1: London collections

London is almost certainly the best place in the world to be researching early film history (and indeed many other aspects of history). Britain was the leading world power in the late nineteenth century, thus generating copious records, and this, combined with the centralization of numerous archives and libraries in the capital, makes London a research Mecca.

An obvious place to start is the British Film Institute (BFI), which has the best collection of early British films,[34] plus most of the contemporary film books and many secondary histories, though arguably even more film books may be found in the British Library. The BFI also holds hundreds of 'related material' documents concerned with early film, and several Special Collections (now computer indexed). These include collections from or about: Percy Smith, the London Film Company, George Pearson, Tom Williamson, Percy Mumford, Rosemary Heaward, William Haggar, C.J.A. Langman and Harry Rowson. The James Anderson collection includes an interesting manuscript co-authored by John Montgomery, *The Romance of British Films, 1889–1928*. The BFI's cataloguing department holds the memoirs of film pioneers Alfred West and Dave Aylott, while the BFI's museum collections include James Williamson's and Cecil Hepworth's photograph albums, and G.A. Smith's cashbooks for 1897 to 1909.

The BFI holds the Merritt Crawford papers on microfilm, which include correspondence with some British pioneers; also on microfilm are several foreign trade journals, which carried occasional articles about the British film industry and its personnel. Such articles can sometimes be located through the *Film Index* bibliography or the index to personalities in the *Moving Picture World*.[35] The *Moving Picture News* (also American) was edited by a Brit, Alfred Saunders, formerly of the *Magic Lantern Journal*, and has something of an anglophile slant.[36]

The British Library (BL) is too rarely visited by film historians. The newspaper department in Colindale holds the finest collection of early British film periodicals anywhere, including a uniquely complete run of *Kinematograph and Lantern Weekly* from 1909 to 1915, and several journals with a more specialized focus, including the *Film Censor* (1912–16), *The Rinking World and Picture Theatre News* (1909–10), continued as *Picture Theatre News* (1910–12), *Scottish Cinema*

(1919–20) and *Express Overseas Mail* (1914–16). As London was the centre of the world's film trade at this time the latter title would be especially valuable in a study of international film distribution.[37] Trade journals are the richest source for early film history, and it is good news that some of the Colindale runs are now available on microfilm (at the BFI, for example).[38]

The BL's central London departments hold most early British film books. The Manuscript Department has collections of the Authors' Cinematograph Agency, 1913–17, as well as eight volumes of typescript film scenarios, 1913–24, deposited with the British Museum for copyright purposes.[39] Historians of film apparatus should know that the BL has one of the best collection of British and foreign patents anywhere in the world, while the library's collection of Goad's fire insurance maps might reveal unique information on cinema buildings.[40]

The Public Record Office, now keyword searchable through the web, holds many records of early British film companies (and British-based foreign ones) and picture palaces.[41] The Colonial Office and Foreign Office files contain records about film policy and censorship overseas, especially from the teen years onwards. Many early films were copyrighted and photographic frames and associated information survive in the COPY records.

Other institutions in London also hold valuable resources relating to early film. The London County Council records include correspondence from little-known early exhibitors and programmes of film venues (currently being brought to light by Tony Fletcher).[42] A leading source for early news film is the Newsreel Project at the British Universities Film and Video Council, which has computer-indexed British newsreels from 1910 to 1979 (and their cameramen).[43] Charles Urban's papers are in the Science Museum, while the Fawcett Library has the papers of Beatrice Heron-Maxwell, a silent film author, and the Victoria and Albert Museum's poster collection includes a couple of early British examples.[44] The Museum of London, the Theatre Museum and the City of Westminster archives centre have yet to be fully explored for film materials.

Private institutions are also worth investigating, such as the British Kodak archives; and several commercial film and photo archives have images relating to early cinema, including the Hulton, Mary Evans, Kobal, Illustrated London News and Pathé. The Cinema Museum has some unique material, including the most complete run anywhere of *The Cinema* from 1912, and such rarities as the records of an Aberdeen cinema from 1913 onwards. Numerous unique items also reside in the private collections of the Barnes brothers, David Robinson, John Huntley and David Francis.

2: Regional collections

British cinemagoing in the period before the First World War was at least as dynamic outside London as in the capital, especially in the industrial cities of the north, and some of the richest collections for early British film research are in the regions. The National Fairground Archive at Sheffield University is *the* source for information and photographs on bioscope shows, while the National Museum of Photography Film and Television in Bradford holds the collection of early showman William Slade. The University of Exeter's Bill Douglas Centre contains unique early and pre-cinema material and one of the best assortments of film books anywhere, collected by Bill Douglas and Peter Jewell. Eadweard Muybridge's legacy is held in Kingston Museum, while the Royal Photographic Society in Bath owns the largest collection in the world of nineteenth- and early twentieth-century photographic periodicals.

As well as conserving films about their areas, several of the regional film archives also have fascinating written deposits about early cinema: the Northwest Film Archive has material on Lancashire cinema, and the Scottish Film Archive has collections about showmen George Kemp, George Green and the Robello family. The Southeast Film Archive has acquired many items about pioneer cameraman Emile Lauste, and about the 'Brighton School'.

The most interesting discoveries may often be made in collections that on the surface are not film-related. Several documents, posters and brochures related to film may be found in the John Johnson ephemera collection at Oxford University, for instance, while Reading University's Rickards ephemera collection may hold similar surprises.

The humble public library should not be overlooked, as many local history collections will contain material on how cinema came to their region; some local newspapers have been indexed, which may lead to more discoveries. Many British towns published entertainment listings journals from the late nineteenth century, with titles like *Manchester Amusements* and *What's On*, including details about cinema in their region.[45] The Harold Manning music-hall collection in Birmingham Public Library would also be worth investigating for cinema information. Municipal and regional archives are often worth exploring —several have deposits about former picture palaces in their area.[46] For example, the Lancashire Record Office has records of Colne Amusements Ltd, cinema proprietors 1911–20, while in the Oxfordshire Archives there are the accounts and records of the Palace Cinema and Witney Electric Theatre from 1912 through the 1920s. Just as London's LCC records contain much precious film-related material, other British cities may also have entertainment licensing records that would include information on cinema. Hull Record Office, for example, preserves a cinema licence register from 1914 to 1919.

3: Collections outside Britain

Early films were widely distributed around the world; as a result a film made in one country may often turn up in the archive of another. Film historians, aided by a volume of 'Magliozzi', thus often need to travel internationally to view film prints.[47] The same may also apply to documentation, and material on British early cinema turns up in the most unlikely places. A beautiful illustrated brochure for the opening in 1913 of the Kensington Picture Theatre is held in the Lisbon film archive, while in the Canadian Center for Architecture is another unique British brochure, *The Modern Electric Picture Theatre*—from around 1910. Many issues of *Pictures* magazine (London, 1911–13), Britain's first ever specialist film fan magazine, are held uniquely in UCLA library. (The other main fan magazine of the period, *Picturegoer*, began in 1913.[48]) The only known copy of the *Bioscope Annual and Diary* for 1909 is in George Eastman House, Rochester, along with unique copies of James Williamson catalogues, dating from 1899 and 1902. One of the greatest film collectors of all time was Will Day, and his collection now resides in Paris, with documents on several British pioneers including R.W. Paul, Matt Raymond and Arthur Malden.[49]

The Museum of Natural History in Los Angeles seems an unlikely repository for early cinema memorabilia, but this was once the main museum for the city and received several collections from film pioneers and collectors. These include material on the Biograph company —both the American and British ends of this business—made up of numerous catalogues, reports and press cuttings. Also located here is Florence Turner's scrapbook of her visit to Britain in 1913–14. Just round the corner at the University of Southern California one may consult some early British film material in the Anthony Slide collection, including items on fairground cinema, William Haggar and actress Helena Millais.

Across the city in Beverly Hills the beautiful Academy library holds

Charles Brabin's diaries of his filming trip to Britain in 1913.[50] Also in the Academy library is the Selig Collection, which contains potentially fascinating files, entitled 'English releases, 1911–14' and 'British correspondence'. The latter includes such names as Brockliss, Bromhead, Clarendon, Gaumont (1909), Herkomer, Jury, Paul (1905), Urban, Walturdaw (1908), Warwick Bioscope Chronicle and Williamson.[51]

The New York Public Library (NYPL)'s Billy Rose Theatre collection holds cuttings on British personalities, and its card index has been published.[52] The NYPL also holds the largest collection of American film trade journals, as well as a unique run of the *Photographic Dealer (PD)*. This was a key British photographic periodical with 12,000 subscribers, aimed at the trade. Every year from 1896—usually in August or September—the *PD* had a special 'lantern number', which of course included information on cinema. For some reason little of the *PD* survives in British collections before 1906 (when the BL's collection starts). A few issues from 1896 to 1898 are in the Bibliothèque Nationale in France, but the longest run is in New York, almost complete from 1898 to 1904. This journal had unrivalled coverage of equipment and patents, with numerous illustrations of cinematographs, lanterns and projectors.

Conclusion

I hope to have shown in this survey not only that much has already been achieved in researching early British film history, but that much more is there to be done. While John Barnes's books have covered the period to 1901 in detail, Barnes himself has rightly proposed that the next major historical task for early British cinema studies would be the Edwardian era, from 1901 to the First World War. This was a crucial period for British cinema, when continuing achievements were accompanied by ominous signs of decline. More work could usefully be done in examining why the early promise of the British cinema ran out of steam, and more generally in comparing the British experience of early cinema with that in other countries.[53]

Other areas which remain under-researched include the use of film by religious organizations, and by scientists and explorers, fields of cinema in which Britons were especially active. Early British film companies worthy of further research include Clarendon, Butchers, and Williamson. It is strange that, while a marginal figure in film history, Hubert von Herkomer, has been the subject of a fine booklet, no book has appeared about producers Bamforth or the Riley Brothers.[54] Also strong candidates for a book-length study would be the Mottershaws of the Sheffield Photo Co., who were important producers in the Edwardian period, even selling films to the Americans.[55]

But as well as these particular gaps in research, there is a more general problem with British early film history. Much of the British work has been done by isolated amateurs, and this has been both a strength and a weakness. A strength in that labours of love often produce rich and satisfying books, a weakness in that so much more could have been achieved if institutions had lent their resources to this work. Film historians in several other European countries (Italy, France and Germany, to name but three) have formed themselves into national associations, and in these countries there has been more institutional support for film history, particularly in the regions. One hopes that such institutional involvement may now be developing in Britain.[56]

Notes

1. Rachael Low and Roger Manvell, *The History of the British Film, 1896–1906* (London: George Allen and Unwin, 1948), and Low, *The History of the British Film, 1906–1914* (London: George Allen and Unwin, 1949).
2. John Barnes, *The Beginnings of the Cinema in England, 1894–1901* (Exeter: University of Exeter Press, 1997 etc.), five volumes.
3. Richard Brown and Barry Anthony, *A Victorian Film Enterprise: the History of the British Mutoscope and Biograph Company, 1897–1915* (Trowbridge: Flicks Books, 1999).
4. Roger Holman, ed., *Cinema 1900–1906: An Analytical Study* (Brussels: FIAF, 1982); Barry Salt, *Film Style and Technology: History and Analysis* (London: Starword, 1992); Michael Chanan, *The Dream That Kicks* (London/New York: Routledge, 1980): a disappointing second edition appeared in 1996, with little reference to more recent publications. Noël Burch, *Life To Those Shadows* (London: BFI, 1990).
5. Ian Christie, *The Last Machine: Early Cinema and the Birth of the Modern World* (London: BBC Education/BFI, 1994), based on a BBC television series.
6. Christopher Williams, ed., *Cinema: the Beginnings and the Future* (London: University of Westminster, 1996).
7. John Hawkridge, 'British Cinema from Hepworth to Hitchcock,' in Geoffrey Nowell-Smith, ed., *The Oxford History of World Cinema* (Oxford: Oxford University Press, 1996), pp. 130–6.

8. See e.g. Hiley, 'At the Picture Palace: The British Cinema Audience, 1895–1920,' in John Fullerton, ed., *Celebrating 1895: The Centenary of Cinema* (Sydney: John Libbey, 1998).

9. Stephen Herbert and Luke McKernan, *Who's Who of Victorian Cinema* (London: BFI, 1996). Denis Gifford, *The British Film Catalogue, Vol. 1: The Fiction Film, 1895–1994* and *Vol. 2: The Non-Fiction Film, 1895–1994* (both London: Fitzroy Dearborn Publishers, 2001; Vol. 1 was first published by David & Charles, 1973).

10. Cecil Milton Hepworth, *Animated Photography. The ABC of the Cinematograph* (London: The Amateur Photographer's Library, 1897, 2nd edn 1900); Henry Hopwood, *Living Pictures* (London: The Optician and Photographic Trades Review, 1899/1915); Frederick A. Talbot, *Moving Pictures, How They Are Made and Worked* (London: William Heinemann, 1912); Harry Furniss, *Our Lady Cinema. How and Why I Went Into the Photo-play World and What I Found There* (Bristol: J.W. Arrowsmith, 1914). Other contemporary publications are listed in the Bibliography elsewhere in this volume.

11. Colin N. Bennett, ed., *The Handbook of Kinematography: The History, Theory and Practice of Motion Photography and Projection* (London: The Kinematograph Weekly, 1911; 2nd edn 1913).

12. Stephen Herbert, ed., *A History of Early Film*, three volumes (London: Routledge, 2000).

13. Colin Harding and Simon Popple, eds, *In the Kingdom of Shadows: a Companion to Early Cinema* (London: Cygnus Arts, 1996).

14. George Pearson, *Flashback* (London: Allen and Unwin, 1957); Cecil Hepworth, *Came the Dawn* (London: Phoenix House, 1951).

15. A.C. Bromhead, 'Reminiscences of the British Film Trade,' *Proceedings of the British Kinematograph Society*, no. 21, December 1933. See the same journal, no. 38, 1936, pp. 2–16, for 'Before 1910: Kinematograph Experiences'—Paul, Hepworth and Barker's reminiscences.

16. John H. Bird, *Cinema Parade: Fifty Years of Film Shows* (Birmingham: Cornish Brothers Ltd, *c.*1946). Further historical items may be found in the Bibliography at the end of this volume.

17. Kevin Scrivens and Stephen Smith, *The Travelling Cinematograph Show* (Tweedale: New Era Publications, 1999). Geoff Weedon and Richard Ward, *Fairground Art: the Art Forms of Travelling Fairs, Carousels and Carnival Midways* (New York/London: Abbeville/White Mouse, *c.*1981). Vanessa Toulmin's articles include: 'Telling the Tale: The Story of the Fairground Bioscope Shows and the Showmen who Operated Them,' *Film History*, vol. 6, 1994, pp. 219–37.

18. See the MLS website: http://www.magiclantern.org.uk.

19. John Fullerton, ed., *Celebrating 1895: the Centenary of Cinema* (Sydney: John Libbey and Co., 1998). See especially the essays by Alan Burton, Richard Crangle, Andrew Higson and Nicholas Hiley.

20. Linda Fitzsimmons and Sarah Street, eds, *Moving Performance: British Stage and Screen, 1890s–1920s* (Trowbridge: Flicks Books, 2000).

21. Simon Popple and Vanessa Toulmin, eds, *Visual Delights: Essays on the Popular and Projected Image in the 19th Century* (Trowbridge: Flicks Books, 2001).

22. Gerry Turvey, 'Weary Willie and Tired Tim Go Into Pictures: The Comic Films of the British and Colonial Kinematograph Company,' in Alan Burton and Laraine Porter, eds, *Pimple, Pranks and Pratfalls: British Film Comedy Before 1930* (Trowbridge: Flicks Books, 2000), pp. 69–75; and Turvey, 'The Battle of Waterloo (1913): The First British Epic,' in Burton and Porter, eds, *The Showman, the Spectacle, and the Two-minute Silence: Performing British Cinema Before 1930* (Trowbridge: Flicks Books, 2001), pp. 40-7.

23. Ray Allister, *Friese-Greene: Close-up of an Inventor* (London: Marsland Publications, 1948). David Robinson and Raymond Newport's material on Rudge is in *New Magic Lantern Journal*, vol. 8, no. 2, October 1997.

24. See e.g. Hauke Lange-Fuchs, *Der Kaiser, der Kanal und die Kinematographie: Begleitheft zur Ausstellung im Landesarchiv Schleswig-Holstein, Birt Acres—100 Jahre Film in Schleswig-Holstein* (Schleswig: Landesarchiv Schleswig-Holstein, 1995).

25. See Frank Gray, *The Hove Pioneers and the Arrival of Cinema* (Brighton: University of Brighton, 1996), and Martin Sopocy, *James Williamson: Studies and Documents of a Pioneer of the Film Narrative* (Cranbury: Associated University Presses, 1998).

26. See especially my own edited issues, vol. 10, no. 1, 1998, and vol. 11, no. 3, 1999.

27. Subjects covered included: early film in Leicester (vol. 1, no. 4, 1961), London and Eastbourne (vol. 1, no. 9, 1964), Hull (vol. 2, no. 1, 1965) and Birmingham (vol. 2, no. 5, 1967); Birt Acres (vol. 1, nos 6 and 7, 1962, 1963), Dave Aylott (vol. 2, no. 1, 1965) and William Haggar (vol. 2, no. 4, 1967).

28. Flicks Books began publishing *Living Pictures* in Spring 2001.

29. http://www.shef.ac.uk/uni/projects/nfa/;
    http://website.lineone.net/~luke.mckernan/Urban.htm.

30. Barry Anthony, *The Kinora—Motion Pictures For the Home, 1896–1914* (London: The Projection Box, 1996); Stephen Herbert, *Theodore Brown's Magic Pictures* (London: The Projection Box, 1997); Stephen Herbert, *Industry, Liberty, and a Vision . . . Wordsworth Donisthorpe's Kinesigraph* (London: The Projection Box, 1998); Luke McKernan, ed., *A Yank in Britain: The Lost Memoirs of Charles Urban, Film Pioneer* (London: The Projection Box, 1999; see also McKernan's chapter 4 in this volume; he is also planning a full biography of Urban); Stephen Bottomore, *The Titanic and Silent Cinema* (Hastings: The Projection Box, 2000). Also from the same publisher: *Victorian Film Catalogues . . . Reprinted From the*

W.D. Slade Archive (London: The Projection Box, 1996); Vanessa Toulmin, *Randall Williams—King of Showmen: From Ghost Show to Bioscope* (London: The Projection Box, 1998). See Flicks's website: http://easyweb.easynet.co.uk/ ~s-herbert/ProjectionBox.htm.

31. Geoffrey James Mellor, *Picture Pioneers: the Story of the Northern Cinema, 1896–1971* (Newcastle upon Tyne: Frank Graham, *c.* 1971); Geoffrey James Mellor, *Movie Makers and Picture Palaces: A Century of Cinema in Yorkshire, 1896–1996* (Bradford: Bradford Libraries, 1996); Robert Benfield, *Bijou Kinema: A History of Cinema in Yorkshire* (Sheffield: Sheffield City Polytechnic/Yorkshire Arts, 1976); Ned Williams, *Cinemas of the Black Country* (Wolverhampton: Uralia Press, 1982); Frank Manders, *Cinemas of Gateshead* (Gateshead: Portcullis Press, 1995); Graham Nutt, *Tuppenny Rush: the Arrival of Cinemas and Film-making in Swadlincote* (Burton-on-Trent: Trent Valley, *c.* 1992); William Shenton, 'Manchester's First Cinemas 1896–1914,' *Manchester Region History Review*, vol. 4, Autumn 1990–1, pp. 3–11; David Mayall, 'Palaces for Entertainment in Birmingham, 1908–1918,' *Midland History*, vol. 10, 1985; Sam Mullins, 'Market Harborough and the Movies, 1901–1940,' *Leicestershire Historian*, vol. 3, 1987; David Williams, *Cinema in Leicester, 1896–1931* (Loughborough: Heart of Albion Press, 1993). (Williams is now working on early cinema in Durham.)

32. Stephen Peart, *The Picture House in East Anglia* (Lavenham: Lavenham Press, 1980); Paul J. Marriott, *Early Oxford Picture Palaces* (Oxford: The author, 1978); Ken George, *'Two Sixpennies Please': Lewisham's Early Cinemas* (London: Lewisham Local History Society, 1987); O'Brien, 'Picture Shows: The Early British Film Industry in Walthamstow,' *History Today*, vol. 37, 1987, pp. 9–15.

33. David Berry, *Wales and Cinema: The First Hundred Years* (Cardiff: University of Wales Press, 1994). As far as Scotland goes, Aberdeen has been well covered, with Michael Thomson's *Silver Screen in the Silver City* (Aberdeen: Aberdeen UP, 1988).

34. For catalogues of film holdings, see Elaine Burrows, Janet Moat, David Sharp and Linda Wood, eds, *The British Cinema Source Book: BFI Archive Viewing Copies and Library Materials* (London: BFI, 1995); and Bryony Dixon and Luke McKernan, eds, *British Silent Comedy Films: Viewing Copies in the National Film and Television Archive* (London: BFI Collections, 1999); see also the BFI's website (http://www.bfi.org.uk).

35. *The Film Index, a Bibliography* (New York: WPA, 1940); Annette M. D'Agostino, *Filmmakers in the Moving Picture World: An Index of Articles, 1907–1927* (Jefferson: McFarland and Company, Inc., 1997).

36. *Moving Picture News, Motography* and *Moving Picture World* are held at the BFI on microfilm.

37. The best existing work on this theme is Kristin Thompson's *Exporting*

Entertainment: America in the World Film Market, 1907–1934 (London: BFI, 1985).

38. The BL's unique run of *Kinematograph and Lantern Weekly* should also be microfilmed in the near future. The Colindale journals are listed at their website: http://www.bl.uk/collections/newspaper/cinema.html#g. I am currently working on an international database of early film journals. The British Cinema History Research Project based at the University of East Anglia, is currently producing an index to *Kinematograph and Lantern Weekly* (and its preceding and succeeding titles).

39. Classmarks are: Add. MSS 54910; Add. MSS 71938-71945.

40. Fire insurance records held at London's Guildhall Library are also worth investigating.

41. Companies at classmark BT31 include: Biograph, Gaumont, Hepworth, Ideal, Jury's, Kinemacolor, Kinora, Nordisk, Selig, Universal, Vitagraph, Williamson. The PRO's website is at http://www.pro.gov.uk/about/search.htm.

42. Some of Fletcher's remarkable research will be published in *Living Pictures*. He has also researched cinema in Lambeth and Southwark to 1909.

43. Available on CD-Rom and at www.bufvc.ac.uk. See also www.footage.net.

44. Posters of *Land and Sea* (Cricks & Martin, 1913) and *His Little Son* (Clarendon, 1910).

45. At least a dozen titles are listed, for towns from Paignton to Glasgow, in Carl J. Stratman, *Britain's Theatrical Periodicals, 1720–1967: A Bibliography* (New York: NYPL, 1972). A computer search of the British Library's newspaper catalogue reveals 'What's On . . .' guides to nine cities in the early film era, including Wigan and Manchester.

46. Such deposits may sometimes be located via NIDS (National Inventory of Documentary Sources) on CD-Rom.

47. Ronald S. Magliozzi, *Treasures from the Film Archives: A Catalog of Short Silent Fiction Films Held by FIAF Archives* (Metuchen: Scarecrow Press, 1988).

48. The BL holds a few issues for 1913–14.

49. A detailed finding aid is available in Bibliothèque du Film in Paris; Day's equipment is at the Cinémathèque Française; Day's films are at Centre Nationale de la Cinématographie. See Stephen Bottomore, 'Will Day: the Story of Rediscovery,' *Film Studies*, no. 1, Spring 1999, pp. 81–91.

50. This was not an altogether happy experience for Brabin, and he regularly notes that dull weather has led to filming being cancelled! I am editing the Brabin diaries for publication.

51. Selig Collection catalogue numbers 514–18, and 544–61.

52. New York Public Library, *Catalog of the Theatre and Drama Collections* (Boston: G.K. Hall, 1967–76): 51 volumes, including 6 volumes of

author listings, 9 of books on the theatre, and 30 of the non-book collection.

53. Though we should recall Charles Musser's advice: 'Comparative histories are only possible—and fruitful—when a critical mass of data has been assembled.' Musser, 'Reading Local Histories of Early Film Exhibition,' *Historical Journal of Film, Radio and Television* vol. 19, no. 2, June 1999, p. 250.

54. Michael Pritchard, *Sir Hubert von Herkomer: Film Pioneer and Artist* (Bushey: Bushey Museum Trust, 1987). Richard Brown's unpublished paper (held in the BFI) 'On the Nomenclature and Dating of some Early Bamforth Films' (1994) is a useful beginning.

55. Some material on the Mottershaws is available in Sheffield Public Library, and much more would undoubtedly be discovered via a trawl through local newspapers. Some information on these and other Yorkshire pioneers may be found in Benfield, *Bijou Kinema*, Allan T. Sutherland, 'The Yorkshire Pioneers,' *Sight and Sound*, Winter 1976/77, pp. 48–51, and Lawrence Sutcliffe, 'A Daring Daylight Film Company: A History of the Sheffield Photo Company,' unpublished MA dissertation, University of East Anglia, 2001.

56. One ambitious project in which such support would prove vital was suggested some years ago by Richard Brown: to study the early years of film in London. More recently a similar venture has independently been proposed by Ian Christie of Birkbeck, University of London. Much information about early cinema in London is surely there to be found, for several film production companies were active in the city in this period, and by 1913 there were around 500 cinemas (according to the LCC's annual *London Statistics*). A crucial resource in this project would be the nearly 200 newspapers which were published in the early film period in the eighty districts of Greater London, and perhaps this research might fruitfully be run in collaboration with the many history organizations in London. There are precedents for such group research in film history: institutions in other countries have organized teams of researchers to comb for information on early film, such as André Gaudreault's GRAFICS group in Canada, or the research department at the Nederlands Filmmuseum.

22

A Guide to Bibliographical and Archival Sources on British Cinema from the First World War to the Coming of Sound

Jon Burrows

Recent Critical Literature

There is a quite striking difference between the amount of recent published research concerned with British cinema and British cinema culture of the 1890s and 1900s, and the years which this biblio-graphical essay will focus upon: 1914 to 1930. Whereas British filmmakers in the first decade or so of cinema were incontrovertibly pioneers, influential on an international scale, many commentators on British films of the 1910s and 1920s perceived them as backward, insular and commercially unsuccessful.[1] As a result, until very recently, film historians have paid little attention to this period. The notable exception to this rule is, of course, Rachael Low whose (recently reissued) multi-part *History of the British Film* series contains separate volumes dealing with the years 1914 to 1918 (first published in 1950) and 1918 to 1929 (first published in 1971).[2] The historian of silent British cinema has a number of reasons to be grateful for her efforts. As others have pointed out, Low had an unusually catholic under-standing of what constituted film history, and endeavoured to document British film culture of the period in its entirety.[3] There are, therefore, extended and invaluable sections devoted not just to production, but also to the distribution and exhibition sectors of the industry. Low also treats non-fiction filmmaking as a subject worthy of as much serious attention as feature film production, and details the cinema-related activities of leading educationalists and moral reform movements.

These distinctive strengths do not, however, altogether compensate for the rather one-dimensional and oppressively dismissive assessment which British fiction filmmaking in this era is subjected to. Low very diligently lists all the major production concerns of the period and offers a pen portrait of their output, but the tone of this appraisal is overwhelmingly negative. Indeed, the volume dealing with the years 1918 to 1929 ends with a short chapter which attempts to explain why 'British films were generally felt to be bad even at the time'.[4] It is worth highlighting this dimension of the series because it is my experience that a detailed survey of the kinds of (usually written) sources upon which Low bases this sweeping indictment is apt to reveal that her marshalling of supporting evidence has been somewhat selective. In this respect, Low's work can be a problematic and even misleading source of information.

To be fair, this colossal enterprise was undertaken at a time when relatively few surviving British films made in the post-pioneer era were accessible to researchers. The same cannot be said of the only other published monograph to focus on British cinema of the 1920s, Kenton Bamford's *Distorted Images*.[5] The National Film and Television Archive has succeeded over the last couple of decades in making prints of over 150 feature films from the era available as viewing copies. Despite this fact, Bamford's study somewhat perversely insists that too many of the relevant films 'have either disappeared or been destroyed'.[6] Rather than examine the considerable amount of extant filmic evidence, he has endeavoured to build up a picture of British film production predominantly through contemporary trade paper reviews. Again, there is a problem here of reductive selectivity, since Bamford only quotes sources which confirm his thesis that British cinema of the time was elitist, unpopular and creatively bankrupt. There is no corresponding consideration of the discourse of appreciation and sympathetic explication of British films that might almost as easily be discovered in the trade press and fan magazines of the era.

In contrast to this approach, there have been some notable recent attempts to write revisionist versions of film history in order to explain and understand the peculiarities of British fiction film production in the mid-1910s and 1920s. Andrew Higson, for example, has offered a contextual reading of Cecil Hepworth's 1924 literary adaptation *Comin' Thro' The Rye* in the light of contemporary trends in other media and particular socio-economic imperatives.[7] As part of an ongoing project that will eventually be published in book-length form, Christine Gledhill has sought to explain characteristic differences between British and American films of the 1920s in terms of contrasting melodramatic antecedents.[8] Stephen Bottomore points out in the preceding chapter that proceedings from two of the annual British Silent Cinema weekends held at the Broadway Media Centre in Nottingham have now been published as edited collections; they contain chapters on British cinema of the 1920s written by Higson and Gledhill, along with a number of other pieces which cover topics relevant to this period. These include essays on Ivor Novello, Betty Balfour, Adrian Brunel, Pathé's *Eve's Film Review* cinemagazine, and the output of both B&C and Ideal in the latter half of the 1910s.[9]

This new scholarship represents the tip of a small iceberg of concentrated research into this era of British filmmaking. Several recent Ph.D. theses have dealt with such subjects as the ties between theatre and cinema in Britain in the 1910s, exhibition strategies and audience tastes during the First World War, 'middlebrow' British film culture in the 1920s, avant-garde British film culture in the 1920s, and the films of Ivor Novello.[10]

Government-sponsored British propaganda films of the First World War have not suffered quite the same critical neglect as their mainstream contemporaries. Aside from the numerous articles listed in the Bibliography, one can point to a standard reference work, written by Nicholas Reeves, and now also a comprehensive catalogue listing all the Imperial War Museum's holdings which relate to the conflict.[11] In general filmographic terms there is still no more authoritative list of British fiction and non-fiction films in this period than the late Denis Gifford's monumental *British Film Catalogue*.[12] Researchers should also be aware of two unpublished catalogues, *British Silent Comedy Films* and *British Feature Films of the Twenties*, recently issued by the National Film and Television Archive.[13] Not only are these very comprehensive listings of surviving British films which the archive holds, they also provide substantially more technical data about the condition of the viewing materials than the official specialist archive catalogue.[14] This latter work should not be ignored, however, not least because it includes a useful index of relevant books and special collections accessible at the BFI National Library. (There is also a computerised catalogue of the BFI's Special Collections available for consultation in the Reading Room of the Library.)

Contemporary Periodicals

The relatively short-lived nature of the vast majority of British production companies from this period, as compared with some of the
bigger French and American equivalents, means that hardly any
corporate records have been preserved. This makes researchers of silent
British cinema all the more reliant on the vast array of trade periodicals
that reported on industry affairs. There were something like twenty
specialist trade papers in existence between 1914 and 1930. Rather
than list them all here, I would advise the reader to consult the online
index of titles held at the British Newspaper Library in Colindale.[15]
The Newspaper Library holds complete runs of all but a few of the
trade papers that are known to me. The three most important of these
remained, as in the earlier part of the 1910s, the *Kinematograph and
Lantern Weekly* (shortened to the *Kinematograph Weekly* in 1919), the
Bioscope and the *Cinema*.

The silent period presents a striking contrast with the later 'talkie'
era in the sheer size of the market for competing trade papers. This can
be explained partly by the fact that there was no comparable
standardization of exhibition practices. In the absence of uniform
synchronized sound technology written sources of suggestions for
appropriate exhibition strategies tended to proliferate at an exponential
rate. It is surely no coincidence that once the take-up of sound
gained an unstoppable momentum, the *Bioscope* was merged with
Kinematograph Weekly, and the *Cinema* was reformatted to provide a
more straightforward news update service.

Where these trade papers largely duplicated the same kind of information and coverage in the later sound era, it can be very rewarding to
take the time to peruse several periodical titles from the silent period
rather than just one. It is not just the advice on exhibition topics that
can vary substantially: for example, even the nature and significance of
a supposedly landmark historical event like the notorious 'British Film
Slump' of November 1924 was interpreted in completely different ways
by the editorial staff of the *Kinematograph Weekly* and the *Bioscope*.[16]
There are other distinctive features of the trade press in these years that
make them an incredibly fertile resource. Throughout most of the
1910s the major titles retained and took care to address a non-specialist
audience which was not quite as well catered for by fan magazines
as in subsequent years. Letters from regular filmgoers continued to
be received and published, and certain kinds of promotional articles
were printed in the trade press predominantly for their benefit.

Furthermore, during the First World War, broadsheet newspapers, which had just begun to send their dramatic critics to review film premieres, dramatically curtailed their film coverage in the face of increasing paper shortages and the demands of accommodating news from the front. For a time, therefore, trade papers attempted to compensate for this by providing a form of serious film criticism which was far more elaborate and detailed than the capsule reviews, aimed primarily at showmen, which predominate in later years. For the researcher most interested in such reviews, some were made more handily accessible in the *Kinematograph Weekly* spin-off publication, the *Kinematograph Weekly Monthly Alphabetical Film Record* (renamed the *Kinematograph Monthly Record* after 1919). The *Kinematograph Weekly*, the *Bioscope* and, to a lesser extent, the *Cinema* also published annual Year Books or Trade Diaries (in the same vein, see also the annual Cinematograph Exhibitors' Diary). These can be invaluable reference sources because (a) they usually provide a detailed month-by-month summary of industry events over the previous year, which serve as a rough 'index' to the weekly papers; (b) they include full lists of all the films released in the previous twelve months, arranged by title and distributor; and (c) they attempt an updated exhaustive listing of all the country's picture theatres, arranged by town and also, in later years, according to the chain of cinemas they might belong to.

Each of the three main trade periodicals covered production, distribution and exhibition affairs as well as extensively reporting provincial news. There was also a large number of complementary publications with a more specialist focus. Several of these concentrated on region-specific coverage, such as the *Biogram* (1919–23; Wales), *Films* (1915–23; Birmingham), and the *Trade Show Critic* (1919–30; Liverpool). The *Film Renter*, a London-based paper for much of its life, actually began in Manchester as *Pictures and Pleasures*, and remained predominantly focused upon the distribution and exhibition scene in the North of England between 1914 and 1922. Other trade papers supplied unique in-depth reports on one particular branch of the industry. The *Motion Picture Studio*, for example, was principally devoted to the British production sector and functioned as a forum for the exchange of views between directors, producers, actors and designers between 1921 and 1924. The *Express Overseas Mail* (1914–16) contained monthly coverage of the British export trade (at a fascinating time, incidentally, when London was beginning to lose its status as the world's international film distribution centre).[17] The *Cinematograph Times* was begun in 1928 as the official organ of the

Cinematograph Exhibitors Association. There was also enough confidence and ambition in the British film industry in the late 1910s and 1920s for two of the leading film companies to produce their own in-house trade papers. The Ideal Film Renting Co., a major distributor and producer in Britain from 1913 until the end of the 1920s, produced its *Idealetter* for nearly a decade. Sadly, none of our major libraries seem to have received or preserved it, but the Bill Douglas Centre for the History of Cinema and Popular Culture at the University of Exeter holds a few random copies. Happily, the Stoll Film Company's house organ, *Stoll's Editorial News*, still exists in a compete run (1919–24) at the Newspaper Library, and, in a more partial form, at the BFI National Library. This meaty publication contains provocative articles, interviews with key creative personnel, detailed reports of production schedules, minutes of shareholders' meetings, exhibitors' exploitation pages, and—very handily—reprints of any and every review (from even the smallest of provincial news-papers) of the films which Stoll distributed during this five-year period.

This abundance of useful trade papers in Britain was unfortunately not particularly well matched by a wealth of fan magazines. Again, the online British Newspaper Library index contains the most com-prehensive inventory available—though few of these magazines are actually identified as such. The relevant titles include the *Cinema World Illustrated* (1927–9), *Film Flashes* (1915–16), *Girls' Cinema* (1920–32), *Photo Bits and Cinema Star* (1923–6), the *Picture Palace News* (1915–17) and *Picture Show* (1919–60). By far the longest serving and most important British film fan magazine is the one usually referred to as *Picturegoer*. Begun in 1913 under that name, its cover title actually went through a number of changes in the silent period (becoming *Pictures and the Picturegoer* and just plain *Pictures* at various points); there were also several switches from weekly to monthly formats. As one might expect, the lion's share of *Picturegoer*'s pages was devoted to interviews and promotional articles concerning American stars and films. The magazine nevertheless seems to have had a fairly patriotic readership (it certainly had a patriotic editorial board) and there are frequent, substantial profiles of British stars and native productions. Perhaps most valuably, regular space was devoted in the corres-pondents' letters pages to discussion about the contrasting merits of British and American films and personalities. *Picturegoer* also organized readers' polls to ascertain who the most popular British film stars of the era were.[18] The most revealing data in this respect, however, is probably that disclosed in the readers' polls conducted by *Picture Palace*

News in the 1910s and Sidney Bernstein's 1927 and 1929 audience questionnaires, since these measured the relative popularity of British stars against their American rivals.[19]

One British producer, the Hepworth Manufacturing Company, enterprisingly published its own fan magazine, the *Hepworth Picture-Play Paper*, which ran in 1915 and 1916 before war shortages forced it to be discontinued; it was later revived in the early 1920s. Both of these short runs are accessible at the BFI National Library.

A more highbrow literature of film appreciation did, of course, make its first appearance in this period, with the monthly journal *Close Up*, which began in July 1927. Famously scathing about the vast majority of British films that it deigned to review, the magazine nevertheless represents one of the most visible signs, and interesting manifestations, of the first wave of interest in the cinema as an art form on the part of British intellectuals (see Section E of this volume for a fuller discussion of this development). Conveniently, a selection of writings from the journal has recently been reprinted.[20] Turning to non-specialist periodicals, earlier mainstream newspaper journalism about films and filmmaking was an early casualty of the war in the 1910s, as I mentioned, but the immediate post-war era presents a very different story. The *Daily News*, the *Evening News* and the *Westminster Gazette* all appointed professional film correspondents in 1919. Most of the major broadsheet newspapers followed suit during the 1920s. The more noteworthy examples, in retrospect, include the *Daily Mail*, which employed Iris Barry in 1925 (discussed by Haidee Wasson in chapter 20, above), and the *Sunday Times*, which hired Ivor Montagu in 1927 (he had previously written for *The Observer*; see chapter 19, above). The theatrical trade paper the *Era* continued to cover film industry affairs in a new formalized column from 1917 onwards. It should be noted, however, that this came to represent little more than a potted version of reports from the specialist press, and was not the unique source of film information that it had been in the cinema's first decade. Other arts-related journals began to show a serious interest in the medium as the 1920s wore on, though, and one can even find articles relating to the alternative wing of British film culture written by Oswell Blakeston in the *Architectural Review*.[21]

Contemporary Monographs and Reports

Book-length studies of the cinema published in this period can be roughly divided into three basic categories: works of film theory, works of technical instruction and industry analysis, and what one might loosely term 'reform manifestos' concerned with the social effects of the cinema.

Indigenous British works of film theory did not really emerge until the latter half of the 1920s, and the list of theorists is almost entirely made up of regular contributors to *Close Up*. Oswell Blakeston's *Through a Yellow Glass*, Ernest Betts' *Heraclitus, or the Future of Films* and Eric Elliott's *Anatomy of Motion Picture Art* were all published in 1928, and all fall into this category. Perhaps the only notable exceptions to this trend are Gerard Fort Buckle's *The Mind and the Film* and Eric Walter White's *Parnassus to Let: An Essay about Rhythm in the Films*. The former, a now-forgotten attempt to study the psychological dimension of film spectatorship, was published in 1926, but largely written in the first half of the decade. The latter was published by Leonard and Virgina Woolf's Hogarth Press in 1928 and articulates a plea for future cinematic experimentation modelled on the aesthetics of poetry.

A fairly substantial literature of technical instruction was published in this period. Much of it is useful to the modern-day researcher in ways that might not be immediately apparent. There were, for instance, at least eight British guides to the art of film acting published in this period. The books are often less instructive for what they tell us about standard industry practices (most of these self-proclaimed courses of training conspicuously downplay or avoid altogether any specific discussion of what the actual craft of screen acting involved on a technical level) than for the ways in which they attempt to *mystify* the phenomenon of screen stardom and seek to instruct readers on how to interpret the activities of their favourite players. There are an even larger number of 'How To' guides aimed at initiating a general readership into the arcane techniques of writing and selling screenplays. Several of these, such as Colden Lore's *The Modern Photoplay and its Construction* and Arrar Jackson's *Writing for the Screen* were actually written by successful British screenwriters, and do offer some revealing glimpses of their aesthetic philosophies.[22] Harold Weston's *The Art of Photo-Play Writing* is particularly interesting in this respect. Weston was one of B&C's top directors in the 1910s, and was frequently responsible for films that broached socially contentious themes. His book lays out something of the rationale behind his progressive intentions, but also defends a somewhat anomalous stylistic conservativeness, most notably his aversion to the 'run-in' tracking shot.[23] There are similar insights into the mindsets of British film directors (albeit of a more journeyman calibre) in L.C. Macbean's *Kinematograph Studio Technique* and Meyrick Milton's *The Malady of the British Film*.[24]

The category that I have called 'reform manifestos' contains only a handful of published titles, but their significance and usefulness should not be underestimated. In November 1916 the Cinematograph Trade Council invited the National Council of Public Morals to undertake a formal investigation of the charge made by hostile commentators that the cinema exerted an immoral influence on British society. The specially convened Cinema Commission, which included such pillars of the community as Baden-Powell and Marie Stopes, interviewed forty-two witnesses for this purpose, including filmmakers, legislators, exhibitors, teachers, doctors, censors and even schoolchildren. The transcripts of the enquiry were published in book form in 1917, and this 372-page document represents an invaluable source of information about the social history of the cinema in Britain, with testimony ranging from the articulation of fears about the cinema's potential incitement of juvenile crime and its potentially deleterious effects upon eyesight, to explanations of the workings of the British Board of Film Censorship, American influences in the film industry, and even the class composition of cinema audiences in both general and particular circumstances.[25] In 1925 the Cinema Commission was active again, although on this occasion its work has a more limited usefulness for historians. It published the results of a subsequent investigation of potential educational uses of the cinema.[26] This was, curiously, a surprisingly popular topic, and there were three other books published on the subject in the period.[27]

Archival Collections

The most extensive single source of unpublished papers relating to this period of British film history is undoubtedly the Special Collections division of the BFI National Library. Over twenty separate collections contain relevant materials and documents. The most substantial of these are undoubtedly the Film Society and Ivor Montagu Collections. The former comprises some 24 boxes relating to this pioneering institution, which represented the central hub of Britain's avant-garde film culture between 1925 and 1939 (see chapter 18, above, for a fuller discussion of the Film Society). The collection includes screening programmes, correspondence between the Society's highly distinguished membership (which included H.G. Wells and Julian

Huxley), and also papers relating to its various infamous legal battles. Ivor Montagu was the driving force behind the formation of the Film Society, but the enormous Montagu Collection (representing twelve shelves' worth of files) also reflects his role within the industry as a professional film editor in the 1920s. Correspondence files (where telegrams from Michael Balcon nestle alongside letters from Pudovkin) make up the bulk of this archive, but not the least valuable of its contents are documents pertaining to Montagu's (troubled) role as the cutter on Hitchcock's *The Lodger* (1927).

Michael Balcon's own enormous Collection is arguably the jewel in the crown of the BFI National Library, but it has to be said that the papers relating to his tenureship at Gainsborough in the 1920s are not nearly as comprehensively preserved as the chapters in his later career. Less illustrious names have made their own unique and invaluable contributions to posterity. The James Anderson Special Collection is another huge mini-archive which represents the legacy of a film memorabilia collector who took particular care to build up scrapbooks filled with publicity materials for British feature films of the 1910s and 1920s in particular. The William F. Jury Collection contains indentures and agreements charting the formation of one of Britain's most important exhibition and distribution combines in this era, as well as documents stemming from Jury's high-level role in the government's war propaganda activities. There is an unfortunate scarcity of detailed information about most of Britain's other early cinema chains, but the Provincial Cinematograph Theatres Collection does at least contain shareholders' reports and the minutes of this circuit management's AGMs between 1914 and 1920. An additional source of exhibition-related information is the Sunday Opening Collection which contains scrapbooks of newspaper cuttings revealing how this contentious issue was reported in 1914, 1915 and 1922.

Extremely useful cuttings scrapbooks form the core of collections which document the early careers of Anthony Asquith, Betty Balfour, Clive Brook, Walter Forde and George Pearson. Sydney Carroll, an important newspaper film critic of the 1920s has bequeathed scrapbooks which collate not only his own writings but seemingly any and every item he came across, from June 1926 onwards, relating to British cinema, and these include many items from regional and colonial papers. Other notable figures active in this era are represented by collections of unpublished memoirs (Dave Aylott, Victor Saville, Harry Rowson), or, in Mabel Poulton's case, two unpublished autobiographical novels.[28] Although his name is now largely forgotten,

Benedict James (the pseudonym of prominent lawyer Bertram Jacobs) was one of the most prolific and successful British scriptwriters of the late 1910s and early 1920s and the Benedict James Collection includes contracts and shooting scripts from the latter part of his career. Going much further down the ranks of British film industry personnel, it may be that there are as yet undiscovered illuminating gems in the shooting diaries contained in the collection of Teddy Baird, who worked as an extra in British films between 1917 and 1918.

No other archival collections contain such a vast array of relevant materials as this, but several other institutions can be extremely fruitful places to pursue research on this period. Among many relevant items held at the aforementioned Bill Douglas Centre is a vast and largely uncharted array of pressbooks and cinema programmes, many of which can be considered unique. The Public Record Office at Kew is an essential stop-off point when investigating any branch of the British film industry which might have come under the scrutiny of, or had regular dealings with, a government ministry.[29] Home Office Files HO 45/10811 and HO 45/10812, for example, allow one to build up a fascinating picture of how close Britain came to instituting a state-controlled form of film censorship in 1916. The Board of Trade's company files contain records relating to every kind of production, distribution or exhibition concern registered in Britain, although there appears to be an element of luck as to how much material has been deposited in individual folders.

The Theatre Museum at Covent Garden contains materials that are generally speaking of more tangential interest for the British cinema researcher. The bulk of its unpublished papers consist of folders (mostly made up of programmes and cuttings, though sometimes also original correspondence) organized by the name, date and venue of a particular theatrical production or by the name of a particular theatrical personality. In cases where one is researching the history of a stage production adapted for the screen this will always throw up a considerable amount of useful background information. But occasionally rare or unique documents relating to the spin-off film production can be found there as well.

Other collections of interest tend to be scattered in a more eccentric fashion. The Imperial War Museum holds large quantities of papers and dope sheets recording the activities of First World War actuality cameramen. The University of Stirling's John Grierson Archive is an invaluable source of unpublished information about the formation of the documentary movement in the late 1920s. Slightly more unexpectedly, the film contracts of Matheson Lang now reside in the Cinema Museum in Kennington, whilst papers of the poet H.D. held at the Beinecke Rare Book and Manuscript Library at Yale University reportedly document her involvement with *Close Up*.[30] Michael Hammond's chapter 8 in this book reveals the existence of a cache of letters sent in the latter half of the 1910s by British exhibitors to the London offices of Selig; these letters are now held by the Margaret Herrick Library at the Academy of Motion Picture Arts and Sciences in Beverly Hills. It may well be that other American archives have ended up as the repositories of materials relating to the distribution and exhibition of Hollywood films in Britain.

Perhaps the most substantial uninvestigated sources of information about British film culture in this period lie in the surviving records of individual cinemas. Whilst the production and personality-related papers within national collections have been relatively well catalogued and publicized there is every likelihood that provincial archives have a lot to tell us about the history of film exhibition in Britain between 1914 and 1930. Sarah Street has recently highlighted the fact that a local history facility like the Tyne and Wear Archives Service possesses ledgers and cashbooks dating back to the First World War for cinemas in Jarrow and North Shields.[31] If such resources are duplicated across the country, it is not inconceivable that the extant information about audiences and exhibition practices which remains untapped will actually outnumber the precious few detailed records of production practices upon which most researchers have hitherto concentrated their energies.

Notes

1. See for example, John Hawkridge, 'British Cinema from Hepworth to Hitchcock,' in Geoffrey Nowell-Smith, ed., *The Oxford History of World Cinema* (Oxford: Oxford University Press, 1996), pp. 131–2.
2. Low, *The History of the British Film, 1914–1918* (London: Allen and Unwin, 1950; London, Routledge, 1997), and *The History of the British Film, 1918–1929* (London: Allen and Unwin, 1971; London: Routledge, 1997).
3. Ian Christie makes a very eloquent case for seeing Low as a significant pioneer of new film historiographical methods in his review of the reprinted volumes in the *Journal of Popular British Cinema*, Issue 2 (1999), pp. 136–40.
4. Low, *The History of the British Film, 1918–1929* (London: George Allen & Unwin, 1971), p. 298.

5. Kenton Bamford, *Distorted Images: British National Identity and Film in the 1920s* (London: I.B. Tauris, 1999).
6. Bamford, *Distorted Images*, p. xi.
7. See Andrew Higson, *Waving the Flag: Constructing a National Cinema in Britain* (Oxford: Oxford University Press, 1995), pp. 28–97.
8. See, for instance, Christine Gledhill, 'Between Melodrama and Realism: Anthony Asquith's *Underground* and King Vidor's *The Crowd*,' in Jane Gaines, ed., *Classical Hollywood Narrative: The Paradigm Wars* (Durham and London: Duke University Press, 1992), pp. 129–68.
9. Alan Burton and Laraine Porter, eds, *Pimple, Pranks and Pratfalls: British Comedy Before 1930* (Trowbridge: Flicks Books, 2000); Burton and Porter, eds, *The Showman, The Spectacle and the Two-Minute Silence: Performing British Cinema Before 1930* (Trowbridge: Flicks Books, 2001).
10. My own Ph.D. thesis, '"The Whole English Stage to be Seen for Sixpence": Theatrical Actors and Acting Styles in British Cinema, 1908–1918,' was completed at the University of East Anglia in 2000; the other thesis topics listed above have been investigated by, respectively, Michael Hammond at Nottingham Trent University (2001), and Lawrence Napper, Jamie Sexton and Michael Williams, all at the University of East Anglia (all 2001).
11. Nicholas Reeves, *Official British Film Propaganda During the First World War* (London: Croom Helm, 1986); Roger Smither, ed., *Imperial War Museum Film Catalogue, Volume One: The First World War Archive* (Trowbridge: Flicks Books, 1994).
12. Gifford's final, long-awaited updated edition of this work is entitled *The British Film Catalogue, Vol. 1: The Fiction Film, 1895–1994* (London: Fitzroy Dearborn, 2001; 3rd edn); there is now also a comparable exhaustive listing of non-fiction films of the era in a new companion volume compiled by Gifford, *The British Film Catalogue, Vol. 2: The Non-Fiction Film, 1895–1994* (London: Fitzroy Dearborn, 2001).
13. Bryony Dixon and Luke McKernan, eds, *British Silent Comedy Films: Viewing Copies in the National Film and Television Archive* (London: BFI Collections, 1999); Bryony Dixon and John Oliver, eds, *British Feature Films of the Twenties: Viewing Copies Held in the National Film and Television Archive* (London: BFI Collections, c.2000). The former is also available on the British Film Institute website (http://www.bfi.org.uk), which also provides details of other holdings in BFI Collections.
14. Elaine Burrows, Janet Moat, David Sharp and Linda Wood, eds, *The British Cinema Source Book: BFI Archive Viewing Copies and Library Materials* (London: BFI, 1995).
15. www.minos.bl.uk/collections/newspaper/cinema.html.
16. See *Kinematograph Weekly*, 13 November 1924; the *Bioscope*, 27 November 1924.

17. I am grateful to Stephen Bottomore for bringing this title to my attention.
18. See, for example, *Pictures and the Picturegoer*, 3 July 1915.
19. See *Picture Palace News*, 31 January 1916, 24 April 1916; the *Bioscope*, 4 August 1927, 3 April 1929. The results of the Bernstein questionnaires are also held at the BFI National Library.
20. James Donald, Anne Friedberg and Laura Marcus, eds, *Close Up: Cinema and Modernism* (London: Cassell, 1998).
21. I am grateful to Jamie Sexton for pointing this fact out to me.
22. Lore, *The Modern Photoplay and its Construction* (London and Sydney: Chapman & Dodd, 1923); Jackson, *Writing for the Screen* (London: A. & C. Black, 1929).
23. Harold Weston, *The Art of Photo-Play Writing* (London: McBride, Nast & Co., 1916), pp. 40–1.
24. Macbean, *Kinematograph Studio Technique* (London: Pitman's Technical Primer Series, 1922); Milton, *The Malady of the British Film* (London: Austin Leigh, 1925).
25. Cinema Commission, *The Cinema: Its Present Position and Future Possibilities, Being the Report of and Chief Evidence Taken by the Cinema Commission of Inquiry Instituted by the National Council of Public Morals* (London: Williams & Norgate, 1917). Although this report has always been fairly widely accessible, it is also now reprinted in full in volume 3 of Stephen Herbert's *A History of Early Film* (London: Routledge, 2000).
26. Cinema Commission of Inquiry, *The Cinema in Education* (London: George Allen & Unwin, 1925).
27. Mary C. Horne, *The Cinema in Education and as an Amusement and Entertainment* (London: The Challenge Press, 1919); Maurice Jackson Wrigley, *The Film, its Use in Popular Education* (London: Grafton, 1922); Frances Consitt, *The Value of Films in History Teaching* (London: Historical Association, 1931).
28. I am grateful to Christine Gledhill and Luke McKernan for indicating to me that there is also a thinly veiled autobiographical novel by Joan Morgan, which did go to press. *Camera!* (London: Chapman Hall, 1940) apparently offers a remarkably detailed and evocative picture of life in a British studio of the 1920s, coping with the difficulties of accomodating a German co-production and an attempt to develop a British sound system.
29. These resources also include the full history of accumulated memoranda behind all the major Acts of legislation relating to the film industry that were passed in this period. For a full list of such Acts, see James Curran and Vincent Porter (eds), *British Cinema History* (London: Weidenfeld & Nicholson, 1983), pp. 397–402.
30. I am grateful to Tony Fletcher and Jamie Sexton, respectively, for providing me with details of these collections.
31. Sarah Street, *British Cinema in Documents* (London: Routledge, 2000).

23

Bibliography: British Cinema before 1930

compiled by Andrew Higson, Michael Williams and Jo-Anne Blanco

Sections

1. Catalogues, guides, reference books, source books — 372
2. Autobiographies, reminiscences, biographies, interviews — 373
3. Material published in Britain before 1937 — 376
4. Material on British cinema up to 1914 — 380
5. Material on British cinema from the beginning of the First World War to the conversion to sound — 389
6. General histories of British cinema with material on the pre-1930 period — 396
7. Histories of regional cinema developments in Britain with material on the pre-1930 period — 399
8. Websites — 401
9. General works on silent cinema — 401
10. General works on film history with material on silent cinema — 404

1. Catalogues, Guides, Reference Books, Source Books

Ballantyne, James, ed., *Researcher's Guide to British Newsreels* (London: British Universities Film and Video Council, 1983; also vol. 2, 1988 and vol. 3, 1993).

Ballantyne, James, ed., *The Researcher's Guide: British Film, Television, Radio and Related Documentation Collections* (London: British Universities Film and Video Council, 2001).

Brown, Richard, 'The British Film Copyright Archive,' in Colin Harding and Simon Popple, eds, *In the Kingdom of Shadows: a Companion to Early Cinema* (London: Cygnus Arts, 1996).

Burrows, Elaine, Janet Moat, David Sharp and Linda Wood, *The British Cinema Source Book: BFI Archive Viewing Copies and Library Materials* (London: BFI, 1995).

Caughie, John, and Kevin Rockett, *The Companion to British and Irish Cinema* (London: Cassell/BFI, 1996).

Chittock, John, ed., *Researchers' Guide to John Grierson: Films, Reference Sources, Collections, Data* (London: Grierson Memorial Trust, 1990).

Dixon, Bryony and Luke McKernan, eds, *British Silent Comedy Films: Viewing Copies in the National Film and Television Archive* (London: BFI Collections, 1999).

Dixon, Bryony and John Oliver, eds, *British Feature Films of the Twenties: Viewing Copies Held in the National Film and Television Archive* (London: BFI Collections, *c*.2000).

Ellis, Jack C., *John Grierson: A Guide to References and Resources* (Boston: Boston University Press, 1986).

The Film Society Programmes, 1925–1939, introduced by Dr George Amberg (New York: Arno Press, 1972).

Gifford, Denis, *The Illustrated Who's Who in British Films* (London: B.T. Batsford, 1978).

Gifford, Denis, *British Animated Films, 1895–1985: A Filmography* (Jefferson, NC; London: McFarland, 1987).

Gifford, Denis, *Books and Plays in Films, 1896–1915: Literary, Theatrical and Artistic Sources of the First Twenty Years of Motion Pictures* (London and Jefferson, N.C.: Mansell, 1991).

Gifford, Denis, *Entertainers in British Films: A Century of Showbiz in the Cinema* (Trowbridge: Flicks Books, 1998).

Gifford, Denis, *The British Film Catalogue, Vol. 1: The Fiction Film, 1895–1994*, 3rd edn (London: Fitzroy Dearborn Publishers, 2001).

Gifford, Denis, *The British Film Catalogue, Vol. 2: The Non-Fiction Film, 1895–1994* (London: Fitzroy Dearborn Publishers, 2001).

Harding, Colin and Simon Popple, eds, *In the Kingdom of Shadows: A Companion to Early Cinema* (London: Cygnus Arts, 1996).

Hecht, Hermann, *Pre-Cinema History: An Encyclopaedia and Annotated*

Bibliography of the Moving Image before 1896 (London: Bowker-Saur/BFI, 1993).

Herbert, Stephen, ed., *A History of Early Film*, three vols. (London: Routledge, 2000).

Herbert, Stephen and Luke McKernan, eds, *A Who's Who of Victorian Cinema: A Worldwide Survey* (London: BFI, 1996).

Herbert, Stephen, Colin Harding and Simon Popple, eds, *Victorian Film Catalogues: A Facsimile Collection* (London: The Projection Box, 1996; reprinted from the W.D. Slade Archive).

Kirchner, Daniela, ed., *The Researcher's Guide to British Film and TV Collections* (London: British Universities Film and Video Council, 1997).

McKernan, Luke, *The Boer War: The Holdings of the National Film and Television Archive* (London: National Film and Television Archive, 1997; 2nd edn 1999).

Magliozzi, Ronald S., *Treasures from the Film Archives: a Catalogue of Short Silent Fiction Films Held by FIAF Archives* (Metuchen: Scarecrow Press, 1988).

Palmer, Scott, *A Who's Who of British Film Actors* (Metuchen, NJ/London: The Scarecrow Press, 1981).

Palmer, Scott, *British Film Actors' Credits, 1895–1987* (Jefferson, NC/London: McFarland and Co., 1988).

Picturegoer's Who's Who and Encyclopaedia of the Screen Today, The (London: Odhams, 1933).

Salmi, Markku, ed., *Catalogue of Stills, Posters and Designs* (London: BFI, 1982).

Sloan, Jane, *Alfred Hitchcock, A Filmography and Bibliography* (Berkeley: University of California Press, 1995).

Smither, Roger, ed., *Imperial War Museum Film Catalogue Volume One: The First World War Archive* (Trowbridge: Flicks Books, 1994).

Stewart, Heather, ed., *Early and Silent Cinema: A Source Book* (London: BFI, 1996).

Street, Sarah, *British Cinema in Documents* (London: Routledge, 2000).

Winchester, Clarence, ed., *The World Film Encyclopaedia: A Universal Screen Guide* (London: The Amalgamated Press, 1933).

Wood, Linda, *British Films, 1927–1939* (London: BFI, 1986).

2. Autobiographies, Reminiscences, Biographies, Interviews

Allister, Ray, *Friese-Greene: Close-up of an Inventor* (London: Marsland Publications, 1948).

Anthony, Barry, 'Alfred Collins: Britain's Forgotten Filmmaker,' in Alan Burton and Laraine Porter, eds, *Pimple, Pranks and Pratfalls: British Film Comedy Before 1930* (Trowbridge: Flicks Books, 2000), pp. 14–16.

Arliss, George, *On the Stage* (London: John Murray, 1928).

Aylott, Dave, 'Reminiscences of a Showman,' *Cinema Studies*, no. 2/1, June 1965, pp. 3–6.

Balcon, Michael, *Michael Balcon Presents . . . A Lifetime in Films* (London: Hutchinson, 1969).

Benson, Frank, *My Memoirs* (London: Ernest Benn, 1930).

Bird, John H., *Cinema Parade: Fifty Years of Film Shows* (Birmingham: Cornish Brothers Ltd., c.1946).

Bottomore, Stephen, 'Joseph Rosenthal: The Most Glorious Profession,' *Sight and Sound*, vol. 52, no. 4, Autumn 1983, pp. 260–5.

Bouchier, Chili, *Shooting Star: The Last of the Silent Film Stars* (London: Atlantis, 1996).

Bromhead, Alfred Claude, 'Reminiscences of the British Film Trade,' *Proceedings of the British Kinematograph Society*, no. 21, December 1933.

Brown, Geoff, *Walter Forde* (London, 1973).

Brunel, Adrian, *Nice Work: The Story of Thirty Years in British Film Production* (London: Forbes Robertson, 1949).

Bryher, *The Heart to Artemis: A Writer's Memoirs* (London: Collins, 1963).

Chaplin, Charles, *My Wonderful Visit* (London: Hurst and Blocket, 1922).

Chaplin, Charles, *My Autobiography* (London: Bodley Head, 1964).

Collier, Constance, *Harlequinade* (London: John Lane, 1929).

Crespinel, William T., 'Pioneering in Colour Motion Pictures with William T. Crespinel,' in *Film History*, vol. 12, no. 1, 2000, pp. 57–71.

Curtis, James, *James Whale* (London, Metuchen: The Scarecrow Press, 1982).

Danischewsky, Monja, *Michael Balcon's 25 Years in Films* (London: World Film Publications, 1947).

Dean, Basil, *Mind's Eye: An Autobiography, 1927–1972* (London: Hutchinson, 1970).

Fletcher, Tony and Ronald Grant, 'A Lowland Cinderella: Joan Morgan's Silent Career, 1912–1929,' in *Griffithiana*, no. 65, October 1999, pp. 48–87.

Gottlieb, Sidney, ed., *Hitchcock on Hitchcock* (London: Faber and Faber, 1995).

Hardy, Forsyth, *John Grierson: A Documentary Biography* (London: Faber and Faber, 1979).

Henson, Leslie, *My Laugh-story: The Story of My Life up to Date* (London: Hodder and Stoughton, 1926).

Hepworth, Cecil, *Came the Dawn: Memories of a Film Pioneer* (London: Phoenix House, 1951).

Hepworth, Cecil, 'Those Were the Days,' in Roger Manvell, ed., *The Penguin Film Review*, no. 6 (Harmondsworth: Penguin: 1948), pp. 33–9.

Lang, Matheson, *Mr Wu Looks Back: Thoughts and Memories* (London: S. Paul, 1941).

Lejeune, Caroline A., *Thank You for Having Me* (London: Hutchinson, 1964).

McKernan, Luke, ed., *A Yank in Britain: The Lost Memoirs of Charles Urban, Film Pioneer* (London: The Projection Box, 1999).

Malins, Geoffrey H., edited by Low Warren, *How I Filmed the War: a Record of the Extraordinary Experiences of the Man who Filmed the Great Somme Battles etc.* (London: Imperial War Museum, Department of Printed Books, 1993; first published by Herbert Jenkins: London, 1919).

Montagu, Ivor, *The Youngest Son: Autobiographical Sketches* (London: Lawrence and Wishart, 1970).

Montagu, Ivor, 'Old Man's Mumble: Reflections on a Semi-centenary,' *Sight and Sound*, vol. 44, no. 4, Winter 1975/76, pp. 220–4, 247.

Moorehead, Caroline, *Sidney Bernstein: A Biography* (London: Jonathan Cape, 1984).

Morley, Sheridan, *Gladys Cooper: A Biography* (London: Heinemann, 1979).

Nares, Owen, *Myself and Some Others: Pure Egotism* (London: Duckworth, 1925).

Noble, Peter, *Ivor Novello: Man of the Theatre* (London, New York, Sydney, Toronto: White Lion Publishers Limited, 1975).

Paul, Robert W., Cecil Hepworth and W. G. Barker, 'Before 1910: Kinematograph Experiences,' *Proceedings of the British Kinematograph Society*, no. 38, 1936, pp. 2–16.

Pearson, George, 'Memories—Into the Twilight Twenties, and What Then?' *Royal Academy Bulletin*, no. 13, (London: 1951).

Pearson, George, *Flashback: The Autobiography of a British Film-maker* (London: George Allen and Unwin, 1957).

Peet, Stephen, 'George Pearson and His "Two Minutes Silence," ' in Alan Burton and Laraine Porter, eds, *The Showman, the Spectacle and the Two-Minute Silence: Performing British Cinema Before 1930* (Trowbridge: Flicks Books, 2001), pp. 73–5.

Ponting, Herbert, *The Great White South; or With Scott in the Antarctic* (London: Duckworth and Co., 1921).

Powell, Michael, *A Life in Movies: An Autobiography* (London: Heinemann, 1986).

Russell Taylor, John, *Hitch: The Life and Work of Alfred Hitchcock* (London: Faber and Faber, 1978).

Spoto, Donald, *The Life of Alfred Hitchcock: The Dark Side of Genius* (London: Collins, 1983).

Thomas, Lowell, *Sir Hubert Wilkins: His World of Adventure* (London: Arthur Baker, 1961/62).

Truffaut, François, *Hitchcock* (London: Secker and Warburg, 1968).

Wilcox, Herbert, *Twenty-five Thousand Sunsets: The Autobiography of Herbert Wilcox* (London: The Bodley Head, 1967).

Wood, Linda, *The Commercial Imperative in the British Film Industry: Maurice Elvey, a Case Study* (London: BFI, 1987).

3. Material Published in Britain Before 1937

Allan, G.A.T., *The Nurserymatograph, by a Lawyer, with Sillystrations by a Person* (London, 1921).

Allen, Gertrude M., *How to Write a Film Story* (London: George Allen and Unwin, 1926).

Anon., *The Modern Electric Picture Theatre: Its Popularity and Its Commercial Aspect* (London: Premier Electric Theatres Ltd, *c.*1910).

Anon., *The Modern Bioscope Operator* (London: Ganes, 1910; revised edn. 1911).

Anon., *How to Run a Picture Theatre* (London: The Kinematograph Weekly, *c.*1911).

Anon., *International Kinematograph Exhibition and Conference* (London: The Oldfield Advertising Co., 1913).

Anon., *Cinema Acting as a Profession* (London: G. Charisse and Sons, 1915).

Anon., *How to Write Moving Picture Plays* (Hull: Success School, 1915).

Anon., *A Guide to Cinema Acting and Course of Training* (London: W. and G. Foyle, 1920).

Anon. ('A Cinema Actor'), *Film-Land: How to Get There* (London: Reeder and Walsh, 1921).

Ball, Eustace Hale, *Cinema Plays: How to Write Them, How to Sell Them* (London: Stanley Paul and Co., 1917).

Bamburgh, Lilian, *Film Acting as a Career* (London: Foulsham's Utility Series, 1929).

Barber, James W., *The Bioscope Electrician's Handbook* (London: 1911–16).

Barkas, Natalie, *Behind the Camera* (London: Geoffrey Bles, 1934).

Barry, Iris, *Let's Go To The Movies* (New York: Arno Press, 1972; first published 1926).

Bennett, Colin N., *The Handbook of Kinematography: The History, Theory and Practice of Motion Photography and Projection* (London: The Kinematograph Weekly, 1911; new edition, 1913, reprinted in Stephen Herbert, ed., *A History of Early Film*, vol. 2, London: Routledge, 2000).

Bennett, Colin N., *The Guide to Kinematography* (London: E.T. Heron, 1917).

Betts, Ernest, *Heraclitus, or the Future of Film* (London: Kegan Paul, 1928).

Birkenhead Vigilance Committee, *The Cinema and the Child: a Report of Investigations (June–October 1931)* (Birkenhead: The Committee, 1931).

Blakeston, Oswell, *Through a Yellow Glass: A Study of Film Technique* (London: POOL, 1928).

Boughey, Davidson, *The Film Industry* (London: Pitman's Common Commodities and Industries, 1921).

Brunel, Adrian, *Filmcraft: The Art of Picture Production* (London: George Newnes, 1933).

Buchanan, Andrew, *Films, The Way of the Cinema* (London: Pitman, 1932).

Buckle, Gerard Ford, *The Mind and the Film: A Treatise on the Psychological Factors in the Film* (London: George Routledge and Sons, 1926).

Buckley, Kevin P., *The Orchestral and Cinema Organist* (London: Hawkes and Son, 1923).

Camiller, E., *How to Get Film Work* (London: Reeder and Walsh, 1921).

Carter, Huntley, *New Spirit in the Cinema* (London: Harold Shaylor, 1930).

Causton, Bernard and Gordon G. Young, *Keeping it Dark: or the Censor's Handbook* (London: Mandrake Press, 1930).

Cinema Commission of Inquiry, *The Cinema: its Present Position and Future Possibilities, Being the Report of and Chief Evidence Taken by the Cinema Commission of Inquiry Instituted by the National Council of Public Morals* (London: Williams and Norgate, 1917; reprinted in Stephen Herbert, ed., *A History of Early Film*, vol. 3, London: Routledge, 2000).

Cinema Commission of Inquiry (National Council of Public Morals), *The Cinema in Education* (London: George Allen and Unwin, 1925).

Consitt, Frances, *The Value of Films in History Teaching* (London: Historical Association, 1931).

Dell, Drycot Montagu, *Cinema Stars: More than 200 Photographs of the Most Famous Film Players of the World* (London: Fleetway House, 1915).

Dench, E.A., *Playwriting for the Cinema* (London: Adam and Charles Black, 1914).

Dickinson, Harold, *How to Write a Picture Play* (Hythe: New Kinema Publishing Co., 1914).

Dickson, William Kennedy-Laurie, *The Biograph in Battle* (Trowbridge: Flicks Books, 1997; first published 1901).

Donaldson, L., *Cinematography for Amateurs* (London: Iliffe, 1916).

Elliot, Eric, *Anatomy of Motion Picture Art* (London: POOL, 1928).

Elliott, William J., *How to Become a Film Actor* (London: Picture Palace News Co., 1917).

Fawcett, L'Estrange, *Films: Facts and Forecasts* (London: Geoffrey Bles, 1927).

Federation of British Industries, *The Activities of the British Film Industry, Presented to the Delegates to the Monetary and Economic Conference of the Federation of British Industries, London 12 July 1933* (London: Federation of British Industries, 1933).

Field, Mary and Percy Smith, *Secrets of Nature* (London: Faber and Faber, 1934).

Forman, H.J., *Our Movie-Made Children* (London: Macmillan, 1933).

Foss, Kenelm, Eliot Stannard, Aurele Sydney, Stewart Rome, Violet Hopson, et al., *Cinema, A Practical Course in Ten Lessons* (London: Standard Art Book Company, 1920).

Furniss, Harry, *Our Lady Cinema. How and Why I went into the Photo-play World and What I Found There* (Bristol: J.W. Arrowsmith, 1914).

Furse, Sir William, 'The Imperial Institute and the Films of the Empire Marketing Board,' *Sight and Sound*, vol. 2, no. 7, Autumn 1933, pp. 78–9.

Gehrts, Emma Auguste (Meg), *A Camera Actress in the Wilds of Togoland* (London: Seely, Service and Co., 1915).

Hallen, Russell, *The Way to the Studio [Advice to Cinema Actors]* (London: Wardour Publishing Co., 1926).

Hanson, Albert, *Hanson Method for Cinema Orchestras* (Leeds: no publisher listed, 1921).

Hepworth, Cecil Milton, *Animated Photography. The ABC of the Cinematograph* (London: The Amateur Photographer's Library, 1897; 2nd edn 1900).

Herbert, Stephen, Colin Harding and Simon Popple, eds, *Victorian Film Catalogues: A Facsimile Collection* (London: The Projection Box, 1996; reprinted from the W.D. Slade Archive).

Herbert, Stephen, ed., *A History of Early Film*, three vols (London: Routledge, 2000).

Herring, Robert, *Films of the Year, 1927–1928* (London: The Studio, 1928).

Hopwood, Henry, *Living Pictures* (London: The Optician and Photographic Trades Review, 1899/1915).

Horne, Mary C., *The Cinema in Education and as an Amusement and Entertainment* (London: The Challenge Press, 1919).

Hunter, William, *Scrutiny of the Cinema* (London: Wishart and Co., 1932).

Ibbetson, W.S., *The Kinema Operator's Handbook, Theory and Practice* (London: E. and F. Spon, 1921).

Jackson, Arrar, *Writing for the Screen* (London: A. and C. Black, 1929).

Jones, Bernard E., *The Cinematograph Book: A Complete Practical Guide to the Taking and Projecting of Motion Pictures* (London: Cassell and Co., 1915 and 1920 editions).

Kirkland, Charles H., *Photoplay Writing For Profit* (Hull: C.H. Kirkland, 1918).

Knowles, Dorothy, *The Censor, the Drama and the Film, 1900–1934* (London: Allen and Unwin, 1934).

Lambert, Richard Stanton, ed., *For Film-goers Only* (London: British Institute of Adult Education, 1934).

Lejeune, C.A., *Cinema* (London: Alexander Maclehouse, 1931).

Lescarboura, A. C., *The Cinema Handbook* (London: Sampson Low and Co., 1922).

Lomas, Harold M., *Picture Play Photography* (London: H. Ganes and Co., 1914).

Lore, Colden, *The Modern Photoplay, and its Construction* (London, Sydney: Chapman and Dodd, 1923).

MacBean, L.C., *Kinematograph Studio Technique* (London: Pitman's Technical Primer Series, 1922).

Macneil, Duncan, *Is the Cinema Commendable?* (London: Pickering and Inglis, 1920).

Messel, Rudolf, *This Film Business* (London: Ernest Benn, 1928).

Milton, Meyrick, *The Malady of the British Film: Its Cause and Cure* (London: Austin Leigh, 1925).

Montagu, Ivor, *The Political Censorship of Films* (London: Victor Gollancz, 1929).

Muddle, E.J., *Picture Plays and How to Write Them* (London, 1911).

Platt, Agnes, *Practical Hints on Acting for the Cinema* (London: Stanley Paul and Co., 1921).

Pudovkin, Vsevolod I., *On Film Technique: Three Essays and an Address*, translated and annotated by Ivor Montagu (London: Victor Gollancz, 1929).

Pyke, Montagu A., *Focussing the Universe* (London: Waterlow Bros and Layton, 1910).

Ramsaye, Terry, *A Million and One Nights* (New York: Simon and Schuster 1986; first published 1926).

Reed, Langford, *The Picture Play* (London: Standard Art Book Company, 1920).

Reed, Langford and Hetty Spiers, *Who's Who in Filmland* (London: 1928).

Rotha, Paul, *The Film Till Now* (London: Jonathan Cape, 1930; and subsequent editions).

Rotha, Paul, *Celluloid: The Film Today* (London: Longmans, 1931).

Settle, Alfred Towers and Frank Henry John Baber, *The Law of Public Entertainments: Theatres, Music and Dancing, Stage Plays, Cinematographs . . .* (London: Sweet and Maxwell, 1915).

Skirrow, William Waite, *The Kinema Operator's Handbook* (London: E. and F.N. Spon, 1921).

Steer, Valentia, *The Romance of the Cinema: A Short Record of the Development of the Most Popular Form of Amusement of the Day* (London: C.A. Pearson, 1913).

Steer, Valentia, *The Secrets of the Cinema* (London: C.A. Pearson, 1920).

Talbot, Frederick A., *Moving Pictures: How They are Made and Worked* (London: William Heinemann, 1912; revised edn 1923).

Talbot, Frederick A., *Practical Cinematography and its Applications* (London: William Heinemann; Philadelphia: Lippincott, 1913).

Tyacke, George W., *Playing to Pictures: A Guide for Pianists and Conductors of Motion Picture Theatres* (London: The Kinematograph and Lantern Weekly, 1912; 2nd edn E.T. Heron, 1914).

Urban, Charles, *The Cinematograph in Science, Education, and Matters of State* (London: Charles Urban Trading Company, 1907).

Warren, Low, *The Showman's Advertising Book* (London: E.T. Heron and Co., Kine Weekly, 1914).

Warren, Low, *The Film Game* (London: T. Werner Laurie, 1937).

Weston, Harold, *The Art of Photoplay-Writing* (London, McBride, Nast and Company, 1916).

White, Eric Walter, *Parnassus to Let: An Essay About Rhythm in the Films* (London: L. and V. Woolf, 1928).

Wood, Leslie, *Romance of the Movies* (London: Heinemann, 1937).

Woolf, Virginia, 'The Cinema,' in Virginia Woolf, *The Captain's Death Bed and Other Essays* (London: Hogarth Press, 1950; first published 1926).

Wrigley, Maurice Jackson, *The Film, Its Use in Popular Education* (London: Grafton, 1922).

4. Material on British Cinema up to 1914

Allister, Ray, *Friese-Greene: Close-up of an Inventor* (London: Marsland Publications, 1948).

Anthony, Barry, 'Shadows of Early Films', *Sight and Sound*, vol. 59, no. 3, Summer 1990, pp. 194–7.

Anthony, Barry, *The Kinora: Motion Pictures For the Home, 1896–1914* (London: The Projection Box, 1996).

Anthony, Barry, 'Disreputable Ghosts: British Synchronised Sound Films Before the First World War,' in Alan Burton and Laraine Porter, eds, *The Showman, the Spectacle and the Two-Minute Silence: Performing British Cinema Before 1930* (Trowbridge: Flicks Books, 2001), pp. 12–20.

Barnes, John, *The Beginnings of the Cinema in England: Volume One, 1894–1896* (Exeter: University of Exeter Press, 1998, revised and enlarged edition; first published 1976, as *The Beginnings of The Cinema in Britain*).

Barnes, John, *The Beginnings of the Cinema in England: Volume Two, 1897* (Exeter: University of Exeter Press, 1996; first published 1983, as *The Rise of the Cinema in Britain*).

Barnes, John, *The Beginnings of the Cinema in England: Volume Three, 1898* (Exeter: University of Exeter Press, 1996; first published 1988, as *Pioneers of the British Cinema*).

Barnes, John, *The Beginnings of the Cinema in England: Volume Four, 1899* (Exeter: University of Exeter Press, 1996; first published 1992, as *Filming The Boer War*).

Barnes, John, *The Beginnings of the Cinema in England: Volume Five, 1900* (Exeter: University of Exeter Press, 1997).

Barr, Charles, 'Before *Blackmail*: British Silent Cinema,' in Robert Murphy, ed., *The British Cinema Book* (London: BFI, 1997), pp. 5–16.

Berry, David, 'William Haggar: Film Pioneer, Actor and Showman,' in Linda Fitzsimmons and Sarah Street, eds, *Moving Performance: British Stage and Screen, 1890s–1920s* (Trowbridge: Flicks Books, 2000), pp. 112–22.

Berry, David, 'William Haggar and *The Sheep Stealer* (1908),' in Alan Burton and Laraine Porter, eds, *The Showman, the Spectacle and the Two-Minute*

Silence: Performing British Cinema Before 1930 (Trowbridge: Flicks Books, 2001), pp. 48–52.

Berry, David, and Simon Horrocks, eds, *David Lloyd George: The Movie Mystery* (Cardiff: University of Wales Press, 1998).

Bottomore, Stephen, 'Frederick Villiers: War Correspondent,' *Sight and Sound*, vol. 49, no. 4, Autumn 1980, pp. 250–5.

Bottomore, Stephen, ' "The Collection of Rubbish." Animatographs, Archives and Arguments: London, 1896–97,' *Film History*, vol. 7, no. 3, 1987, pp. 291–7.

Bottomore, Stephen, 'Shots in the Dark: The Real Origins of Film Editing,' *Sight and Sound*, vol. 57, no. 3, Summer 1988, pp. 200–4.

Bottomore, Stephen, 'An Exotic Plant in Unfriendly Soil: British Cinema in 1913,' *Griffithiana*, no. 5, May 1994, pp. 87–95.

Bottomore, Stephen, 'The Biograph in Battle,' in Karel Dibbets and Bert Hogenkamp, eds, *Film and the First World War* (Amsterdam: Amsterdam University Press, 1995), pp. 28–35.

Bottomore, Stephen, ' "She's Just Like My Granny! Where's Her Crown?" Monarchs and Movies, 1896–1916,' in John Fullerton, ed., *Celebrating 1895: The Centenary of Cinema* (Sydney: John Libbey, 1998), pp. 172–81.

Bottomore, Stephen, 'Will Day: The Story of Rediscovery,' *Film Studies*, no. 1, Spring 1999, pp. 81–91.

Brown, Geoff, ' "Sister of the Stage": British Film and British Theatre,' in Charles Barr, ed., *All Our Yesterdays: 90 Years of British Cinema* (London, BFI, 1986), pp. 143–67.

Brown, Richard, 'England's First Cinema,' *British Journal of Photography*, 24 June 1977.

Brown, Richard, 'England's First Film Shows,' *British Journal of Photography*, 31 March and 7 April 1977.

Brown, Richard, 'Marketing the Cinematographe in Britain,' in Christopher Williams, ed., *Cinema: the Beginnings and the Future: Essays Marking the Centenary of the First Film Show Projected to a Paying Audience in Britain* (London: University of Westminster Press, 1996), pp. 63–71.

Brown, Richard, ' "England is not Big Enough . . ." American Rivalry in the Early English Film Business: The case of Warwick v Urban,' in *Film History*, vol. 10, no. 1, 1998, pp. 21–34.

Brown, Richard, and Barry Anthony, *A Victorian Film Enterprise: The History of the British Mutoscope and Biograph Company* (Trowbridge: Flicks Books, 1999).

Burrows, Jonathan, *'The Whole English Stage to be Seen for Sixpence!': Theatrical Actors and Acting Styles in the British Cinema, 1908–1918* (Norwich: unpublished Ph.D. thesis, University of East Anglia, 2000).

Burton, Alan, 'The Emergence of an Alternative Film Culture: Film and the British Consumer Co-operative Movement before 1920,' *Film History*, vol. 8, no. 4, 1996, pp. 446–57.

Burton, Alan, ' "To Gain the Whole World and Lose Our Soul": Visual Spectacle and the Politics of Working-class Consumption before 1914,' in Simon Popple and Vanessa Toulmin, eds, *Visual Delights: Essays on the Popular and Projected Image in the 19th Century* (Trowbridge: Flicks Books, 2001).

Burton, Alan, and Laraine Porter, eds, *Pimple, Pranks and Pratfalls: British Film Comedy Before 1930* (Trowbridge: Flicks Books, 2000).

Burton, Alan, and Laraine Porter, eds, *The Showman, the Spectacle and the Two-Minute Silence: Performing British Cinema Before 1930* (Trowbridge: Flicks Books, 2001).

Burton, Alan, and Laraine Porter, eds, *Crossing the Pond: Anglo-American Film Relations before 1930* (Trowbridge: Flicks Books, 2002).

Chanan, Michael, *The Dream That Kicks: The Prehistory and Early Years of Cinema in Britain* (London: Routledge and Kegan Paul, 1980; revised edn, 1996).

Chanan, Michael, 'The Emergence of an Industry,' in James Curran and Vincent Porter, eds, *British Cinema History* (London: Weidenfeld and Nicolson, 1983), pp. 39–58.

Clay, Andrew, 'True Crime? Charles Peace and the British Crime Film,' in Linda Fitzsimmons and Sarah Street, eds, *Moving Performance: British Stage and Screen, 1890s–1920s* (Trowbridge: Flicks Books, 2000), pp. 123–36.

Coe, Brian, 'William Friese Green and the Origins of Cinematography,' in three parts, *Screen*, vol. 10, no. 2, pp. 25–41; no. 3, pp. 72–83; and nos. 4–5, pp. 129–47.

Collick, John, 'Silent Shakespeare and British Cinema,' from his *Shakespeare, Cinema and Society* (Manchester: Manchester University Press, 1989) pp. 33-57.

Crangle, Richard, 'Saturday Night at the X-Rays—The Moving Picture and "The New Photography" in Britain, 1896,' in John Fullerton, ed., *Celebrating 1895: The Centenary of Cinema* (Sydney: John Libbey, 1998), pp. 138–44.

Dinsmore, Uma, 'Films at Home: Putting Domestic Audiences in the Picture,' in Linda Fitzsimmons and Sarah Street, eds, *Moving Performance: British Stage and Screen, 1890s–1920s* (Trowbridge: Flicks Books, 2000), pp. 137–50.

East, John M., 'The Codmans,' *The Silent Picture*, no. 13, Winter–Spring 1972, pp. 24–6.

East, John M., 'Lancelot Speed,' in F. Maurice Speed, ed., *Film Review 1972–73* (London: W.H. Allen, 1972), pp. 39–42.

East, John M., 'The Forgotten Pioneer,' in F. Maurice Speed, ed., *Film Review 1973–74* (London: W.H. Allen, 1973), pp. 73–8.

East, John M., 'A Film Pioneer,' in F. Maurice Speed, ed., *Film Review 1974–75* (London: W.H. Allen, 1974), pp. 21–8.

East, John M., 'We Saw The Dawn', in F. Maurice Speed, ed., *Film Review 1976–77* (London: W.H. Allen, 1976), pp. 59–65.

Fitzsimmons, Linda, and Sarah Street, *Moving Performance: British Stage and Screen, 1890s–1920s* (Trowbridge: Flicks Books, 2000).

Fletcher, Tony, 'British Film Production in 1913,' *Griffithiana*, no. 5, May 1994, pp. 96–101.

Fletcher, Tony, 'British Comedy Films in the Silent Period: A Production Survey,' in Alan Burton and Laraine Porter, eds, *Pimple, Pranks and Pratfalls: British Film Comedy Before 1930* (Trowbridge: Flicks Books, 2000), pp. 10–13.

Fletcher, Tony, 'Sound Before *Blackmail* (1929),' in Alan Burton and Laraine Porter, eds, *The Showman, the Spectacle and the Two-Minute Silence: Performing British Cinema Before 1930* (Trowbridge: Flicks Books, 2001), pp. 6–11.

Gifford, Denis, 'Fitz: The Old Man of the Screen,' in Charles Barr, ed., *All Our Yesterdays: 90 Years of British Cinema* (London: BFI, 1986), pp. 314–20.

Gray, Frank, ed., *The Hove Pioneers and the Arrival of Cinema* (Brighton: University of Brighton, Faculty of Art, Design and Humanities, 1996).

Gray, Frank, 'Smith the Showman: The Early Years of George Albert Smith,' in *Film History*, vol. 10, no. 1, 1998, pp. 8–20.

Gray, Frank, 'James Williamson's "Composed Picture": Attack on a China Mission—Bluejackets to the Rescue (1900),' in John Fullerton, ed., *Celebrating 1895, The Centenary of Cinema* (Sydney: John Libbey, 1998), pp. 203–11.

Gray, Frank, 'Smith versus Melbourne-Cooper: History and Counter-History,' in *Film History*, vol. 11, no. 3, 1999, pp. 246–61.

Gray, Frank, 'George Albert Smith's Comedies of 1897,' in Alan Burton and Laraine Porter, eds, *Pimple, Pranks and Pratfalls: British Film Comedy Before 1930* (Trowbridge: Flicks Books, 2000), pp. 17–23.

Gray, Frank, 'George Albert Smith's Visions and Transformations: The Films of 1898,' in Simon Popple and Vanessa Toulmin, eds, *Visual Delights: Essays on the Popular and Projected Image in the 19th Century* (Trowbridge: Flicks Books, 2001), pp. 170–80.

Hammond, Michael, ' "A Soul Stirring Appeal to Every Briton": The Reception of Birth of a Nation in Britain (1915–1916),' *Film History*, vol. 11, no. 3, 1999, pp. 353–70.

Harding, Colin, and Simon Popple, eds, *In the Kingdom of Shadows: a Companion to Early Cinema* (London: Cygnus Arts, 1996).

Hawkridge, John, 'British Cinema from Hepworth to Hitchcock,' in Geoffrey Nowell-Smith, ed., *The Oxford History of World Cinema* (Oxford: Oxford University Press, 1996), pp. 130–6.

Heard, Mervyn, ' "Come in Please, Come Out Pleased": The Development of British Fairground Bioscope Presentation and Performance,' in Linda

Fitzsimmons and Sarah Street, eds, *Moving Performance: British Stage and Screen, 1890s–1920s* (Trowbridge: Flicks Books, 2000), pp. 101–11.

Hepworth, Cecil, *Came The Dawn: Memories of a Film Pioneer* (London: Phoenix House, 1951).

Herbert, Stephen, *Theodore Brown's Magic Pictures* (London: The Projection Box, 1997).

Herbert, Stephen, *Industry, Liberty, and a Vision . . . Wordsworth Donisthorpe's Kinesigraph* (London: The Projection Box, 1998).

Herbert, Stephen, ed., *A History of Early Film*, three vols. (London: Routledge, 2000).

Higson, Andrew, 'Heritage Discourses and British Cinema Before 1920,' in John Fullerton, ed., *Celebrating 1895: Proceedings of the International Conference on Film Before 1920* (Sydney: John Libbey, 1998), pp. 182–9.

Hiley, Nicholas, 'The British Cinema Auditorium,' in Karel Dibbets and Bert Hogenkamp, eds, *Film and the First World War* (Amsterdam: Amsterdam University Press, 1994), pp. 160–70.

Hiley, Nicholas, 'Fifteen Questions about the Early Film Audience,' in Daan Hertogs and Nico de Klerk, eds, *Uncharted Territories: Essays on Early Non-Fiction Films* (Amsterdam: Stichting Nederlands Filmmuseum, 1997), pp. 105–18.

Hiley, Nicholas, 'At the Picture Palace: The British Cinema Audience, 1895–1920,' in John Fullerton, ed., *Celebrating 1895: The Centenary of Cinema* (Sydney: John Libbey, 1998), pp. 96–103.

Hiley, Nicholas, ' "No mixed bathing": the creation of the British Board of Film Censors in 1913,' in Ian Conrich and Julian Petley, eds, *Journal of Popular British Cinema*, no. 3, 2000, pp. 5–19.

Honri, Baynham, 'From Glasshouse to Gimmick Palace,' *Kinematograph Weekly*, 3 May 1956, pp. 47, 49 and 51.

Honri, Baynham, 'Milestones in Motion Picture Production,' *British Kinematography, Sound and Television Journal*, vo. 51, no. 4, April 1969, pp. 94–104.

Honri, Baynham, 'The Samuelson Saga,' *The Silent Picture*, no. 5, Winter 1969–70, pp. 3–6.

Honri, Baynham, 'Cecil M. Hepworth—his Studios and Techniques,' *British Journal of Photography*, 15 January 1971, p. 48.

Hunningher, Joost, 'Premiere on Regent Street,' in Christopher Williams, ed., *Cinema: the Beginnings and the Future* (London: University of Westminster Press, 1996), pp. 41–54.

Kember, Joe, 'Face to Face: The Facial Expressions Genre in Early British Film,' in Alan Burton and Laraine Porter, eds, *The Showman, the Spectacle and the Two-Minute Silence: Performing British Cinema Before 1930* (Trowbridge: Flicks Books, 2001), pp. 28–39.

Kember, Joe, ' "It Was Not the Show, It Was the Tale that You Told": Film Lecturing and Showmanship on the British Fairground,' in Simon

Popple and Vanessa Toulmin, eds, *Visual Delights: Essays on the Popular and Projected Image in the 19th Century* (Trowbridge: Flicks Books, 2001), pp. 61–70.

Kindem, Gorham, 'The Demise of Kinemacolor: Technological, Legal, Economic, and Aesthetic Problems in Early Cinema History,' *Cinema Journal*, no. 2, Spring 1981, pp. 3–13.

Kuhn, Annette, *Cinema, Censorship and Sexuality, 1909–1925* (London/New York: Routledge, 1988).

Lange-Fuchs, Hauke, *Birt Acres* (Kiel: Walter G. Mühlau, 1987).

Lange-Fuchs, Hauke, *Der Kaiser, der Kanal und die Kinematographie: Begleitheft zur Ausstellung im Landesarchiv Schleswig-Holstein, Birt Acres—100 Jahre Film in Schleswig-Holstein* (Schleswig: Landesarchiv Schleswig-Holstein, 1995).

Low, Rachael, *The History of the British Film, 1906–1914* (London: Allen and Unwin, 1949; London: Routledge, 1997).

Low, Rachael, and Roger Manvell, *The History of the British Film, 1896–1906* (London: Allen and Unwin, 1948; London: Routledge, 1997).

Lynch, Dennis, 'The Worst Location in the World: Herbert G. Ponting in the Antarctic,' *Film History*, vol. 3, 1989, pp. 291–306.

McKernan, Luke, 'Sport and the First Films,' in Christopher Williams, ed., *Cinema: the Beginnings and the Future* (London: University of Westminster Press, 1996), pp. 107–16.

McKernan, Luke, 'A Scene—*King John*—Now Playing at Her Majesties Theatre,' in Linda Fitzsimmons and Sarah Street, eds, *Moving Performance: British Stage and Screen, 1890s–1920s* (Trowbridge: Flicks, 2000), pp. 56–68.

McKernan, Luke, 'How to Make *Ben-Hur* Look Like an Epic,' in Alan Burton and Laraine Porter, eds, *Pimple, Pranks and Pratfalls: British Film Comedy Before 1930* (Trowbridge: Flicks Books, 2000), pp. 7–9.

McKernan, Luke, ' "That Slick Salesman in the Silk Hat": Charles Urban Arrives in Britain,' in Simon Popple and Vanessa Toulmin, eds, *Visual Delights: Essays on the Popular and Projected Image in the 19th Century* (Trowbridge: Flicks Books, 2001), pp. 116–26.

Mayer, David, 'Eighteen Minutes,' in Alan Burton and Laraine Porter, eds, *The Showman, the Spectacle and the Two-Minute Silence: Performing British Cinema Before 1930* (Trowbridge: Flicks Books, 2001), pp. 21–7.

Medhurst, Andy, 'Music Hall and British Cinema,' in Charles Barr, ed., *All Our Yesterdays: 90 Years of British Cinema* (London: BFI, 1986), pp. 168–88.

Monaghan, Garrett, 'Performing the Passions: Comic Themes in the Films of George Albert Smith,' in Alan Burton and Laraine Porter, eds, *Pimples, Pranks and Pratfalls: British Film Comedy Before 1930* (Trowbridge: Flicks Books), pp. 24–32.

Montgomery, John, *Comedy Films 1894–1954* (London: George Allen and Unwin, 1954).

Newey, Katherine, 'Women and Early British Film: Finding a Screen of Her Own,' in Linda Fitzsimmons and Sarah Street, eds, *Moving Performance: British Stage and Screen, 1890s–1920s* (Trowbridge: Flicks Books, 2000), pp. 151–65.

Newport, Raymond, 'The Motion Picture Experiments of John Arthur Roebuck Rudge,' *New Magic Lantern Journal*, vol. 8, no. 2, October 1997, pp. 1–3.

Pitt, Peter, 'The Oldest Studio,' *Films and Filming*, no. 342, March 1983, pp. 29–31.

Popple, Simon, 'The Diffuse Beam: Cinema and Change,' in Christopher Williams, ed., *Cinema: the Beginnings and the Future* (London: University of Westminster Press, 1996), pp. 97–106.

Popple, Simon, ' "Cinema Wasn't Invented, It Growed": Technological Film Historiography Before 1913,' in John Fullerton, ed., *Celebrating 1895: The Centenary of Cinema* (Sydney: John Libbey, 1998), pp. 19–26.

Popple, Simon, and Vanessa Toulmin, eds, *Visual Delights: Essays on the Popular and Projected Image in the 19th Century* (Trowbridge: Flicks Books, 2001).

Pritchard, Michael, *Sir Hubert von Herkomer: Film Pioneer and Artist* (Bushey: Bushey Museum Trust, 1987).

Pritchard, Michael, *Sir Hubert von Herkomer and His Film-making in Bushey 1912–1914* (Bushey: Bushey Museum/Allm Books, 1987).

Robinson, David, 'Rudge and Friese-Greene's Lantern Experiments—Some Technical Considerations,' *New Magic Lantern Journal*, vol. 8, no. 2, October 1997, pp. 4–7.

Rossell, Deac, 'A Slippery Job: Travelling Exhibitors in Early Cinema,' in Simon Popple and Vanessa Toulmin, eds, *Visual Delights: Essays on the Popular and Projected Image in the 19th Century* (Trowbridge: Flicks Books, 2001), pp. 50–60.

Sadoul, Georges, *British Creators of Film Technique: British Scenario Writers, the Creators of the Language of D.W. Griffith, G.A. Smith, Alfred Collins, and Some Others* (London: BFI, 1948).

Salt, Barry, *Film Style and Technology: History and Analysis*, 2nd edn (London: Starword, 1992).

Salt, Barry, 'Cut and Shuffle,' in Christopher Williams, ed., *Cinema: the Beginnings and the Future: Essays Marking the Centenary of the First Film Show Projected to a Paying Audience in Britain* (London: University of Westminster Press, 1996), pp. 171–83.

Sanderson, Michael, *From Irving to Olivier: A Social History of the Acting Profession in England, 1880–1983* (London: Athlone, 1984).

Scheide, Frank, 'Fred Karno's Music-Hall, Copyright and Silent Film Comedy,' in Alan Burton and Laraine Porter, eds, *Pimple, Pranks and*

Pratfalls: British Film Comedy Before 1930 (Trowbridge: Flicks Books, 2000), pp. 51–7.

Scheide, Frank, 'The Influence of the English Music–hall on Early Screen Acting,' in Linda Fitzsimmons and Sarah Street, eds, *Moving Performance: British Stage and Screen, 1890s–1920s* (Trowbridge: Flicks Books, 2000), pp. 69–79.

Scrivens, Kevin, and Stephen Smith, *The Travelling Cinematograph Show* (Tweedale: New Era Publications, 1999).

Scullion, Adrienne, ' "The Cinematograph Still Reigns Supreme at the Skating Palace": The First Decades of Film in Scotland,' in Linda Fitzsimmons and Sarah Street, eds, *Moving Performance: British Stage and Screen, 1890s–1920s* (Trowbridge: Flicks, 2000), pp. 80–100.

Seton, Marie, 'The British Cinema, 1896–1907,' *Sight and Sound*, vol. 6, no. 21, Spring 1937, pp. 5–8.

Seton, Marie, 'The British Cinema, 1907–1914,' *Sight and Sound*, vol. 6, no. 22, Summer 1937, pp. 64–7.

Seton, Marie, 'The British Cinema, 1914,' *Sight and Sound*, vol. 6, no. 23, Autumn 1937, pp. 126–8.

Sheils, Trish, '*Trilby* (1914): Theatre to Film,' in Alan Burton and Laraine Porter, eds, *Pimple, Pranks and Pratfalls: British Film Comedy Before 1930* (Trowbridge: Flicks Books, 2000), pp. 42–50.

Smith, Emma, ' "Sir J. and Lady Forbes-Robertson Left for America on Saturday": Marketing the 1913 *Hamlet* for Stage and Screen,' in Linda Fitzsimmons and Sarah Street, eds, *Moving Performance: British Stage and Screen, 1890s–1920s* (Trowbridge: Flicks Books, 2000), pp. 44–55.

Smith, Trevor, 'British Film Pioneers. Part 1: 1896–1908,' *Flickers*, no. 34, October 1976, pp. 17–19.

Smith, Trevor, 'British Film Pioneers. Part 2: 1908–1914,' *Flickers*, no. 35, February 1977, pp. 16–19.

Sobchack, Thomas, 'Gypsies, Children, and Criminals: Anti-authority Themes in Early British Silent Film,' *Journal of Popular Film and Television*, vol. 17, no. 1, 1989, pp. 15–19.

Sopocy, Martin, 'A Narrated Cinema: The Pioneer Story Films of James A. Williamson,' *Cinema Journal*, vol. 18, no. 1, Fall 1978, pp. 2–27.

Sopocy, Martin, 'French and British Influences in Porter's *American Fireman,*' *Film History*, vol. 1, no. 2, 1987, pp. 137–48.

Sopocy, Martin, 'The Role of the Intertitle in Film Exhibition, 1910–1914,' in Christopher Williams, ed., *Cinema: The Beginnings and the Future*, London: University of Westminster Press, 1996, pp. 123–34.

Sopocy, Martin, *James Williamson: Studies and Documents of a Pioneer of the Film Narrative* (London: Associated University Presses, 1998).

Strebel, Elizabeth Grottle, 'Primitive Propaganda: The Boer War Films,' *Sight and Sound*, vol. 46, no. 1, Winter 1976/7, pp. 45–7.

Sutcliffe, Lawrence, 'A Daring Daylight Film Company: A History of the

Sheffield Photo Company' (Norwich: unpublished M.A. dissertation, University of East Anglia, 2001).

Sutherland, Allan T., 'The Yorkshire Pioneers,' *Sight and Sound*, Winter 1976/77, pp. 48–51.

Thomas, D.B., *The First Colour Motion Pictures* (London: HMSO, 1969).

Toulmin, Vanessa, 'Telling the Tale: The Story of the Fairground Bioscope Shows and the Showmen who Operated Them,' *Film History*, vol. 6, no. 2, 1994, pp. 219–37.

Toulmin, Vanessa, 'The Fairground Bioscope,' in Colin Harding and Simon Popple, eds, *In the Kingdom of Shadows: A Companion to Early Cinema* (London: Cygnus Arts, 1996), pp. 191–3.

Toulmin, Vanessa, 'Travelling Shows and the First Static Cinemas,' *Picture House*, Summer 1996, pp. 5–12.

Toulmin, Vanessa, *Randall Williams—King of Showmen: From Ghost Show to Bioscope* (London: The Projection Box, 1998).

Toulmin, Vanessa, 'Women Bioscope Proprietors—Before the First World War,' in John Fullerton, ed., *Celebrating 1895: The Centenary of Cinema* (Sydney: John Libbey, 1998), pp. 55–65.

Tummel, H., 'Birt Acres,' *Cinema Studies*, 1: 4, June 1963, pp. 157–60.

Turvey, Gerry, 'Weary Willie and Tired Tim Go Into Pictures: The Comic Films of the British and Colonial Kinematograph Company,' in Alan Burton and Laraine Porter, eds, *Pimple, Pranks and Pratfalls: British Film Comedy Before 1930* (Trowbridge: Flicks Books, 2000), pp. 69–75.

Turvey, Gerry, '*The Battle of Waterloo* (1913): The First British Epic,' in Alan Burton and Laraine Porter, eds, *The Showman, the Spectacle and the Two-Minute Silence: Performing British Cinema Before 1930* (Trowbridge: Flicks Books, 2001), pp. 40–7.

Weedon, Geoff, and Richard Ward, *Fairground Art: The Art Forms of Travelling Fairs, Carousels and Carnival Midways* (New York/London: Abbeville/White Mouse, c.1981).

Whalley, Robin and Peter Warden, 'Forgotten Firm: A Short Chronological Account of Mitchell and Kenyon, Cinematographers,' in *Film History*, vol. 10, no. 1, 1998, pp. 35–51.

Williams, Christopher, ed., *Cinema: The Beginnings and the Future: Essays Marking the Centenary of the First Film Show Projected to a Paying Audience in Britain* (London: University of Westminster Press, 1996).

Williams, David R., 'The Cinematograph Act of 1909: An Introduction to the Impetus Behind the Legislation and Some Early Effects,' in *Film History*, vol. 9, no. 4, 1997, pp. 341–50.

Winston, Sue, 'Great Exhibitions: Representing the World at the Great Exhibition, the Sydenham Crystal Palace and Early British Film Shows' (Norwich: unpublished Ph.D. thesis, University of East Anglia, 1996).

5. Material on British Cinema from the Beginning of the First World War to the Conversion to Sound

Badsey, Stephen. D., 'Battle of the Somme: British War-propaganda,' in *Historical Journal of Film, Radio and Television*, vol. 3, no. 2, 1983, pp. 99–115.

Bamford, Kenton, *Distorted Images: British National Identity and Film in the 1920s* (London: I.B. Tauris, 1999).

Barr, Charles, '*Blackmail*: Silent and Sound,' *Sight and Sound*, vol. 52, no. 2, Spring 1983, pp. 122–6.

Barr, Charles, 'Hitchcock's British Films Re-visited,' in Andrew Higson, ed., *Dissolving Views: Key Writings on British Cinema* (London: Cassell, 1996), pp. 9–19.

Barr, Charles, 'Before *Blackmail*: British Silent Cinema,' in Robert Murphy, ed., *The British Cinema Book* (London: BFI, 1997), pp. 5–16.

Barr, Charles, 'Desperate Yearnings: Victor Saville and Gainsborough,' in Pam Cook, ed., *Gainsborough Pictures* (London: Cassell, 1997), pp. 47–59.

Barr, Charles, *English Hitchcock* (Moffat: David & Charles, 1999).

Berry, David, and Simon Horrocks, eds, *David Lloyd George: The Movie Mystery* (Cardiff: University of Wales Press, 1998).

Brown, Geoff, ' "Sister of the Stage": British Film and British Theatre,' in Charles Barr, ed., *All Our Yesterdays: 90 Years of British Cinema* (London: BFI, 1986), pp. 143–67.

Burrows, Jon, ' "Our English Mary Pickford": Alma Taylor and Ambivalent British Stardom in the 1910s,' in Bruce Babington, ed., *British Stars and Stardom: from Alma Taylor to Sean Connery* (Manchester: Manchester University Press, 2001).

Burrows, Jon, ' "That Type of Picture Which Appeals to the Best Instincts": *The Vicar of Wakefield* (1916) and the Vagaries of the Heritage Film in the 1910s,' in Alan Burton and Laraine Porter, eds, *The Showman, the Spectacle and the Two-Minute Silence: Performing British Cinema Before 1930* (Trowbridge: Flicks Books, 2001), pp. 63–72.

Burton, Alan, 'The Emergence of an Alternative Film Culture: Film and the British Consumer Co-operative Movement Before 1920,' in *Film History*, vol. 8, no. 4, 1996, pp. 446–57.

Burton, Alan, and Laraine Porter, eds, *Pimple, Pranks and Pratfalls: British Film Comedy Before 1930* (Trowbridge: Flicks Books, 2000).

Burton, Alan, and Laraine Porter, eds, *Crossing the Pond: Anglo-American Film Relations before 1930* (Trowbridge: Flick Books, 2002).

Chanan, Michael, 'The Emergence of an Industry,' in James Curran and Vincent Porter, eds, *British Cinema History* (London: Weidenfeld and Nicolson, 1983), pp. 39–58.

Collick, John, 'Silent Shakespeare and British Cinema,' in John Collick,

Shakespeare, Cinema and Society (Manchester: Manchester University Press, 1989), pp. 33–57.

Cook, Ann-Marie, 'The Adventures of the 'Vitagraph Girl' in England,' in Alan Burton and Laraine Porter, eds, *Pimple, Pranks and Pratfalls: British Film Comedy Before 1930* (Trowbridge: Flicks Books, 2000), pp. 33–41.

Cook, Pam, ed., *Gainsborough Pictures* (London: Cassell, 1997).

Cosandey, Roland, 'On Borderline,' *Afterimage*, no. 12, Autumn 1985, pp. 66–84.

Cricks, R.H., 'Sixty Years of Techniques,' *Kinematograph Weekly*, 3 May 1956, pp. 69, 71 and 73.

Curnow, Wystan, 'Len Lye and *Tusalava*: Interview,' *Cantrills Filmnotes*, 29/30, February 1979, pp. 38–41.

Dickinson, Margaret, and Sarah Street, *Cinema and State: The Film Industry and the British Government, 1927–84* (London: BFI, 1985).

Donald, James, Anne Friedberg and Laura Marcus, eds, *Close Up: Cinema and Modernism*, (London: Cassell, 1998).

Fitzsimmons, Linda, and Sarah Street, eds, *Moving Performance: British Stage and Screen, 1890s–1920s* (Trowbridge: Flicks Books, 2000).

Fletcher, Tony, 'British Comedy Films in the Silent Period: A Production Survey,' in Alan Burton and Laraine Porter, eds, *Pimple, Pranks and Pratfalls: British Film Comedy Before 1930* (Trowbridge: Flicks Books, 2000), pp. 10–13.

Fletcher, Tony, 'Sound Before *Blackmail* (1929),' in Alan Burton and Laraine Porter, eds, *The Showman, the Spectacle and the Two-Minute Silence: Performing British Cinema Before 1930* (Trowbridge: Flicks Books, 2001), pp. 6–11.

Fluegel, Jane, ed., *Michael Balcon: The Pursuit of British Cinema* (New York, Museum of Modern Art, 1984).

Gifford, Denis, 'Pimple,' *Silent Picture*, no. 6, Spring 1970, pp. 8–9 and 11.

Gifford, Denis, 'The Early Memoirs of Maurice Elvey,' *Griffithiana*, no. 60–61, October 1997, pp. 77–119.

Gledhill, Christine, 'Between Melodrama and Realism: Anthony Asquith's *Underground* and King Vidor's *The Crowd*,' in Jane Gaines, ed., *Classical Hollywood Narrative: The Paradigm Wars* (Durham and London: Duke University Press, 1992), pp. 129–68.

Gledhill, Christine, 'Taking it Forward: Theatricality and British Cinema Style in the 1920s,' in Linda Fitzsimmons and Sarah Street, eds, *Moving Performance: British Stage and Screen, 1890s–1920s* (Trowbridge: Flicks Books, 2000), pp. 5–25.

Gledhill, Christine, 'Wit and the Literate Image: The Adrian Brunel/A.A. Milne Collaborations,' Alan Burton and Laraine Porter, eds, *Pimple, Pranks and Pratfalls: British Film Comedy Before 1930* (Trowbridge: Flicks Books, 2000), pp. 82–8.

Hammerton, Jenny, 'Letters to the Editor of *Pathe Pictorial* and *Eve's Film Review*,' *Journal of Popular British Cinema*, 1999, no. 2, pp. 128–31.

Hammerton, Jenny, 'Performers in the News: Stars of Stage and Screen in Early Pathe Newsreels and Cinemagazines,' in Alan Burton and Laraine Porter, eds, *The Showman, the Spectacle and the Two-Minute Silence: Performing British Cinema Before 1930* (Trowbridge: Flicks Books, 2001), pp. 93–4.

Hammerton, Jenny, *For Ladies Only? Eve's Film Review: Pathe Cinemagazine, 1921–33* (Hastings: The Projection Box, 2001).

Hammond, Michael, ' "Cultivating Pimple": Performance Traditions and the Film Comedy of Fred and Joe Evans,' in Alan Burton and Laraine Porter, eds, *Pimple, Pranks and Pratfalls: British Film Comedy Before 1930* (Trowbridge: Flicks Books, 2000), pp. 58–68.

Hammond, Michael, 'The Men Who Came Back: Anonymity and Recognition in Local British Roll of Honour Films (1914–1918),' *Scope: An Online Film Journal*, Autumn 2000, www.nottingham.ac.uk/film/journal/index.htm.

Hammond, Michael, ' "The Big Show": Cinema Exhibition and Reception in Britain in The Great War,' (Nottingham: unpublished Ph.D. thesis, Nottingham Trent University, 2001).

Hardy, Forsyth, ed., *Grierson on Documentary* (London: Faber and Faber, 1966).

Hardy, Forsyth, ed., *Grierson on the Movies* (London: Faber and Faber, 1981).

Hawkridge, John, 'British Cinema from Hepworth to Hitchcock,' in Geoffrey Nowell-Smith, ed., *The Oxford History of World Cinema* (Oxford: Oxford University Press, 1996).

Hepworth, Cecil, *Came The Dawn: Memories of a Film Pioneer* (London: Phoenix House, 1951).

Higson, Andrew, 'The Victorious Re-cycling of National History: Nelson (1918),' in Karel Dibbets and Bert Hogenkamp, eds, *Film and the First World War* (Amsterdam: Amsterdam University Press, 1995), pp. 108–15.

Higson, Andrew, *Waving the Flag: Constructing a National Cinema in Britain* (Oxford: Clarendon Press, 1995).

Higson, Andrew, ' "A Film League of Nations": Gainsborough, Gaumont and "Film Europe",' in Pam Cook, ed., *Gainsborough Pictures* (London: Cassell, 1997), pp. 60–79.

Higson, Andrew, 'Heritage Discourses and British Cinema Before 1920,' in John Fullerton, ed., *Celebrating 1895: The Centenary of Cinema* (Sydney: John Libbey, 1998), pp. 182–9.

Higson, Andrew, 'Polyglot Films for an International Market: E.A. Dupont, the British Film Industry, and the Idea of a European Cinema, 1926–1930,' from Andrew Higson and Richard Maltby, eds, '*Film*

Europe' and 'Film America': Cinema, Commerce and Cultural Exchange, *1920–1939* (Exeter: University of Exeter Press, 1999), pp. 274–301.

Higson, Andrew, 'Figures in a Landscape: The Performance of Englishness in Cecil Hepworth's *Tansy* (1921),' in Alan Burton and Laraine Porter, eds, *The Showman, the Spectacle and the Two-Minute Silence: Performing British Cinema Before 1930* (Trowbridge: Flicks Books, 2001), pp. 53–62.

Higson, Andrew, '*The Flag Lieutenent*: Waving the Flag Differently in Britain and America,' in Alan Burton and Laraine Porter, eds, *Crossing the Pond: Anglo-American Film Relations before 1930* (Trowbridge: Flick Books, 2002).

Hiley, Nicholas, '*The British Army Film, You!* and *For the Empire*: Reconstructed Propaganda Films, 1914–1916,' *Historical Journal of Film, Radio and Television*, vol. 5, no. 2, 1985, pp. 165–82.

Hiley, Nicholas, 'Hilton DeWitt Girdwood and the Origins of British Official Filming,' *Historical Journal of Film, Radio and Television*, vol. 13, no. 2, 1993, pp. 129–48.

Hiley, Nicholas, 'At the Picture Palace: The British Cinema Audience in the 1920s and 1930s,' in John Fullerton, ed., *Celebrating 1895: The Centenary of Cinema* (Sydney: John Libbey, 1998), pp. 96–103.

Hiley, Nicholas, ' "Let's Go to the Pictures": The British Cinema Audience in the 1920s and 1930s,' *Journal of Popular British Cinema*, vol. 2, 1999, pp. 39–53.

Historical Journal of Film, Radio and Television, Special Issue on 'Britain and the Cinema in the First World War,' vol. 13, no. 2, 1993.

Hogenkamp, Bert, *Deadly Parallels: Film and the Left in Britain, 1929–1939* (London: Lawrence and Wishart, 1986).

Honri, Baynham, 'The Samuelson Saga,' *Silent Picture*, no. 5, Winter 1969–70, pp. 3–6.

Honri, Baynham, 'Cecil M. Hepworth—his Studios and Techniques,' *British Journal of Photography*, 15 January 1971, p. 48.

Jones, Stephen, *The British Labour Movement and Film, 1918–1939* (London: Routledge and Kegan Paul, 1987).

Kemp, Philip, 'Not For Peckham: Michael Balcon and Gainsborough's International Trajectory in the 1920s,' in Pam Cook, ed., *Gainsborough Pictures* (London: Cassell, 1997), pp. 13–30.

Kimbley, D., 'How the B.K.S. Began: The Developments of 1928–32,' *BKSTS Journal*, no. 63, January 1981, p. 123.

Kuhn, Annette, *Cinema, Censorship and Sexuality, 1909–1925* (London/New York: Routledge, 1988).

Lejeune, Anthony, ed., *The Caroline Lejeune Film Reader* (Manchester: Carcanet, 1991).

LeMahieu, D.L., *A Culture for Democracy: Mass Communication and the Cultivated Mind in Britain Between the Wars* (Oxford: Clarendon Press, 1988).

Lindgren, Ernest, 'The Early Feature Film,' in Michael Balcon, Ernest Lindgren, Forsyth Hardy and Roger Manvell, *Twenty Years of British Films 1925–1945* (London: The Falcon Press, 1947), pp. 13–28.

Low, Rachael, *The History of the British Film, 1914–1918* (London: Allen and Unwin, 1950; London, Routledge, 1997).

Low, Rachael, *The History of the British Film, 1918–1929* (London: Allen and Unwin/BFI, 1971; London: Routledge, 1997).

Low, Rachael, *The History of the British Film, 1929–1939: Documentary and Educational Films of the 1930s* (London: Allen and Unwin/BFI, 1979; London: Routledge, 1997).

Low, Rachael, *The History of the British Film, 1929–1939: Films of Comment and Persuasion of the 1930s* (London: Allen and Unwin/BFI, 1979; London: Routledge, 1997).

McKernan, Luke, *Topical Budget: The Great British News Film* (London: BFI, 1992).

McKernan, Luke, ed., *A Yank in Britain: The Lost Memoirs of Charles Urban, Film Pioneer* (London: The Projection Box, 1999).

McKernan, Luke, 'How to Make Ben-Hur Look Like an Epic,' in Alan Burton and Laraine Porter, eds, *Pimple, Pranks and Pratfalls: British Film Comedy Before 1930* (Trowbridge: Flicks Books, 2000), pp. 7–9.

McLaren, Judith, ' "My Career Up To Now": Betty Balfour and the Background to the *Squibs* Series,' in Alan Burton and Laraine Porter, eds, *Pimple, Pranks and Pratfalls: British Film Comedy Before 1930* (Trowbridge: Flicks Books, 2000), pp. 76–81.

Macnab, Geoffrey, 'The Not-So-Roaring 20s: Ivor Novello and Betty Balfour,' in Geoffrey Macnab, *Searching for Stars* (London and New York: Cassell, 2000), pp. 34–58.

Medhurst, Andy, 'Music Hall and British Cinema,' in Charles Barr, ed., *All Our Yesterdays: 90 Years of British Cinema* (London: BFI, 1986), pp. 168–88.

Minney, R.J., *'Puffin' Asquith: A Biography of the Hon Anthony Asquith, Aesthete, Aristocrat, Prime Minister's Son and Film Maker* (London: Leslie Frewin, 1973).

Montgomery, John, *Comedy Films 1894–1954* (London: George Allen and Unwin, 1954).

Murphy, Robert, 'The Coming of Sound to the Cinema in Britain,' *Historical Journal of Film, Radio, and Television*, vol. 4, no. 2, 1984, pp. 143–60.

Murphy, Robert, 'Hitchcock the Joker,' in Alan Burton and Laraine Porter, eds, *Pimple, Pranks and Pratfalls: British Film Comedy Before 1930* (Trowbridge: Flicks Books, 2000), pp. 107–10.

Napper, Lawrence, 'The Middlebrow, "National Culture" and British Cinema, 1920–1939,' (Norwich: unpublished Ph.D. thesis, University of East Anglia, 2001).

Napper, Lawrence, and Michael Williams, 'The Curious Appeal of Ivor

Novello,' in Bruce Babington, ed., *British Stars and Stardom: from Alma Taylor to Sean Connery* (Manchester: University of Manchester Press, 2001).

Newey, Katherine, 'Women and Early British Film: Finding a Screen of Her Own,' in Linda Fitzsimmons and Sarah Street, eds, *Moving Performance: British Stage and Screen, 1890s–1920s* (Trowbridge: Flicks Books, 2000), pp. 151–65.

Noble, Peter, *Anthony Asquith* (London: BFI, 1952).

O'Dell, Henri, Margaret Dickinson, Michael Balcon and Anthony Slide, 'George Pearson,' *Silent Picture*, no. 2, Spring 1969, pp. 2–18.

O'Pray, Michael, ed., *The British Avant-Garde Film, 1926–1995: An Anthology of Writings* (Luton: University of Luton Press/The Arts Council of England, 1996).

Paris, Michael, *Warrior Nation: Images of War in British Popular Culture, 1850–2000* (London: Reaktion, 2000).

Petrie, Duncan and Robert Kruger, eds, *A Paul Rotha Reader* (Exeter: University of Exeter Press, 1999).

Rapp, Dean and Charles W. Weber, 'British Film, Empire and Society in the Twenties: The *Livingstone* Film, 1923–1925,' in *Historical Journal of Film, Radio and Television*, vol. 9, no. 1, 1989, pp. 3–17.

Reeves, Nicholas, 'Film Propaganda and its Audience: The Example of Britain's Official Films During the First World War,' in *Journal of Contemporary History*, vol. 18 no. 3, July 1984, pp. 15–28.

Reeves, Nicholas, *Official British Film Propaganda during the First World War* (London: Croom Helm, 1986).

Reeves, Nicholas, 'The Power of Film Propaganda: Myth or Reality,' *Historical Journal of Film, Radio and Television*, vol. 13, no. 2, 1993, pp. 181–202.

Reeves, Nicholas, 'Cinema, Spectatorship and Propaganda: *Battle of the Somme* (1916) and its Contemporary Audience,' *Historical Journal of Film, Radio and Television*, vol. 17, no. 1, 1997, pp. 5–28.

Reeves, Nicholas, 'Official British Film Propaganda,' in Michael Paris, ed., *The First World War and Popular Cinema* (Edinburgh: Edinburgh University Press, 1999)

Reeves, Nicholas, *The Power of Film Propaganda: Myth or Reality?* (London: Cassell, 1999).

Robertson, James C., '*Dawn* (1928): Edith Cavell and Anglo-German Relations,' in *Historical Journal of Film, Radio and Television*, vol. 4, no. 1, 1984, pp. 15–28.

Rollins, Cyril B., and Robert J. Wareing, *Victor Saville* (London: BFI, 1972; pamphlet).

Ryall, Tom, *Blackmail* (BFI Film Classics; London: BFI, 1993).

Ryall, Tom, *Alfred Hitchcock and the British Cinema* (London: Croom Helm, 1996).

Samson, Jen, 'The Film Society, 1925–1939,' in Charles Barr, ed., *All Our Yesterdays: 90 Years of British Cinema* (London: BFI, 1986), pp. 306–13.

Sanders, Michael L., 'British Film Propaganda in Russia, 1916–1918,' in *Historical Journal of Film, Radio and Television*, vol. 3, no. 2, 1983, pp. 117–29.

Sanders, Michael L, and Philip M. Taylor, eds, *British Propaganda During the First World War, 1914–1918* (London: Macmillan, 1982).

Sanderson, Michael, *From Irving to Olivier: A Social History of the Acting Profession in England, 1880–1983* (London: Athlone, 1984).

Sexton, Jamie, 'Parody on the Fringes: Adrian Brunel, Minority Film Culture and the Art of Deconstruction,' in Alan Burton and Laraine Porter, eds, *Pimple, Pranks and Pratfalls: British Film Comedy Before 1930* (Trowbridge: Flicks Books, 2000), pp. 89–95.

Sexton, Jamie, 'The Emergence of an Alternative British Film Culture in the Inter-War Period,' (Norwich: unpublished Ph.D. thesis, University of East Anglia, 2001).

Shafer, Stephen C., *British Popular Films, 1929–1939: The Cinema of Reassurance* (London: Routledge, 1997).

Smith, Trevor, 'British Film Pioneers. Part 3: 1914–1918,' *Flickers*, no. 36, January 1978, pp. 3–8.

Smith, Trevor, 'British Film Pioneers. Part 4: 1919–1923,' *Flickers*, no. 37, October 1978, pp. 3–11.

Smith, Trevor, 'British Film Pioneers. Part 5: 1919–1923 (cont.),' *Flickers*, no. 38, January 1979, pp. 3–12.

Smith, Trevor, 'British Film Pioneers. Part 6: 1924–1928,' *Flickers*, no. 39, January 1980, pp. 15–18.

Smith, Trevor, 'British Film Pioneers. Part 7: 1924–1928 (cont.),' *Flickers*, no. 40, March 1980, pp. 16–20.

Smith, Trevor, 'British Film Pioneers. Part 8: A New Melting Pot,' *Flickers*, no. 41, June 1980, pp. 8–10.

Smither, Roger, 'A Wonderful Idea of the Fighting: the Question of Fakes in the *Battle of the Somme*,' *Historical Journal of Film, Radio and Television*, vol. 13, no. 2, 1993, pp. 149–68.

Smither, Roger, and Daniel Walsh, 'Unknown Pioneer: Edward Foxen Cooper and the Imperial War Museum Film Archive, 1919–1934,' in *Film History*, vol. 12, no. 2, 2000, pp. 187–203.

Street, Sarah, 'The Memoir of Harry Rowson: David Lloyd George, M.P.: "The Man Who Saved the Empire" (1918),' in *Historical Journal of Film, Radio and Television*, vol. 7, no. 1, 1987, pp. 55–68.

Street, Sarah, 'British Film and the National Interest, 1927–1939,' in Robert Murphy, ed., *The British Cinema Book* (London: BFI, 1997), pp. 17–26.

Swann, Paul, *The British Documentary Film Movement 1926–1946* (Cambridge: Cambridge University Press, 1989).

Thomas, D.B., *The First Colour Motion Pictures* (A Science Museum Monograph [on Kinemacolor]), HMSO, 1969.

Turvey, Gerry, 'That Insatiable Body: Ivor Montagu's Confrontation with British Film Censorship,' *Journal of Popular British Cinema*, Issue 3, 2000, pp. 31–44.

Walton, Jean, 'White Neurotics, Black Primitives and the Queer Matrix of *Borderline*,' in Ellis Hansen, ed., *Out Takes: Essays on Queer Theory and Film* (Durham, NC and London: Duke University Press, 1999), pp. 243–70.

Williams, David R., 'Ladies of the Lamp: The Employment of Women in the British Film Trade During World War I,' in *Film History*, vol. 9, no. 1, 1997, pp. 115–27.

Williams, David R., 'The *Five Nights* Affair', *Journal of Popular British Cinema*, no. 3, 2000, pp. 20–30.

Williams, Michael, 'A Sequestered Poodle-faker: Droll, Camp and Ivor Novello,' in Alan Burton and Laraine Porter, eds, *Pimple, Pranks and Pratfalls: British Film Comedy before 1930* (Trowbridge: Flicks Books, 2000), pp. 101–6.

Williams, Michael, ' "England's Apollo": Ivor Novello—Post-war Icon, Matinée-idol and "Ambassador of the British Film",' (Norwich: unpublished Ph.D. thesis, University of East Anglia, 2001).

Wood, Linda, *The Commercial Imperative in the Film Industry: Maurice Elvey, a Case Study* (London: BFI, 1987).

Yacowar, Maurice, *Hitchcock's British Films* (Hamden: Connecticut, Archon, 1977).

6. General Histories of British Cinema with Material on the Pre-1930 Period

Aitken, Ian, *Film and Reform: John Grierson and the Documentary Film Movement* (London: Routledge, 1990).

Aitken, Ian, ed., *The Documentary Film Movement: An Anthology* (Edinburgh: Edinburgh University Press, 1998).

Anstey, Edgar, 'Development of Film Technique in Britain,' in Roger Manvell, ed., *Experiment in the Film* (London: Greywalls Press, 1949), pp. 234–65.

Armes, Roy, *A Critical History of British Cinema* (London: Secker and Warburg, 1978).

Atwell, David, *Cathedrals of the Movies: A History of British Cinemas and their Audiences* (London: Architectural Press, 1980).

Babington, Bruce, ed., *British Stars and Stardom: from Alma Taylor to Sean Connery* (Manchester: University of Manchester Press, 2001).

Barr, Charles, 'Introduction: Schizophrenia and Amnesia,' in Charles Barr, ed., *All Our Yesterdays: 90 Years of British Cinema* (London: BFI, 1992).

Barr, Charles, ed., *All Our Yesterdays: 90 Years of British Cinema* (London: BFI, 1986).

Barr, Charles, *English Hitchcock* (Moffat, Scotland: Cameron and Hollis, 1999).

Berry, David, *Wales and Cinema: The First Hundred Years* (Cardiff: University of Wales Press: 1994).

Betts, Ernest, *The Film Business: A History of British Cinema, 1896–1972* (London: Allen and Unwin, 1973).

Bird, John H., *Cinema Parade: Fifty Years of Film Shows* (Birmingham: Cornish Brothers Ltd., *c*.1946).

Burrows, Elaine, 'Live Action: A Brief History of British Animation,' in Charles Barr, ed., *All Our Yesterdays: 90 Years of British Cinema* (London: BFI, 1986), pp. 272–85.

Butler, Ivan, *Cinema in Britain: An Illustrated Survey* (London: Tantivy Press, 1973).

Caughie, John, with Kevin Rockett, *The Companion to British and Irish Cinema* (London: Cassell/BFI, 1996).

Cook, Pam, ed., *Gainsborough Pictures* (London: Cassell, 1997).

Curran, James, and Vincent Porter, eds, *British Cinema History* (London: Weidenfeld and Nicolson, 1983).

Dick, Eddie, ed., *From Limelight to Satellite: A Scottish Film Book* (London: BFI/Scottish Film Council, 1990).

Dickinson, Margaret, and Sarah Street, *Cinema and State: The Film Industry and the British Government, 1927–84* (London: BFI, 1985).

Dixon, Wheeler W., *Re-Viewing British Cinema, 1900–1992: Essays and Interviews* (New York: State University of New York Press, 1994).

Fluegel, Jane, ed., *Michael Balcon: The Pursuit of British Cinema* (New York: Museum of Modern Art, 1984).

Higson, Andrew, *Waving the Flag: Constructing a National Cinema in Britain* (Oxford: Clarendon Press, 1995).

Higson, Andrew, ed., *Dissolving Views: Key Writings on British Cinema* (London: Cassell, 1996).

Higson, Andrew, 'British Cinema,' in John Hill and Pamela Church-Gibson, eds, *The Oxford Guide to Film Studies* (Oxford: Oxford University Press, 1998), pp. 501–9.

Houston, Penelope, *Keepers of the Frame: The Film Archives* (London: BFI, 1994).

McFarlane, Brian, 'A Literary Cinema? British Films and British Novels,' in Charles Barr, ed., *All Our Yesterdays: 90 Years of British Cinema* (London: BFI, 1986), pp. 120–42.

MacNab, Geoffrey, 'Looking for Lustre: Stars at Gainsborough,' in Pam Cook, ed., *Gainsborough Pictures* (London: Cassel, 1997), pp. 99–117.

MacNab, Geoffrey, *Searching for Stars* (London: Cassell, 2000).

Medhurst, Andy, 'Music Hall and British Cinema,' in Charles Barr, ed., *All Our Yesterdays: 90 Years of British Cinema* (London BFI, 1986), pp. 168–88.

Murphy, Robert, 'Under the Shadow of Hollywood,' in Charles Barr, ed., *All Our Yesterdays: 90 Years of British Cinema* (London: BFI, 1986), pp. 47–71.

Murphy, Robert, ed., *The British Cinema Book* (London: BFI, 1997).

Oakley, Charles, *Where We Came In: 70 Years of the British Film Industry* (London: Allen and Unwin, 1964).

O'Pray, Michael, ed., *The British Avant-Garde Film, 1926–1995: An Anthology of Writings* (Luton: University of Luton Press/The Arts Council of England, 1996).

Perry, George, *The Great British Picture Show* (London: Hart-Davis and MacGibbon, 1974).

Petley, Julian, 'The Lost Continent,' in Charles Barr, ed., *All Our Yesterdays: 90 Years of British Cinema* (London: BFI, 1986), pp. 98–119.

Petrie, Duncan, 'Innovation and Economy: The Contribution of the Gainsborough Cinematographer,' in Pam Cook, ed., *Gainsborough Pictures* (London: Cassell, 1997), pp. 118–54.

Petrie, Duncan, *The British Cinematographer* (London: BFI, 1996).

Pronay, Nicholas, 'The First Reality: Film Censorship in Liberal England,' in K.R.M. Short, ed., *Feature Films as History* (London: Croom Helm, 1981), pp. 113–37.

Richards, Jeffrey, *Films and British National Identity: From Dickens to Dad's Army* (Manchester: Manchester University Press, 1997).

Robertson, James, *The British Board of Film Censors, 1896–1956* (London: Croom Helm, 1985).

Robertson, James, *The Hidden Cinema: British Film Censorship in Action, 1913–1975* (New York: Routledge, 1989).

Ryall, Tom, *Britain and the American Cinema* (London: Sage Publications, 2001).

Scottish Film Council, *Fifty Years at the Pictures* (Glasgow: Scottish Film Council, 1946).

Smith, Trevor, 'Luxuriant Splendour: The Early Picture Palaces, Part 1,' *Flickers*, no. 42, October 1980, pp. 12–16.

Smith, Trevor, 'Luxuriant Splendour: The Early Picture Palaces, Part 2,' *Flickers*, no. 43, January 1981, pp. 14–18.

Smith, Trevor, 'Luxuriant Splendour: The Early Picture Palaces, Part 3,' *Flickers*, no. 44, June 1981, pp. 13–17.

Street, Sarah, *British National Cinema* (London: Routledge, 1997).

Street, Sarah, *British Cinema in Documents* (London: Routledge, 2000).

Warren, Patricia, *The British Film Collection 1896–1984: A History of the British Cinema in Pictures* (London: Elm Tree Books, 1984).

Wood, Linda, *British Film, 1927–1939* (London: BFI, 1986).

Wood, Robin, *Hitchcock's Films Revisited* (London: Faber and Faber, 1989).

Yacowar, Maurice, *Hitchcock's British Films* (Hamden: CT: Archon, 1977).

7. Histories of Regional Cinema Developments in Britain with Material on the Pre-1930 Period

Bayer, Miranda, 'The Showman, the Barker and the Cicerone: A Show in Three Acts—Film Exhibition and Reception on Three East Anglia Fairgrounds,' (Norwich: unpublished MA dissertation, University of East Anglia, 2001).

Benfield, Robert, *Bijou Kinema: a History of Cinema in Yorkshire* (Sheffield: Sheffield City Polytechnic/Yorkshire Arts, 1976).

Brooker, Amy, 'Make 'Em Laugh? Film Exhibition in Croydon, 1896–1910,' (Norwich: unpublished MA dissertation, University of East Anglia, 2001).

Brown, Richard, 'The Kinetoscope in Yorkshire: Exploitation and Innovation,' in Simon Popple and Vanessa Toulmin, eds, *Visual Delights: Essays on the Popular and Projected Image in the 19th Century* (Trowbridge: Flicks Books, 2001), pp. 105–15.

Carroll, Kevin, 'The Cinematograph in the London Music Hall,' *Cinema Studies*, vol. 1, no. 2, June 1964, pp. 212–21.

Dewes, R.H., 'My Nottingham Venture: Recalling a Cinema Development of 1921,' *Focus on Film*, no. 32, April 1979, pp. 43–7.

East, John M., 'The Birth of the Cinema Trade in Scotland,' *Scotland's Magazine*, no. 69, December 1973, pp. 27–9.

East, John M., 'The Discovery of Boreham Wood: Film Capital of Britain', in F. Maurice Speed, *Film Review 1975–76* (London: W.H. Allen, 1975), pp. 52–6.

East, John M., 'Looking Back: When Croydon was Film Capital of Britain', in F. Maurice Speed, *Film Review 1977–78* (London: W.H. Allen, 1977), pp. 102–9.

Eyles, Allen, Frank Gray and Alan Readman, *Cinema in West Sussex: the First Hundred Years* (Chichester: Phillimore, 1996)

George, Ken, *'Two Sixpennies Please': Lewisham's Early Cinemas* (London: Lewisham Local History Society, 1987).

Honri, Baynham, 'The Blackburn Pioneers,' *British Journal of Photography*, vol. 11, no. 3, 1977, pp. 205–7.

Manders, Frank, *Cinemas of Gateshead* (Gateshead: Portcullis Press, 1995).

Marriott, Paul J., *Early Oxford Picture Palaces* (Oxford: The author, 1978).

Mayall, David, 'Palaces for Entertainment in Birmingham, 1908–1918,' *Midland History*, vol. 10, 1985, pp. 94–109.

Mellor, Geoffrey James, *Picture Pioneers: The Story of the Northern Cinema, 1896–1971* (Newcastle upon Tyne: Frank Graham, *c*.1971).

Mellor, Geoffrey James, *Movie Makers and Picture Palaces: A Century of Cinema in Yorkshire, 1896–1996* (Bradford: Bradford Libraries, 1996).

Mullins, Sam, 'Market Harborough and the Movies, 1901–1940,' *Leicestershire Historian*, vol. 3, 1987.

Nutt, Graham, *Tuppenny Rush: The Arrival of Cinemas and Film-making in Swadlincote* (Burton-on-Trent: Trent Valley, c.1992).

O'Brien, Margaret and Allen Eyles, eds, *Enter the Dream-House: Memories of Cinemas in South London from the Twenties to the Sixties* (London: Museum of the Moving Image/BFI, 1985).

O'Brien, Margaret and Julia Holland, 'Picture Shows: The Early British Film Industry in Walthamstow,' *History Today*, vol. 37, February 1987, pp. 9–15.

Peart, Stephen, *The Picture House in East Anglia* (Lavenham: Lavenham Press, 1980).

Price, Cecil, 'Early Cinemas in Wales,' *Dock Leaves*, vol. 8, no. 21, 1957, pp. 45–9.

Scullion, Adrienne, ' "The Cinematograph Still Reigns Supreme at the Skating Palace": The First Decades of Film in Scotland,' in Linda Fitzsimmons and Sarah Street, *Moving Performance: British Stage and Screen, 1890s–1920s* (Trowbridge: Flicks Books, 2000), pp. 80–100.

Shaw, Clifford H. and Stuart R. Smith, *The Early Years of Cinema in Sheffield, 1896–1911* (Sheffield: Sheffield Cinema Society, 1993).

Sheffield Cinema Society, *The A.B.C. of the Cinemas of Sheffield* (Sheffield: Sheffield Cinema Society, 1993).

Shenton, William, 'Manchester's First Cinemas 1896–1914,' *Manchester Region History Review*, vol. 4, Autumn 1990/91, pp. 3–11.

Slide, Anthony, 'Bioscope Shows at Hull Fair,' *Cinema Studies*, no. 2, June 1965, pp. 7–9.

Standley, Philip, 'Cinemas in Bedford, 1898–1978,' *Bedfordshire Magazine*, no. 17, Winter 1979, pp. 122–7.

Sutherland, Allan T., 'The Yorkshire Pioneers,' *Sight and Sound*, vol. 46, no. 1, Winter 1976/7, pp. 48–51.

Thomson, Michael, *Silver Screen in the Silver City* (Aberdeen: Aberdeen UP, 1988).

Toulmin, Vanessa, 'Moving Images: The Early Days of Cinema in Yorkshire,' *Yorkshire Journal*, issue 12, 1995, pp. 32–41.

Toulmin, Vanessa, 'The Cinematograph at the Nottingham Goose Fair, 1896–1911,' in Alan Burton and Laraine Porter, eds, *The Showman, the Spectacle and the Two-Minute Silence: Performing British Cinema Before 1930* (Trowbridge: Flicks Books, 2001), pp. 76–86.

Weybridge Museum, *If it Moves—Film it: a History of Film-making in Walton-on-Thames, 1900–1939, Commemorating the Work of Cecil Hepworth and Clifford Spain* (Weybridge: Weybridge Museum, 1973).

White, Bill, Sheila Jemima and Donald Hyslop, eds, *Dream Palaces: Going to the Pictures in Southampton* (Southampton: Southampton City Council, 1996).

Williams, David, *Cinema in Leicester, 1896–1931* (Loughborough: Heart of Albion Press, 1993).

Williams, Ned, *Cinemas of the Black Country* (Wolverhampton: Uralia Press, 1982).

Wolters, N.E.B., *Bungalow Town: Theatre and Film Colony* (Shoreham: The author, 1985).

8. Websites

Alfred West F.R.G.S.—Film Pioneer, *http://mcs.open.ac.uk/dac3/ournavy/*

Bill Douglas Centre for the History of Cinema and Popular Culture, *http://info.ex.ac.uk/billdouglas/mainmenu.html*

British Film Institute, *http://www.bfi.org.uk/*

British Library Periodicals on Film, *http://www.bl.uk/collections/newspaper/cinema.html#g.*

British Pathe, *http://www.britishpathe.com.*

British Universities Film and Video Council, *http://www.bufvc.ac.uk/databases/newsreels.html/.*

earlycinema.com, *http://www.earlycinema.com/*

Elmbridge Museum, *http://www.datanet.co.uk/enterprise/elm-mus/*

The Magic Lantern Society, *http://www.magiclantern.org.uk.*

National Fairground Archive, *http://www.shef.ac.uk/uni/projects/nfa/.*

National Museum of Photography, Film and Television, *http://www.nmpft.org.uk/*

Performing Arts Data Service, *http://www.pads.ahds.ac.uk/pads.html.*

The Projection Box, *http://easyweb.easynet.co.uk/~s-herbert/ProjectionBox.htm.*

Quellen zur Filmgeschichte, *http://www.unibw-muenchen.de/campus/Film/pro.html*

Screening the Past, *http://www.latrobe.edu.au/www/screeningthepast*

The Silent Film Bookshelf, *http://cinemaweb.com/silentfilm/bookshelf/*

The Silents Majority, *http://www.mdle.com/ClassicFilms/*

Silent Film Sources, *http://www.cinemaweb.com/silentfilm/*

Charles Urban, *http://website.lineone.net/~luke.mckernan/Urban.htm.*

9. General Works on Silent Cinema

Abel, Richard, ed., *Silent Film* (New Brunswick, NJ: Rutgers University Press, 1996).

Abel, Richard, ed., *The Cine Goes to Town: French Cinema, 1896–1914* (Berkeley and London: University of California Press, 1994).

Ball, Robert Hamilton, *Shakespeare on Silent Film* (London: George Allen and Unwin, 1968).

Bottomore, Stephen, *I Want to See This Annie Mattygraph: A Cartoon History of the Coming of the Movies* (Pordenone: Giornate del Cinema Muto, 1995).

Bottomore, Stephen, *The Titanic and Silent Cinema* (Hastings: Projection Box, 2000).

Bowser, Eileen, *The Transformation of Cinema* (History of the American Cinema, 1907–1915) (New York: Scribner's, 1990).

Brewster, Ben and Lea Jacobs, *Theatre to Cinema: Stage Pictorialism and the Early Feature Film* (Oxford: Oxford University Press, 1997).

Burch, Noël, *Life To These Shadows* (London: BFI, 1990).

Christie, Ian, *The Last Machine: Early Cinema and the Birth of the Modern World* (London: BBC/BFI, 1994).

Dibbets, Karel, and Bert Hogenkamp, eds, *Film and the First World War* (Amsterdam: Amsterdam University Press, 1995).

Elsaesser, Thomas, with Adam Barker, eds, *Early Cinema: Space, Frame, Narrative* (London: BFI, 1990).

Elsaesser, Thomas, with Michael Wedel, *A Second Life: German Cinema's First Decades* (Amsterdam: Amsterdam University Press, c.1996).

Fell, John, ed., *Film before Griffith* (Berkeley: University of California Press, 1983).

Film History, Special Issue on 'Silent Cinema,' vol. 9, no. 1, 1997.

Film History, Special Issue on 'International Cinema of the 1910s,' vol. 9, no. 4, 1997.

Film History, Special Issue on 'Cinema Pioneers,' vol. 10, no. 1, 1998.

Film History, Special Issue on 'Early Cinema,' vol. 11, no. 3, 1999.

Film History, Special Domitor Issue on 'Global Experiments in Early Synchronous Sound,' vol. 11, no. 4, 1999.

Fuller, Kathryn H., *At the Picture Show: Small Town Audiences and the Creation of Movie Fan Culture* (Washington and London: Smithsonian Institution Press, 1996).

Fullerton, John, ed., *Celebrating 1895: Proceedings of the International Conference on Film Before 1920* (Sydney: John Libbey, 1998).

Gunning, Tom, 'The Cinema of Attractions: Early Film, its Spectator and the Avant-Garde,' in Thomas Elsaesser with Adam Barker, eds, *Early Cinema: Space, Frame, Narrative* (London: BFI, 1990), pp. 56–62.

Guzman, Anthony Henry, 'The Exhibition and Reception of European Films in the US during the 1920s' (Los Angeles: unpublished Ph.D. thesis, University of California, 1993).

Hake, Sabine, *Cinema's Third Machine: Writing on Film in Germany 1907–1933* (Lincoln: University of Nebraska Press, 1993).

Hansen, Miriam, *Babel and Babylon: Spectatorship in American Silent Film* (Cambridge, MA: Harvard University Press, 1991).

Herbert, Stephen, *When the Movies Began: Chronology of the World's Film*

Production and Film Shows before May 1896 (London: Projection Box, 1994; pamphlet).

Hertogs, Daan, and Nico de Klerk, eds, *Uncharted Territories: Essays on Early Non-fiction Films* (Amsterdam: Stichting Nederlands Filmmuseum, 1997).

Higson, Andrew, and Richard Maltby, eds, *'Film Europe' and 'Film America': Cinema, Commerce and Cultural Exchange, 1920–1939* (Exeter: University of Exeter Press, 1999).

Hofman, Charles, *Sounds for Silents* (New York: DBS Publications, 1970).

Holman, Roger, ed., *Cinema 1900–1906: An Analytical Study by FIAF* (Brussels: FIAF, 1982).

Kirby, Lynne, *Parallel Tracks: The Railroad and Silent Cinema* (Exeter: University of Exeter Press, 1997).

Koszarski, Richard, *An Evening's Entertainment* (History of the American Cinema, 1915–1928) (New York: Scribner's, 1990).

McKernan, Luke, 'Lo Sport Nel Cinema Muto/Sport and the Silent Screen,' *Griffithiana*, no. 64, October 1998, pp. 80–141.

Marks, Martin Miller, *Music and the Silent Film: Contexts and Case-studies* (New York and Oxford: Oxford University Press, 1997).

Mayne, Judith, *The Woman at the Keyhole: Feminism and Women's Cinema* (Bloomington: Indiana University Press, 1990).

Mitchell, Glenn, *A–Z of Silent Film Comedy* (London: Batsford, 1998).

Morley, Sheridan, *Tales from the Hollywood Raj: The British Film Colony On Screen and Off* (London: Weidenfeld and Nicolson, 1983).

Musser, Charles, *The Emergence of Cinema: The American Screen to 1907* (New York: Scribner's, 1990).

Musser, Charles, *Before the Nickelodeon: Edwin S. Porter and the Edison Manufacturing Company* (Berkeley: University of California Press, 1991).

Ramsaye, Terry, *A Million and One Nights* (New York: Simon and Schuster, 1926).

Robinson, David, *From Peepshow to Palace: The Birth of American Film* (New York and Chichester: Columbia University Press, 1996).

Rossell, Deac, 'A Chronology of Cinema 1889–1896,' special issue of *Film History*, vol. 7, no. 2, 1995.

Rossell, Deac, *Living Pictures: The Origins of the Movies* (Albany, NY: State University of New York, 1998).

Thompson, Kristin, 'National or International Films? The European Debate During the 1920s,' in *Film History*, vol. 8, no. 3, 1996, pp. 281–96.

Tsivian, Yuri, *Early Cinema in Russia and its Cultural Reception* (Chicago, IL and London: University of Chicago Press, 1998).

Usai, Paolo Cherci, *Burning Passions: An Introduction to the Study of Silent Cinema* (London: BFI, 1994), reprinted in a revised edition as, *Silent Cinema: An Introduction* (London: BFI, 2000).

Williams, Christopher, ed., *Cinema: the Beginnings and the Future: Essays*

Marking the Centenary of the First Film Show Projected to a Paying Audience in Britain (London: University of Westminster Press, 1996).

10. General Works on Film History with Material on Silent Cinema

Allen, Robert, and Douglas Gomery, *Film History: Theory and Practice* (New York: Knopf, 1985).

Arts Council of Great Britain, *Film as Film: Formal Experiment in Film 1920–1975* (London: Arts Council of Great Britain, 1979).

Bordwell, David, Janet Staiger and Kristin Thompson, *The Classical Hollywood Cinema: Film Style and Mode of Production to 1960* (London: Routledge and Kegan Paul, 1985).

Brownlow, Kevin, *The Parade's Gone By* (London: Secker and Warburg, 1968).

Hill, John and Pamela Church-Gibson, eds, *The Oxford Guide to Film Studies* (Oxford: Oxford University Press, 1998).

Horak, Jan-Christopher, ed., *Lovers of Cinema: The First American Film Avant-Garde 1919–1945* (Madison: University of Wisconsin Press, 1995).

Jarvie, Ian, *Hollywood's Overseas Campaign: The North Atlantic Movie Trade, 1920–50* (Cambridge: Cambridge University Press, 1992)

Kelly, Andrew, *Cinema and the Great War* (London and New York: Routledge, 1997).

Montagu, Ivor, *The Film World: A Guide to Cinema* (Harmondsworth: Penguin, 1964).

Nowell-Smith, Geoffrey, ed., *The Oxford History of World Cinema* (Oxford: Oxford University Press, 1996).

Pronay, Nicholas and Derek W. Spring, *Propaganda, Politics and Film 1918–1945* (London: Macmillan, 1982).

Salt, Barry, *Film Style and Technology: History and Analysis*, 2nd edn (London: Starword, 1992).

Thompson, Kristin, *Exporting Entertainment: America in the World Film Market, 1907–1934* (London: BFI, 1985).

Thompson, Kristin, and David Bordwell, *Film History: An Introduction* (New York: McGraw-Hill, 1994).

Notes on Contributors

Charles Barr is Professor of Film Studies at the University of East Anglia. His many publications on British film history include *Ealing Studios* (original publication 1977; third edition, Berkeley: University of California Press, 1999), *English Hitchcock* (Moffat, Scotland: Cameron and Hollis, 1999), and, as editor, *All Our Yesterdays: 90 Years of British Cinema* (London: British Film Institute, 1986). He is currently completing *The Film at War: British Cinema 1939–1945*, for publication by the British Film Institute in 2002.

Stephen Bottomore runs a television production company and has been researching the early cinema for over twenty years. His interests include the social and cultural contexts of early film, as well as non-fiction film in this period, and the work of travelling and expedition cameramen. Among his recent publications are 'The panicking audience?: Early cinema and the "train effect",' in the *Historical Journal of Film, Radio and Television* (vol. 19, no. 2, 1999), and *The Titanic and Silent Cinema* (Hastings: The Projection Box, 2000). Future plans include a book on the relationship between war and early cinema and a biography of pioneer cameraman Joseph Rosenthal.

Neil Brand is a composer and writer who has worked with silent cinema for over sixteen years as an improvising pianist, performing throughout the world and writing scores for BFI Video releases. He regularly accompanies films at the National Film Theatre, London, at the Pordenone Silent Film Festival in Italy, and at the annual British Silent Cinema Weekend at Broadway, Nottingham. He is the author of *Dramatic Notes: Foregrounding Music in the Dramatic Experience* (Luton: Arts Council Publications/University of Luton Press, 1998) and contributed to *David Lloyd George: The Movie Mystery* (Cardiff: University of Wales Press, 1998).

Jon Burrows is a Lecturer in the Department of Film and Television Studies at the University of Warwick. His Ph.D. thesis was on actors and acting styles in British cinema of the 1910s. He has contributed essays on Alma Taylor and British film stars of the 1910s to Bruce Babington, ed., *British Stars and Stardom* (Manchester: Manchester University Press, 2001) and on British studios of the early 1920s to Robert Murphy, ed., *The British Cinema Book* (London: BFI, 2nd edn, forthcoming 2002).

Frank Gray is a Principal Lecturer in Art and Media History at the University of Brighton and the Director of the South East Film and Video Archive. His research is devoted to early English cinema, especially the emergence of film culture in Sussex before 1914. He has contributed to Simon Popple and Vanessa Toulmin, eds, *Visual Delights: Essays on the Popular and Projected Image in the 19th Century* (Trowbridge: Flicks Books, 2001) and to *Film History* and *Kintop*; he co-authored the exhibition catalogue, *The Hove Pioneers and the Arrival of Cinema* (Brighton: University of Brighton, 1996).

Jenny Hammerton, a graduate of the University of East Anglia's Film Archiving MA, is Senior Cataloguer at British Pathe, specializing in silent cinemagazines and documentaries. Her publications include *For Ladies Only? Eve's Film Review: Pathé Cinemagazine, 1921–33* (Hastings: The Projection Book, 2001), and articles in Alan Burton and Laraine Porter, eds, *Pimple, Pranks and Pratfalls: British Film Comedy before 1930* (Trowbridge: Flicks Books, 2000), the *Journal of Popular British Cinema* (issue 2, 1999), *Viewfinder Magazine* (February, 1999) and Alan Burton, ed., *Beyond Grierson: Studies in the British Non-Fiction Film* (forthcoming from Flicks Books).

Michael Hammond is a Lecturer in Film Studies in the English Department at the University of Southampton. His work on British cinema culture and reception includes contributions to *Film History* (vol. 11, no. 3, 1999), Alan Burton and Laraine Porter, eds, *Pimple, Pranks and Pratfalls: British Film Comedy before 1930* (Trowbridge: Flicks Books, 2000) and Gaylyn Studlar and Kevin Sandler, eds,

Titanic: Anatomy of a Blockbuster (Rutgers, NJ: Rutgers University Press, 1999). He completed his doctoral thesis, entitled 'The Big Show: Cinema Exhibition and Reception in Britain in the Great War', in 2001.

Sylvia Hardy was formerly a Senior Lecturer in English and is now Research Associate at the University College of Northampton. She edited H.G. Wells's *Ann Veronica* for Everyman Press (London: J.M. Dent, 1993), was the editor of *The Wellsian* for a number of years and is currently Chairman of the H.G. Wells Society. Publications include several articles on Wells, including 'The Time Machine and Victorian Mythology', in Patrick Parrinder, George Slusser and Danièle Chatelain, eds, *H.G. Wells's The Perennial Time Machine* (Athens, GA: University of Georgia Press, 2001).

Andrew Higson is Professor of Film Studies at University of East Anglia, and Director of the British Cinema History Research Project. He is author of *Waving the Flag: Constructing a National Cinema in Britain* (Oxford: Clarendon Press, 1995), editor of *Dissolving Views: Key Writings on British Cinema* (London: Cassell, 1996) and co-editor of *'Film Europe' and 'Film America': Cinema, Commerce and Cultural Exchange, 1920–1939* (with Richard Maltby; Exeter: University of Exeter Press, 1999) and *British Cinema, Past and Present* (with Justine Ashby; London: Routledge, 2000). He has recently completed *English Heritage, English Cinema* for Oxford University Press.

Nicholas Hiley is a social historian who has published numerous articles on the early history of the British mass media. In 1995 he started the British Universities Newsreel Project, a database of 160,000 newsreel stories, with more being added under the second stage of the project, which he launched in 1999 (*http://www.bufvc.ac.uk/databases/newsreels.html*). Since 2000 he has been Head of the Centre for the Study of Cartoons and Caricature at the University of Kent, which has a database of 40,000 newspaper cartoons (*http://library.ukc.ac.uk/cartoons/*). In 2001 he launched a new project to add a further 70,000 political cartoons.

Luke McKernan is Head of Information at the British Universities Film and Video Council. He is the author of *Topical Budget: The Great British News Film* (London: BFI, 1992), and co-editor of *Walking Shadows: Shakespeare in the National Film Archive* (London: BFI, 1994) and *Who's Who of Victorian Cinema* (London: BFI, 1996). His most recent publication is *A Yank in Britain: The Lost Memoirs of Charles Urban, Film Pioneer* (Hastings: The Projection Box, 1999). He is currently studying the life and films of Charles Urban for a research degree.

Alex Marlow-Mann, a graduate of the University of East Anglia MA in Film Archiving, is now researching a Ph.D. on Neopolitan cinema at the University of Reading. He specializes in Italian cinema and has published a study of the four versions of *The Last Days of Pompeii* produced in Italy between 1908 and 1926, in *La Valle dell'Eden* (no. 6, January 2001).

Roberta E. Pearson is a Reader in Media and Cultural Studies at Cardiff University. She is the author of *Eloquent Gestures: The Transformation of Performance Style in the Griffith Biograph Films* (Berkeley: University of California Press, 1992), the co-author of *Reframing Culture: The Case of the Vitagraph Quality Films* (New Jersey: Princeton University Press, 1993), and the co-editor of *The Critical Dictionary of Film and Television Studies* (London: Routledge, 2000) and *American Cultural Studies: A Reader* (Oxford: Oxford University Press, 2000).

Simon Popple is Senior Lecturer in Media History at the University of Teesside. He has written widely on the popular visual culture of the nineteenth and early twentieth centuries, including *In The Kingdom Of Shadows—A Companion To Early Cinema* (London: Cygnus Arts Press, 1997), co-authored with Colin Harding. He is joint editor of *Living Pictures: The Journal of the Popular and Projected Image before 1914* and is currently working on a major project examining the visual culture of the Anglo-Boer war.

Lise Shapiro Sanders is Visiting Assistant Professor of Literature and Cultural Studies at Hampshire College in Amherst, Massachusetts. Recent publications include 'The Failures of the Romance' (*Modern Fiction Studies*, March 2001) and *Embodied Utopias: Gender, Social Change, and the Modern Metropolis* (London: Routledge, 2001), a collection of essays co-edited with Amy Binagman and Rebecca Zorach. She is presently working on a book entitled *Consuming Fantasies: Labor, Leisure, and the London Shopgirl, 1880-1914.*

Emma Sandon teaches Film Studies at Birkbeck, University of London. Her publications include 'Projecting Africa, Two British Travel Films of the 1920s', in Elizabeth Hallam and Brian V. Street, eds, *Cultural Encounters, Representing 'Otherness'* (London: Routledge, 2000). She has been a contributor to *Vertigo* and *Everywoman* magazines, writing about women's filmmaking; she has also produced documentary and educational films and videos, specializing in camera-lighting. She is currently writing her doctorate on British television, 1936–52.

Jamie Sexton completed his Ph.D., entitled 'The Emergence of an Alternative British Film Culture in the Inter-War Period', at the University of East Anglia in 2001, where he has also taught Film Studies. He is currently a Junior Research Fellow at the AHRB Research Centre for British Film and Television Studios at Birbeck College, London. His essay 'Parody on the Fringes: Adrian Brunel, Minority Film Culture and the Art of Deconstruction' appeared in Alan Burton and Laraine Porter, eds, *Pimple, Pranks and Pratfalls: British Film Comedy Before 1930* (Trowbridge: Flicks Books, 2000).

Gerry Turvey teaches Sociology and Film at Kingston University. His current research interests include the films and filmmaking activities of the British and Colonial Kinematograph Company, 1908–24, and Ivor Montagu's contribution to British film culture between 1925 and the late 1940s. Recent publications include ' "That Insatiable Body": Ivor Montagu's confrontation with British film censorship', in the *Journal of Popular British Cinema* (no. 3, 2000) and 'Weary Willie and Tired Tim Go into Pictures: The Comic Films of the B&C Company', in Alan Burton and Laraine Porter, eds, *Pimple, Pranks and Pratfalls: British Film Comedy before 1930* (Trowbridge: Flicks Books, 2000).

Mike Walsh is Senior Lecturer in Screen Studies at Flinders University in Adelaide, Australia. He has contributed to anthologies such as *Post-Theory* (Madison: University of Wisconsin Press, 1996) and *'Film Europe' and 'Film America': Cinema, Commerce and Cultural Exchange, 1920-1939* (Exeter: University of Exeter Press, 1999) and to journals such as *Film History* (vol. 8, no. 1, Spring 1996), the *Velvet Light Trap* (no. 40, Fall 1997) and the *Journal of Popular British Cinema* (no. 3, 2000). He is currently working on a history of Hollywood's foreign distribution operations.

Haidee Wasson is Assistant Professor in the Department of Cultural Studies and Comparative Literature, University of Minnesota. Her book on the early history of the Museum of Modern Arts' Film Library is forthcoming with University of California Press. She has published articles on new technologies, film and museums, and film archives in journals such as *Convergences* (vol. 4, no. 3, Fall 1998), *Continuum* (vol. 12, no. 3, November 1998), the *Canadian Journal of Film Studies* (vol. 9, no. 1, Spring 2000) and *The Moving Image: Journal of the Association of Moving Image Archivists* (vol. 1, no. 1, Spring 2001).

Michael Williams is a Lecturer in Film Studies in the Modern Languages Department at the University of Southampton. He completed his Ph.D. on the film career of Ivor Novello at the University of East Anglia in 2001. He has published on Novello in Alan Burton and Laraine Porter, eds, *Pimple, Pranks and Pratfalls: British Film Comedy Before 1930* (Trowbridge: Flicks Books, 2000), and, with Lawrence Napper, in Bruce Babington, ed., *British Stars and Stardom* (Manchester: University of Manchester Press, 2001).

Index

Acres, Birt, 344
acting, 4
  pantomime, 80, 83–89, 91
  for the screen, 79, 81–89
  for the theatre, 79–80
actuality films *see* non-fiction films
adaptations *see* literature
Adventures of Deadwood Dick, The (1915)
  (series), 151
Adventures of Dick Turpin, The (1912)
  (series), 149, 153
Adventures of Dorcas Dene, Detective, The
  (1919) (series), 151
Adventures of Kathlyn, The (1913) (serial),
  128, 130–134, 148
Adventures of Sherlock Holmes, The (1921)
  (series), 152, 156
  Dying Detective, The (1921), 154
Adventurous Voyage of 'The Arctic' (1903),
  60
advertising, promotional material, 130
Affaire Dreyfus, L' (1899), 57
Aladdin and the Wonderful Lamp (1899), 51
Alice in Wonderland (1903), 4, 42–61
Alliance, 278
Amalgamated Cinematograph Theatres
  Limited, 122
Amazing Quest of Mr Ernest Bliss, The
  (1920) (semi-serial), 151
American cinema
  export of, 271–277
  reception and distribution in Britain, 8,
  128–142
American Prisoner, The (1929), 237
American Roller Rink Company, 113, 115
Anderson, Benedict, 178

Anderson, G.M., 294
Anderson, James, 365
Angle Pictures, 300
Argus (journal), 283
Armes, Roy, 243
Around the Town (cinemagazine/
  travelogue), 163
  Series, 110 (1922) 182–183
As Seen Through the Telescope (1900), 29, 55
Asquith, Anthony, 235, 293, 301
Associated Electric Theatres Limited, 122
Atlantic (1929), 284
Attack on a China Mission—Bluejackets to
  the Rescue (1900), 28, 29–31
Attack on a Mission Station (1900), 30
Aubert, Charles, 83, 88
audiences *see* reception
Ault, Marie, 265
Australasian Films, 278, 283, 284
Australian cinema
  and British film distribution, 278–285
  and cultural identity, 271–277
  as national cinema, 271–277
avant-garde cinema, 198–199, 295, 301,
  313, 314, 318
Avery, Jack, 68

B&C *see* British and Colonial (B&C)
B&D *see* British and Dominions (B&D)
Bachelard, Gaston, 37
Baechlin, Peter, 166, 167
Bairnsfather, Captain Bruce, 186
Balcon, Michael, 235, 258, 293, 306, 307,
  308, 365
Balfour, Betty, 258, 358
Bamford, Kenton, 181, 357

Bamforth, James, 103
Bannister Howard, J., 116
Barabas (1920) (series), 156
Barker, W.G., 80
Barnes, John, 1, 341, 349
Barr, Charles, 5, 227–241
Barrie, J.M., 47
Barry, Iris, 8, 182, 258, 293, 297, 321–337
  and the *Daily Mail* (newspaper), 321,
    322, 323, 324, 329–332, 362
  and the Film Society, 321, 322, 323, 333
  and the *Spectator* (journal), 321, 322,
    324–329, 330
*Battle of the Ancre and the Advance of the
  Tanks, The* (1916), 137
Battle of the Somme, The (1916), 137
Battling Bruisers (1925), 298, 299
Baucus, Joseph, 67
BBFC *see* British Board of Film Censors
  (BBFC)
BDF *see* British Dominions Films (BDF)
Beau Geste (1926), 280
Beerbohm Tree, Sir Herbert, 80–81, 85
Ben Hur (1925), 331
Bennett, Billy, 315
Bennett, Charles, 232
Benson, Frank R., 4, 78, 81, 86, 90, 91
Bentley, Thomas, 236
Berger, Ludwig, 311
Bernstein, Sidney, 164, 293, 362
Betts, Ernest, 297, 363
BFI *see* British Film Institute (BFI)
Big Parade, The (1926), 312, 315
Biograph Company, 21, 24–25
Biograph Theatres Limited, 122
Bioscope Annual (journal), 119
Bioscope (journal), 156, 359, 360
Bioscope projector, 66, 68
BIP *see* British International Pictures (BIP)
Birth of a Flower (1910), 71
Birth of a Nation (1915), 29, 135, 136
Blackmail (1929), 237
Blakeston, Oswell, 299, 302, 362, 363
Bluebottles (1928) (short), 251, 252, 300,
  301, 309
Blunderland of Big Game, The (1925), 298
Boer War, 4
  abuse of war conventions, 17–19
  film exhibition in Leeds, 23–25
  patriotic displays, 17, 24, 25
  representations of, 13–15, 22–23
  staged images, 15, 15–17, 19–20, 22
  topical films, 21–22
Bond, Ralph, 302
Bordwell, David, 39–40, 234, 318
Bostock, Edward, 116

Bottomore, Stephen, 4, 341–355, 358
Boxer Rebellion (China), 29–31
Boy Scouts Be Prepared (1917) (serial), 151,
  153, 156, 158
Bramble, A.V., 234–235, 236
Brand, Neil, 7, 208–224
Breslau Fire Department in Action (1900), 35
Brewster, Ben, 83
Britain Prepared (1915), 73
British Board of Film Censors (BBFC),
  106, 294, 307, 308, 309, 364
British cinema, 181–182, 248–249
  and alternative film culture, 291–294
  Australian distribution of, 5, 278–285
  export of, 271–285
  as national cinema, 6, 234, 258
  periodisation of, 5–6
  standardization of, 6, 106–107
  transitional period, 78
  and William Shakespeare, 7, 176, 179,
    181–182, 185, 186–188
  and working class representations,
    300–301
British Cinema Company, 112
British and Colonial (B&C), 149, 151,
  155, 156, 358, 363
British documentary movement, 168, 173,
  302, 307
British and Dominions (B&D), 282
British Dominions Films (BDF), 282, 283
British Film Institute (BFI), 345, 358, 361,
  362, 364–366
British Filmcraft, 152
British Gaumont Company, 244, 245
British International Pictures (BIP), 229,
  237, 282, 284
British Newspaper Library (Colindale),
  345–346, 359, 361
British Pathe, 173
British Screen Classics, 176
British Screen Tatler (cinemagazine), 163
Brittain, Vera, 264, 266
Brooke, Rupert, 260, 262, 263
Brown, Theodore, 68, 74
Bruce, Stanley, 275
Brunel, Adrian, 8, 250, 256, 334, 358
  and the Film Society, 293, 294, 298,
    299, 301
  and Ivor Montagu, 307, 308, 309, 316,
    318
Brunel and Montagu Limited, 308, 309,
  310, 318
Bryan, Jane, 149
Buchanan, Andrew, 168
Buckley, Reginald R., 177, 179–180
Buffalo Bill's Wild West show, 29

Bullock, William, 200
Burch, Noël, 47, 204
Burgess, Charles (exhibitor), 130–131
Burrows, Jon, 4, 78–93, 356–369
Burton, Langhorne, 152

Cabinet of Dr Caligari, The (1919), 293, 295, 297, 312
CAF see Cinema Art Films (CAF)
Call of the Blood, The (1919) (L'appel du sang), 256, 263
Carlton, Frank, 151
Carnival (1921), 256
Carré, Michele, 84–85
Carroll, Lewis, 42, 45–47, 54, 56
Carroll, Sydney, 262
Castle, Hugh, 302
Cavalcanti, Alberto, 312
Cazabon, Albert, 208, 215–217, 218, 219, 222
CEA see Cinematograph Exhibitors' Association (CEA)
Celio Company (Italy), 85
censorship, 100, 104, 106–107, 309–310
Champagne (1928), 229
Champion Charlie (1916) (short), 295, 316
Chaplin, Charles, 248, 295, 313, 325, 327
  and the Film Society, 311, 312, 316, 317
Charles Urban Trading Company, 69, 71, 72
Charles XII (1925), 315
chase film, 53, 55
Chasing De Wet (1901), 20
Chowl, Hay, 191
Churchill, Winston (American novelist), 135, 137
Cinderella and the Fairy Godmother (1898), 51
Cinema Art Films (CAF), 282, 283, 284
cinema of attractions, 7, 102, 154–155, 169–173, 198, 204
  and Alice in Wonderland (1903), 43, 52–54, 58
cinema collections, 347–349
Cinema Commission, 364
Cinema (journal), 359, 360
cinema journals, 344
Cinema News and Property Gazette, 122
Cinema Quarterly (journal), 168, 297, 302
cinemagazines, 7, 162–173, 198
Cinematograph Act (1909), 119
Cinematograph Exhibitors' Association (CEA), 122
Cinematograph Films Act (1927), 280
Cinématographe, 66
Clarendon, 149, 156

classical Hollywood cinema, 6
Close Up (journal), 8, 362, 367
  and the Film Society, 297, 299, 300, 302, 322, 323
Co-operative Film Company, 78, 80, 81, 86, 92
C.O.D.—A Mellow Drama (1929) (short), 299, 300
Coleby, A.E., 152
Collick, John, 79
Collins, Alf, 47
Comin' Thro' The Rye (1916), 43
Comin' Thro' The Rye (1923), 43, 48, 357
Committee on Public Information, 74
Conan Doyle, Sir Arthur, 152, 154, 156, 158
continuity editing, 54–55
Coombes, Annie, 202
Cornford, Frances, 262
Corsican Brothers, The (1898), 51
Court Treatt, Major C. and Stella, 191, 192
Courtship, 104
Covered Wagon, The (1923), 278
Crawford, Chester, 113, 115
Crisis, The (1916), 128, 131, 135–139
Croise, Hugh, 152
Crossing the Great Sagrada (1924), 298, 299
Crossing the Great Sahara (1924), 299
Cut It Out (1925), 298, 299, 301
Cutts, Graham, 256, 263, 334

Daily Films Renter (journal), 282
Daily Mail (newspaper), and Iris Barry, 8, 293, 321, 322, 323, 324, 329–332, 362
Dalrymple, Ian, 307, 308, 310
Dane, Clemence, 183–184
Daring Daylight Burglary, A (1903), 53, 55
Darling, Alfred, 68, 71
Daydreams (1928) (short), 251, 300
De Mille, Cecil B., 311, 312, 331–332
Death of Nelson, The (1897), 59
Desperate Poaching Affray, A (1903), 55
Devant, David, 151
Dick Whittington (1899), 51
Dickens, Charles, 51, 59, 178, 200
Dickson, W.K.L., 21
distribution, 8, 128–142, 278–285
Dobson, Frank, 293
documentary films see non-fiction films
Don Q (1912) (series), 151, 156, 158
Don Q (1925), 327
Dorothy's Dream (1903), 60
Dotheboys Hall, or Nicholas Nickleby (1903), 59
Downhill (1927), 256

Doyle, Stuart, 284
Dr Sing Fang Dramas (1928) (series), 152
Drifters (1929), 302
Duckworth, Joshua (exhibitor), 112
Duncan, F. Martin, 68, 70, 74
Dyer, Richard, 258–259, 266, 267

Eagle, The (1925), 310
East Lynne (1902), 59
Ebbutt, P.G., 149
Eclipse (France), 69, 70
Edison, Thomas, 66
Edison Company, 34, 35, 67, 85, 102, 147
Education Week—Newcastle on Tyne (1911)
    (newsreel), 185
Edwards, Henry, 151, 215
Eggeling, Viking, 313
Eisenstein, Sergei, 227, 228, 232, 236,
    295, 296–297, 311, 318
Elliot, Eric, 297, 363
Elstree Studios, 237
Elvey, Maurice, 152, 233–234, 235, 236,
    256, 334
  and *The Flag Lieutenant* (1926), 208, 215
  and *The Passionate Friends* (1922), 245,
    247–248
En Rade (1928), 312
Enfant Prodigue, L' (1907 & 1911), 84
Enfant Prodigue, L' (play), 85
English Nell (1900), 59
Entertainments Tax (1916), 129, 141
Epic of Everest, The (1924), 326–327
Era, The (trade paper), 362
Essanay company, 294, 316
ethnographic representations, 192, 199–205
Evans, Fred, 149, 158, 159
Everyday (1929) (unreleased), 295
Eve's Film Review (cinemagazine), 163,
    164, 165–166, 167, 169, 170, 358
  Bride of the Black Forest, The (1929), 169
  Eve's Home Hint—A Silver Cleaning Tip
    (1921), 169
  Fishergirls of Ostend (1920's), 169
  Flower Girls of Lincolnshire (1929), 169
  Gadgets! (1929), 169
  Hair Fashions (c.1921), 170, 171
  Keep Fit Brigade, The (1927), 172
  Lens Liar, The (c.1921), 172
  Light on Turkish Delight (1924), 169
  Miss Japan Takes Up Billiards (1929), 169
  Odds and Ends (early 1920's), 169
  Sealing-Wax Stunts (1930), 169
exhibition, 8
  of American films in Britain, 128–142
  Boer War films in Leeds, 23–25
  patriotic displays, 24, 25

standardization of, 100–101, 106–107
exhibitors
  audience response, 136–138, 139–142
  promotional campaigns, 135–136
Exploding Motor Car, The (1900), 48
Exploits of Three-Fingered Kate, The
    (1909–1912) (series), 149, 155, 158

Fairbanks, Douglas, 214, 279–280, 312,
    327
faked films *see* staged films
Falsely Accused (1905), 44
fan magazines, 361–362
Fantomas (1913) (series), 151, 156
Farmer's Wife, The (1928), 236
Faust and Mephistopheles (1898), 51
Felix the Cat, 327
Fencing Contest from 'The Three Musketeers'
    (1898), 59
Feuillade, Louis, 147, 154, 156
FIAF conference (Brighton 1978), 3,
    233–234, 341
Fighting the Fire (1897), 34
Film Art (journal), 297, 302
Film Arts Guild (New York), 294
film conferences, 343
Film d'Art (France), 81
film serials, 7, 74, 128, 130–134, 147–160
Film Society, The, 8, 252, 364–365
  and alternative film culture, 291–294
  and critical discourse, 297–303
  and Iris Barry, 321, 322, 323
  and Ivor Montagu, 306–318
  programmes of, 294–297
Fire! (1901), 28, 31–38, 55
fire culture, 31–34
Fire Drills at Breslau, Germany (1900), 35
Fire Rescue Scene (1894), 34
Firemen—Departure of Fire Engine (1897),
    34
Firemen—Getting Ready (1897), 34
Firemen—Life Saving (1897), 34
Firemen—Playing at the Fire (1897), 34
First Men in the Moon, The (1919), 245
Flag Lieutenant, The (1926), 7, 208–210,
    215–223, 279
Flaherty, Robert, 204
Folly Films, 149
Fort Buckle, Gerard, 363
Foss, Kenelm, 235
Franco-British Film Company, 151
Friedberg, Anne, 300
Friese-Green, William, 73, 343
Fuller, John (exhibitor), 274
Further Adventures of Dr Fu Manchu, The
    (1924) (series), 152

Further Adventures of the Flag Lieutenant
(1928), 215
Further Adventures of Sherlock Holmes, The
(1922) (series), 152
Fussell, Paul, 265

Gainsborough, 229, 235, 251, 258, 282
   and Ivor Novello, 256, 257, 262
   and Adrian Brunel, 295, 299, 308–309
Galsworthy, John, 228
Garden of Allah, The (1917), 128, 139–141
Garrick, David, 178
Gaumont British, 282
Gaumont Company, 84
Gaumont Film Company, 182
Gaumont Graphic, The
   (cinemagazine/newsreel), 164, 167
   Shakespeare's Birthday (1930), 182
   Twelfth Night (1916), 185–186
Gaumont Mirror (newsreel), 163
Gaumont-Victory, 151, 156
General Theatres Corporation (GTC), 284
German cinema, 312
   expressionism, 295–296, 301
Gielgud, John, 293
Gifford, Denis, 233, 358
Gilliat, Sidney, 237
Gish, Lillian, 214
Gledhill, Christine, 358
Globe Theatre, The, 177, 178, 179
Godal, Edward, 249
Going to the Fire (1897), 34
Gold Rush (1925), 327
Goodbye Mr Chips (play), 216
Goodwin Norton, Charles, 34–35
Gordon, Edward R., 152
Gordon, Leslie Howard, 248
Grahame, Kenneth, 47
Grand Guignol (1921), 149
Grandma's Reading Glass (1900), 29, 55
Grass (1925), 192
Gray, Frank ,4, 28–41
Great London Mystery, The (1920) (serial),
   151, 153
Great Train Robbery, The (1903), 55, 155
Greater Australasian Films *see* Australasian
   Films
Grierson, John, 168, 302, 366
Griffith, D.W., 237, 256–257, 311, 312,
   321, 325, 327
   film style of, 228, 232, 234
Grock (clown), 315
Grossmith, George and Weedon, 37
Grüne, Karl, 325
GTC *see* General Theatres Corporation
   (GTC)

Gunning, Tom, 169–173, 198

Haddon, A.C., 204–205
Haggar, William, 47
Haigh, Ernest, 152, 156
Hamilton Ball, Robert, 79, 81, 86, 88
Hamilton, Harry H., 25
Hammerton, Jenny, 7, 162–175
Hammond, Michael, 8, 128–143, 367
Hands off the Flag (1901), 20
Hansen, Miriam, 193, 201
Hardy, Sylvia, 5, 242–255
Harris, Sam, 114, 122
Harrison, Lt Col. J., 200
Hate Ship, The (1929), 237
Hathaway, Anne, 178, 183, 184, 185, 188
Hawkridge, John, 155
Haynes, Manning, 334
Hearst, William Randolph, 74
Helen of Troy (1927), 327
Henry VIII (1911), 80, 81, 85–86
Hepworth, Cecil, 1, 4, 6, 39, 68, 159, 234,
   237, 306, 357
   and *Alice in Wonderland* (1903), 42–61
Hepworth (Imperial), 151
Hepworth Manufacturing Company, 42,
   180–181, 184, 278, 362
heritage cinema, 79, 181–182, 184, 234
Herring, Robert, 302
Hiawatha (1903), 59, 60
Higson, Andrew, 4, 42–61, 79, 90, 181,
   234, 357, 358
Hiley, Nicholas, 8, 106, 111–127
Histoire d'un Pierrot (1913), 85
Hitchcock, Alfred, 1–2, 5, 227–230, 311,
   313, 322, 334
   and Eliot Stannard, 230–232, 235–238
   and *The Lodger* (1926), 256, 257, 295,
   301, 308
Hitchens, Robert, 139
Hobsbawm, Eric, 178
Holman, W.A., 274
Houlston, Denis, 164–165
House That Jack Built, The (1900), 29
How Broncho Billy Left Bear Country
   (1912), 294
How It Feels to be Run Over (1900), 48
Howitt, William, 178
Howkins, Alun, 186–187
Hoyts (exhibition circuit), 282–283, 284
Huxley, Julian, 293

I Do Like to be Beside the Seaside (1928), 299
Ideal Pictures, 151, 228, 251, 358
   Ideal Cinemagazine, 163, 168
   Idealetter (journal), 361

Independence Day (1996), 29
Indian and the Maid, The, 91
interest films *see* supporting programme
International Federation of Film Archives, 321
Interrupted Courtship, An (1899), 104
intertextuality, 43–44, 45–46, 48, 53, 140
intertitles, 57, 187, 252, 299, 310–311
Invisible Voleur, L' (1909), 244
Irving, H.B., 81
Irving, Washington, 185
Isaacs, Walter, 66

Jackson, Arrar, 363
Jacobs, Lea, 83
James, Henry, 243, 244
Jannings, Emil, 295, 311
Jazz Singer, The (1927), 236
Jeffs, Waller (exhibitor) ,112
John Wrench and Son 67
Joy, Henry, 68, 74
Jury, William F., 365
Justice (1917), 228, 229, 232, 233

Kaes, Anton, 263
Keating, Peter, 243
Keaton, Buster, 317, 327
Keep the Home Fires Burning (song), 5, 258, 260, 261
Keystone, 316
Khaki-Covered Camera, The (song), 15–17
Kinemacolor, 69, 71–73
Kinematograph Weekly (journal), 210, 230, 231, 232, 236, 359, 360
Kineto Company, 69, 184
Kineto Company of America, 74
Kinetoscope, 66, 67, 101
King John (1899), 59
Kinograms (newsreel), 74
Kipps (1921), 5, 245–247
Kirshenblatt-Gimblett, Barbara, 200
Kiss in the Tunnel (1899), 55, 102–104
Kissing Couple, The, 102
kissing films, 102–104
Kruger's Dream of Empire (1900), 20–21

Lahue, Kalton, 148
Lambert, Albert, 81
Lambert, Gavin, 237
Lanchester, Elsa, 251, 301, 309
Lang, Fritz, 325
Last Adventures of Sherlock Holmes, The (1923) (series), 152
Laughton, Charles, 251, 309
Le Bargy, Charles, 81
Lear, Edward, 47

Leaves of My Life (1921) (series), 152, 156
Leavis, Q.D., 243
lecturers, 57, 58, 113
Lee, F. Marshall, 71
Lee, Sidney, 178
Lehman, Ernest, 232
Lejeune, C.A., 323
Leni, Paul, 295, 311
Leslie, Rolf, 152
Let Me Dream Again (1900), 29
Levy, Louis, 210
Lewis, Wyndham, 325, 328
Lieutenant Daring (1911–14) (series), 149, 156, 158
   Lieutenant Daring and the Plans of the Minefield (1912), 155
   Lieutenant Daring Quells A Rebellion (1912), 154–155
Lieutenant Rose (1910–14) (series), 149, 153, 154, 156, 158
Lieutenant Rose R.N. and the Boxers (1911), 150
Life of an American Fireman, The (1902), 37
Lindsay, Vachel, 313–318
literature
   adaptations of, 5, 43, 45–48, 55, 59, 233, 234, 242–252
   see also Shakespeare adaptations
Little Lord Fauntleroy (play), 216
live acts *see* supporting programme
live music *see* supporting programme
Lloyd, Harold, 214, 317
Lodger: A Tale of the London Fog, The (1926), 236, 259, 365
   and Alfred Hitchcock, 256, 257, 295, 301, 308
   and Ivor Novello, 260, 261, 264, 265, 266–267
London Cinematograph Company, 81
London's Burning (TV series), 29
Lore, Colden, 363
Lorraine, Harry, 149
Low, Rachael, 153, 159, 205, 210, 233, 235, 321, 324
   and *The History of British Film* series, 1, 51, 54, 79, 341, 356
   and *Richard III* (1911), 81, 86, 88
Lubitsch, Ernst, 311, 325
Lumière Company, 34, 66, 67, 204, 242
Lye, Len, 302
Lyons, H. Agar, 152

Macbeth (1911), 91
McClure's Ladies World (magazine), 147
McFarlane, Brian, 245
McKernan, Luke, 4, 5, 65–76

McLaren, Norman, 302
MacPhail, Angus, 307, 308, 310, 315
Macphershon, Kenneth, 302
MacQueen-Pope, W., 261
magic lantern industry, 33
Maguire and Baucus (Continental
    Commerce Company), 67, 69
Maguire, Franck, 67
Main Rouge, La (1908), 84
Manvell, Roger, 51, 54
Manxman, The (1929), 237
Marchbanks, Albert, 210
Marks, Walter, 282
Marle, Clifford, 149
Marlow-Mann, Alex, 7, 147–161
Marriage Circle, The (1924), 325
Marshall, Emma, 177
Martinek, H.O., 151
Martinek, Ivy, 151
Masefield, John, 177
Master Films, 152
Masterman, Charles, 73
Mathers, Helen, 43
May Irwin–John C. Rice Kiss, The (1896)
    102
Melbourne Age (journal), 283
Méliès, Georges, 55, 57, 59, 68, 172
Menschen Company (Germany), 85
Mercanton, Louis, 256
Miarka: Daughter of the Bear (1920)
    (*Miarka, Fille de L'Ourse*), 256
Michigan Electric Company, 66
Millais, John, 31
Miller, Hugh, 293, 307
Miller and the Sweep, The (1897), 53
Miracle, The (1912), 85
Mitchell and Kenyon Company, 18, 19,
    20, 30
mode of address, 193–197
Modern Bioscope Operator, The (journal), 117
montage, 228, 233, 234
    Soviet, 227, 228, 295, 296–297, 299,
    301, 302
Montagu, Ivor, 8, 250–252, 267, 293, 300,
    301
    and the Film Society, 297, 302, 306–318,
    364–365
Moran, Percy, 149, 151
Morin, Pilar, 85
Morning Alarm, A (1897), 34
Morrell, Henry, 85
Morrison, Lee, 152
Mort du Duc de Guise, La (1908), 81
Morton, H.V., 180–181
Mother (1926), 227, 233
Motion Picture Music Company, 217

Motion Picture Producers and Distributors
    of America (MPPDA), 275, 277
Mottershaw, Frank, 47
Movie Chats (serial), 74
MPPDA *see* Motion Picture Producers
    and Distributors of America
    (MPPDA)
Mr Bumble the Beadle (1898), 59
Mr Pickwick's Christmas at Wardle's (1901),
    59
Muller-Strauss, Maurice, 166, 167
musical directors, 211–214, 216, 218, 223
Musical Dog (1929) (newsreel), 166
Musical Mirror (journal), 223
Musser, Charles, 43, 204
Mutoscope, 101
Mutoscope and Biograph Company, 59
Mycroft, Walter, 293
Mystery of Dr Fu Manchu, The (1923)
    (series), 152

Nanook of the North (1922), 192, 204
narrative films, 152–155, 204
    continuity and causality, 29, 56
    development of, 34–35, 42–61, 154–155
    effects on audience, 107
    rescue narratives, 28–40
Nash, Percy, 151
National Council of Public Morals,
    106–107, 158, 364
National Film and Television Archives
    (NFTVA), 102, 182, 184, 185, 217,
    357
Natural Color Kinematograph Company,
    69, 72
Neal, Mary, 180
Nelson (1918), 228, 229, 233, 234
Nepean, Edith, 259, 260, 263, 264, 267,
    268
New Era, 282
newsreels, 7, 74, 163, 165–167, 211, 299
    Shakespeare themed, 176, 177, 182–184,
    185–186, 188
NFTVA *see* National Film and Television
    Archives (NFTVA)
Nick Carter—Le Roi des Détectives (1908),
    158
Nietzsche, Friedrich, 260
Nionga (1925), 7, 191–197, 198, 199,
    200–205
non-fiction films
    actuality films, 15, 68, 76, 192–193, 201,
    204
    documentary films, 70, 76, 192, 204
    scientific films, 69, 70
    topical films, 21–22

Norgate, P.G., 149
North American Phonograph Company, 66
Norwood, Eille, 152, 154
Novarro, Ramon, 258
Novello, Ivor, 5, 256–270, 293, 301, 358
    and star image, 261–268

Observer (newspaper), 8, 293, 310, 315,
    316, 323
October (1927), 227, 297
Official War Review (newsreel), 74
Old Bill Through the Ages (1924), 186–188
Old Man in the Corner, The (1924) (series),
    152
Only a Sister, 91
Only Way, The (1925), 313
Opera 2, 3 and 4 (1923–25) (shorts), 294
Orczy, Baroness, 152
Ormiston-Smith, Frank, 68
Our New Errand Boy (1905), 53
Owen, Wilfred, 267

Pabst, G.W., 296
Parkinson, Harry B., 176
Passion Play (1897 & 1898), 59
Passionate Friends, The (1922), 5, 245–248
Pathé, Charles, 244
Pathé Company, 84, 163
Pathé Gazette (newsreel), 299
The Shakespeare Memorial Theatre
    Foundation Stone Laying at Stratford
    on Avon on July 2nd, 1929 (1929), 182
Pathé Pictorial (cinemagazine), 163–164,
    164, 167, 168, 171
Pathetic Gazette (1924), 298, 299
Pathétone Weekly (cinemagazine), 171
Patriotic Film Corporation, 73
Paul, Fred, 149, 151, 152
Paul, R.W., 1, 20–21, 34, 51, 59, 67, 242,
    344
Pearson, George, 151, 293, 334
Pearson, Roberta E., 7, 90, 176–190
performance, Boer War film programmes,
    25–26
Perry, George, 80
phantom rides, 102, 184, 194
Phillips Oppenheim, E., 151, 152
Phonograph, 66
Picture Show (journal), 258, 259, 261, 262,
    264
Picture Theatre News (journal), 116
Pimple (film series, 1910s), 149, 159
    Lieutenant Pimple films, 158
Pioneer, 152
Pixie at the Wheel (1924) (series), 152
Pleasure Garden, The (1926), 235, 236, 313

Poisoning the Well (1901), 19
Popple, Simon, 4, 13–27
Porter, Edwin S., 37, 43, 155
Pound, Ezra, 325
Pritchard, Hesketh, 156
Propaganda, 73–74
Pudovkin, Vsevelod I., 227, 228, 232, 234
    and the Film Society, 295, 296, 306–307,
    311, 318
purpose-built cinemas
    construction of, 111, 121–124, 129
    investment in, 114–124
    resistance to, 112–113
Pygmalion (play), 216
Pyke, Montague, 114–115, 118

Quiller Couch, Arthur, 187
Quota Act (1927), 313

Raleigh, Walter, 187
Ramsaye, Terry, 242–243
Raskolnikov (1923), 295
Rat, The (1925), 257, 260, 262, 263–265
Raymond, Charles, 151
reception
    of American films, 132–134, 136–142
    audience composition, 8, 46–48, 90–92,
        99–100, 129, 138
    of Boer War images, 24, 25
    demand for purpose-built sites, 121–124
    familiarity with source-text, 43–44,
        45–46, 48, 53
    habitual audiences, 112
    social control and regulation of, 97–98
Recreations Limited, 115
Redford, G.A., 106
Reeves, Nicholas, 358
Reinhardt, Max, 85, 296
Renault, Felix Louis, 204
Rescue 999 (TV series), 29
Rescued by Rover (1905), 39, 44, 56
Reville, Alma, 231
Richard III (1911), 4, 78–92
Richter, Hans, 295, 296, 313
Riley Brothers, 103
Ring, The (1927), 229, 235
Rinking and Rinks (trade journal), 114
Rinking World (trade journal), 114, 116
Rip Van Winkle (1903), 59
Robin Hood (1922), 279–280
Rogers, George, 69
Rohmer, Sax, 152, 154, 156
Rolfe, William James, 177
roller-skating, 113–116
Rose, Winifred, 151
Rosenthal, Joseph, 68, 69

Rotha, Paul, 297
Rothermere, Lord, 330
Royal Shakespeare Company (RSC), 178
RSC *see* Royal Shakespeare Company
    (RSC)
Russo-Japanese War (1904–5), 69
Ruttman, Walter, 294, 296, 313
Ryall, Tom, 230, 301

Sally of the Sawdust (1925), 327
Salt, Barry, 55, 57
Sandon, Emma, 7, 191–207
Sandow, Eugene, 25
Santa Claus Without His Whiskers (1921)
    (newsreel), 166
Schneider, Eberhard, 35
scientific films *see* non-fiction films
Scrooge (1901) (*Marley's Ghost*), 51, 59
Searle, Luscombe, 25
Seastrom, Victor, 311, 325
Selde, Gilbert, 313–318
Selig Polyscope, 128–142, 367
Sennett, Mack, 316
*Set-to Between John Bull and Paul Kruger,
    The* (1900), 20
Séverin (mime artist), 84
Sexton Blake (1928) (series), 152
Sexton, Jamie, 8, 291–305
Shakespeare Memorial Theatre, 178, 182,
    184
Shakespeare, William 7, 176–188
    adaptations of 4, 78–92
Shakespeare's Land (1910) (travelogue), 184
Shapiro Sanders, Lise, 8, 97–110
Shaw, Harold, 245, 246
Shelling the Red Cross (1900), 19, 20
Sherlock Holmes (1912) (series), 151
Shohat, Ella, 199
Shooting Stars (1928), 235
Showalter, Elaine, 266
Singer, Ben, 132, 153, 158
Singing Fool, The (1928), 284
Skin Game, The (1931), 229, 295
Sloan, Jane, 238
Smith, George Albert, 29, 37, 51, 59, 68,
    71, 102–103
Smith, Percy, 68, 70–71
Sneaky Boer, A (1900), 19
So This Is Jollygood (1925), 298, 299
Sopocy, Martin, 57
Sorel, Cecile, 81
Sorrel and Son (1927), 279–280
Soviet montage *see* montage
Spectator (journal), 8
    and Iris Barry, 321, 322, 324–329, 330
Spirograph (projector), 74, 75

Stage Struck (1925), 212
Stagecoach (1939), 29
staged films
    Boer War, 15, 16–17, 19–20, 22
    Boxer Rebellion (China), 30–31
Staiger, Janet, 234
Stam, Robert, 199
Stampede (1929), 7, 191–192, 197–199,
    200–205
Stannard, Eliot, 5, 229–230, 233–235
    and Alfred Hitchcock, 235–238
    and montage theory, 230–233
stardom
    and Ivor Novello, 258–268
    theatre stars on screen, 80
Starting for the Fire (1897), 34
Stedman, Raymond William, 148
Stevens, Gilbert R., 210, 214, 215, 217,
    222
Stoll Film Productions, 152, 200, 245,
    248, 278, 300
Stoll's Editorial News (journal), 361
Stow, Percy, 42, 149
Strachey, John, 293, 324
Stratford on Avon (1925) (travelogue),
    180–181, 184
Street, Sarah, 367
Sumners, Walter, 334
supporting programme
    interest films, 7, 198
    live acts, 91
    live music, 7, 208–214
    see also cinemagazines; film serials;
        newsreels; travelogues
Swaffer, Hannen, 261
Swanson, Gloria, 311
Sydney, Aurele, 151
Sylvester Music, 217

Taylor, D.F., 162, 168–169
Ten Commandments, The (1923), 278, 280
Ten Commandments, The (1956), 29
Tenniel, Sir John, 45, 48, 49, 50, 52, 56, 58
Theatre Museum (Covent Garden), 366
Thomae, Robert L., 66, 67
Thompson, F.M.L., 37
Thompson, Kristen, 234
Tilly Girls (film series, 1910s), 48
Tilly's Party (1911), 53
Times, The (newspaper), 30, 293
Tipping, Jessica, 266
Tonic, The (1928) (short), 251, 300
Tonnies, Ferdinand, 158
Topical Budget (newsreel), 164, 166, 167,
    299
    Soviet's Salute to Shakespeare (1926), 182

To Shakespeare's Memory (1927), 182
topical films *see* non-fiction films
Torquay and Paignton Photoplay
    Productions, 151
trade journals, 342, 360–361
Transatlantic Film Company, 151
travelogues, 7, 68, 193, 198, 204
    Shakespeare themed, 176, 177, 180–182,
    184–185, 188
Trevelyan, Laurence, 84
Treville, Georges, 151
trick films, 20–21, 50–52, 172, 198
Triumph of the Rat (1926), 259
Truffaut, François, 236
Turner, Edward R., 71
Turvey, Gerry, 8, 306–318
Two Little Waifs (1905), 28, 38–39
Typical Budget (1925), 294–295, 298–299

Ufa, 282
Ultus (1915–17) (series), 151, 153, 156, 158
    Ultus and the Grey Lady (1916), 157
Uncle Tom's Cabin (1903), 43
Underground (1928), 301, 302
Union Theatres (UT) (exhibition circuit),
    278, 282–284
Union Theatres Film Exchange *see*
    Australasian Films
United Artists (UA), Australian subsidiary,
    274, 279
Urban, Charles, 4, 5, 65–76, 344
Urban Motion Picture Industries
    Incorporated, 75
Urban-Duncan Micro-Bioscope, 70
Urban-Kineto Corporation, 75
Uricchio, William, 90
UT *see* Union Theatres (UT)

Valentino, Rudolph, 258, 266, 310
Vampires, Les (1915) (series), 156
Variety (1925), 311
Veidt, Conradt, 295
Vieux Colombier (Paris), 294
Vitagraph company, 90
Vitaphone, 223

Vitascope, 66
von Arnim, Elizabeth, 248
von Stroheim, 223

Walls, Ernest, 177
Walsh, Mike, 5, 271–287
War of the Worlds, The (1953), 242
Warwick Trading Company, 20, 23, 34,
    68, 71, 103, 201
Washing Boer Prisoners (1900) (*Washing A
    Boer Prisoner in Camp*), 19
Wasson, Haidee, 8, 321–337, 362
Waxworks (1924), 295, 312
Wells, Frank, 250–252, 300, 301
Wells, H.G., 5, 242–255, 300
    *The King Who Was a King: the Book of the
    Film*, 249–250, 251–252
Welsh Pearson, 278
Weston, Harold, 363
What Happened to Mary? (serial), 147, 152
Wheels of Chance, The (1922), 245
Whirlpool of War (cinemagazine), 163
White, Eric Walter, 363
White Flag Treachery (1900), 19
White Rose, The (1924), 256
Wiene, Robert, 325
Wiener, Martin J., 179, 180
Wiffle's Best Friend, 91
Wilcox, Herbert, 282, 311, 313
Wilking Film, 295
Wilkins, Fred, 113, 115
Williams, Kathlyn, 131
Williams, Michael, 5, 256–270
Williamson, James, 1, 4, 28–40, 68, 201
Winter, Jay, 261
Wonderful Britain (serial), *Shakespeare's
    Country* (1926), 176, 177, 184–185
Worth, Peggy, 152
Wrestling with a Lion (1930) (newsreel),
    166
Wright, Stanley (exhibitor), 277
Wullschläger, Jackie, 45–46, 47–48

Ypres (1925), 327